Spenser and Donne

Manchester University Press

The Manchester Spenser

The Manchester Spenser is a monograph and text series devoted to historical and textual approaches to Edmund Spenser – to his life, times, places, works and contemporaries.

A growing body of work in Spenser and Renaissance studies, fresh with confidence and curiosity and based on solid historical research, is being written in response to a general sense that our ability to interpret texts is becoming limited without the excavation of further knowledge. So the importance of research in nearby disciplines is quickly being recognised, and interest renewed: history, archaeology, religious or theological history, book history, translation, lexicography, commentary and glossary – these require treatment for and by students of Spenser.

The Manchester Spenser, to feed, foster and build on these refreshed attitudes, aims to publish reference tools, critical, historical, biographical and archaeological monographs on or related to Spenser, from several disciplines, and to publish editions of primary sources and classroom texts of a more wide-ranging scope.

The Manchester Spenser consists of work with stamina, high standards of scholarship and research, adroit handling of evidence, rigour of argument, exposition and documentation.

The series will encourage and assist research into, and develop the readership of, one of the richest and most complex writers of the early modern period.

General Editors Joshua Reid, Kathryn Walls and Tamsin Badcoe
Editorial Board Sukanta Chaudhuri, Helen Cooper, Thomas Herron, J. B. Lethbridge, James Nohrnberg and Brian Vickers

Also available
Literary and visual Ralegh   Christopher M. Armitage (ed.)
The art of The Faerie Queene   Richard Danson Brown
A Concordance to the Rhymes of The Faerie Queene   Richard Danson Brown & J.B. Lethbridge
A Supplement of the Faery Queene: By Ralph Knevet   Christopher Burlinson & Andrew Zurcher (eds)
A Companion to Pastoral Poetry of the English Renaissance   Sukanta Chaudhuri
Pastoral poetry of the English Renaissance: An anthology   Sukanta Chaudhuri (ed.)
Spenserian allegory and Elizabethan biblical exegesis: A context for The Faerie Queene
Margaret Christian
Monsters and the poetic imagination in The Faerie Queene: 'Most ugly shapes and horrible aspects'
Maik Goth
Celebrating Mutabilitie: Essays on Edmund Spenser's Mutabilitie Cantos   Jane Grogan (ed.)
Spenserian satire: A tradition of indirection   Rachel E. Hile
Castles and Colonists: An archaeology of Elizabethan Ireland   Eric Klingelhofer
Shakespeare and Spenser: Attractive opposites   J.B. Lethbridge (ed.)
Dublin: Renaissance city of literature   Kathleen Miller and Crawford Gribben (eds)
A Fig for Fortune: By Anthony Copley   Susannah Brietz Monta
Spenser and Virgil: The pastoral poems   Syrithe Pugh
The Burley manuscript   Peter Redford (ed.)
Renaissance psychologies: Spenser and Shakespeare   Robert Lanier Reid
European erotic romance: Philhellene Protestantism, renaissance translation and English literary politics   Victor Skretkowicz
Rereading Chaucer and Spenser: Dan Geffrey with the New Poete   Rachel Stenner, Tamsin Badcoe and Gareth Griffith (eds)
God's only daughter: Spenser's Una as the invisible Church   Kathryn Walls
William Shakespeare and John Donne: Stages of the soul in early modern English poetry   Angelika Zirker

Spenser and Donne
Thinking poets

EDITED BY YULIA RYZHIK

Manchester University Press

Copyright © Manchester University Press 2019

While copyright in the volume as a whole is vested in Manchester University Press, copyright in individual chapters belongs to their respective authors, and no chapter may be reproduced wholly or in part without the express permission in writing of both author and publisher.

Published by Manchester University Press
Altrincham Street, Manchester M1 7JA
www.manchesteruniversitypress.co.uk

British Library Cataloguing-in-Publication Data is available

ISBN 978 1 5261 1735 9 hardback
ISBN 978 1 5261 1737 3 paperback

First published by Manchester University Press in hardback 2019

This edition first published 2021

The publisher has no responsibility for the persistence or accuracy of URLs for any external or third-party internet websites referred to in this book, and does not guarantee that any content on such websites is, or will remain, accurate or appropriate.

Typeset by Servis Filmsetting Ltd, Stockport, Cheshire

Contents

Notes on contributors		*page* vii
Acknowledgements		x
Note on the texts		xi
	Introduction: Spenser, Donne, and the trouble of periodization *Yulia Ryzhik*	1
1	Caring to turn back: overhearing Spenser in Donne *Richard Danson Brown*	13
2	Comparing figures: figures of comparison and repetition in Spenser's *Cantos of Mutabilitie* and Donne's *Anniversaries* *Christopher D. Johnson*	32
3	Refiguring Donne and Spenser: aspects of Ramist rhetoric *Niranjan Goswami*	62
4	*Artes poeticae*: Spenser, Donne, and the metaphysical sublime *Patrick Cheney*	85
5	Spenser and Donne look to the Continent *Anne Lake Prescott*	108
6	Ovidian Spenser, Ovidian Donne *Linda Gregerson*	118
7	Cosmic matters: Spenser, Donne, and the philosophic poem *Ayesha Ramachandran*	137
8	'Straunge characters': Spenser's Busirane and Donne's 'A Valediction of my name, in the window' *Elizabeth D. Harvey*	157
9	Marriage and sacrifice: the poetics of the Epithalamia *Ramie Targoff*	171
10	Spenser's and Donne's devotional poetics of scattering *David Marno*	183

11 Eliot, Yeats, Joyce, and the modernist reinvention of Spenser and Donne   200
    Anne Fogarty and Jane Grogan

Index   225

Notes on contributors

Richard Danson Brown is Professor of English Literature at the Open University, and has published monographs on Spenser, including *The Art of* The Faerie Queene (2019) and *The New Poet: Novelty and Tradition in Spenser's 'Complaints'* (1999), and on MacNeice (2009), as well as the *Concordance to the Rhymes of* The Faerie Queene, with J.B. Lethbridge (2013), and several edited collections.

Patrick Cheney is Edwin Erle Sparks Professor of English and Comparative Literature at Penn State University. His most recent publications include *English Authorship and the Early Modern Sublime: Spenser, Marlowe, Shakespeare, Jonson* (2018) and 'Donne's Literary Career' in *John Donne in Context* (2019).

Anne Fogarty is Professor of James Joyce Studies at University College Dublin, co-founder with Luca Crispi of the *Dublin James Joyce Journal*, and Academic Director of the *Dublin James Joyce Summer*. She is co-editor of *Joyce on the Threshold* (2005), *Bloomsday 100: Essays on 'Ulysses'* (2009), *Imagination in the Classroom: Teaching and Learning Creative Writing in Ireland* (2013) and *Voices on Joyce* (2015). She has edited special issues of the *Irish University Review* on Spenser and Ireland, Lady Gregory, Eiléan Ní Chuilleanáin, and Benedict Kiely and has published widely on aspects of twentieth- and twenty-first-century Irish literature.

Niranjan Goswami is Associate Professor of English at Chandernagore College. His publications include 'The Theatre of Death: Executions in Kyd, Marlowe and Shakespeare' in *Offstage and Onstage* (2015); 'Peter Ramus, William Ames and the New England Way: Investigations into Theologia Timocratica' in *Anthropological Reformations* (2015); 'The Theory of Truth in Valla's "Repastinatio" and Its Legacy in the Logic of Agricola and Ramus' in *La Diffusione Europea del Pensiero del Valla* (2013) and 'Translation as Transfer: Thomas Hoby's The Book of the Courtier' in *Travels and Translations* (2013).

Linda Gregerson is Caroline Walker Bynum Distinguished University Professor of English and Creative Writing at the University of Michigan. She is the author of *The Reformation of the Subject: Spenser, Milton, and the English Protestant Epic* and the editor, with Susan Juster, of *Empires of God: Religious Encounters in the Early Modern Atlantic*. She has also published six books of poetry and a volume of essays on the contemporary American lyric. Her essays on Milton, Spenser, Shakespeare, Wyatt,

Donne, and Jonson appear in numerous journals and anthologies. Gregerson is a chancellor of the Academy of American Poets.

Jane Grogan is Associate Professor in the School of English, Drama, Film and Creative Writing at University College Dublin. She is the author of two monographs, *The Persian Empire in English Renaissance Writing, 1549–1622* (2014), and *Exemplary Spenser: Visual and Poetic Pedagogy in 'The Faerie Queene'* (2009) and editor of *Celebrating Mutabilitie: Essays on Edmund Spenser's* Mutabilitie Cantos (2010) and *Beyond Greece and Rome: Reading the Ancient Near East in Early Modern Europe* (2019). She is working on an edition of William Barker's translation of Xenophon's *Cyropaedia* for the MHRA Tudor and Stuart Translations series.

Elizabeth D. Harvey is Professor of English at the University of Toronto. She is the author of *Ventriloquized Voices: Feminist Theory and Renaissance Texts,* and, most recently, editor of *Sensible Flesh: On Touch in Early Modern Culture,* and co-editor of *Luce Irigaray and Premodern Culture.* She is currently completing a book (with Timothy Harrison), *John Donne's Physics.*

Christopher D. Johnson is Associate Professor at the School of International Letters and Cultures, Arizona State University. He is the author of *Memory, Metaphor, and Aby Warburg's Atlas of Images* (2012) and *Hyperboles: The Rhetoric of Excess in Baroque Literature and Thought* (2010), and also translated and edited *Selected Poetry of Francisco de Quevedo* (2009). He is currently working on a book provisionally entitled *Baroque Expression: On Seventeenth-Century Literature, Art, and Thought.*

David Marno is Associate Professor of English at the University of California, Berkeley. He is the author of *Death Be Not Proud: The Art of Holy Attention* (2016), and has published numerous articles on literature and religious practices in the aftermath of the Reformation, including prayer, meditation, and spiritual exercises.

Anne Lake Prescott is Helen Goodhart Altschul Professor of English (Emerita) at Barnard College. She is the author of *Imagining Rabelais in the English Renaissance* (1978) and *French Poets and the English Renaissance: Studies in Fame and Transformation* (1998), editor of *Renaissance Historicisms: Essays in Honor of Arthur F. Kinney,* with J. Dutcher (2008), and *Female and Male Voices in Early Modern England,* with B. Travitsky (2000). For some years a trustee of the Renaissance Society of America and previously president of the International Spenser Society, she is currently president of the Sixteenth Century Society and co-editor of *Spenser Studies.*

Ayesha Ramachandran is Associate Professor of Comparative Literature at Yale University. She is the author of *The Worldmakers* (2015) and has also published on Spenser, Lucretius, Tasso, Petrarch, Montaigne, on postcolonial drama and cosmopolitanism in various venues including *NLH, Spenser Studies, MLN, Forum Italicum,* and *Anglistik.* Together with Melissa Sanchez, she is the co-editor of 'Spenser and the Human', a special issue of *Spenser Studies.* Her new book in progress is tentatively entitled *Lyric Thinking: Humanism, Selfhood, Modernity.*

Yulia Ryzhik is Assistant Professor of English (CLTA) at the University of Toronto, Scarborough. Her publications include 'Complaint and Satire in Spenser and Donne: Limits of Poetic Justice' (*ELR*, 2017), 'Spenser and Donne Go Fishing' (*Spenser Studies*, 2018), and 'Books, Fans, and Mallarmé's Butterfly' (*PMLA*, 2011). She is completing a monograph entitled *Donne's Spenser: Between Allegory and Metaphor*.

Ramie Targoff is Professor of English, co-chair of Italian Studies, and the Jehuda Reinharz Director of the Mandel Center for the Humanities at Brandeis University. She is the author of *Renaissance Woman: The Life of Vittoria Colonna* (2018), *Posthumous Love: Eros and the Afterlife in Renaissance England* (2014), *John Donne, Body and Soul* (2008), *Common Prayer: The Language of Public Devotion in Early Modern England* (2001), and 'Traducing the Soul: Donne's *Second Anniversarie*' (*PMLA*, 2006).

Acknowledgements

This volume would not have come into existence if it were not for Gerard Passannante's kind invitation for me to present at the roundtable discussion 'Spenser's Donne and Done' the 2014 MLA convention in Chicago, and for Julian Lethbridge's generosity in approaching me after the panel to continue the conversation and recommending that I pursue publication with Manchester University Press. Julian's enthusiasm and guidance were essential in the early stages of this project's conceptualization, and even more so in my first forays into editing and commenting on the newly arrived chapters. His sage, refreshingly direct, and extensive advice helped me avoid many missteps, both professional and scholarly. I also extend my thanks to Joshua Reid, who provided crucial support for the project in the submission and review stages, and to Kathryn Walls for her attentive reading of the manuscript and detailed comments. I am grateful to all the contributors to this volume for their painstaking work and patience, but especially to Linda Gregerson and Elizabeth D. Harvey, who came on board the earliest and took a chance on a novice editor when this collection was but a seedling of an idea, and to Jane Grogan, who was willing to impart her wisdom as an experienced editor for MUP when it came time to write the proposal. I want to thank Mary Harper and Susan Stewart at the Princeton Society of Fellows for helping me navigate the soliciting of chapters, as well as Sarah Townsend, my colleague at the University of New Mexico, and Katherine Larson, my colleague and chair at the University of Toronto Scarborough, for their advice on handling inevitable snags in the timeline of editing. As always, I am grateful to Gordon Teskey for his bracing encouragement and vision that helped me keep a straight, if not always speedy, course.

Note on the texts

Citations from Spenser's works are from A.C. Hamilton's edition of *The Faerie Queene* and from the Yale *Shorter Poems* edited by William A. Oram et al. For citations from Donne's works, this volume adheres to contributors' individual preferences as to the edition. The use of unmodernised or modernised spellings, except in the Index, follows these editions.

Introduction: Spenser, Donne, and the trouble of periodization

Yulia Ryzhik

The names Edmund Spenser and John Donne are rarely seen together in a scholarly context, and even more rarely seen together as an isolated pairing. When the two are brought together, it is usually for contrast rather than for comparison, and even the comparisons tend to be static rather than dynamic or relational. Spenser and Donne find themselves on two sides of a rift in English Renaissance studies that separates the sixteenth century from the seventeenth and Elizabethan literature from Jacobean.[1] In the simplest terms, Spenser is typically associated with the Elizabethan Golden Age, Donne with the 'metaphysical' poets of the early seventeenth century.

Critical discourse overlooks, or else takes for granted, that Spenser's and Donne's poetic careers and chronologies of publication overlapped considerably. Hailed as the Virgil of England, and later as its Homer, Spenser was the reigning 'Prince of Poets', and was at the height of his career when Donne began writing in the early 1590s. Both poets, at one point, hoped to secure the patronage of the Earl of Essex, Donne by following him on expeditions to Cadiz and the Azores, Spenser by hailing his victorious return in *Prothalamion* (1596). The second instalment of Spenser's *The Faerie Queene* (also 1596) gives a blistering account in Book V of the European wars of religion in which Ireland, where he lived, was a major conflict zone, but it is Donne who travelled extensively on the Continent, including places where 'mis-devotion' reigned.[2] Spenser died in 1599 and was buried with much pomp at Westminster Abbey as if poetry itself had died with him. Yet Spenser's voice would be heard again from beyond the grave, in the seventeenth century, with the publication of the first full edition of *The Faerie Queene*, including the *Cantos of Mutabilitie*, by Matthew Lownes in 1609. By 1609 the greater part of Donne's poetry had already been written, but not his most ambitious poems, the two *Anniversaries*, *An Anatomy of the World* (1611), and *Of the Progresse of the Soul* (1612).

For all their many and major differences as poets, it is unusual for two canonical authors whose careers overlapped as closely as Spenser's and Donne's to have been so significantly separated in scholarly discourse. Yet literary-historical and pedagogical conventions have for a long time rendered the pairing as seemingly unnatural as apples and oranges.[3] The influence of Spenser on Milton – more openly acknowledged yet also more remote – has received much critical attention,[4] while the more immediate relation between Donne and Spenser has remained largely neglected. To date, books that treat both Spenser and Donne treat them more or less in isolation from each other, as discrete examples of a common theme.[5] *The Oxford Handbook of Edmund Spenser* mentions Donne only three times, none of which refer to poetry. *The Oxford Handbook of John Donne* mentions Spenser fifteen times, of which ten are more than passing mentions, but only seven include a substantive comparison of the two poets' works.[6]

The traditional view of Spenser and Donne in terms of contrast rather than comparison has been cultivated from the earliest critical commentators forward, and is not unjustified.[7] Donne himself, in his radical and almost certainly deliberate departure from Spenser's poetics, may have been partly responsible. Thomas Carew, in his 'Elegy on the Death of Dr. Donne' (1633), praised Donne for his 'giant fancy', which proved 'too stout' for the 'soft melting phrases' of his predecessors, and for having purged the Muses' garden of classical deities, 'tales i' th' Metamorphoses' and other 'pedantic weeds' that had 'stuff[ed the] lines, and swell[ed] the windy page' of Elizabethan poetry. Milton, conversely – as Dryden tells us – declared his allegiance to Spenser, calling him his 'original',[8] and in 'At a Vacation Exercise' (1628) dismissed the shallow tricks of 'our late fantastics' – presumably imitators of Donne. Dryden himself took exception to Donne's 'affect[ing] the metaphysics' and 'perplex[ing] the minds of the fair sex with nice speculations of philosophy, when he should engage their hearts, and entertain them with the softnesses of love', as was done before him in the Elizabethan age and after him during the Restoration.[9] Spenser remained influential alongside Milton, and continued to be imitated, through the eighteenth century. The Romantic poets' favourable reception of Spenser's prophetic vision is well known, as is the appreciation of Spenser among the Victorians.[10] Donne had his admirers in the nineteenth century, but the sometimes rapturous responses of Samuel Taylor Coleridge, Thomas De Quincey, and Robert Browning were exceptions rather than the rule.[11] When T.S. Eliot, with the indispensable aid of H.J.C. Grierson, resurrected Donne and the metaphysical poets from centuries-long critical obscurity, he did it at the expense of the epic poets, Spenser and Milton – although as Anne Fogarty and Jane Grogan show in Chapter 11, Eliot's alienated allusions to Spenser often prove more definitive of Eliot's self-conscious modernism than his emulative allusions to Donne.

The pattern has held in the contemporary academy, where, until recently, Donne studies and Spenser studies have tended to rise and fall in an inverse relation, and primary critical concerns and scholarly approaches associated with each poet have run on separate tracks. Proponents of New Criticism idolized Donne, while Spenser studies have inclined towards philology and later theory, especially in the heyday of deconstruction.[12] Donne studies have, of necessity, focused on manuscripts, archival research, and textual criticism, and the ongoing project of the Donne *Variorum* highlights the enormity and complexity of the task.[13] The *Oxford Handbook* devotes its entire first section to research tools and resources in Donne studies, approximately 11 per cent of the total page count excluding the frontmatter and index. Spenser studies, by contrast, have focused on publication history, which takes up 5.7 per cent of the page count in its respective *Oxford Handbook*.[14] Spenser might be discussed in the context of Neoplatonism, Donne in the context of new science, or 'new philosophy'.[15] Such examples are myriad. Although some scholars have published on both Spenser and Donne, there has been little crossover work that engages these poets concurrently and extensively; articles and book chapters that put the two in conversation are few and far between, focusing mostly on the few sites of Donne's direct allusion to or parody of Spenser.[16]

The trouble here of course is one of periodization, the convenient divide at the turn of the sixteenth century, between the reigns of Elizabeth I and James I, who came to the throne upon the Queen's death in 1603. Spenser's death in 1599 places him firmly on one side. Donne's dates are not so neat, but his career is often described as twofold, divided between the early satires and amatory poems of 'Jack' Donne and the devotional poems and sermons of 'Doctor' Donne – a separation encouraged by Donne himself and immortalized in Izaak Walton's hagiographical account of Donne's life.[17] The same split has for a long time defined the careers of Shakespeare, divided roughly around the time of *Hamlet* (1601), and of Ben Jonson, with a line of division drawn between his poems and city comedies and his masques.

Not only literary-historical but also historical accounts of the period can be prone to this perception of rupture, and the 1590s can be viewed as a particularly turbulent time, an end of one era and the beginning of another. A confluence of disasters – famine, pestilence, wars of religion, internal rebellions – made the 1590s seem a veritable crisis, not only in England but all over Europe, and England's crisis was exacerbated by the uncertainty of succession.[18] Making matters worse, scientific and intellectual upheavals of the sixteenth century called into doubt long-held beliefs about the workings of the body, the world, the universe. Paracelsian chemistry displaced the long-standing theory of humours; Vesalian anatomy and medicine challenged the Galenic, showing the body to be a complex and highly specific machine; Copernican, heliocentric cosmology shook the foundations of the geocentric Ptolemaic system; astronomical findings of Kepler and Galileo, with the use of a telescope, showed that the superlunary world, previously held to be permanent, was subject to change.[19] The belief in a universal correspondence based on the analogy of macrocosm to microcosm – a foundational principle of natural philosophy in the West from late antiquity (and later a crucial concept in the critical movement focusing on the history of ideas) – was becoming increasingly untenable.[20] Both Spenser and Donne viewed the scientific revolution with studied suspicion, but Donne's famously hyperbolic pronouncement in the *First Anniversary* – over a decade after the turn of the century – that all was 'in pieces, all coherence gone' once again aligned him in critical discourse with 'new philosophy' against Spenser's old.[21] While it would be anachronistic to attribute the unrest of the 1590s to '*fin de siècle* malaise',[22] and while the dichotomous view of the broader period fostered by Michel Foucault and others has since been scaled back, it is clear – and it must have been clear to people living at the time – that a dramatic change was afoot.

The very terms by which we refer to the literary-historical period contain in themselves a rhetoric of disruption and division. The terms 'Renaissance' and 'early modern', which we use almost interchangeably to describe the broader period in English literature, are not the same.[23] 'Renaissance' implies a retrospective idealism dependent on the 'rebirth' of classical antiquity, relegating the time in between to the 'dark' or 'middle' ages. 'Early modern' implies a beginning of something new, a looking ahead (if not necessarily looking optimistically forward) to what we now call modernity.

Both terms, 'Renaissance' and 'early modern', are questionable (indeed often questioned) in that both discount what came immediately before. The term 'early modern', intended to correct the teleological, exceptionalist view of the 'Renaissance', only substituted one teleology for another, heightening the sense of rupture and sharpening the implicit distinction between the new and timely on the one hand and the obsolete and irrelevant on the other.[24] The separation is especially detrimental to medieval studies, but is damaging to early modern studies as well, whether we consider the period a bounded one on both sides, markedly different from both before and after, or an open-ended one, inaugurating an increasingly distant 'modernity'.[25] One effect of the narrative of rupture on either end of the English literary Renaissance is fragmentation within the field.[26] In this respect too, Spenser and Donne seem to stand on opposite sides of the divide, and this perception is symptomatic of the receding present in relation to the 'early modern' moment. It is Donne who is traditionally associated with modern innovation, but it is worth remembering that Spenser too was at one point the 'new poet'.[27] The misconception of Spenser as 'old' and Donne as 'new' is only furthered by Spenser's self-conscious medievalism that prompted Jonson to quip that Spenser 'in affecting the Ancients writ no language'.[28] Jonson played a part as well in calcifying Donne's role as a seventeenth-century 'metaphysical' opposed to the 'Cavalier' poets, the so called 'Sons of Ben'. The opposition between 'metaphysical' and 'Cavalier' drives Donne even further forward in the seventeenth century, over a decade beyond his lifetime, as 'Cavalier' came to signify one of the sides of the English Civil Wars.

To be sure, conventions of periodization are recognized as such and acknowledged to be functionally useful yet ultimately arbitrary.[29] The outer boundaries of the period continue to blur and shift as new scholarship tightens the links between the medieval and early modern and challenges long-standing markers of the period's end.[30] The internal divisions within the field are likewise becoming less stark, and certainly gestures have been made to complicate the well-worn dichotomies between sixteenth- and seventeenth-century literature and history.[31] Studies in early modern English literature have produced unusual and illuminating pairings between major authors: Shakespeare and Spenser, Shakespeare and Donne, Milton and Donne, and even Spenser and Jonson.[32] Likewise encouraging are recent re-evaluations of Spenser and Donne individually that question the standard view of each author[33] and fresh, unconventional pairings of their works in article-length studies.[34] Spenser studies and Donne studies are thriving fields of scholarly enquiry, but the legacy of periodization that imposed a sharp break between them remains palpable. For one, there is not yet a holistic book-length study of Spenser and Donne together, apart from other authors,[35] and insights still need to be gleaned from works that address one of the authors but mention the other only in passing.

The rift between Spenser and Donne is deep, and we are only just beginning to fill it. In recent years concerted efforts have been made to merge the interests of Donne and Spenser scholars more closely, as evidenced in the roundtable sessions, sponsored jointly by the International Spenser Society and the John Donne Society, at the MLA conventions of 2012 and 2014.[36] It is at the latter roundtable that this present volume had its beginning. Abstracts for these roundtables emphasize 'conversation' and 'dialogue' about the 'relation(s)' between the two poets, the work of poetic making and transformation, and a continuity, or at least a comparableness, of thought that enables reading Spenser and Donne both backwards and forwards.[37] In my own conversations with colleagues, I have heard an enthusiastic consensus that the Spenser–Donne pairing could prove to be a treasure trove for new research in early modern literature, but has been sorely understudied. Gradually, the conversation on Donne's Spenser and Spenser's Donne is emerging. This collection of essays, then, brings together scholars working on either side of the divide to put this nascent conversation into print.

The aim of this conversation is to move beyond the convenient but unfruitful contrast between Spenser and Donne that has dominated critical discourse. To be sure, the differences between the two poets are profound. Donne's verse was rough where Spenser's was mellifluous, stark and short where Spenser's was florid and expansive.[38] Spenser's poetic persona was retiring, Donne's was brash. Spenser thought allegorically, Donne metaphorically. Spenser presented his works to the world in print, Donne in manuscript.[39] Donne at times casts a resentful glance in Spenser's direction (as, for instance, in the 'Epithalamion Made at Lincoln's Inn'), but not an anxious one in the Bloomian sense.[40] Spenser is not a distant precursor whose memory Donne needs to repress, but a contemporary, a mere generation older, regularly publishing new work – sometimes provoking an immediate satirical response from Donne. If Donne felt any anxiety of influence towards Spenser, it is probably in the simpler, historical sense suggested by Walter Jackson Bate in *The Burden of the Past and the English Poet*.[41] Yet no poet's break from a competitor, predecessor, or past tradition can be reduced to a table of antonyms.

We take, therefore, a more relational view of Donne and Spenser, and, although Spenser was probably unaware of Donne's work, the relation is not necessarily unidirectional. The chapters engage critically with both poets not only at the sites of allusion, imitation, or parody but also in terms of common preoccupations and continuities of thought. Bearing in mind the subtitle 'Thinking Poets', the aim is not merely to compare what Spenser and Donne thought about certain subjects, such as contemporary events and politics, science, philosophy, love, marriage, or religious devotion. Rather, these chapters explore and meditate on *how* these poets thought: how they directed their rhetorical and figurative processes, how they crafted their verses, their authorial personae, and their literary careers, and how they navigated the rich landscape available to them of literary conventions, innovations, and influences both ancient and modern. A close analysis of Spenser and Donne together complicates and challenges the conventional wisdom of literary history.

To the extent that Spenser and Donne present scholars and critics with fundamentally different textual and intellectual problems, a comparative, relational study may seem at best indirect.[42] A significant part of this project, therefore, is establishing the appropriate terms to define the Spenser–Donne connection. Richard Danson Brown calls it 'overhearing'; my preferred term is 'engagement'; Ayesha Ramachandran suggests 'encounter'; David Marno uses 'foreshadowing'; I might also add 'interplay'. This volume showcases a multiplicity of approaches and points of entry into this area of research, but a robust theoretical model remains somewhat elusive. Here too, the solution is 'thinking poets' – that is, thinking of Spenser and Donne as poets *qua* poets. To achieve a more holistic view of the relation, the scope of the evidence must be broadened, allowing not only the scattered moments of concrete linguistic borrowing or parody but also the more generalized sense of the pressure Spenser exerted on early modern poetry and Donne's more generalized response to that pressure.[43] The historical context can help situate the two poets within the larger social, political, and intellectual pressures of the time. To what extent should we consider the political and intellectual unrest of the late sixteenth century as a crisis of poetic imagination? Where do Spenser's and Donne's reactions to this crisis coincide, and where do they diverge? What insights might be gained from juxtaposing two poets so apparently unlike one another for comparison rather than contrast? How might this juxtaposition change our understanding of each poet individually? Reading Donne in the context of Spenser not only modifies our view of Donne as a poet but also illuminates important, if less conspicuous, aspects of Spenser's poetry. We see what Donne saw in it, what he rejected outright and what he considered worthy of imitation or of parody. We also see how Spenser's poetics may have aligned with, anticipated, or foreshadowed Donne's.

Certain loci in the two poets' respective oeuvres prove to be particularly generative: Spenser's *Mother Hubberds Tale*, the *Cantos of Mutabilitie*, *Fowre Hymnes*, and perhaps Book I of *The Faerie Queene*; Donne's *Metempsychosis*, the two *Anniversary* poems, three *Epithalamia* (especially 'Epithalamion Made at Lincoln's Inn'), and to a lesser extent the *Satires*. The sometimes unconventional pairings between Spenser's and Donne's works – for instance, Brown's juxtaposition of *Mother Hubberds Tale* and Donne's *Satire IV*, or David Marno's examination of devotional poetics in the *Fowre Hymnes* as a precursor of Donne's *Holy Sonnets* – yield surprising results and new connections. Another fruitful method is situating Spenser and Donne within a broader intellectual or literary tradition – for example, Ramist rhetoric (Niranjan Goswami) or philosophical poetry (Ayesha Ramachandran), treating them as part of the same continuum rather than separate points and finding that their places on the continuum are closer together than we think. Chapters that approach Donne and Spenser vis-à-vis genre and mode tend to perform a productive crossover, in which at least one of the poets is revealed as engaging a genre not typically associated with him: Spenser as a satirist (Brown), Donne as harbouring epic career ambitions (Patrick Cheney).[44] Finally, several chapters illuminate aspects of the Spenser–Donne relation by way of a triangulation with a third author, and in most cases that third author has turned out to be Ovid (Cheney, Anne Lake Prescott, Linda Gregerson). The Ovidian renaissance has been a critical growth area in early modern studies, but here for the first time Ovid proves instrumental to bridging a gap between two major English poets.[45]

The eleven chapters are arranged to construct an overarching narrative, moving from the more formal considerations of Spenser and Donne to the more thematic and philosophical readings, and returning, towards the end, to the issues of genre and the legacies of the two poets. The chapters by Richard Danson Brown, Christopher Dean Johnson, and Niranjan Goswami concern themselves with style, figuration, and rhetoric, respectively. In making a case for Spenser's 'rough' style and for the overheard notes of Spenser in Donne, Brown progresses from a detailed metrical analysis to a more philosophical discussion of the ways in which Spenser and Donne negotiate the tension between sentence and poetic line, particularly in the context of dialogue and debate. Comparing Spenser's and Donne's figures of comparison, Christopher Johnson's chapter performs an astonishing chiasmus. Spenser's *Cantos of Mutabilitie* push against the limits of *comparatio* but resolve the conflict through an uncharacteristic dramatic syncrisis; conversely, Johnson makes a case for the importance of *similitudo* in Donne's *Anniversaries* to temper and balance the extremes of syncrisis for which the poems are notorious. Niranjan Goswami counters the long-standing Spenser–Donne binaries by examining the two poets' use of binaries as the underlying structure of their poetry, following the strategies of Ramist logic and rhetoric. The argument is particularly innovative with respect to Spenser, as his rhetorical methods have hitherto been overlooked in scholarship. Patrick Cheney's chapter caps off this section by taking a broader view of Spenser's and Donne's literary careers, but also anticipates the prevailing approaches in the rest of the book, finding an inclusive conceptual framework to comprehend both poets: the question of the sublime. Donne, Cheney argues, 'thinks about Spenser sublimely across the literary topics of genre, immortality, and career'. Whereas Spenser may be England's first 'sublime' poet, Donne produces a 'metaphysical sublime' – a coinage that conveys both a sense of continuity and a sense of departure.

Three chapters that follow, by Anne Lake Prescott, Linda Gregerson, and Ayesha Ramachandran, look beyond the English borders to establish the place of Spenser and Donne within the geographical region, the world, and the cosmos. Prescott deftly traces myriad potential lines and configurations as she looks at Spenser and Donne looking across the English Channel to the Continent, its history, its literature, its philosophy. In comparing the two poets' overall methods of appropriating Continental literature, however, she focuses on an 'ancient author, Ovid, and [on] one geographical feature, the hill'. Both Ovid and the hill – Arlo Hill, to be precise – feature prominently in Linda Gregerson's chapter. Using Ovid's Pythagoras as a point of departure, the chapter sees both Spenser and Donne questioning and subverting (although not quite levelling) nature's traditional hierarchies and boundaries to hint at an alternative 'vision of connection and interdependence that we now call ecological', or even 'post-humanist'.[46] If Gregerson's chapter concerns primarily earthly ecologies and worldly matters, Ramachandran's takes Spenser and Donne beyond the sphere of the moon to address cosmic matters – both in the sense of 'cosmos' as an orderly universe and in the sense of formal aesthetics. Situating Spenser's *Fowre Hymnes* and Donne's *Anniversaries* within the rich continental tradition of philosophical poetry, Ramachandran makes a strong case for both poets' poetic practice as an effort to repair the cosmological rupture brought about by new science, restoring its circularity through repetition.

The chapters by Elizabeth Harvey and Ramie Targoff can be considered companion pieces in that both address the issue of eroticism and sexual violence in the poetry of Spenser and Donne, albeit through vastly different lenses and points of comparison. Targoff looks to the classical tradition of the epithalamion, or marriage hymn, arguing that Spenser's mythological allusions, just before his glorious *Epithalamion* reaches the moment of consummation, hint at 'the bride's involuntary role as sacrifice as the telos of the marriage ritual' – a barely concealed violence that Donne's parodic 'Epithalamion Made at Lincoln's Inn' brings rather graphically into focus. Harvey examines a different kind of 'graphic' violence: the breach of bodily and psychic integrity implicit in the common Petrarchan figure of writing on the beloved's heart. Although Spenser's and Donne's representations of that violence differ according to their preferred figurative devices, in both cases 'bounded subjectivity is sacrificed in the service of an eroticism that continually courts its own undoing'. With reference to psychology and the changing early modern notions of 'character' Harvey sees each poet fashioning a distinctive poetic 'signature'. Like Harvey, David Marno turns to a Petrarchan topos (informed by Augustine's influence) as a triangulating point between Donne and Spenser, elucidating a shared devotional poetics of distraction. Spenser, he argues, first appropriates this poetics in the *Fowre Hymnes*, moving from inattention towards a gradual correction of error. Donne's elaboration of this progression in the *Holy Sonnets* in turn plays a crucial role in the development of a meditative, author-oriented devotional lyricism of the seventeenth century.

Anne Fogarty and Jane Grogan conclude the book by returning to the question of the two poets' legacies and afterlives, focusing on the reception of Spenser and Donne among three major modernist writers: T.S. Eliot, William Butler Yeats, and James Joyce. In all three cases, the triangulation reveals unusual findings: for instance, Spenser is revealed to be a more generative source of allusion and poetic innovation for Eliot (compared to Donne's more 'functional' role), whereas Joyce, Fogarty and Grogan argue, deploys Spenser with the deepest of ironies and recasts Donne as essentially 'medieval'. Through these several complex triangulations, the chapter links the transitional period at the turn of the sixteenth century with another transitional period in English literary history, one that helped entrench the very scholarly paradigm that we are working to counter.

This book, I believe, breaks new ground, sustaining an extensive and multifaceted discussion of the Spenser–Donne relation, establishing new directions in the study of two canonical poets at a pivotal point in literary history and in the process compiling a much-needed critical bibliography. The implications of the Spenser–Donne relation are potentially far-reaching in understanding the literary culture of early modern England, particularly in the late Elizabethan and early Jacobean periods. These chapters will bring a remarkable convergence of lines of enquiry into focus and illuminate possible avenues for further exploration. We hope that this book will become an important starting point for scholars and students continuing to cultivate this fruitful field of research. When it comes to Donne's relation to Spenser, we are not done, for surely we must have more.

Notes

1 For instance, Spenser and Donne are treated in separate volumes of the Oxford literary histories: C.S. Lewis, *English Literature in the Sixteenth Century, Excluding Drama* (Oxford: Clarendon, 1954), and Douglas Bush, *English Literature in the Earlier Seventeenth Century, 1600–1660*, 2nd ed. (Oxford: Clarendon, 1962).
2 See Anne Lake Prescott, Chapter 5 below.

3 The same has been said of another unlikely pairing, Spenser and Shakespeare. Robert Lanier Reid, *Renaissance Psychologies: Spenser and Shakespeare* (Manchester: Manchester University Press, 2017), 35.
4 See, for instance, Harold Bloom, *A Map of Misreading*, 2nd ed. (New York: Oxford University Press, 2003); Maureen Quilligan, *Milton's Spenser: The Politics of Reading* (Ithaca: Cornell University Press, 1983); Linda Gregerson, *The Reformation of the Subject: Spenser, Milton, and the English Protestant Epic* (Cambridge: Cambridge University Press, 1995); Gordon Teskey, 'From Allegory to Dialectic: Imagining Error in Spenser and Milton', *PMLA*, 101.1 (Jan. 1986), 9–23.
5 Frank Kermode, *Shakespeare, Spenser, Donne: Renaissance Essays* (London: Routledge and Kegan Paul, 1971); A.C. Partridge, *The Language of Renaissance Poetry: Spenser, Shakespeare, Donne, Milton* (London: Deutsch, 1971); Louis Martz, *From Renaissance to Baroque: Essays on Literature and Art* (Columbia: University of Missouri Press, 1991); Murray Roston, *Tradition and Subversion in Renaissance Literature: Studies in Shakespeare, Spenser, Jonson, and Donne* (Pittsburgh: Duquesne University Press, 2007); Terry G. Sherwood, *The Self in Early Modern Literature: For the Common Good* (Pittsburgh: Duquesne University Press, 2007); Adam Potkay, 'Spenser, Donne, and the Theology of Joy', *Studies in English Literature 1500–1900*, 46.1 (2006 Winter), 43–66; Esther Gilman Richey, 'The Intimate Other: Lutheran Subjectivity in Spenser, Donne, and Herbert', *Modern Philology*, 108.3 (2011 February), 343–74; David Landreth, *The Face of Mammon: The Matter of Money in English Renaissance Literature* (Oxford: Oxford University Press, 2012); Daniel D. Moss, *The Ovidian Vogue: Literary Fashion and Imitative Practice in Late Elizabethan England* (Toronto: University of Toronto Press, 2014); Judith H. Anderson, *Light and Death: Figuration in Spenser, Kepler, Donne, Milton* (New York: Fordham University Press, 2017).
6 Richard A. McCabe (ed.), *The Oxford Handbook of Edmund Spenser* (Oxford: Oxford University Press, 2010); Jeanne Shami, Dennis Flynn, and M. Thomas Hester (eds), *The Oxford Handbook of John Donne* (Oxford: Oxford University Press, 2011).
7 See, for instance, Edmund Gosse, *The Life and Letters of John Donne, Dean of St. Paul's*, 2 vols (New York: Dodd, Mead and Company; London: W. Heinemann, 1899), II.329–41, 351.
8 John Dryden, Preface to *Fables Ancient and Modern, Translated into Verse from Homer, Ovid, Boccaccio, and Chaucer, with Original Poems*, in *'Of Dramatic Poesy' and Other Critical Essays*, ed. George Watson, 2 vols (London: J.M. Dent & Sons, 1962), 2.270–1.
9 Dryden, 'Discourses on Satire and on Epic Poetry' in *'Of Dramatic Poesy' and Other Critical Essays*, 2.76.
10 Michelle O'Callaghan, 'Spenser's Literary Influence', in McCabe (ed.), *The Oxford Handbook of Edmund Spenser*, 664–83. On Spenser's influence in the eighteenth century, see R.C. Frushell, *Edmund Spenser in the Early Eighteenth Century: Education, Imitation, and the Making of a Literary Model* (Pittsburgh: Duquesne University Press, 1999). On Spenser among the Romantics, see Greg Kucich, *Keats, Shelley, and Romantic Spenserianism* (University Park: Pennsylvania State University Press, 1991). For Victorian receptions of Spenser, see David Hill Radcliffe, *Spenser: A Reception History* (Columbia: Camden House, 1996), 114–48.
11 Albert C. Labriola, 'Style, Wit, Prosody in the Poetry of John Donne', in Shami et al. (eds), *The Oxford Handbook of John Donne*, 704–17. On the reception of Donne in the nineteenth century, see Dayton Haskin, *John Donne in the Nineteenth Century* (Oxford: Oxford University Press, 2007), and 'Donne's Afterlife' in Achsah Guibbory (ed.), *The Cambridge Companion to John Donne* (Cambridge: Cambridge University Press, 2006), 233–46. Coleridge, De Quincey, and Browning admired even Donne's much maligned *Metempsychosis*, which also earned the unlikely appreciation of Alexander Pope. See A.J. Smith (ed.), *John Donne: The Critical Heritage* (London: Routledge and Kegan Paul, 1975), 2.154, 274; 347–50.
12 One outlier is Thomas Docherty's *John Donne, Undone* (New York: Methuen, 1986), a deconstructionist reading of Donne.
13 Shami et al. (eds), *The Oxford Handbook of John Donne*, 12–95.
14 Wayne Erickson, 'Spenser's Patrons and Publishers', and Joseph Loewenstein, 'Spenser's Textual History', in McCabe (ed.), *The Oxford Handbook of Edmund Spenser*, 106–24, 637–63. See also Elisabeth Chaghafi, 'Spenser and Book History', in Paul J. Hecht and J.B. Lethbridge (eds), *Spenser in the Moment* (Madison: Fairleigh Dickinson University Press, 2015), 67–99; Andrew Zurcher, 'The Printing of the *Cantos of Mutabilitie* in 1609', in Jane Grogan (ed.), *Celebrating Mutabilitie: Essays on Edmund Spenser's* Mutabilitie Cantos (Manchester: Manchester University Press, 2010), 40–60.
15 On Spenser, Platonism, and Neoplatonism see Robert Ellrodt, *Neoplatonism in the Poetry of Spenser* (Folcroft: Folcroft Press, 1969); Frances Yates, *Elizabethan Neoplatonism Reconsidered: Spenser and Francesco Giorgi* (London: Society for Renaissance Studies, 1977); Jon A. Quitslund, *Spenser's Supreme*

Fiction: Platonic Natural Philosophy and The Faerie Queene (Toronto: University of Toronto Press, 2001); Spenser and Platonism [Special Issue], ed. and introd. Kenneth Borris, Jon Quitslund, and Carol Kaske, Spenser Studies, 24 (2009); Kenneth Borris, Visionary Spenser and the Poetics of Early Modern Platonism (Oxford: Oxford University Press, 2017). Studies on Donne and (Neo-)Platonism tend to focus on 'The Ecstasy'; see, for instance, Catherine Gimelli Martin, 'The Erotology of Donne's "Extasie" and the Secret History of Voluptuous Rationalism', Studies in English Literature 1500-1900, 44.1 (2004 Winter), 121-47. On Donne and science, Charles M. Coffin, John Donne and the New Philosophy (New York: Humanities Press, 1958); Marjorie Nicolson, The Breaking of the Circle: Studies in the Effect of the 'New Science' upon Seventeenth-Century Poetry, rev. ed. (New York: Columbia University Press, 1960); William Empson, Essays on Renaissance Literature, Vol. 1: Donne and the New Philosophy, ed. John Haffenden (Cambridge: Cambridge University Press, 1995); Elizabeth D. Harvey and Timothy M. Harrison, 'Embodied Resonances: Early Modern Science and Tropologies of Connection in Donne's Anniversaries', English Literary History [ELH], 80.4 (2013 Winter), 981-1008. For recent work on Spenser and science, see Mary Thomas Crane, 'Spenser's Giant and the New Science', in Judith H. Anderson and Joan Pong Linton (eds), Go Figure: Energies, Forms, and Institutions in the Early Modern World (New York: Fordham University Press, 2011), 19-37; Sarah Powrie, 'Spenser's Mutabilitie and the Indeterminate Universe', Studies in English Literature 1500-1900, 53.1 (2013 Winter), 73-89.

16 Among the few articles that take a more holistic view of Donne's relation to Spenser are Kenneth Gross, 'Shapes of Time: On the Spenserian Stanza', Spenser Studies, 19 (2004), 27-35; and Elizabeth D. Harvey, 'Nomadic Souls: Pythagoras, Spenser, Donne', Spenser Studies, 22 (2007), 257-79. See also Anne Lake Prescott, 'Menippean Donne', in Shami et al. (eds), The Oxford Handbook of John Donne, 158-79.

17 Izaak Walton, The Lives of John Donne, Sir Henry Wotton, Richard Hooker, George Herbert and Robert Sanderson (London: Oxford University Press, 1927).

18 See, for instance, Trevor Aston (ed.), Crisis in Europe, 1560-1660: Essays from Past and Present, introd. Christopher Hill (London: Routledge & Kegan Paul, 1965); Peter Clark (ed.), The European Crisis of the 1590s: Essays in Comparative History (London and Boston: G. Allen & Unwin, 1985).

19 Allen G. Debus, Man and Nature and Chemistry, Alchemy and the New Philosophy, 1550-1700: Studies in the History of Science and Medicine (London: Variorum, 1987); Frank Lestringant, L'atelier du cosmographe: ou l'image du monde à la Renaissance (Paris: A. Michel, 1991); James J. Bono, The Word of God and the Languages of Man: Interpreting Nature in Early Modern Science and Medicine (Madison: University of Wisconsin Press, 1995).

20 George Boas, 'Macrocosm and Microcosm', in Philip P. Wiener (ed.), Dictionary of the History of Ideas: Studies of Selected Pivotal Ideas (New York: Charles Scribner's Sons, 1973); Michel Foucault, The Order of Things: An Archaeology of Human Sciences (New York: Vintage Books, 1970). See also Leo Spitzer, Classical and Christian Ideas of World Harmony; Prolegomena to an Interpretation of the Word 'Stimmung', ed. Anna Granville Hatcher, pref. René Wellek (Baltimore: Johns Hopkins University Press, 1963); S.K. Heninger, Touches of Sweet Harmony: Pythagorean Cosmology and Renaissance Poetics (San Marino: Huntington Library, 1974); and Leonard Barkan, Nature's Work of Art: The Human Body as Image of the World (New Haven: Yale University Press, 1975).

21 The analogy of macrocosm to microcosm received its fullest enunciation belatedly, in Robert Fludd's Utriusque Cosmi. Allen G. Debus (ed.), Robert Fludd and His Philosophicall Key: Being a Transcription of the Manuscript at Trinity College, Cambridge (New York: Science History Publications, 1979).

22 Margreta de Grazia, 'Fin-de-Siècle Renaissance England', in Elaine Scarry (ed.), Fins de Siècle: English Poetry in 1590, 1690, 1790, 1890, 1990 (Baltimore: Johns Hopkins University Press, 1995), 37-63, shows that historical periodization by century (which in the 1590s could signify any unit of 100, not just years) did not arise until the French Revolution.

23 See Gordon Teskey, 'Renaissance Theory and Criticism', in Michael Groden, Martin Kreiswirth, and Imre Szeman (eds), Johns Hopkins Guide to Literary Theory and Criticism, 2nd ed. (Baltimore: Johns Hopkins University Press, 2005); Leah S. Marcus, 'Renaissance/Early Modern Studies', in Stephen Greenblatt and Giles Gunn (eds), Redrawing Boundaries: The Transformation of English and American Literary Studies (New York: Modern Language Association of America, 1992), 41-63; Heather Dubrow and Frances E. Dolan, 'The Term Early Modern', PMLA, 109.5 (1994 October), 1025-7.

24 Margreta de Grazia, 'The Modern Divide: From Either Side', Journal of Medieval and Early Modern Studies, 37.3 (2007 Fall), 453-66; Jeffrey Jerome Cohen, 'In the Middle of the Early Modern', Journal for Early Modern Cultural Studies, 13.3 (2013 Summer), 128-32.

25 De Grazia, 'The Modern Divide', 456-7, 461, 463; Cohen, 'In the Middle', 128-9.

26 The professional division of the field into sub-specializations, dramatic and non-dramatic literature, can be considered another effect of this fragmentation.

Introduction 11

27 Richard Danson Brown, *'The New Poet': Novelty and Tradition in Spenser's Complaints* (Liverpool: Liverpool University Press, 1999).
28 Ben Jonson, *The Complete Poems*, ed. George Parfitt (London; New York: Penguin Books, 1975), 428. On Spenser's medievalism and archaism see, for example, Judith H. Anderson, *The Growth of a Personal Voice: 'Piers Plowman' and 'The Faerie Queene'* (New Haven: Yale University Press, 1976), and *Reading the Allegorical Intertext* (New York: Fordham University Press, 2008); Andrew Zurcher, 'Spenser's Studied Archaism: the Case of "Mote"', *Spenser Studies*, 21 (2006), 231–40; Helen Cooper, *Pastoral: Medieval into Renaissance* (Ipswich: D.S. Brewer, 2012); Andrew King, 'Spenser, Chaucer, and Medieval Romance', in McCabe (ed.), *The Oxford Handbook of Edmund Spenser*, 553–72; William Kuskin, *Recursive Origins: Writing at the Transition to Modernity* (Notre Dame: Notre Dame University Press, 2013); Kathryn Walls, 'Spenser and the "Medieval" Past: A Question of Definition', in Hecht and Lethbridge (eds), *Spenser in the Moment*, 35–66.
29 Helen Cooper, 'The Origins of the Early Modern', *Journal for Early Modern Cultural Studies*, 13.3 (2013 Summer), 133–7; *On Periodization: Selected Essays from the English Institute*, ed. Virginia Jackson (Cambridge, MA: The English Institute, 2010), http://hdl.handle.net/2027/heb.90047.0001.001, especially Caroline Levine, 'Infrastructuralism, or the Tempo of Institutions', and Marshall Brown, 'The Din of Dawn'.
30 James Simpson, *1350–1547: Reform and Cultural Revolution* (Oxford: Oxford University Press 2004); Steven N. Zwicker, 'Is There Such a Thing as Restoration Literature?', *Huntington Library Quarterly*, 69.3 (2006 September), 425–50.
31 See, for instance, Curtis Perry, *The Making of Jacobean Culture: James I and the Renegotiation of Elizabethan Literary Practice* (Cambridge: Cambridge University Press, 1997); Heather Dubrow, *Echoes of Desire: English Petrarchism and Its Counterdiscourses* (Ithaca: Cornell University Press, 1995), 221.
32 J.B. Lethbridge (ed.), *Shakespeare and Spenser: Attractive Opposites* (Manchester and New York: Manchester University Press, 2008); Anita Gilman Sherman, *Skepticism and Memory in Shakespeare and Donne* (New York: Palgrave Macmillan, 2007); Catherine Gimelli Martin, 'Milton's and Donne's Stargazing Lovers, Sex, and the New Astronomy', *Studies in English Literature 1500–1900*, 54.1 (2014 Winter), 143–71; James A. Riddell and Stanley Stewart, *Jonson's Spenser: Evidence and Historical Criticism* (Pittsburgh: Duquesne University Press, 1995).
33 Rachel E. Hile, *Spenserian Satire: A Tradition of Indirection* (Manchester: Manchester University Press, 2017), reveals Spenser as a major influence on English satire; Hugh Grady, *John Donne and Baroque Allegory: The Aesthetics of Fragmentation* (Cambridge: Cambridge University Press, 2017) places Donne within an allegorical tradition, typically the province of Spenser.
34 Theresa M. DiPasquale, 'Anti-Court Satire, Religious Polemic, and the Many Faces of Antichrist: An Intertextual Reading of Donne's "Satyre 4" and Spenser's *Faerie Queene*', *Studies in Philology*, 112.2 (2015 Spring), 264–302.
35 My own monograph in progress, *Donne's Spenser: Between Allegory and Metaphor*, aims to correct this gap. Segments from this project have been published in article form: Yulia Ryzhik, 'Complaint and Satire in Spenser and Donne: Limits of Poetic Justice', *English Literary Renaissance*, 47.1 (2017 Spring), 110–35, and 'Spenser and Donne Go Fishing', *Spenser Studies*, 31–2 (2018), 417–37.
36 'Spenser, Donne, and the Work of Poetry' (45) at the 2012 MLA in Seattle (speakers: Judith H. Anderson, Theresa DiPasquale, Heather Dubrow, Anne Lake Prescott, and Melissa E. Sanchez; Sean H. McDowell presiding), and 'Spenser's Donne and Done' (330) at the 2014 MLA in Chicago (speakers: Joseph A. Campana, Jeff Dolven, Linda Gregerson, and Yulia Ryzhik; Gerard Passannante presiding).
37 *PMLA*, 126.5 (2011 November), 1258–9; *PMLA*, 128.5 (2013 November), 1169.
38 However, see Richard Danson Brown, Chapter 1 below, on Spenser's 'rough' style.
39 See Patrick Cheney, Chapter 4 below, on what these choices entail for Spenser's and Donne's literary careers.
40 Harold Bloom, *The Anxiety of Influence: A Theory of Poetry*, 2nd ed. (New York: Oxford University Press, 1997 [1973]).
41 W. Jackson Bate, *The Burden of the Past and the English Poet* (Cambridge, MA: Harvard University Press, 1970).
42 On potential methodological problems when approaching Spenser and Donne, see J.B. Lethbridge, 'Spenser, Donne, I.A. Richards and the Limitations of Practical Criticism', *Ranam: Recherches Anglaises et Nord-Américaines*, 49 (2016), 29–42, 207–8.
43 J.B. Lethbridge, 'Introduction: Spenser, Marlowe, Shakespeare: Methodological Investigations', in Lethbridge (ed.), *Shakespeare and Spenser: Attractive Opposites*, 1–53, esp. 2–4, 49, 52–3.

44 See also Raymond-Jean Frontain, 'Donne, Spenser, and the Performative Mode of Renaissance Poetry', *Explorations in Renaissance Culture*, 32.1 (2006 Summer), 76–102.
45 Lynn Enterline, *The Rhetoric of the Body from Ovid to Shakespeare* (Cambridge: Cambridge University Press, 2000); Syrithe Pugh, *Spenser and Ovid* (Aldershot and Burlington: Ashgate, 2005); Daniel D. Moss, *The Ovidian Vogue: Literary Fashion and Imitative Practice in Late Elizabethan England* (Toronto: University of Toronto Press, 2014). Moss's book contains chapters on both Spenser and Donne, but never draws the third line between Spenser and Donne to complete the triangle.
46 See also Joseph A. Campana and Scott Maisano (eds), *Renaissance Posthumanism* (New York: Fordham University Press, 2016), and Ayesha Ramachandran and Melissa E. Sanchez (eds), *Spenser and 'The Human'* [*Spenser Studies* 30] (New York: AMC Press, 2015).

1

Caring to turn back: overhearing Spenser in Donne

Richard Danson Brown

It is in terms of form that conventional literary history sees the starkest contrast between Spenser and Donne. This is a narrative of complacent smoothness being righteously usurped by avant-garde roughness, as the Monarch of Wit ousts 'Englands Arch Poet'.[1] Thomas Carew's supercharged elegy for Donne as the 'Promethean' pioneer of a new poetic who purges 'The Muses garden' (lines 386–7) remains prophetically at the heart of this literary-historical narrative. As recently as the *Oxford Handbook of John Donne* (2011), for leading scholars the space between Donne and Spenser can seem almost an ontological chasm. In an essay on the genres of Donne's love lyrics and their problematic description in literary history, Dayton Haskin reaches for a binary characterization of the two poets, which is, as he is well aware, of long duration: 'Modernist poets found vital inspiration in Donne's having made so productive a break with his predecessors. Even today, to come upon Donne's voice after hearing Spenser's can seem a difference as great as between night and day.'[2] The night/day opposition is another way of putting what John Carey stated less tactfully thirty years earlier: 'In place of Spenser's dreamy conservatism', a completed *Metempsychosis* would have been 'not only progressive and contentious in its intellectual cast, but also wedded to immediacy and the real world'.[3] The assumptions are, in their different forms, analogous. Donne's voice is individual and contentious where Spenser's is monolithic and conservative; a new Donne day emerges out of old Spenserian [k]night, in which the immediacy of the real is proleptic of the intellectual adventure of the empirical seventeenth century as it brushes aside dusty chivalric absurdities.[4] Of course these are broad-brush characterizations – pedagoguish metaphors intended to provoke reflection on the experience of reading very different poets – which few literary historians would defend without qualification.[5] They do nevertheless provide a useful sighter for a chapter which aims to take another look at the formal affiliations between Spenser and Donne. My contention is a simple one: Donne learned much about verse form and verse shape from his reading of Spenser; the dialogic connections and resonances of tone between their works are richer and less negative than is conventionally assumed. Indeed, Donne's *Satires* are more thoroughly Spenserian than is often thought, which in turn underlines the extent to which satire is an important, often neglected facet of Spenser's work. I contend that Donne's poetry covertly and explicitly 'leans and hearkens after' Spenserian forms and discoveries about poetic form.[6] This is not to say that Donne writes like Spenser so much as to suggest that

Donne's innovations of form, metre, and morphology have significant Spenserian precedents. By characterizing Donne as a bold stylistic innovator, conventional literary history has neglected Spenser as himself a risky, innovative writer, thus muting the rich dialogue which exists between their works.[7]

I want to overhear Spenser in Donne, and to suggest through this critical eavesdropping that the latter owes the former a more significant debt both in terms of poetic forms and in terms of genre. 'Overhear' of course is different from 'trace the influence of', or 'establish the debt to'. The traditional view has been that Donne reacts against Spenser more than he builds upon him. His lyric forms have been seen as either testament to his individuality – in which a new voice imposes itself on tradition – or, more persuasively, as a continuation with difference of a tradition of short poems not written for music.[8] But to overhear Spenser in Donne offers a different approach, which suggests not so much influence as a way in which the textures of Donne's poetry may be seen to echo, and intersect with, Spenser's. Above all, it suggests a different way of thinking about literary affiliations. Rather than Bloom's still influential anxious conversation between competing 'strong' poets intent upon 'misreading' the work of their coercive parents, the reader who overhears Spenser in Donne's formal structures is attentive to an alternative literary history, in which formal resonances, variations around similar melodies, may be as important as direct, frictive, filial allusion. In brief, to understand the relationship between Donne and Spenser we need a model of reading which is intertextual, Andersonian, rather than anxious, Bloomian.[9]

How did Donne hear Spenser, and to what extent is it possible to overhear Spenser in Donne? Donne's *Metempsychosis* is the orthodox place to begin this enquiry, since it has long been read as a Donnean response to, or parody of, *The Faerie Queene*, written in a stanza form based on the Spenserian.[10] As a number of scholars have highlighted, *Metempsychosis* has several Spenserian echoes, not only of *The Faerie Queene*.[11] Consider an intertext which has not received as much significant comment: the description of the proud swan, which rechannels an image from *Prothalamion*.[12] Spenser describes a pair of swans of staggering, supra-Jovian whiteness:

> With that I saw two Swannes of goodly hewe,
> Come softly swimming downe along the Lee;
> Two fairer Birds I yet did never see:
> The snow which doth the top of *Pindus* strew,
> Did never whiter shew,
> Nor *Jove* himselfe when he a Swan would be
> For love of *Leda*, whiter did appeare:
> Yet *Leda* was they say as white as he,
> Yet not so white as these, nor nothing neare;
> So purely white they were,
> That even the gentle streame, the which them bare,
> Seem'd foule to them
>
> (lines 37–49)[13]

Prothalamion is worth quoting at length, because it is only at length that we get the dazzling sense of the swans' overbearing whiteness: fair birds become the snow on

Pindus become Jove-as-swan mating with the über-white Leda, yet not even these lovers were 'so white as these'; Spenser launders his swans beyond previous example and any sense of realism. Donne takes in these emblems of purity when describing his own swan: 'A swan, so white that you may unto him / Compare all whitenesse, but himselfe to none, / Glided along' (lines 232–4).[14] At one level, Donne's swan confirms Carew's analysis: where Spenser seems 'windy', Donne laconically juxtaposes a very white swan with its predatory instincts: 'And with his arched necke this poore fish catch'd' (line 235). Yet as John B. Bender long ago commented, Spenser's superficially prolix description is emblematically functional: 'the extreme whiteness of the swans removes them from the realm of ordinary worldly birds, or even ordinary mythological birds'.[15] Donne's side-swipe remembers *Prothalamion* in a different fictional setting: where Spenser's birds emblematically represent the mysteries of marriage, Donne presents a symbol of pride, opportunistically gobbling the fish which is the current resting place of the wandering soul.

A more complex exchange takes place in stanza XL. Donne's version of this 'familiar elephant lore', ultimately deriving from a contemporary Portuguese account of India, looks back to Spenser's *Visions of the Worlds Vanitie* sequence from *Complaints* (1591): a huge elephant is destroyed either by an ant (Spenser) or by a mouse (Donne).[16] Spenser's version concentrates on the elephant's 'foolish vanitie' and, like the rest of the sequence, issues a compact warning against the 'surquedrie', or arrogant pride, of the powerful (*Visions of the Worlds Vanitie*, lines 103, 105). For Donne, the same source materials furnish a sardonic reflection on the mouse's self-destructive malice: 'thus he made his foe, his prey, and tombe: / Who cares not to turn back, may any whither come' (*Metempsychosis*, lines 399–400). What is provocative about Donne's version is that it fails to repudiate Spenser's; unlike the allusion to *Prothalamion*, this one has no sense of teasing or parody. Rather, Donne's focus on the mouse (another incarnation of the wandering soul) enables a related form of moralizing. Despite the anti-Spenserian claim of the Epistle that he 'would have no such readers as [he] can teach', this stanza shows a Donne able to work ambiguously within the constraints of the moralizing tradition.[17] Not caring to turn back is certainly reckless, and yet the line is pitched between admiration and warning. The mouse destroys itself, but the speaker enjoys the mouse's daring while at the same time building on Spenser's satirical depiction in the *Visions* sequence of the high and mighty being undone by the apparently insignificant.[18] The next sonnet in the *Visions* concludes with a couplet which is akin to Donne's line in its ambivalence about the catastrophes it describes: 'Straunge thing me seemeth, that so small a thing / Should able be so great an one to wring' (lines 125–6). The nod to Spenser invites the reader to enjoy the spectacle of Donne inhabiting the Spenserian tradition; to paraphrase T.S. Eliot, mature poets care to turn back.[19] This example also shows Donne mimicking a key facet of Spenser's form. The aphoristic alexandrine follows the pattern of two equal hemistichs of six syllables each, a permutation used numerous times in *The Faerie Queene*.[20] Donne's line is congruent with the antithetical, summarizing function Spenser frequently gives to his alexandrines. Donne's stanza suggests the sophistication of his reading of Spenser. As the didactic aesthetic of *The Faerie Queene* is more complex than the programme sketched in the Letter to Raleigh, so Donne's adaptation of Spenser's poems – juxtaposing a form adapted from the epic with content borrowed from the significantly less celebrated *Visions of the Worlds Vanitie* – indicates a supple responsiveness to Spenserian modes alongside an omnivorous curiosity about the Spenser's oeuvre.

Metempsychosis remains problematic in terms of tone, genre, and intent. Anne Lake Prescott's description of the poem – 'fifty-two quasi-Spenserian stanzas of nine pentameter lines and one alexandrine' – raises the relationship between *Metempsychosis* and *The Faerie Queene*.[21] Is it a parody, a tribute, or something else? One answer may be numerological: as Prescott and Yulia Ryzhik have suggested, *Metempsychosis* may have a deliberate 'temporal patterning' (on the fifty-two weeks of the year), which would recall the complex horological play in *Epithalamion* and other contemporaneous poems.[22] None the less, numerology would not wholly clarify the question of the kind of intertextual relationship which exists between Donne's poem and Spenser's. Indeed, there has been little detailed consideration of what might be called the 'quasi-ness' of Donne's stanza – that is, its problematic relationship with its apparent parent. In this context, one is reminded of Spenser's DuBellayan description of 'bitter step-dame Nature' in *Ruines of Rome* (line 114), a description which perhaps conveys some of the tensions between the two forms. Elizabeth D. Harvey has recently suggested that Donne's stanza adds 'a vitalizing anomaly' to a Spenserian ruin in the form of its tenth line which thus refuses 'the stately confines of the Spenserian architecture'.[23] There are indeed significant distinctions between the two stanzas, which I go on to explore. At the same time, it is important to recognize that in many respects Donne relies on tricks of phrasing and metrical transposition borrowed from Spenser. The first stanza of *Metempsychosis* features a knowing Spenserism in line 5: 'And the great world t'his aged evening' rhymes with 'sing', thus requiring 'evening' to be sounded as a trisyllable. Spenser provides a precedent for this in rhyming 'Euening' with monosyllables like 'King' and 'bring'.[24] In evolving a *Faerie Queene*-like (or perhaps -lite, since the *Metempsychosis* stanza is less demanding than the Spenserian) stanza of his own, Donne necessarily had recourse to such Spenserian rhyming devices. This example is particularly striking, since it is a paragoge to satisfy the demands of the metre, whereby the word is extended from its usual form.[25] Linguistic distortion to satisfy metre is one of the hallmarks of Spenser's style. That Donne follows Spenser's practice suggests the poetic utility of this kind of swelling of the windy page.[26]

Although the *Metempsychosis* stanza responds to the Spenserian precedent, it organizes syntax into different units. Consider stanza XXIX, Donne's bravura defence of fish, in the context of a stanza on monstrous fish from Guyon's journey to the Bower of Bliss:

> Is any kinde subject to rape like fish?
> Ill unto man, they neither doe, nor wish:
> Fishers they kill not, nor with noise awake,
> They doe not hunt, nor strive to make a prey
> Of beasts, nor their yong sonnes to beare away;
> Foules they pursue not, nor do undertake
> To spoile the nests industrious birds do make;
> Yet them all these unkinde kinds feed upon,

> To kill them is an occupation,
>   And lawes make Fasts, and Lents for their destruction.
>   (Donne, *Metempychosis*, lines 281–90)

> The dreadfull Fish, that hath deseru'd the name
>   Of Death, and like him lookes in dreadfull hew,
>   The griesly Wasserman, that makes his game
>   The flying ships with swiftnes to pursew,
>   The horrible Sea-satyre, that doth shew
>   His fearefull face in time of greatest storme,
>   Huge *Ziffius*, whom Mariners eschew
>   No lesse, then rockes (as trauellers informe,)
> And greedy *Rosmarines* with visages deforme.
>   (*FQ* II.xii.24)

Donne's phrasing is again markedly Spenserian. Lines 286–7 share Spenser's fondness for verbal rhymes in the form of auxiliary + infinitive: 'do undertake' and 'do make', which are mirrored by 'to pursew' and 'doth shew' in Spenser. Since the *b*-rhyme is the first triplet rhyme in the *Metempsychosis* stanza, it is perhaps unsurprising to find Donne using one of Spenser's favourite tricks for satisfying the rhyme scheme by avoiding inflected verb endings.[27] The organization of syntax shows the biggest differences between the two stanza forms. Spenser's *ababbcbcc* stanza is a braided, imbricated form which serves to connect the disparate semantic elements. In William Empson's classic description, it falls into two unequal halves connected by the pivotal fifth line, which may supplement the *abab* pattern, introduce the *cbcc* conclusion, or offer further variations.[28] The Spenserian stanza above is a list of oceanic horrors, where the fifth line provides an additive connection between the first and second quatrains; as such, the first couplet's climax is muted as the fifth line introduces a new monster. Similarly, the couplet in lines 8 and 9 is shared between two different creatures – Ziffius and the Rosemarines – with the effect that, though the rhymes are clearly audible, they do not impose themselves on to what is an aptly fluid syntax, controlled more by the dynamic of itemization than by argument or formal design. Although the Spenserian is a technically demanding form by virtue of its triple and fourfold rhymes, it is also – as most readers of *The Faerie Queene* come to recognize – supremely flexible, allowing huge syntactic variety within a shape which is simultaneously constricting and plastic.[29] In contrast, the *Metempsychosis* stanza is less interlaced: it is constructed on a base of couplets and triplets, with the interlacing *b*-rhyme providing the only real equivalence to the delicate involutions of the Spenserian. The *aabccbbddd* structure is more like the couplet- and triplet-driven forms of Donne's lyrics, such as 'The Anniversarie' (ten lines rhyming *aabbccdddd*), 'The Flea' (nine lines rhyming *aabbcddd*), and particularly 'The Relique' (eleven lines rhyming *aabbcddceee*), which resembles *Metempsychosis* in having a single interlacing rhyme.[30] Donne's form has consequences for his syntax. *Metempsychosis* is more committed to (sometimes violent) enjambment, with the effect that lineation is frequently subordinated to the authority of the phrase: 'But if my dayes be long, and good enough, / In vaine this sea shall enlarge, or enrough / It selfe'; 'he had swallow'd cleare / This, and much such, and unblam'd devour'd there / All' (lines 51–3; 238–40). As in the shorter poems, the 'masculine, persuasive force' of the individual speaking voice threatens to override verse form, with the effect that, although Donne's stanza commits him to more couplet and triplet climaxes, these are not felt in the same way that they are in Spenser.[31] Where the Spenserian stanza labours to conceal its artifice in a permissive syntax built out of strongly individuated lines, the *Metempsychosis* stanza, like most of Donne's work, continuously strives to make the reader conscious of the painful subordination of language to poetic form.[32]

This problematic kinship between the two forms is vividly shown by Donne's *d*-rhyme, the second triplet in his stanza. While individual alexandrines may be reminiscent of alexandrines in *The Faerie Queene*, the stanza's syntactic structure serves to isolate its last three lines from the body of the stanza. In the stanza quoted above, the first line introduces a question – 'Is any kinde subject to rape like fish?' – which is then expanded in the next six. Syntax is largely contained within the couplet structure, as in 'Foules they pursue not, nor do undertake / To spoile the nests industrious birds do make'. The first seven lines prove the case outlined in the opening: fish are abused more than any other species. The pause at the end of line 287 is conclusive: the narrator has carried his point through a number of related examples, which means that the last three lines take on a different function from that performed by the *c*-rhymes in *The Faerie Queene*. This structure occurs throughout *Metempsychosis*: as many as twenty of the poem's fifty-two stanzas have in the 1633 edition a strong pause between lines 7 and 8.[33] The final triplet thus takes on a pointed, summarizing quality, as Donne's defence of fish turns into a quip about the Elizabethan legislation of fish-eating days in the wake of religious change; a potentially recherché question about piscine rights turns into a quasi-satiric epigram about 'Fasts, and Lents'.[34] In contrast, the *c*-rhymes in *The Faerie Queene* seldom work like this because the seventh line interlaces with the main body of the stanza; the list which runs through II.xii.24 shows that the *c*-rhyme is neither structured nor felt as an epigrammatic triplet. As noted above, when Spenser wants to clinch his stanza with a summary, this is typically done through either the final couplet or an antithetical alexandrine.

This sense of difficult kinship is also apparent in the ways that Donne and Spenser handle debate and dialogue through their stanzas. As the fish stanza indicates, *Metempsychosis* is – as befits its subject matter – driven more by intellectual debate than by narrative; the latter aspect, arguably, interested Donne the least, which may have contributed to his failure to get any further with the poem. As with the love lyrics, there is a sense in which Donne is most excited by his poem when he can use it as a framework for discursive exploration rather than story-telling. Stanza XI debates the meaning of Original Sin in the voice of a 'curious Rebell':

> So fast in us doth this corruption grow,
> That now wee dare aske why wee should be so.
> Would God (disputes the curious Rebell) make
> A law, and would not have it kept? Or can
> His creatures will, crosse his? Of every man
> For one, will God (and be just) vengeance take?
> Who sinn'd? 'twas not forbidden to the snake

> Nor her, who was not then made; nor is't writ
> That Adam cropt, or knew the apple; yet
>   The worme and she, and he, and wee endure for it.

(lines 101–10)

The first couplet is again a closed unit which introduces the point at issue: why do we suffer under the sentence of Original Sin?[35] In the rest of the stanza, syntax is shaped by phrase rather than by line, with the result that the questions repeatedly infringe line boundaries. This characteristically Donnean writing maybe be compared with the anxious, question-driven syntax of poems such as Holy Sonnet 5 ('If poysonous mineralls') and 'The Indifferent'. Pierre Legouis long ago commented that the aesthetic tension in such writing means that 'When it seems to have given itself most rope, it proves to have tied itself tightest'.[36] Yet in this stanza, the rope is almost slackened. The accumulation of oracular questions is barely contained by the triplet which seems to peter out inconclusively. This impression is suggested by the *yet: it* half rhyme (unused in *The Faerie Queene*),[37] and the insistent internal rhymes of the alexandrine – 'The worme and *she*, and *he*, and *wee* endure for it' – which show the curious Rebel in the process of assembling his argument, groping for emphasis, an impression confirmed by the narrator's repudiation of this position in the next stanza, 'Arguing is heretiques game' (line 118).[38] Nevertheless, Donne makes his stanza a vehicle for argument: though the *Metempsychosis* stanza alludes to the Spenserian, in practice the abrasion of syntax against lineal structure is symptomatic of Donne's writing.

Spenser's dialogic stanzas tend to be less contorted, although what is at issue between the Redcrosse Knight and Despair in the following example is no less pointed than the contention between heresy and orthodoxy in Donne. Where the latter undermines his stanza's line structure with the force of insistent questions, Spenser exploits his interlaced stanza to capture the insidious nature of Despair's challenge:

> The knight much wondred at his suddeine wit,
>   And said, The terme of life is limited,
>   Ne may a man prolong, nor shorten it;
>   The souldier may not moue from watchfull sted,
>   Nor leaue his stand, vntill his Captaine bed.
>   Who life did limit by almightie doome,
>   (Quoth he) knowes best the termes established;
>   And he, that points the Centonell his roome,
> Doth license him depart at sound of morning droome.

(*FQ* I.ix.41)

Syntactically, the contrast between these two stanzas underlines the different formal approaches Donne and Spenser took to stanzaic writing. Spenser's stanza eloquently exemplifies Empson's observation of the significance of couplet climaxes, and Alpers's model of the sovereignty of the individual line. Each line is strongly end-stopped: Spenser wants the reader to register the limits of those lines in a passage which is existentially concerned with the question of what is or is not legitimately 'limited'. We read the exchange better once we attend to how the debate is managed within and across the constraints of line shape and rhyme scheme. In the first five lines, the astonished Redcrosse musters a defence against Despair, clinched in the couplet between lines 4–5 in the image of the watchman who may not leave his post. Despair then reworks the same image, and in the queasy *c*-rhyme – hideously underlined by the one-off morphological distortion *droome* – unpicks Redcrosse's argument.[39] Where Donne's syntax works against his stanza form, Spenser uses all the permutations – including distortion and one-off rhymes – possible within his stanza and within the limits of his stanza.

Finally, this passage has another Donnean intertext in *Satire III*, which recycles the commonplace of the individual believer as a 'Centonell': 'O desperate coward, wilt thou seeme bold, and / To thy foes and his (who made thee to stand / Sentinell in his worlds garrison) thus yeeld, / And for forbidden warres, leave th'appointed field?' (lines 29–32).[40] Some manuscripts have 'Souldier' for 'Sentinell', providing if anything a stronger link between Donne and Spenser, since the correction of 'souldier' to 'Centonell' is a key part of Despair's revisionary strategy in repointing Redcrosse's metaphor through the process of the stanza.[41] At any event, the remembering of Despair's 'Centonell' in the highly charged theological and autobiographical contexts of *Satire III* is strong evidence of Donne's appreciative reading of Spenser in the 1590s as a writer wrestling with analogous pressures, albeit in very different genres.[42]

Such a reading partly reinforces the binary between 'rough' Donne and 'smooth' Spenser which I began by problematizing, and it remains the case in terms of versification and lineation that Donne continues to *feel* rougher, less regular, than Spenser. Nevertheless, the model of an exclusively 'smooth' Spenser remains problematic, and it was not the only way in which Donne and his contemporaries read Spenser.[43] Theresa DiPasquale's recent work on Donne's *Satire IV* and Spenser's House of Pride is exemplary of Donne's receptivity to the complex tonalities within Spenser's works, and does valuable work in suggesting 'the compelling overlap between Spenser's late Elizabethan and early Jacobean readership'.[44] However, she overlooks Spenser's own verse satire. I turn now to the parallels between *Satire IV* and *Mother Hubberds Tale* from the *Complaints* volume (1591). Though *Mother Hubberd* is not typically considered as part of the surge of verse satire written in the 1590s, the poem contains strong satiric elements and is written in the same verse form later employed by Donne, Guilpin, Marston, and Hall.[45] The poem was a *cause célèbre* in the 1590s, when it was officially suppressed, or 'called in' – meaning that unsold copies were publicly destroyed – apparently because of its attack on Burghley. In the final episode, in which the Fox masquerades as chief minister, Spenser attacks Burghley's nepotism through the manipulation of preferments: 'He crammed them with crumbs of Benefices, / And fild their mouthes with meeds of malefices' (lines 1153–4).[46] Such satire of Burghley's control of juicy opportunities finds a ready analogue in *Satire IV*, where the speaker is told 'That offices are entail'd, and that there are / Perpetuities of them, lasting as farre / As the last day' (lines 123–5). Robin Robbins's note, which makes the connection with Burghley's grooming of Robert Cecil to succeed him as chief minister, authoritatively glosses 'entail'd' as '[p]redetermined to be inherited': in both texts, the influential parent socially engineers his children's succession.[47] The word may also contain a suppressed pun on the Ape in *Mother Hubberd*, who plays the false king to the Fox's false first minister. The Ape's tail figures prominently in the poem's climax, when Mercury cuts it off as punishment for his impersonation; 'Since which, all Apes ... of their tailes are utterlie bereft', as the narrator drily comments, reflecting that the Ape will look more human without his tail than previously (lines 1380-5).[48] This intertextual play suggests Donne's receptivity to Spenser's poem and its jaundiced view of the Elizabethan court.

Mother Hubberd is a provocative text to reread in the light of the smooth Spenser/ rough Donne dichotomy. The kinship between their work can be discerned in the way in which the two poets conceptualize poetic language as they update the heroic couplet. As a term from Dryden's criticism, 'heroic couplet' is problematic: at this period of stylistic change and experiment, narrative poems written in decasyllabic couplets are best thought of as Elizabethan recastings of the *Canterbury Tales* couplet.[49] Questions of appropriate style circulate in both the dedication to *Mother Hubberd* and its narrative frame. This document asserts that the poem was '*long sithens composed in the raw conceipt of my youth*', which many scholars have taken at face value, often in the hopes of shedding light on either the relationship with Burghley or possible motivations behind Spenser's emigration to Ireland.[50] The point at issue is what the function of this remark was when the poem was published in 1591. Spenser and Ponsonby (or Ponsonby alone, if we accept Jean Brink's theory that *Complaints* was an unofficial publication)[51] would have fully recognized the inflammatory potential of the poem, so the dedication serves to draw the reader's attention away from that possibility.[52] This is old words dressed new, Spenser is saying, with the effect that the dedication, like the framing device, is an elegant, self-protecting modesty topos. Spenser presents the poem as an exercise in deliberate simplicity: '*Simple is the device, and the composition meane, yet carrieth some delight, even the rather because of the simplicitie and meannesse thus personated*'.[53] Though no reference is made to satire, Spenser's terminology, with the connection of aesthetic delight to '*simplicitie and meannesse*', anticipates the Juvenalian aggression characteristic of 1590s satire, and long since diagnosed by Alvin Kernan.[54] Similarly, the poem's Chaucerian framing device explicitly derogates from classical decorum through its failure to invoke a muse. The 'termes' of this gesture are complex. The poet-narrator self-consciously, and with a degree of humour, passes over chivalric tales 'of Ladies, and their Paramoures ... of the Faeries and their strange attires / And some of Giaunts hard to be beleeved' (lines 28-31). I am not, this seems to say, proposing on this occasion to stick to trusted formulae from my back catalogue – you won't find Orgoglio or Argante *here*:

> Amongst the rest a good old woman was,
> Hight Mother *Hubberd*, who did farre surpas
> The rest in honest mirth, that seem'd her well:
> She when her turne was come her tale to tell,
> Tolde of a strange adventure, that betided
> Betwixt the Foxe and th' Ape by him misguided;
> The which for that my sense it greatly pleased,
> All were my spirite heavie and diseased,
> Ile write in termes, as she the same did say,
> So well as I her words remember may.

> No Muses aide me needes heretoo to call;
> Base is the style, and matter meane withall.
>
> (lines 33–44)

To an extent, Spenser keeps his neoclassical credentials in order. Though Mother Hubberd's 'honest mirth ... seem'd her well', this does not detract from the fact that her tale, like her style, remains 'Base'. The narrator's resolution to record her tale suggests that the text we read is a pellucid redaction of what she actually said; as W.L. Renwick commented long ago, *Mother Hubberd* displays Spenser's understanding of 'how verse must on occasion approach (but not become) the everyday cadence of prose'.[55] Spenser implies that Chaucerian rhyming couplets are an almost natural speech idiom that requires no help from the Muses. This mirrors Puttenham's characterization of the form of *The Canterbury Tales* as 'but riding rhyme, nevertheless very well becoming the matter of that pleasant pilgrimage in which every man's part is played with much decency'.[56] Elizabethan scansion of Chaucer – hampered by a lack of awareness of the likely sounding of the terminal -e in Middle English – was problematic. At one level, the *Mother Hubberd* frame deploys poetic modesty to disguise satiric intent ('how could anyone be upset by such inconsequentialities?'). At another, it is seriously invested in a notion of the Chaucerian idiom which holds that Chaucer's forms were less distinguished than his matter; this is '*but* riding rhyme', so the reader is being warned not to expect any of the stylistic sophistication of the 1590 *Faerie Queene* in this new-yet-old poem (emphasis mine).[57] Some knowing stylistic crudeness is evident in this passage. Although, as Jeff Dolven notes, Spenser usually aims for and achieves iambic regularity, there are moments throughout this poem which eschew the stylistic regularity and polish of *The Faerie Queene*.[58] Consider the bumpy, mimetic repetition of related terms for story-telling: 'She when her turne was come her *tale* to *tell*, / *Tolde*' (emphases mine). Spenser is always unafraid of functional redundancy, but in this case, the inelegance underlines the tale's oral character.

Similarly, the recurring pairs of feminine rhymes in lines 37–40 are remarkable because the 1590 *Faerie Queene* almost entirely banishes them.[59] In the context of a disavowal of the Muses, such rhymes convey something of the 'meannesse' highlighted by the dedication. The rapid conjunction of 'misguided' and 'diseased' in rhyming positions, if not in the same key as Marston's 'sharp-fang'd Satyrist', manifests a poetic distinct from the vatic tone and aureate diction of the opening of *The Faerie Queene*, which deliberately throws the emphasis of rhyme on to negative terminology.[60] The sheer preponderance of such rhymes – including other instances of successive feminine rhymes (e.g. lines 1129–32; 1191–6) – indicates Spenser's cultivation of the low style in *Mother Hubberd*, alongside a permissiveness in respect of diction and metre which in some measure anticipates Donne.[61] Consider a related example from the end of the poem: as Jove resolves to unseat the Ape from his usurped kingship, he wants to 'blot his brutish name / Unto the world, that never after anie / Should of his race be voyd of infamie' (lines 1240–2). The rhyme on 'anie' is disyllabic, so the line scans as an iambic hendecasyllabic with a feminine ending. Yet this is paired with a iambic decasyllabic, in which the accent is placed on the first and third syllables of 'infamie'; additionally, there is an imperfect consonantal join between 'a*n*ie' and 'infamie' in the rhyme. Such slippage of accent between rhyming terms is unusual for Spenser, and underlines both the raw style of the poem as a whole and the comedy of this episode.[62] Crucially, this is a Spenser unafraid of roughness.

Like the other *Complaints*, *Mother Hubberds Tale* is stealthily concerned with the ethos of poetry in cultural contexts felt to be inimical to its practice.[63] The narrator's commentary about style is as revelatory of Spenserian ambiguity as the later passage about court poetry which tries – in my view, with only limited success – to demarcate the 'right' practice of the art from the seductive confections perpetrated by the Ape in amoral mimicry of poetry as a reformative art 'whose onely pride / Is vertue to advaunce, and vice deride' (lines 811–12).[64] This is an attitude and style – a self-conscious scepticism about the very poetic means through which satire exists – which is related to the persona Donne produces for the court described in *Satire IV*. To turn to this poem is then not like turning from night to day, but is rather to see the continuation of related stylistic motifs and intellectual agendas in similarly dangerous fictional contexts, where the line between the imagined and the real is equivocal, to use a word which highlights the ideological jeopardy in which Donne's speaker stands as a Catholic sympathizer in a Protestant court.[65] As *Mother Hubberd* begins with the juxtaposition of Mother Hubberd's 'base' orality with the narrator's more urbane linguistic standards, so *Satire IV* begins with the encounter between the narrator and 'A thing' of the court that turns on questions of register, tone, and implication, while radically manipulating the couplet form (line 18). As in *Metempsychosis*, Donne privileges syntax above line shape. Immediately before this encounter, the speaker violently ruptures line and morphology to secure a rhyme: 'of good as forget- / full, as proud, as lustfull, and as much in debt' (lines 13–14).[66] Traditional commentary has seen such gestures as almost proto-modernist, as though Donne was impatient with the bonds of the couplet and was working towards a kind of free verse. It would be more apt to suggest that Donne's attitude to word form is Spenserian: like Spenser, Donne is ready to distort morphology and accent for poetic effect. Again, my point is not that Donne writes like Spenser, but rather that in engineering his own rough style he draws on the possibilities afforded by Spenser's promiscuous and experimental poetic practice.[67] In this sense, there is a broad congruence between Donne's encounter with the 'thing' and the framing device of *Mother Hubberds Tale*. Donne's narrator objects to this figure for precisely the kind of stylistic infractions which many readers have complained about in the satires:

> This thing hath travail'd, and saith, speakes all tongues,
> And only know'th what to all States belongs;
> Made of th'Accents, and best phrase of all these,
> He speakes one language; If strange meats displease,
> Art can deceive, or hunger force my tast,
> But Pedants motley tongue, souldiers bumbast,
> Mountebankes drugtongue, nor the termes of law
> Are strong enough preparatives, to draw
> Me to beare this: yet I must be content
> With his tongue, in his tongue, call'd complement:
> In which he can win widdowes, and pay scores,

> Make men speake treason, cosen subtlest whores,
> Out-flatter favorites, or outlie either
> Jovius, or Surius, or both together.
>
> (*Satire IV*, lines 35–48)

The register of Donne's *Satires* is challenging, and very different from the Chaucerian narrative of *Mother Hubberd*, which is probably why the close proximity between Spenser's work and that of Donne, Marston, and Guilpin has until recently been neglected.[68] Gregory Kneidel summarizes the problems these poems pose: 'Donne's Satires remain difficult poems to understand and appreciate ... there is no strong consensus about what was in his mind when he wrote them'.[69] This passage assumes knowledge of contemporary Catholic historians (Jovius and Surius),[70] the 'coney-catching' pamphlets of Robert Greene, alongside an almost morbid consciousness of a later sixteenth-century Urban Dictionary: 'Pedants motley tongue, souldiers bumbast, / Mountebankes drugtongue'.[71] The thing's 'tongue' is insinuating and polyvalent, capable at once of seduction, flattery, lying, and, most troublingly, of making 'men speak treason'.[72] Where Spenser signposts his deviation from stylistic norms, Donne rushes the reader into a linguistic maelstrom characteristic of the court, which his narrator finds as estranging as the reader. 'Art can deceive' is an appropriate warning from a poem which ventures close to the risks of treason the nearer it gets to the heart of the court, as when the narrator later sees 'One of our Giant Statutes ope his jaw / To sucke me in' (lines 132–3).

It is in this sense of courtly danger that *Mother Hubberd* provides a powerful analogue for *Satire IV*. After the narrator has shaken off the hanger-on, he examines his experience of the court from the comparative safety of home:

> At home in wholesome solitarinesse
> My precious soule began, the wretchednesse
> Of suiters at court to mourne, and a trance
> Like his, who dreamt he saw hell, did advance
> It selfe on mee; Such men as he saw there,
> I saw at court, and worse, and more; Low feare
> Becomes the guiltie, not th'accuser.
>
> (lines 155–61)

As most commentators have agreed, Donne alludes to Dante's *Inferno*.[73] Less obviously, he directly recalls the wording of Spenser's lengthy evocation of the 'Suters state' in *Mother Hubberd*, itself an explicit comparison of the court with hell. Donne needs the intertext partly because it is Spenserian empathy which he edits out of his account of the courtly lowlife: where Donne concentrates on the political jeopardy of being seen as a double agent, Spenser explores the realities of endless waiting at court. Here is Spenser's climactic vision of the realities of attendance at court:

> Full little knowest thou that hast not tride,
> What hell it is in suing long to bide:
> To loose good dayes, that might be better spent;
> To wast long nights in pensive discontent;
> To speed to day, to be put back to morrow;

> To feed on hope, to pine with feare and sorrow;
> To have thy Princes grace, yet want her Peeres;
> To have thy asking, yet waite manie yeeres;
> To fret thy soule with crosses and with cares;
> To eate thy heart through comfortlesse dispaires;
> To fawne, to crowche, to waite, to ride, to ronne,
> To spend, to give, to want, to be undonne.
>
> (lines 895–906)

The hell of the Spenserian court is one in which the infinitives of verbal action are all shown to be equally unavailing. There is nothing you can do. Even when you think you 'have' what you need – 'thy Princes grace' – the reality resolves having into further waiting, and finally, in a verb which Donne would in all probability have relished, 'to be undonne'. There are necessary pitfalls to this observation. As Gary A. Stringer remarks, 'Manuscript copyists … saw puns on Donne's name everywhere, and constantly draw attention to this possibility by spelling "done" as "donne"'.[74] Nevertheless, the close proximity between *Mother Hubberd* and *Satire IV* suggests that Donne remembered the line enough to take it to heart. Though *Satire IV* does not include any 'don[n]es', it revolves around the risks the Donne-like speaker takes in coming near to the court.[75] Simply by evoking 'the wretchednesse / Of suiters at court', Donne explicitly nods to Spenser's 'pitifull' account of the suitor, so that the submerged Spenserian intertext becomes a way of reinforcing the 'hell' of the 1590s court, particularly for a writer with Donne's complex religious affiliations.

Reading *Satire IV* in the light of *Mother Hubberds Tale* stresses, in ways which are congruent with DiPasquale's work, the resonances between Spenser and Donne as satirists. Both poems explicitly repudiate the ethos and ethics of the court; Donne's outburst shortly after the passage quoted above – 'hast thou seene, / O Sunne, in all thy journey, Vanitie, / Such as swells the bladder of our court?' (lines 166–8) – chimes with Spenser's depiction of the suitor's state as a living hell, and indeed the broader satiric agenda of the *Complaints* volume against the vanities of the rich and powerful.[76] Donne's radical, inventive couplet form, with its disregard for neatness of expression and its readiness to force rhyme to adapt to the poem's floating, unfixed, garrulous idiom, takes some of its impetus from the low style of *Mother Hubberd*. The persona who rails against courtly vanity and desperately fears the hazard of 'Becoming Traytor' (line 131) would scarcely have read Spenser's equally risky, transgressive, and censored poem as the voice of an outmoded literary generation.

Through the observation of formal and generic intertexts, I have argued that Donne may legitimately be read as operating within a Spenserian tradition. Our literary-historical narratives, indeed, should be forced to register that the affiliations between so-called 'Metaphysicals' and so-called Spenserians are significantly more complex than the truisms repeated by twentieth-century literary historians. Consider a couple of final examples: George Herbert's poetry shows a pervasive awareness of Spenserian forms and modes of allegory. Coburn Freer's magisterial *Spenser Encyclopedia* entry gives plausible grounds for believing that Herbert was deeply receptive to Spenser, even though we lack the sort of concrete evidence Abraham Cowley gives us of his delighted childhood reading of *The Faerie Queene*.[77] The recent publication of Ralph

Knevet's *Supplement of the Faery Queene* (1635) suggests the emerging complexity of literary generations in the early seventeenth century, since, as well as this homage to *The Faerie Queene* in orthodox Spenserian stanzas, Knevet wrote the manuscript collection *A Gallery to the Temple*, which is modelled on Herbert and which deploys a wide range of lyrical stanza forms.[78] Knevet was an accomplished poet, and clearly felt no tension between writing in the styles of Herbert and Spenser. Literary history nevertheless still prefers a less nuanced narrative. To a significant extent, the formal history of English poetry, particularly the complex liaisons between Spenser and his successors, has been scripted by the hyperbole of Thomas Carew, and later by John Dryden, who, in the preface to *Fables Ancient and Modern* (1700), articulated a model of formal history which is not that far removed from twentieth-century paradigms. For Dryden, Spenser and Edward Fairfax were 'Great Masters in our Language ... who saw much farther into the Beauties of our Numbers, than those who immediately followed them'.[79] Where Carew praises Donne as a radical gardener, Dryden damns him by omission, suggesting that Spenser and Fairfax, as more metrically regular writers, are the true harbingers of the kind of poetry Dryden himself was writing.[80] Yet rereading Donne in the light of Spenserian resonances suggests the limitations of both these views. *Metempsychosis* shows on a formal level the deep affiliations between Donne and Spenser as stanzaic writers, their different voices notwithstanding. And though Spenser was a less 'rough' stylist than Donne – less inclined to let the authority of the phrase overwrite the cadence of the individual line – he was certainly capable of stylistic 'baseness', as *Mother Hubberds Tale* demonstrates. At the beginning of this chapter, I adopted a line from 'A Valediction: Forbidding Mourning', implicitly casting Spenser in the role of the subject/wife, to whom the poet/speaker 'leans and hearkens after' in the conceit of the 'stiff twin compasses'. My intention was not to suggest any sexual, or indeed matrimonial, subtext to this neglected literary relationship, but rather to pick up on the image of feet which underpins the conceit. Spenser as 'the fixed foot' to Donne's 'obliquely' running twin nicely inclines to my argument that Donne's experimentalism builds on and develops Spenser's formal innovations. As in the poem, the oblique is a necessary product of the fixed; Donne's inventive deviations from the metrical norms of the 1580s and 1590s presume the manifold ways in which Spenser worked to extend and stretch what was possible in the iambic line. In this sense, it is not inappropriate to close as Donne closes his poem, in regular yet flexible iambic tetrameter: 'Thy firmness makes my circle just, / And makes me end where I begun'.[81]

Notes

1 Thomas Carew, 'An Elegie upon the death of the Deane of Pauls, Dr. Iohn Donne', in J[ohn] D[onne], *Poems* (London: John Marriot, 1633; facsimile ed. Menston: Scolar, 1969), 388; Edmund Spenser, *The faerie queen: The shepheards calendar: together with the other [H]works / of England's arch-poët, Edm. Spencer* (London: Matthew Lownes, 1611), title page.
2 Dayton Haskin, 'The Love Lyric [Songs and Sonets]', in Jeanne Shami, Dennis Flynn, and M. Thomas Hester (eds), *The Oxford Handbook of John Donne* (Oxford: Oxford University Press, 2011), 198.
3 John Carey, *John Donne: Life, Mind and Art* (London: Faber & Faber, 1981), 157.
4 See ibid., 10, for Donne deeming *The Faerie Queene* absurd because chivalric. The irresistible pun is

anticipated by a celebrated misprint on the lyric sheet of Richard and Linda Thompson's classic *I Want To See The Bright Lights Tonight* LP (1974): 'A couple of drunken knights / Rolling on the floor / Is just the kind of mess I'm looking for'.
5 See Douglas Bush, *English Literature in the Earlier Seventeenth Century 1600–1660* (Oxford: Oxford University Press, 1962). Although Bush's historical narrative is shaped by dichotomies between Spenser's successors and those of Jonson and Donne (see Yulia Ryzhik's Introduction above), his discriminations between Spenser and Donne are more complex than, say Carey's, as when he cautions against the view that 'Elizabethan orthodoxy, as represented by Spenser, was effete' (130).
6 Donne, 'A Valediction: Forbidding Mourning', l. 31, in *The Complete Poems*, ed. Robin Robbins (Harlow: Longman, 2008; revised ed., 2010), 261.
7 For a reading of Spenser as a fundamentally experimental writer, see Andrew Hadfield, *Edmund Spenser: A Life* (Oxford: Oxford University Press, 2012). Hadfield's corrective to conventional literary criticism opens new ways of reading Spenser as a literary figure in his times and beyond.
8 See Haskin, 'The Love Lyric', 186–7.
9 Harold Bloom, *The Anxiety of Influence: A Theory of Poetry*, 2nd ed. (New York: Oxford University Press, 1997). Bloom has little to say about Spenser or Donne: Spenser is chiefly discussed as the 'major precursor' of Milton (11), and Donne in the context of reaction to the Copernican revolution (43). Judith Anderson's work, particularly the essays collected in *Reading the Allegorical Intertext: Chaucer, Spenser, Shakespeare, Milton* (New York: Fordham University Press, 2008), offers a more powerful set of analytical tools for understanding the formal interrelationships between early modern poets than Bloom's.
10 The fifty-two-stanza poem is analogous to a canto of *The Faerie Queene*. In the 1633 edition under the title, the text has the designation '*First Song*', which reinforces the family relationship between Donne's poem and Spenser's; Donne, *Poems*, 1. For recent accounts of this intertextual relationship, see Elizabeth D. Harvey, 'Nomadic Souls: Pythagoras, Spenser Donne', *Spenser Studies*, 22 (2007), 257–79, and Anne Lake Prescott, 'Menippean Donne', in Jeanne Shami, Dennis Flynn, and M. Thomas Hester (eds), *The Oxford Handbook of John Donne* (Oxford: Oxford University Press, 2011), 160–4. For recent work on the complexity of naming conventions around subdivisions in Elizabethan long poems, see Kenneth Borris and Meredith Donaldson Clark, 'Hymnic Epic and *The Faerie Queene*'s Original Printed Format: Canto-Canticles and Psalmic Arguments', *Renaissance Quarterly*, 64 (2011), 1148–93, especially 1158–9.
11 See Prescott, 'Menippean Donne', 160–4; Carey, *John Donne*, 157; and Harvey, 'Nomadic Souls', who suggests that the chief Spenserian intertexts for *Metempsychosis* are *Visions of the Worlds Vanitie*, *Mother Hubberds Tale*, and the Castle of Alma, as Donne picks up on both 'Spenser's representation of body-soul relations' and his metaphorical 'depictions of animals' (257).
12 Yulia Ryzhik, 'Spenser and Donne Go Fishing', *Spenser Studies*, 31–2 (2018), 427–8, compares these passages in relation to her focus on the two poets' use of fishing as a political metaphor.
13 Edmund Spenser, *The Yale Edition of the Shorter Poems of Edmund Spenser*, ed. William A. Oram et al. (New Haven: Yale University Press, 1989), ll. 39–46. All quotations from the shorter poems of Spenser are from this edition unless otherwise stated; line references are given parenthetically in the text; hereafter it is referred to as *The Shorter Poems*.
14 John Donne, *The Satires, Epigrams and Verse Letters*, ed. W. Milgate (Oxford: Clarendon, 1967; rpt 2000), ll. 232–4. All quotations from *Metempsychosis* and the *Satires* are from this edition, unless otherwise stated; line references are given parenthetically in the text.
15 John B. Bender, *Spenser and Literary Pictorialism* (Princeton: Princeton University Press, 1972), 91.
16 W. Milgate, 'A Difficult Allusion in Donne and Spenser', *Notes and Queries*, 13.1 (1966), 12–14 (12). See also Harvey, 'Nomadic Souls', 262–4.
17 Donne, *The Satires*, 26. Donne's repudiation of didacticism picks up on the Letter to Raleigh, appended to the 1590 *Faerie Queene*, with its claim that '*The generall end therefore of all the booke is to fashion a gentleman or noble person is vertuous and gentle discipline*'; in Spenser, *The Faerie Queene* (revised 2nd ed.), ed. A.C. Hamilton, textual ed. Hiroshi Yamashita and Toshiyuki Suzuki (Harlow: Longman, 2007), 714. All quotations from *The Faerie Queene* are from this edition unless otherwise stated; book, canto, and stanza references are given parenthetically in the text.
18 See Harvey, 'Nomadic Souls', 267–8, for a reading of these texts in the context of contemporaneous debates about anatomy and the relationship between the animal and the rational soul.
19 T.S. Eliot, 'Philip Massinger', in *Selected Essays* (London: Faber and Faber, 1980), 206 ('mature poets steal').
20 See John Hollander, 'Alexandrine', in A.C. Hamilton et al. (ed.), *The Spenser Encyclopedia* (Toronto: University of Toronto Press, 1990; rpt 1997), 15–16.

21 Prescott, 'Menippean Donne', 162.
22 Prescott, 'Menippean Donne', 163, building in part on A. Kent Hieatt's classic, *Short Time's Endless Monument: The Symbolism of the Numbers in Edmund Spenser's Epithalamion* (New York: Columbia University Press, 1960), suggests that as well as the allusion to the weeks in the year, *Metempsychosis* may exhibit a pattern of twelve opening stanzas followed by forty on the actual metamorphoses which 'could, to those so inclined, recall the forty years of that earlier wandering towards the Promised Land'. As her wording suggests, such analyses remain to an extent speculative. Ryzhik ('Spenser and Donne Go Fishing', 426-7, 432), posits a different number-based scheme around *Metempsychosis*'s three episodes where the soul inhabits a succession of fish.
23 Harvey, 'Nomadic Souls', 262. For ruin as a pervasive trope in Spenser, see Rebeca Helfer, *Spenser's Ruins and the Art of Recollection* (Toronto: University of Toronto Press, 2012).
24 See Richard Danson Brown and J.B. Lethbridge, *A Concordance to the Rhymes of The Faerie Queene with Two Studies of Spenser's Rhymes* (Manchester: Manchester University Press, 2013), 234, 361, citing III.iii.27. 'Euening' is a rare rhyme for Spenser, with only two examples in all *The Faerie Queene*; the unambiguously trisyllabic 'euentide' (and variants) are more frequent, with five examples in total. The point is perhaps that precisely because the rhyme is unusual it may have lodged itself in Donne's ear.
25 'Autumnal', l. 21, shows that Donne usually scanned this word disyllabically: 'Here, where still Evening is; not noon, nor night'; see Donne, *The Complete Poems*, ed. Robbins, 359. For Spenser's usual scansion of the word, see I.i.35, 'With faire discourse the euening so they pas'.
26 Though it could be possible to read Donne's line as a knowing parody of Spenser, since the stanza as a whole alludes to the start of the *Aeneid* ('I sing the progresse of a deathlesse soule'), this seems implausibly specific. Donne wants the start of his poem to sound epic, and inflates his diction accordingly; paragoge is a useful device in signalling the epic style rather than a more specific allusion.
27 For details, see Brown and Lethbridge, *A Concordance*, 66-71; for other examples in *Metempsychosis*, see lines 86, 88, 96-7 and 256-7.
28 William Empson, *Seven Types of Ambiguity* (1930; rpt London: Hogarth, 1984), 33-4. See also Kenneth Gross, 'Shapes of Time: On the Spenserian Stanza', *Spenser Studies*, 19 (2004), 27-35.
29 See David Scott Wilson-Okamura, *Spenser's International Style* (Cambridge: Cambridge University Press, 2013), 18-49, for the argument that the Spenserian stanza transposes 'what was best about classical prosody into a native idiom' (48). See further Richard Danson Brown, *The Art of The Faerie Queene* (Manchester: Manchester University Press, 2019), 139-91, for my discussion of the stanza as a new and permissive form of poetic technology.
30 Like *Metempsychosis* and *The Faerie Queene*, these lyrics vary line lengths, but to much more pronounced effect (I give the usual numbers of stresses): 'The Anniversarie' takes the form 4a4a5b5b5c4d5d5d6d; 'The Flea' 4a5a4b5b4c5c4d5d5d; and 'The Relique' 4a4a4b4b3c5d3d5c5e5e. See Pierre Legouis, *Donne the Craftsman: An Essay upon the Structure of the Songs and Sonnets* (1928; rpt New York: Russell & Russell, 1962), 14-16, for a still useful tabulation of the different stanza forms in Donne's love lyrics.
31 Donne, 'To his Mistress on Going Abroad', line 4, in *The Complete Poems*, ed. Robbins, 341.
32 For the strength of the individual line in Spenser, see Paul J. Alpers, *The Poetry of The Faerie Queene* (Princeton: Princeton University Press, 1967; rpt 1982), 37.
33 My list (checked against the text in J[ohn] D[onne], *Poems* [1633], 1-27) includes stanzas I, II, IV, V, VI, IX, X, XII, XVI, XXI, XXII, XXVI, XXVII, XXIX, XXX, XXXI, XXXIII, XXXIV, XLI, LII. Other stanzas have heavy pauses half-way through line 8, which creates an analogous effect; see stanzas XIX, XXV, XXXVII, XXXIX, XLII; XLIII, XLIV, and XLVII.
34 See Milgate's note, in Donne, *The Satires*, 182. The Reformation reduced the number of fasts, leading to a decline in the fishing industry; this was rectified in 1564 by the imposition of statutory fish-eating days on Wednesdays and Saturdays.
35 Milgate notes that the rebel 'would not be very daring' in the context of contemporary theological debates, although Donne takes pains to talk this up as heresy in the next stanza; in Donne, *The Satires*, 178.
36 Legouis, *Donne the Craftsman*, 34.
37 Brown and Lethbridge, *A Concordance*, 263-4, 348. Spenser has many rhymes on *it* and several on *yit* (though not with *it*). Donne's decision not to distort morphology to fit with the rhyme here is further suggestive of his desire to keep this stanza close inconclusive.
38 My emphases. For the use of legal language in Donne's poetry, see Jeremy Maul's brilliant 'Donne and the Words of the Law', in David Colclough (ed.), *John Donne's Professional Lives* (Cambridge: D.S. Brewer, 2003).

39 Brown and Lethbridge, *A Concordance*, 229. Interestingly, there are no rhymes on *drum* in *The Faerie Queene*.
40 See Spenser, *The Faerie Queene*, ed. A.C. Hamilton (London: Longman, 1977), 126, for the origins of this image in Cicero and Pythagoras. See also Donne, *The Satires*, 142, for a passage from John of Salisbury, citing Pythagoras and Plotinus.
41 See Donne, *The Satires*, 11, 142; see also http://digitaldonne.tamu.edu/, for a reproduction of the O'Flahertie MS, which has the 'Souldier' variant on sheet 66. Accessed 4 March 2016.
42 I suggest that *Satire III* has another intertext from *The Faerie Queene* I in the celebrated image of Truth standing 'On a huge hill' (lines 79–84). Spenser's description of the old dragon as 'stretcht he lay vpon the sunny side / Of a great hill, himselfe like a great hill' (I.xi.4) may have lodged in Donne's ear because of the metrical distortion in the second line, in which both 'great hills' are spondaic, a pattern partly repeated in Donne's line. See Spenser, *The Faerie Queene*, 137, for Hamilton's note on the metre, and Donne, *The Satires*, 290–2, for Milgate's account of the sources of Donne's hill. More broadly, the theological personifications *Satire III*, particularly of 'Truth' (line 80), suggests Donne's critical engagement with Book I of *The Faerie Queene*, where Una appears as '*Forsaken Truth*' in her emblematic representation of the Church of England (I.iii.Arg.1).
43 See for example *Satire VI* of Everard Guilpin's *Skialetheia* (1598), which records the celebrity of Spenser's 'grandam words' in a Stoic satire of the vagaries of opinion; Guilpin, *Skialetheia Or A Shadowe of Truth, in Certaine Epigrams and Satyres*, ed. D. Allen Carroll (Chapel Hill: University of North Carolina Press, 1974), 90. Though Guilpin has often been seen as part of a generational reaction against Spenser, read in context, Guilpin's target is popular literary opinion; for Guilpin and Donne, see R.C. Bald, *John Donne: A Life* (Oxford: Clarendon, 1970), 74–6.
44 Theresa M. DiPasquale, 'Anti-Court Satire, Religious Polemic, and the Many Faces of Antichrist: An Intertextual Reading of Donne's "Satyre 4" and Spenser's *Faerie Queene*', *Studies in Philology*, 112.2 (2015), 264–302 (267).
45 See for example Michelle O'Callaghan, 'Verse Satire', in Catherine Bates (ed.), *A Companion to Renaissance Poetry* (Oxford: Wiley Blackwell, 2018), 392–6, which rightly contextualizes the satire of the 1590s in terms of 'Satiric Communities' (394), yet without mentioning *Mother Hubberd*.
46 See Hadfield, *Edmund Spenser: A Life*, 265–77, for the historical background. See also Bruce Danner, *Edmund Spenser's War on Lord Burghley* (Houndsmills: Palgrave Macmillan, 2011), particularly 162–5. Overall, Danner problematizes earlier assumptions that *Mother Hubberd* relates to events of the late 1570s, preferring to contextualize the poem in the early 1590s and the moment of its publication; see 5–10, 151–83. See further Rachel E. Hile, *Spenserian Satire: A Tradition of Indirection* (Manchester: Manchester University Press, 2017), 13–14, 108–9.
47 In Donne, *The Complete Poems*, 407. See also Donne, *The Satires*, 157, for Milgate's note.
48 Richard Danson Brown, *The New Poet: Novelty and Tradition in Spenser's Complaints* (Liverpool: Liverpool University Press, 1999), 209–10.
49 See William Bowman Piper, 'Heroic Couplet', in Alex Preminger and T.V.F. Brogan (eds), *The New Princeton Encyclopedia of Poetry and Poetics* (Princeton: Princeton University Press, 1993), 522, for a description of the gradual imposition of 'a regular hierarchy of pauses' on to the looser Chaucerian couplet. Jonson's Conversations with William Drummond of Hawthornden are germane, articulating Jonson's preference for the couplet ('the bravest sort of verses'), alongside his contempt for elaborate, 'forced' stanza forms; see Ben Jonson, *The Complete Poems*, ed. George Parfitt (Harmondsworth: Penguin, 1975), 461.
50 Spenser, *The Shorter Poems*, 334. The classic formulation of this approach is Edwin Greenlaw, *Studies in Spenser's Historical Allegory* (1932; rpt London: Frank Cass, 1967), 104–32. For modern reaction, see Brown, *The New Poet*, 173–5, and Danner, *Edmund Spenser's War*, 5–6. Hadfield, *Edmund Spenser: A Life*, 265–74, is also relevant.
51 For the view that *Complaints* was unauthorised, see Jean R. Brink, 'Who Fashioned Edmund Spenser? The Textual History of *Complaints*', *Studies in Philology*, 88 (1991), 153–68; for the counter view, see Brown, *The New Poet*, 5–6.
52 See Bjorvand and Schell's comments about the related claim – a 'biographical-literary myth' – that the Hymns in Honour of Love and Beautie had been written '*in the greener times of my youth*', in Spenser, *The Shorter Poems*, 683–4, 690.
53 Ibid., 334.
54 Alvin Kernan, *The Cankered Muse: Satire of the English Renaissance* (New Haven: Yale University Press, 1959), 55–8. See also Richard Danson Brown, '"Such ungodly terms": Style, Taste, Verse Satire and Epigram in *The Dutch Courtesan*', *The Dutch Courtesan* website (University of York); www.dutchcourtesan.co.uk/such-ungodly-terms/, accessed 18 March 2016.

55 Edmund Spenser, *Complaints*, ed. W.L. Renwick (London: Scolartis, 1928), 226. Renwick's comments on the poem's debt to Chaucer are also valuable: 'Spenser deliberately roughens his verse in imitation of his master'.
56 See George Puttenham, *The Art of English Poesy*, ed. Frank Whigham and Wayne A. Rebhorn (Ithaca: Cornell University Press, 2007), 149–50, for useful notes on the uncertain term 'riding rhyme'. See Catherine Bates, *Masculinity and the Hunt: Wyatt to Spenser* (Oxford: Oxford University Press, 2013), 120–1, for the plausible suggestion that Gascoigne's uses of the term (both in relation to *The Canterbury Tales* and in *The Adventures of Master F. J.*) are cumulatively 'suggestive of impropriety'.
57 For the complexity of the Elizabethan response to Chaucer's language and style, see Craig A. Berry, '"Sundrie Doubts": Vulnerable Understanding and Dubious Origins in Spenser's Continuation of the Squire's Tale', in Theresa Krier (ed.), *Refiguring Chaucer in the Renaissance* (Gainsville: University Press of Florida, 1998), 106–27.
58 Jeff Dolven, 'Spenser's Metrics', in Richard A. McCabe (ed.), *The Oxford Handbook of Edmund Spenser* (Oxford: Oxford University Press, 2010), 387, 389. Dolven is chiefly describing the metre of *The Faerie Queene*, noting that Spenser was 'at his most experimental near the beginning of his career' in *The Shepheardes Calender* and the Letters to Harvey (387).
59 See Brown and Lethbridge, *A Concordance*, 47–55, for my discussion of the reasons for the introduction of feminine rhyme to the 1596 *Faerie Queene*, and, in particular, their virtual exclusion from the 1590 edition. For comparison, where the 1590 *Faerie Queene* has only one feminine rhyme (II.ix.47c), *Mother Hubberd* has as many as seventy-two; this count includes uncontracted past participles such as *conceived/received* and, here, *pleased/diseased* (lines 3–4, 39–40), since the 1591 quarto includes contracted forms in rhyming positions (such as *constraind/complain'd*, lines 561–2), possibly indicating distinctions in Spenser's manuscript. At any event, the proliferation of feminine rhymes strikes a deliberate contrast with the 1590 *Faerie Queene*. See Spenser, *Complaints* (London: William Ponsonbie, 1591), sig. L3r–v, N3v.
60 John Marston, *The Poems*, ed. Arnold Davenport (Liverpool: Liverpool University Press, 1961), 158.
61 See Wilson-Okamura, *Spenser's International Style*, 74–7, for the three styles (the humble, the middle, and the high) in Renaissance rhetorical and literary criticism. Where *The Faerie Queene* is in the middle style, *Mother Hubberd* self-consciously advertises its lowness. For *Mother Hubberd* as a template for later poets, see Hadfield, *Edmund Spenser: A Life*, 269, 508 n.25, noting the connections between Spenser's poem and the work suppressed by the Bishop's Ban of 1599.
62 For an analogous rhyme in Donne, see *Satire IV* lines 153–4: 'Ran from thence with such or more haste, then one / Who feares more actions, doth make from prison', where the usually trochaic accent of 'prison' is wrested into an iamb to satisfy the rhyme. For the usual Elizabethan scansion of the word, see *The Faerie Queene* I.i.44: 'A diuerse dreame out of his prison darke'.
63 Brown, *The New Poet*, 185–93.
64 Ibid., 197–200.
65 See James Shapiro, *1606: William Shakespeare and the Year of Lear* (London: Faber & Faber, 2015), 178–207, for the use of 'equivocation' in the contexts of the Gunpowder Plot and *Macbeth*.
66 Compare with lines 215–16: 'And whisperd "by Jesu", so'often, that A / Pursevant would have ravish'd him away', which throws an unlikely stress onto the rhyming indefinite article. The capitalization of 'A' in early editions perhaps registers some of the abrasive force of this couplet, also shown in the uncertain metre; see Donne, *Poems* (1633), 344. However, this orthography is not replicated in manuscripts, such as the St Paul's MS, where the line reads 'And whisper'd by *Iesu* soe often, that a'; see the Digital Donne website, http://digitaldonne.tamu.edu/DisplayText, accessed 29 February 2016. For earlier commentary on all the passages cited here, see Donne, *The Variorum Edition of the Poetry of John Donne*, ed. Gary A, Stringer et al., *Volume 3: The Satyres*, ed. Jeffrey S. Johnson et al. (Bloomington: Indiana University Press, 2016), 802–6, 815, 843, 857 (hereafter cited as *Variorum 3*).
67 For archaism as an experimental, modish practice in Spenser, see Andrew Zurcher, *Spenser's Legal Language: Law and Poetry in Early Modern England* (Cambridge: D.S. Brewer, 2007), 31–2; Wilson-Okamura, *Spenser's International Style*, 58–62; and Lucy Munro, *Archaic Style in English Literature, 1590–1674* (Cambridge: Cambridge University Press, 2013), 204–36, and Richard Danson Brown, 'Lucy Munro, *Archaic Style in English Literature, 1590–1674*', *Spenser Review*, 44.2.44 (2014 Fall), www.english.cam.ac.uk/spenseronline/review/volume-44/442/reviews/munro-lucy-archaic-style-in-english-literature-1590-1674, accessed 18 March 2016. For Spenser's broader experimental practice, see Brown, *The Art of The Faerie Queene*, especially 48–102, 139–91.
68 See Hadfield, *Edmund Spenser: A Life*, 269.
69 Gregory Kneidel, 'The Formal Verse Satire', in Shami et al. (eds), *The Oxford Handbook of John Donne*, 122.

70 And potentially Protestant ones: according to some manuscripts, the line reads 'Jovius, or Sleydan, or both together', alluding to John Sleidan. Milgate suggests that this was the earlier version of the line, making the riskier point that Catholic and Protestant writers were equally prone to lying; in Donne, *The Satires*, 153.
71 For glosses on these, see Donne, *The Satires*, 151-3, and *Variorum 3*, 821-3.
72 The difficulties of this passage also include variants. Grierson preferred the reading from several manuscripts in line 38, 'He speaks *no* language', on the grounds that because it was bolder it was more likely to be authoritative, see Donne, *The Poems*, ed. Herbert J.C. Grierson (London: Oxford University Press, 1912; rpt 1938), 2 vols; I.160, II.120; my emphasis. For the counter view, see Milgate in Donne, *The Satires*, 151-2, and more recently (stressing the arbitrariness of Grierson's intervention) Gary A. Stringer, 'Editing Donne's Poetry: from John Marriot to the Donne *Variorum*', in Shami et al. (eds), *The Oxford Handbook of John Donne*, 49.
73 See Milgate's note in Donne, *The Satires*, 159, and *Variorum 3*, 844.
74 Gary A. Stringer, 'Composition and Dissemination of Donne's Writings', in Shami et al. (eds), *The Oxford Handbook of John Donne*, 24; note that Stringer adds the rider '"When thou hast donne thou hast not donne" in ['A Hymn to God the Father'] is almost inevitable'.
75 For the proximity of Donne to the speaker, see line 84, 'I'have but one Frenchman, looke, hee followes mee', and Milgate's note, in Donne, *The Satires*, 155: Donne had a French servant, though probably at a later point than the first drafting of this poem.
76 See *The Ruines of Time*, which also glances at Burghley's preferment of his children (lines 447-58); see Spenser, *The Shorter Poems*, 251, for the suppression of these lines in the 1611 Folio. Consider also the satiric aspects of *Visions of the Worlds Vanitie*; see above for discussion.
77 Coburn Freer, 'Herbert, George (1593-1633)', in Hamilton (ed.), *The Spenser Encyclopedia*, 355. For Cowley, see R.M. Cummings (ed.), *Spenser: The Critical Heritage* (London: Routledge & Kegan Paul, 1971), 185-6.
78 Ralph Knevet, *A Supplement of the Faery Queene*, ed. Christopher Burlinson and Andrew Zurcher (Manchester: Manchester University Press, 2015); for *A Gallery to the Temple*, see Knevet, *The Shorter Poems*, ed. Amy M. Charles (Columbus: Ohio State University Press, 1966), 275-396.
79 John Dryden, *Fables Ancient and Modern* (London: Jacob Tonson, 1700), sig. A1r; see also Cummings (ed.), *Spenser: The Critical Heritage*, 205.
80 See also Dryden's praise of Sandys as 'the best Versifier of the former Age'. Given that Sandys was a contemporary of Donne's (1578-1644), the comment is arguably another pointed gesture of omission; *Fables Ancient and Modern*, sig. A1r.
81 Donne, *The Complete Poems*, ed. Robbins, 260-2. 'A Valediction' is a strikingly regular poem metrically: Robbins marks a single elision (on 'by a') on the nine-syllable line 17: 'But we, by' a love so much refined' (259).

2

Comparing figures: figures of comparison and repetition in Spenser's *Cantos of Mutabilitie* and Donne's *Anniversaries*

Christopher D. Johnson

Grounds for comparison

'Comparisons are odorous.' One of his many acrylogias, Dogberry's unwitting figure of speech in *Much Ado About Nothing* (III.v.19) doubles as a sensuous metaphor which wittily, if unwittingly, remakes the commonplace 'comparison is odious'.[1] Of course, most comparison is invidious as well. Riddled by category mistakes, historical aporias, epistemological and psychological biases, no wonder the task of comparison has troubled thinkers from Aristotle to Kant to Nelson Goodman and beyond.

With succinct scepticism, W.J.T. Mitchell assesses three primary modes of comparison: perceptual, discursive, and disciplinary.[2] While each mode institutes a 'dialectic between similarity and difference', rarely does the comparatist, Mitchell contends, reflect on the nature and limits of comparison.[3] An exception, he notes, is Edmund Burke, whose distinction between 'wit' and 'judgment', adumbrated in *A Philosophical Enquiry into the Origins of Our Ideas Concerning the Sublime and Beautiful* (1754), can help us analyse discursive comparison, 'the process of verbalizing comparative propositions, of making metaphors, similes, conceits, allegories, and other figures'.[4] Yet even if we grant Burke that wit is 'chiefly conversant in tracing resemblances' and judgement involved mainly in 'finding differences', most poets, Mitchell contends, fruitfully ignore this distinction.[5] By way of an example, he cites Donne's *Elegy: The Comparison*.

Arguably, however, this early lyric (ca. 1596) would exhaust more than undermine comparison. Mocking judgement, Donne invidiously compares two beloveds, his and an addressee's. Fifty-five wit-abusing lines are made to yield thirty-two similes, some dilated, some condensed, linked in paratactic chains: 'Like Proserpines whight bewty-keeping chest, / Or Ioue's best fortune's Vrne, is her faire brest. / Thyne like Worme-eaten truncks, clothd in Celes skin, / Or graue that's durt without, and stinch within' (lines 23–6).[6] Concluding this exercise in exorbitant, indecorous comparison, the final couplet uses a ploce to propel a *pointe* that conflates the object of comparison with comparison itself: 'Leaue her, and I will leaue comparing thus / She, and comparisons are odious' (lines 54–5). Granted, Donne's objects of desire change dramatically in the course of his career; still, he never leaves off 'comparing' or self-consciously adducing reasons how and why to compare. In other words, simile here and elsewhere creates first- and second-order meanings. As an ostensive, imaginative, but also synthetic form of comparison, simile works as a thinking figure that remakes ordinary meanings and readerly expectations. It makes 'a process of thinking' palpable, indeed possible, as Judith H. Anderson writes of Spenserian allegory.[7] And while, as Gordon Teskey reminds us, the close work of such figuration is not the only way the 'thinking poet' proceeds, yet, like the other figures I will discuss below, simile forms critical nodes for comparative thought.[8]

More particularly, in this chapter I would compare figures of thought that compare and figures of speech that repeat in Spenser's *Two Cantos of Mutabilitie* and Donne's *Anniversaries*. I will discuss the figures of speech presently; but first I want to indicate two figures of thought, both flying under the banner of *comparatio*: *similitudo* (mainly in the form of simile and analogy) and syncrisis (a comparison, usually invidious, of different things belonging to the same category).[9] Unlike metaphor, which sublates its terms to forge a new identity, *similitudo* and syncrisis stop one step short of sublation as they put their terms and the mechanics of comparison on display. As such they are key to any consideration of how Spenser and Donne negotiate differences and similarities between things and ideas. On a local level, simile institutes a type of comparative thinking which isolates, even reifies *comparanda* and *comparatum* (or *comparata*) only to wittily suggest, but never quite realize, their union. The maker of similes takes Britomart's wisdom to heart: 'Be bolde, be bolde ... Be not too bold' (III.xi.54).[10] Syncrisis undertakes more global comparisons. Thinking etymologically, since a crisis is a 'decision' requiring one 'to judge' (*krinein*), we might say syncrisis is a figurative means of thinking critically about things urgently demanding comparison. Syncrisis may ultimately enlist sophisticated allegories or difficult conceits, but on a more basic level, it is a mode of thought, a form of invention, tasked with comparative judgement.

In the late English Renaissance, to make verse that compares, that thinks, is to figure, refigure, and disfigure language's material and semantic aspects. Such comparative, figurative thinking takes place in determining, though not determinative historical contexts. Analogous contingencies occur when present-day hermeneuts try to parse such thinking. As Anderson observes, when criticism tries to translate poetic figuration, it must find ways to mediate between formal, 'textual concerns' and historicist, material-cultural ones.[11] This balancing act is not unlike what Spenser and Donne undertake. To be a public man or woman, a monarch, a courtier, a clergyman, and/or a poet is to figure oneself and one's world. To please the Queen, Spenser would 'fashion' or figure 'a gentleman'. To win a patron, Donne becomes a Pauline 'Trumpet'. Both poets endeavour to use their figured verse to gain personal fame and 'get a place'.[12] And even when they have less contingent, more conceptual, more self-reflective aims, 'when Renaissance writers use a figure they are simultaneously thinking with the figure and about the figure'.[13]

First published in 1609, the *Cantos of Mutabilitie* were written some time after 1596, probably in the year before Spenser's death in 1599.[14] Marked by the chaos of the colonial conflict in Ireland and expressive of the poet's growing scepticism, they are 'late' poems in numerous ways, especially in the manner they complicate moral allegory, perhaps fatally so, with other figurations.[15] The two *Anniversaries*, the first subtitled *An Anatomie of the World* (1611) and the second *Of the Progres of the Soule* (1612), composed when Donne was nearly forty, courting a patron, and deliberating whether to take holy orders, were the only poems he published, much to his later regret, during his lifetime. Fuelled by an exorbitant *contemptus mundi* and a correspondingly 'insatiate soule' (*Second Anniversarie* (*SA*), line 45) thirsting for higher truths, their cognitive effect and emotional *affectus* depend less on the resolution of witty conceits, as in his lyrics, than on the contemplation of extreme antitheses.

Dialogic, narrative, and mythographic, the *Cantos* recount a titanomachy and a trial: Mutabilitie would metonymically 'displace' (VII.vi.10) Cynthia from her palace and the other gods from 'heauen' (VII.vi.16). The *Anniversaries* offer a dramatic monologue based on the fantastic premise that a fourteen-year-old girl's death has left the present world a 'carkasse' (*First Anniversarie* (*FA*), line 339). The temporalities of the *Cantos* and *Anniversaries* also strikingly diverge. Framed as an act of memory told by an archival narrator who then only occasionally interpolates or apostrophizes, the *Cantos* are veiled, like the rest of *The Faerie Queene*, by archaicizing diction and subtle allegories. Even when they digressively tell the recent history of Ireland or grapple with empirical reality, Graeco-Roman deities play an outsized role. By contrast, the *Anniversaries*, for all their scholastic reasoning and panegyric memorializing, are insistently contemporary and prospective. Via the poet's conceits and sustained dialogue with the reader and, especially in the *Progres*, with himself or his 'soule', they mediate immanent concerns.

Yet despite these and myriad other differences, even a cursory judgement finds significant similarities. Both Spenser and Donne explore the 'decay' and 'mutabilitie' of the world and both ingeniously try to redeem it. Mutabilitie's titanomachy resembles the human overrreaching in the *Anniversaries*, while Spenser's glimpse of eternal *stasis* is the mystical kin to Donne's ephemeral 'ecstasee'.[16] Both the *Cantos* and the *Anniversaries* invidiously compare physics with metaphysics, the sub- and superlunary spheres, and, implicitly, *scientia and sapientia*.[17] Both sets of poems, while diverging wildly in form and content, are deeply Pauline-Augustinian, that is, both poets see through the darkened, material glasses of poetic figures to glimpse eternal spiritual truths. But, again, they also grind different lenses. For all its torsions of literal meaning, Spenser's 'darke conceit' remains attached to a mimetic, scopic regime, whereas Donne's anamorphotic conceits distort or neglect the same in pursuit of other cognitive, aesthetic, and spiritual rewards. Donne precipitates a kind of heurisis that *grosso modo* seems more subjective than the one Spenser crafts – a distinction that may well correspond to the different effect/affects of punctual versus continual metaphor.

All the more reason, then, to explore the common ground of *similitudo* and syncrisis – rather than raking the well-trodden ground of Spenserian allegory or Donnean metaphor. Spenser and Donne use these figures of comparison, respectively, to 'way' and to 'thinke', and ultimately to judge what can and cannot be known. Their stylistic tasks aside, both figures are intrinsically self-reflective. Put another way, the critic's *comparatio*, the similarities and differences he or she finds, mimics the poet's. As imitating poets, Spenser and Donne invite comparison not only for the figures they use but in so far as they reconfigure literary traditions and readerly expectations. Spenser revisits and remakes Chaucerian topoi;[18] Donne does something similar with Petrarchism. But when their *imitatio* approaches *aemulatio*, it verges on syncrisis, too.[19] Conversely, steeped in the rhetorical tradition, much early seventeenth-century critical thought is animated by syncrisis – for example, North's version of Plutarch's *Parallel Lives*, the endless iterations of the *Querelle des anciens et modernes*, Jonson's 'To my Beloved William Shakespeare', or Carew's 'Elegy' for Donne. Further, judgements about poets are largely made on the basis of the decorum, subtlety, and force of their figures. Fraunce's *Arcadian rhetorike* exemplifies the figures with verse from Homer, Virgil, Boscán, Tasso, and Sidney; his *Lawyers Logike* (1588) ransacks the *Shepheardes Calender* to model decorous argumentation.[20] Donne was also read syncritically. As Jasper Mayne's 'On Dr. Donne's Death' (1633) has it, Donne, uniquely among his contemporaries, transforms readers into 'wits' – if they read poems like the 'Anniverse [*sic*]' with understanding, if they figure out his figures, the engine of his 'expression'.[21]

Until very recently, as Yulia Ryzhik notes in the Introduction, to compare Spenser and Donne had typically been in the service of some invidious version of literary history. And while less invidious, more subtle approaches tend to be found in studies dedicated to one poet or the other poet, still, when James Nohrnberg elucidates *The Faerie Queene* as being structured more by analogy than allegory, or when Barbara Lewalski scrutinizes the shifting personae of the speaker in the *Anniversaries*, they implicitly raise the comparative question of how such critical narratives might be joined.[22] For my part, while wanting to avoid *grands récits* about their relative places in literary history, I would argue that Spenser and Donne tend, respectively, towards a visual and a verbal epistemology.[23] Reductively put, Spenser favours figures soliciting *enargeia*; Donne those creating *energeia*.[24] What Sidney calls 'speaking picture[s]' fill the *Cantos*, while the *Anniversaries* appeal more to the mind's synthetic and analytic eye.[25] As Panofsky might say, to read Spenser demands an iconography, to parse Donne an iconology.[26]

Spenser and Donne variously rely on the same figures of thought, *similitudo* and syncrisis, in part to discover the limits of their thinking about a decaying world and their own capacity as poets to think and to remake 'all things' – a phrase that echoes throughout the *Cantos* and the *Anniversaries*. Indeed, this chapter's secondary focus will be on figures of speech involving semantic repetition and permutation, figures that appeal to the ear as well as the mind. Spenser and Donne lean heavily on ploce, *traductio*, and other figures of speech iterating a word or sememe: 'still' and 'all' in the *Cantos*; 'thinke', 'vp', and 'all' in the *Anniversaries*. In this far from frivolous manner, our poets variously express their thirst for identity, stability, unity, and the absolute, even as they hint at their impossibility.[27] Such tintinnabulation gives a hearing to perennial philosophical questions: the nature of human and divine 'Time' for Spenser; the relation between the one and the many, the soul and the body for Donne. In short, figures of speech involving repetition prove to be an essential, catachrestic mode of thought for both poets – especially when figures of thought propelling *comparatio* hit conceptual walls.

Figures

By the late Renaissance, the study of rhetoric consisted largely in learning one's figures, that is, tropes, figures of speech, and figures of thought. The emergence of this *rhétorique restreinte*, as Gérard Genette dubs it, had many causes, including vernacularization, the emphasis on written over oral rhetoric, and the fact that literature was no longer seen mainly as a form of persuasion.[28] School exercises mostly involved practising figures; but even the most refined poets and thinkers sought to display their mastery of figures. The conceptual subtlety and affective power of Shakespeare's drama and the heuristic force of Bacon's encyclopaedic programme reside partially in such mastery.[29]

The poetic use of figures is interpreted in marginalia, paratexts, commentaries, and rhetorical treatises, which in good and bad faith turn to poets for their examples. In other words, as a 'restricted rhetoric' merged with poetics, verse becomes 'as much a set of tools for reading as an art of composition'.[30] More particularly, what most catches the Renaissance reader's eye is how tropes and figures mutate so-called ordinary language. Tropes generally do so at the level of the word, while figures work throughout a sentence or larger discursive structures.[31] There is a consensus, though, that many figures of thought may serve as forms of invention as well as style. By contrast, figures of speech involving, say, artful contortions of syntax or the repetition of a word, typically are not seen as effecting a change in meaning or involving 'ideas'.[32] Some historians of rhetoric distinguish 'between figurative operations that *represent* thought and those that actively *provoke* it', but this surely obtains more in theory than practice.[33] Further, if every figure is to varying degrees a material as well as a semantic creature, then each has a history of being shaped and reshaped in different contexts by situated authors and readers.

Figures and tropes are affective, imaginative, often imitative responses to extraordinary circumstances, things, and ideas. Their success, at least in late Renaissance England, is judged by their decorousness and the quality of their artifice. In *The Garden of Eloquence* (1593), Henry Peacham writes: 'A *Figure* is a forme of words, oration, or sentence, made new by art, differing from the vulgar maner and custome of writing or speaking.'[34] Abraham Fraunce's *Arcadian rhetorike* (1588) treats 'Tropes, or turnings' and 'Figures or fashionings' as ways of producing novel, unusual, 'more elegant and conceipted' forms of 'signification'.[35] Alternatively, George Puttenham's *The Arte of English Poesie* (1589) regards 'figure' as purposefully altering 'ordinarie' language, 'in shape, in sounde, and also in sence, sometime by way of surplusage, sometime by defect, sometime by disorder, or mutation'.[36] And if 'speech ... it selfe is artificiall and made by man', then '*Ornament Poeticall*' – comparable to 'flowers', 'rich Orient coulours', a painting's 'shadowing traits', and a woman's cosmetics – can either furnish 'a delectable varietie' or 'disfigure' when it does not keep 'iust proportion'.[37]

Of the some two hundred figures delineated in the second edition of *The Garden of Eloquence*, Peacham singles out *comparatio*, 'which may stand as the generall head and principall of many figures'.[38] That *comparatio* includes both quantitative and qualitative comparisons, and that it effectively designates reasoning by analogy as well as epic simile, Biblical parable, and, perhaps, poetic *concetto*, justifies Peacham's praise for it:

> This forme of speech is of mightie force and power to move by example, & to persuade by reason, for the parts of the comparison being brought together, their likenesse or unlikenesse, their equalitie or inequalitie is as plainly discerned, as things which are tried and iudged by the ballance. The use thereof is verie great and mightie in whatsoever cause it handelth, whether it be in praising or dispraising, accusing, reprehending, co[n]firming, confuting, moving affection, perswading, or in anie other like: and no one forme of speech more apt and excellent to amplifie.[39]

The performative aspects of Peacham's account aside, I would underscore how *comparatio* and its attendant figures – both *similitudo* and syncrisis fall under its head – can serve both as a form of proof (*inventio*) and ornament (*elocutio*). In intellectual-historical terms, *comparatio* seems to thrive on both sides of Foucault's (in)famous epistemic divide: it enables the play of resemblances, but it also helps bring about the reign of identity and difference.

Simile, for Aristotle, is a metaphor dilated by the word 'like' or 'as'. Like metaphor, it creates *enargeia* and *energeia*.[40] As ornament, *similitudo* is prized, Quintilian notes, for its visual or iconic qualities. Yet its constitutive dilation aims for comparison rather than substitution, a distinction that can have substantial cognitive, ontological, and aesthetic implications.[41] As for simile's decorum, Quintilian warns against choosing a *comparatum* too obscure, unfamiliar, or dissimilar; though sometimes the novelty, sublimity, colour, and surprise produced justify the risk.[42] In effect, the conservative Quintilian, with a wary eye on the mannered prose and verse of his time, offers a scopic criterion to evaluate the *similitudines* of Spenser and Donne.

After defining *similitudo* and quoting several examples from Cicero (which conflate simile and analogy), Peacham praises its great utility and variety, its analytic 'perspicuitie', and the aesthetic 'pleasure' it produces. But he also warns against comparing 'things' with too much dissimilarity or choosing *comparata* that are 'straunge and unknowne', for 'by the one there is an absurditie, by the other obscuritie'.[43] Conversely, he praises *dissimilitudo*, 'a forme of speeche which compareth diverse things in a diverse qualitie', for its 'utilitie in amplification' and epideixis.[44] Luke 9:58, which notably bridges natural history and theology, exemplifies this: 'The foxes have holes, and the fowles of the aire have nests, but the sonne of man hath not where to laie his head.' Yet again Peacham warns: 'The grace of dissimilitude is much impaired, when the unlikenesse is verie little, or when the parts are straunge, or unaptly compared.'[45] This caveat nicely prefigures how and why Samuel Johnson condemns the 'wit' of the 'metaphysical' poets:

> [W]it, abstracted from its effects upon the hearer, may be more rigorously and philosophically considered as a kind of *discordia concors*; a combination of dissimilar images, or discovery of occult resemblances in things apparently unlike. Of wit, thus defined, they have more than enough. The most heterogeneous ideas are yoked by violence together; nature and art are ransacked for illustrations, comparisons, and allusions.[46]

To illustrate this, the neoclassical Johnson cites 'A Valediction: Forbidding Mourning' where 'the comparison of a man that travels, and his wife that stays at home, with a pair of compasses' prompts him to jibe that 'it may be doubted whether absurdity or ingenuity has better claim'.[47] In short, both Peacham and Johnson pretend that the line separating a virtuous *similitudo* from a vicious *dissimilitudo* is clear and distinct. But other criteria can and have been adduced: Homer's similes have been read for their persuasive power and unmatched ingenuity; Shakespeare's for their cognitive, heuristic force; and Milton's for their nimble, self-conscious play with 'disparity'.[48] As for Spenser and Donne, in the close readings below we shall see how they use simile to discover and to play with similarity and difference, even as they would persuade us of the need to reflect on the very nature of comparison.

A more critical form of *comparatio*, syncrisis works to praise and blame, compare and judge, usually in an invidious fashion. Ian Donaldson observes:

> [S]yncrisis is a word which simply denotes a bringing together for comparative analysis ... of objects, events, institutions, of artists, writers, warriors, footballers, politicians, elephants, charioteers – the categories are almost without limit – in order to arrive at a final adjudication of their relative merits, and to persuade the reader or listener that one of these elephants or writers or warriors is superior to the other.[49]

Historically, syncrisis would have been encountered by students in the *progymnasmata*; and, as I suggested above, it also informs many nascent forms of literary criticism and intellectual history.[50] Vividly illustrated by Biblical passages, Peacham's definition stresses brevity: '*Syncrisis*, is a comparison of contrary things, diverse persons in one sentence ... The same use and Caution may serve to this figure, which pertaine to Antithesis.'[51] Then, under *Antithesis*, he observes:

> This is a most excellent ornament of eloquence, serving most aptly to amplification, it graceth and beautifieth the Oration with pleasant varietie, and giveth singular perspicuitie and light by the opposition, it is so generall that it may serve to amplifie and garnish any grave and weightie cause ... In the use of this exornation, it behoveth to moderate the number of comparisons, lest they growe to a great multitude, which bewayeth affectation, a fault which ought to bee shunned. Secondly, to provide that we impaire not the beautie and strength of this figure by opposing things differing, instead of contraries.[52]

By making 'contraries' and not 'things differing' the object of syncritic thought – a distinction Johnson also implicitly urges – and in conflating syncrisis and antithesis, Peacham lends both comparing figures real dialectical force. Further, he helps us see how these figures, with their aesthetic and cognitive virtues of 'perspicuitie' and 'varietie', are the two sides, one more acute, the other more dilated, of the same critical impulse. Scaliger's *Poetices libri septem* (1561), with its encyclopaedic, invidious comparisons of Homer and Virgil, notably exemplifies this critical mode.

Finally, distinct from these figures of comparison are several figures of speech involving the repetition of a word or sememe, such as ploce, *traductio*, anadiplosis, etc. – the nomenclature matters less than the effect – that Spenser and Donne use for surprisingly conceptual ends. While not typically regarded as forms of invention, such figures of speech are treated by Puttenham as 'sententious figures', which may 'serve[ ] as well the ear as the conceit'.[53] This double analogy would explain their cognitive effect:

For like as one or two drops of water perce not the flint stone, but many and often droppings doo: so cannot a few words (be they never so pithie or sententious) in all cases and to all manner of mindes, make so deepe an impression, as a more multitude of words to the purpose discreetly, and without superfluitie uttered: the minde being not lesse vanquished with large loade of speech, than the limmes are with heavie burden.[54]

For the present comparison of Spenser's and Donne's figuration, three of these figures stand out: '*Ploche*, or the doubler, otherwise called the swift repeate' is 'a speedie iteration of one word, but with some little intermissio[n] by inserting one or two words betweene';[55] '*Antanaclasis*, or the rebounde' is the repetition of word whose meaning changes in the second instance by changing a letter or two;[56] and closely related is polyptoton or '*Traductio*, or the tranlacer', 'which is when ye turne and tranlace a word into many sundry shapes as the Tailor doth his garment'.[57] That these figures were central to late Renaissance poetics is confirmed by Alexander Gil, whose *Logonomia Anglica* (1619, 1621) mines examples from *The Faerie Queene* to help teach Latin students grammar and rhetoric. More particularly, after quoting *The Faerie Queene* II.vi.13, Gil praises the great 'artifex' of figures like anaphora and congeries.[58]

As I will argue below, Spenser and Donne exploit figures of speech involving repetition and permutation to grasp after absolute or universal ideas and, in the event, to self-consciously wrestle with inexpressibility. Spenser, of course, favours euphonious figures of speech, especially alliteration; yet close listening of the *Cantos* reveals a poet particularly intent on using figures of speech to instantiate notions of change and *stasis*, even as he invidiously compares the former with the latter. In the *Anniversaries*, the anaphoric 'Thinke' and 'Vp' serve hortatory, meditative ends, while the insistent, increasingly urgent reiteration of 'Shee' and 'all' helps effect a subtle nominalism. In both texts, then, material figures of speech create a kind of conceptual palilalia – which, if Donne had read the *Cantos*, would also be a kind of echolalia.[59]

Figuring Mutabilitie

In figuring 'the euer-whirling wheele / Of *Change*' (*FQ* VII.vi.1), and so natural metamorphosis, historical aetiology, political genealogy, and, ultimately, Christian eschatology, the *Cantos* chiefly draw on Ovid, Chaucer, Natalis Comes, and the New Testament.[60] And while by the time they were published in 1609 the political crises informing them had mostly subsided, the epistemological crisis, which had long troubled Renaissance humanism, had only grown. By this I mean the intellectual and cultural implications of the competing truth claims of *scientia* (concerned with *res*) and *sapientia* (transmitted by *verba*) – whether expressed by Bruno during his English sojourn (1583–85), by Montaigne in the English-tongue lent him by Florio (1603), by Bacon's *Advancement of Learning* (1605), by Harriot and Galileo contemplating the heavens (1609–10), or by the Authorized Version of the Bible (1611). Negotiating these kinds of knowing, Spenser (like Donne after him) was Augustinian or Pauline enough to attempt a *translatio*.[61]

After the publication of the first three books of *The Faerie Queene*, a more sceptical Spenser emerges in the 1591 *Complaints* and then, in 1596, when the next three books of his increasingly melancholic romance appear. Geographically and stylistically removed from London's cosmopolitan, witty literary culture, Spenser is fascinated by 'ruines' and decline, topics which are always comparative, if not superlative. For what is 'wourse' (V.Proem.1) is so in light of something better; the worst exists only compared to things thought best. While such worsening clearly prefigures the syncritic thought and agonistic tone shaping the *Cantos*, its effect on Spenser's 'continued Allegory, or darke conceit' is less clear. In other words, we should not overvalue Mutabilitie as a daemon of disorder, especially given how the vicious inconstancy of various characters in earlier books (e.g., Duessa, Busirane) is balanced by other allegorical figures, whose virtuous constancy may retain some synchronic efficacy as the sceptical materialism of the *Cantos* is pondered. Numerous episodes and characters in the first six books – most obviously, the 'Gardin of Adonis' episode in Book III – furnish positive and negative *comparata* for the natural philosophical and metaphysical concerns encountered in the *Cantos*. Yet with the *Cantos* 'unperfite', with an overreaching Mutabilitie riding an Ovidian wave of metonymies, and with 'the noise of genealogical struggle' distorting allegorical harmonies, a certain amnesia may be forgiven.[62] For in the dramatic course of the *Cantos*, we see Mutabilitie countered by a flawed, imperious Jove and a cryptic, reactionary Nature – figures serving less as agents of allegory's imperious, logical 'violence' than, arguably, as symbols of its metaphysical impotence.

A refiguration of the classical goddess *Fortuna*, whose turning wheel iconographically depicts the limits of human power and understanding, the 'titanesse' Mutabilitie champions an empirical, phenomenological, ultimately ontological truth experienced by everything in the physical, historical, mythographic, and spiritual worlds. A belated titanomachy veiling recent political history and, seemingly, Spenser's own search for certainties, Mutabilitie's audacious, epic self-fashioning is condemned now forthrightly (VII.vi.22–4), now ambivalently (VII.viii.1). More particularly, Spenser may also be allegorizing the history of cosmography, whereby an Aristotelian medieval worldview, which holds sub- and superlunary spheres to be qualitatively different, struggles to forestall a late Renaissance one in which both are subject to change.[63] In any case, like Eve, Mutabilitie is a figure of the Creation, even as she disfigures it.[64] She is made to furnish 'proofe and sad examples' (VII.vi.4) of her less than virtuous desire for 'rule and dominion'; but she is also granted the eloquence, and so the figures, to demonstrate the scope and power of her physics and metaphysics. Conversely, if *exemplum*, serving as a form of *similitudo*, typically works in league with allegory for Spenser (see Letter to Raleigh), then here the narrative constructed about Mutabilitie eschews 'doctrine by ensample' for more ambiguous lessons (e.g., VII.vi.29, VII.vi.32).[65] Swayed by her external 'beauty' (VII.vi.31), Jove is blind to her 'confused' (VII.vi.26) interiority. Moreover, he is granted no inkling of the part he is to play in the eschatological or anagogic allegory gesturing towards the Last Judgement, which Spenser adumbrates in the last stanzas. As for Nature, for all her omnipotence, s/he seems overshadowed by lesser, but more vividly painted characters, who copiously fill the poem's allegorical *Denkraum*.[66]

That the *Cantos* may be partially read through the prism of figures other than allegory is confirmed by Gil's treatise, where Spenser is made to exemplify the whole range of figures.[67] More to the point, after citing verses from Samuel Daniel's *Delia* (sonnet 31) and *FQ* III.iv.8–10 where Britomart allegorizes her life as a perilous sea journey, Gil contrasts the obscurity of allegory with the lucidity of *comparatio*. A simile (*FQ* I.ii.16 is quoted) 'first explicates the metaphor, then afterwards composes the matter'.[68] More dilated and transparent than metaphor, simile invites readers to inspect its workings. Describing the non-verbal marginalia in the Folger copy of *The Faerie Queene* (1609), Andrew Fleck notes the predominance of manicules that 'gesture to extended similes'.[69] And if in the *Cantos* such similes remain tethered, however tenuously, to the microcosmic–macrocosmic analogy, then they also sometimes function as figures of thought which explicitly explore the affective and epistemological limits of this analogy.[70] Even as Spenserian simile dilates meaning by establishing correspondences between different spheres of experience, it reflects on this dilation. In Canto vi, Spenser cultivates a visual, cognitive rhetoric of amazement, as he describes the gods' reactions to Mutabilitie's *Putsch*, e.g., in stanza 13 ('All beeing with so bold attempt amazed'), stanza 16 ('so strange astonishment'), stanza 17 ('At whose strange sight … He wondred much'), stanza 19 ('it did them all exceedingly amate'), and stanza 25 ('inly quaking, seem'd as reft of sense'). This amazement culminates in a fascinating simile about fascination, whose logic is primed by a syncrisis: As 'great *Chaos* child', Mutabilitie boasts, 'I greater am in bloud … / Then all the Gods, though wrongfully from heauen exil'd' (VII.vi.26). The latter experience themselves this difference in the course of this strangely indecorous, perhaps satiric simile:

> Whil'st she thus spake, the Gods that gaue good eare
>   To her bold words, and marked well her grace,
>   Beeing of stature tall as any there
>   Of all the Gods, and beautifull of face,
>   As any of the Goddesses in place,
>   Stood all astonied, like a sort of Steeres;
>   Mongst whom, some beast of strange and forraine race,
>   Vnwares is chaunc't, far straying from his peeres:
> So did their ghastly gaze bewray their hidden feares.
>
> (*FQ* VII.vi.28)

The experience of being 'all astonied' is thus implicitly shared by the reader, who, though, narratively, rhetorically, and perhaps politically identifies with the usurper. Remaking the Homeric epithet of 'ox-eyed' or 'ox-faced' Hera,[71] Spenser simultaneously bestializes 'the Gods' and gives them tangible interiority. In more conceptual terms, as Richard Danson Brown contends, the simile damages their 'credibility … as metaphorical embodiments of Christian providence'.[72] With their allegorical value diminished, Mutabilitie, a 'beast of strange and forraine race' – like the 'impertinent predicate' of metaphor itself – must be reconciled in some other way to the ordinary state of things.[73]

In Canto vii, borrowing heavily from Chaucer's *Parlement of Foules*, Spenser has the 'Gods' assemble at Arlo Hill where '*Natures* Sargeant (that is *Order*)' arranges 'all other creatures' in a 'well disposed' manner. This sets up the antithesis with

Mutabilitie's 'confusion and disorder' (VII.vii.4) which runs throughout the canto. Ambiguously gendered, Nature defies visual description, even as Spenser leaves little doubt of her place in the celestial hierarchy: 'Being far greater and more tall of stature / Then any of the gods or Powers on hie' (VII.vii.5). This *comparatio* then informs three visual similes which paradoxically question the worth of physical vision. The first, perhaps figuring Christ, asserts 'her face did like a Lion shew, / That eye of wight could not indure to view' (VII.vii.6).[74] The second figures Nature's face: 'But others tell that it so beautious was, / And round about such beames of splendor threw, / That it the Sunne a thousand times did pass, / Ne could be seene, but like an image in a glass' (VII.vii.6). Chief of these 'others' is Chaucer, whose own simile seems to inform Spenser's.[75] Tellingly, the comparing poet, not Mutabilitie, has this vision; indeed, with the exception of the last two stanzas of the *Cantos*, these lines show Spenser at his most self-reflective. Here, with a third simile, he emerges from his narrative to feign the failure of comparison:

> That well may seemen true: for, well I weene
>   That this same day, when she on *Arlo* sat,
>   Her garment was so bright and wondrous sheene,
>   That my fraile wit cannot deuize to what
>   It to compare, nor finde like stuffe to that,
>   As those three sacred *Saints*, though else most wise,
>   Yet on mount *Thabor* quite their wits forgat,
>   When they their glorious Lord in strange disguise
> Transfigur'd sawe; his garments so did daze their eyes.
>
> (*FQ* VII.vii.7)

The first of only two direct mentions of Christ in the *Cantos* (see also VII.vii.41), with this re(con)figuration of the Transfiguration Spenser attains Dantesque heights – though ostensibly Nature occasions the theophany. Yet by implicitly invoking Matthew 17:2 ('And [Jesus] was transfigured before them: and his face did shine as the sunne, and his clothes were as white as the light'), Spenser mines his not so 'fraile wit' to audaciously compare Nature and Christ on the basis of a common, if synecdochal, *tertium comparationis*, namely, 'Her garment' = 'his garments'. He thus compares himself both to the '*Saints*' (Peter, James, and John), whose 'wits' are dumbfounded by their sight, and to the author, Paul, who offers the two similes.

Meanwhile, syncrisis works narratively to help structure the comparison of allegorical figures and ideas. It also throws into relief competing visual and verbal epistemologies. While the narrator adopts the fiction of reported speech (VII.vi.1), and while Cantos vi and vii have the same dual structure – first rhetorical argument appeals to the ear, then ekphrastic pageant courts the eye – a *lexis* promoting the basic conceptual metaphor *seeing is knowing* reigns throughout. Presenting her case in Canto vii, Mutabilitie promises ocular proof: 'As, if ye please it [the world] into parts diuide, / And euery parts inholders to conuent, / Shall to your eyes appeare incontinent' (VII.vii.17). Her vivid, eloquent, if sometimes paradoxical (e.g., VII.vii.24) account of the four elements and their interactions (VII.vii.15–27) appeals constantly to the 'eyes'. Likewise, just before Nature's pageant of 'times and seasons' unfolds, Mutabilitie urges: 'iudge thy selfe, by verdit of thine eye, / Whether to me they are not subiect all' (VII.vii.27). Fittingly, then, the critical 'eye' has responded to these scenes with various kinds of iconography, which question the viability of iconological-allegorical meanings.[76]

Goaded by Mutabilitie, who traces her lineage back to 'great *Chaos*' (VII.vi.26), Nature has '*Order*' organize a spectacular *progresse* or pageant of the four seasons, twelve months, and then of Day and Night, Life and Death (VII.vii.27–46). This visual/verbal pageant puts God's greatest 'ornament' (*kosmos*) on display, while figuring a redemptive circle that prefigures Spenser's ultimate solution to the metaphysical problem of 'Short *Time*' (VII.viii.1). The zodiacal symbols of the months are exquisitely detailed visual similes, *icones*, whose physical attributes emblemize and sharpen commonplace humanist notions. But Spenser's great conceptual innovation here is to give verisimilar human figures rule over pagan deities and symbolic animals.[77] Still, if this is a triumph, then it is immanent rather than transcendent. Lauding the copious fruits of human labour and love and so ultimately of divine justice, too, the pageant of the Months leads recursively towards Spring ('hasting Prime'), which here stands for prelapsarian Creation. Spenser's mood is playful, even celebratory, as evidenced by the *exclamatio*: 'Lord! how all creatures laugh' (VII.vii.34). Such delight also informs other figures, such as the Marvellian simile comparing the 'Crab', 'Bargemen', and courtiers on the basis of their common 'backward' motion (VII.vii.35). Propelled by alliteration and other material figures of speech, the pageant eventually results in two antitheses involving natural-temporal phenomena (VII.vii.44–6): Day and Night, then Death and Life. Death merits the striking asyndeton: 'Vnbodied, vnsoul'd, vnheard, vnseene'. 'But Life', which notably comes last, 'was like a faire young lusty boy, / Such as they faine *Dan Cupid* to haue beene, / Full of delightfull health and liuely ioy, / Deckt all with flowres, and wings of gold fit to employ'. With this vivid, if commonplace *similitudo*, Spenser proleptically bolsters Nature's verdict; for like the recurrence of 'Prime', the appearance here of '*Dan Cupid*' testifies to her regenerative power.

As for figures of speech, most remarkable is how Spenser's constant ploce and *traductio* featuring 'all' – an echo perhaps of the Ovidian-Pythagorean account of the cosmos, of *omnia mutantur* or *to pan* – signals a thirst for totality and certainty.[78] After the pageant passes by, Mutability urges Nature: 'now be iudge and say, / Whether in all thy creatures more or lesse / CHANGE doth not raign and beare the greatest sway: / For, who sees not, that *Time* on all doth pray?' (VII.vii.47). Yet Nature says nothing and instead Jove responds by admitting 'that these / And all things else that vnder heauen dwell / Are chaung'd of *Time*, who doth them all disseise / Of being' – an admission he then tries to qualify by adding that 'we gods doe rule' over these same 'things' (VII.vii.48). Nevertheless, the ploce with 'all' underscores how Jove understands Mutabilitie's query as an absolute one. Seizing her advantage, Mutabilitie answers with a rhetorical question (*erotema*) which again distils the poem's visual epistemology: 'But what we see not, who shall vs perswade?' (VII.vii.49).[79] The next six stanzas would furnish this visual proof, as she sketches the 'sundry' and irregular motions of the 'Spheares' or planets. And while these empirical (to say nothing of genealogical and political) implications unfold, a more axiomatic, absolute claim is made: 'all that moueth, doth mutation loue' (VII.vii.55).

This (il)logic shapes Mutabilitie's peroration addressed to Nature as well. Exploiting ploce, *traductio*, anadiplosis, and antithesis, she urges a final syncrisis:

> Then since within this wide great *Vniuerse*
>   Nothing doth firme and permanent appeare,
>   But all things tost and turned by transuerse:
>   What then should let, but I aloft should reare
>   My Trophee, and from all, the triumph beare?
>   Now iudge then (ô thou greatest goddesse trew!)
>   According as thy selfe doest see and heare,
>   And vnto me addoom that is my dew;
> That is the rule of all, all being rul'd by you.
>
> (VII.vii.56)

By lexically and syntactically harping on 'all', Mutabilitie sublimates her vain cosmological ambitions.[80] With a *traductio* and the turn of a few verses, she figures and disfigures the '*Vniuerse*' (lit. 'one turn'), as 'all things' are 'tost and turned by transuerse'.[81] Yet by traducing or turning the '*Vniuerse*' in this entropic direction, and by submitting herself to Nature's judgement, Mutabilitie sets up a final refiguration, too, one that will repeat but also overturn the very terms of her 'Plea'.

After her orderly pageant and Mutabilite's perversion of the same have passed, Nature finally breaks her silence to ingeniously reverse Mutabilitie's argument:

> I well consider all that ye haue sayd,
>   And find that all things stedfastnes doe hate
>   And changed be: yet being rightly wayd
>   They are not changed from their first estate;
>   But by their change their being doe dilate:
>   And turning to themselues at length againe,
>   Doe worke their owne perfection so by fate:
>   Then ouer them Change doth not rule and raigne;
> But they raigne ouer change, and doe their states maintaine.
>
> (VII.vii.58)

Fusing Ovidian physics and Christian eschatology, bolstered by the ploce of 'all' in lines 1–2 (reiterating 'all things' from VII.vii.56) and the polyptoton of 'stedfastnes', 'estate', and 'states' (which solves the chiasmus in lines 8–9),[82] Spenser/Nature animates the axial lines 5–6 which remake the 'tost and turned' in VII.vii.56, such that now 'turning' becomes a form of identity or 'perfection'.[83] Mutabilitie's discourse ('all that ye haue sayd') corresponds to the universe ('all things'), which here, now distilling the lesson of the cosmological pageant, Spenser/Nature subtly transforms, in the space of a stanza, from being ruled by 'Change' to ruling over it. In this respect, the Neoplatonic claim that 'all things ... their states maintaine' informs and justifies the reiteration and variation of semantic forms of *sto/stare* running throughout the *Cantos*. Consequently, the various connotations of 'dilate' are crucial.[84] Indicating both a physical and temporal lengthening, they connote the absence of rupture, the persistence of form, even the triumph of unity over multiplicity. Think Donne's 'A Valediction: Forbidding Mourning': 'Our two soules therefore, which are one, / Though I must goe, endure not yet / A breach, but an expansion, / Like gold to ayery thinnesse beate' (lines 21–4).[85] More, however, is at stake for Spenser than an absent lover's anguish. He and Nature must somehow 'subiect' upstart Mutabilitie. To this end he marshals an absolute antithesis, a chiasmus, another ploce, and of course rhyme: 'But time shall come that all shall changed bee, / And from thenceforth, none no more change shall see' (VII.vii.59). Supported by Scripture – Hamilton reads 1 Corinthians 15:51, 54 as the relevant intertext – and propelled by the skilled, insistent exploitation of figures of speech involving repetition, Spenser's syncrisis thus precipitates a dramatic narrative and thematic peripeteia.[86] Leaning on these figures, the narrative closes with a translingual pun: 'So was the *Titaness* put downe ...'.[87] *Sub-iected* by Nature because she fails to acknowledge differences (e.g., in VII.vii.15), Mutabilitie is silenced by figures of speech. With such figuration, Spenser refines his paradoxical take on phenomenological change. Further, considering that 'figure' can denote also 'geometric shape', we might say that the *Cantos* transforms linear change (Mutabilitie) into circular repetition (Nature). In other words, the conceptual antithesis of Mutabilitie and Nature is sharpened and finally resolved by the introduction of an intuitive, metaphysical claim: Time, for all its destructive effects, is also recursive, regenerative, and, ultimately, providential.

Still, Mutabilitie haunts until the end. The notion of 'being rightly wayd' is picked up in VII.viii.1, where Spenser again would 'way' the truth of her claims. Such weighing, as Peacham suggests with his balance-metaphor, is the essence of *comparatio*. The poet's scale, however, hinges on faith not reason (or decorum), on sound as much as sense. He sets up an antithesis between experience of change and belief in eternity that is resolved less by argument – despite the nod to Scripture – than by material poetic figuration. At first, Spenser sees 'all things' from Mutabilitie's Ovidian perspective:

> When I bethinke me on that speech whyleare,
>   Of *Mutability*, and well it way:
>   Me seemes, that though she all vnworthy were
>   Of the Heav'ns Rule; yet very sooth to say,
>   In all things else she beares the greatest sway.
>   Which makes me loath this state of life so tickle,
>   And loue of things so vaine to cast away;
>   Whose flowring pride, so fading and so fickle,
> Short *Time* shall soon cut down with his consuming sickle.
>
>   (VII.viii.1)

Then, with one last turn, he glimpses eternal permanence:

> Then gin I thinke on that which Nature sayd,
>   Of that same time when no more *Change* shall be,
>   But stedfast rest of all things firmely stayd
>   Vpon the pillours of Eternity,
>   That is contrayr to *Mutabilitie*:

> For, all that moueth, doth in *Change* delight:
> But thence-forth all shall rest eternally
> With Him that is the God of Sabbaoth hight:
> O that great Sabbaoth God, graunt me that Sabaoths sight.
>
> (VII.viii.2)

The pleonastic 'But stedfast rest of all things firmly stayd' pivots, arguably, on 1 Corinthians 15:28, 'And when all things shall be subdued unto him, then shall the Son also himself be subject unto him that put all things under him, that God may be all in all.'[88] And just as line 7 reiterates this 'all', so the paranomasia of 'Sabbaoth' as 'hostes' (Romans 9:29) and 'Sabaoths' as 'rest' makes the nominalist case for apotheosis. Alternatively, with 'sight' as the final note, the last two stanzas of the *Cantos* both confirm and subvert the visual epistemology so dear to Spenser. His *comparatio* of 'Short *Time*' with 'that same time when no more *Change* shall be' envisions a final, future, thoroughly orthodox syncrisis. Shifting mythopoetic gears, Ovidian metamorphosis is transformed into Christian Last Judgement.[89] Semantic repetition works to frustrate, to 'dilate', if you will, 'Short *Time*' (VII.viii.1).

With this tautology, with this figured moment when '*Change*' ceases, Spenser breaks off. Paraphrasing Dante, Giorgio Agamben writes in 'The End of the Poem' that the 'most beautiful way to end a poem' is when 'the last verses fall, rhymed, in silence'.[90] Together with the metaphysics of rhyme, Spenser's 'sententious figures' here signal the primacy of identity over difference. Artificially 'fashioning' certain words (while subjecting others to 'turning'), the poet steadfastly grasps after an understanding of change and God's design. His figures achieve specific aural effects closely linked to the dynamics of stanzaic form, even as they signpost a metaphysics of temporal repetition and ontological perfection.

Figuring 'Shee'

Donne's fascination with mutability runs throughout his career. Early on it takes the form of lyrics like the arch Petrarchan 'Woman's Constancy' where the beloved's inconstancy is outmatched only by the witty poet's 'turnings' and 'fashionings'.[91] In the *Satires* (first three written around 1593, the last two circa 1597), Donne critiques political and cultural decline, confessional and intellectual hypocrisy: 'O Age of rusty iron! Some better wit / Call it some worse name, if ought equall it' (*Satire V*, 35–6). But by 1611, after two decades of playing the courtier and sharpening his wit to exquisite points in the *Songs and Sonets*, *Satires*, *Elegies*, *Holy Sonnets* (mostly written around 1609–10), and in the prose of *Paradoxes and Problems* and *Biathanatos* (1608), Donne, pondering his vocation and future prospects, ponders a kind of Augustinian conversion.[92] This is to say, as 'the finest long poems written in English between *The Faerie Queene* and *Paradise Lost*',[93] the *Anniversaries* mark a liminal moment in Donne's career, a watershed between his life as courtier and clergyman, while also serving as a laboratory in which he discovers a philosophically eclectic, rhetorically exorbitant, but in the end well-travelled mystical solution to the problem of change.

While sympathetic readers have found myriad learned, often ingenious ways to explicate the poems' radical epideixis of Elizabeth Drury, his patron's recently deceased daughter, the best hermeneutic clues come from Donne himself. A 1612 letter touches on his motives in writing and regrets in publishing the *Anniversaries*. There he rejects 'the imputation of having said too much' with a 'defe[n]se' of his own powers of invention: '[M]y purpose was to say as well as I could: for since I never saw the Gentlewoman, I cannot be understood to have bound my self to have spoken just truths, but I would not be thought to have gone about to praise her, or any other in rhyme; except I took such a person, as might be capable of all that I could say.'[94] In other words, as in his other epideictic verse, Donne writes not about a particular death, but rather he sets himself a 'general problem': how to figure the dead.[95] Just as crucial is his reported reply to Ben Jonson, 'that he described the Idea of a Woman and not as she was'.[96] How, then, does Donne figure this 'Idea'? How does he embody 'all that [he] could say'?

To begin with, like Spenser with Mutabilitie, Donne makes a feminine figure the heuristic vehicle for his most difficult thoughts. Yet Drury is not allegorized.[97] Denied any physical attributes or narrative contingencies (*accidentia*) which might lend themselves to allegory, 'Shee' is made to generate meanings that, for all their hyperbole, are treated as literal consequences of her death, which Donne treats as an absolute, universal event – much like Hegel regards Christ's incarnation.[98] Further, the *Anatomie* doubts the kind of synthetic judgements the allegorist exploits to join the literal and figurative: 'What Artist now dares boast that he can bring / Heauen hither, or constellate any thing ... / The art is lost, and correspondence too' (*FA*, lines 391–6). Thus eschewing allegory, Donne favours antithesis, syncrisis, and the conceit's paralogic. If 'The worlds proportion disfigured is', then this truth is countered with 'Shee by whose lines proportion should bee / Examin'd, measure of all Symmetree' (*FA*, lines 309–10, 302). Rather than indicating a literal referent, Donne constructs an abstract figure, a 'patterne' (*SA*, line 524) by which he can 'thinke', invidiously compare, and eventually raise himself 'vp' to 'know' eternal things (*SA*, lines 251–320).[99] Whatever Spenserian mythopoetic agency lingers in the poems does so, ambiguously, in Drury, whom Donne transforms into a generic, pliable 'type' (*FA*, lines 319–20). This 'Shee' may represent, different readers have claimed: the 'image of God', the logos, a logos, Wisdom (*sapientia*), Perfection, *anima mundi*, Christ, Eve, the Virgin Mary, St Lucy, Dante's Beatrice, Petrarch's Laura, Queen Elizabeth, Donne's wife, etc.[100] Further, while 'Shee' is twice cast as an 'example' (*FA*, line 457; *SA*, line 307), remarkably, Donne offers no tangible moral lessons.

Instead, the *Anniversaries* are exemplary for how their various figures of thought and speech, especially as elements in logically contorted conceits, involve the reader in comparing unlike things. Readers become complicit in the task of figuring out the meaning of figures and, as fellow fallen beings, for a 'decayd' (*FA*, line 249) world. Briefly put, when Donne urges his soul to transcend, 'we' are also being addressed and instructed in how to reread the creation or God's book. Cultivating the '[p]leasures of the enthymeme', his conceits produce a sequential maze of *pointes* to be puzzled out.[101] This continual metalepsis is framed, however, by the larger structural syncrisis between this world and the next, a syncrisis motivating both his satiric hyperboles expressing *contemptus mundi* and the exorbitant hyperboles exalting Drury.[102]

Alternatively, as with Spenser, figures of speech involving the repetition and permutation of a word or semene play an outsized role. While by no means exclusive to the *Anniversaries*, such repetition acquires there heuristic power that defies any attempt to dismiss it as mere mannerism.[103]

The *Anatomie*, a 'world of wit' as Bishop Hall's prefatory poem dubs it, is riddled by a great variety of figures. The reader is greeted by a dramatic prosopopoeia: 'So thou, sicke world' (*FA*, lines 23–62); challenged by an aporetic *erotema*: 'How witty's ruine?' (*FA*, line 99); and moved by this elegant combination of paradox and meiosis: 'And all the world would be one dying Swan, / To sing her funerall praise' (*FA*, lines 406–7). Indeed, even as they join with other figures, Donne's *similitudines* flout decorum and strain logic by wildly distorting both *comparandum* and *comparatum*. As for *comparata*, first our 'bodies' are belittled (*FA*, lines 111–12); then, by analogy, our 'mindes' are subject to the same meiosis (*FA*, line 152). Meanwhile, Donne urges a double syncrisis which distorts the terms of the micro-macrocosmic analogy: 'Be more then man, or thou'rt lesse than an Ant. / Then, as mankinde, so is the worlds whole frame / Quite out of joynt, almost created lame' (*FA*, lines 190–2). Quickly, though, distortion becomes disruption. Correspondences no longer exist between 'every man' who 'thinkes he hath got / To be a Phoenix' and the unique 'She' (*FA*, lines 216–38). That this failed *comparatio* is partially driven by astonished scepticism toward the 'new Philosophy' has of course compelled many readers. Less remarked, however, is how Donne's rhetorical-spiritual overreaching mirrors the very cosmographical overreaching he condemns. Dissecting fully the dynamics of this mirroring is beyond this chapter's scope, but I would stress how the memorializing poet displaces man as 'measure' (*FA*, line 310) with Drury, who, being (literally) dead, is a *comparandum* beyond mutability's reach.

This displacing, thinking metonymy fuels each stage of Donne's extreme syncrisis. Crucially though, by sometimes preferring dilated *similitudines* over metaphoric condensation, he protects his *ethos* and preserves a degree of verisimilitude. So, for example, it is '[a]s though heav'n suffred earth-quakes, peace or war' (*FA*, line 261). Similes soften the cognitive blow of surprising figures: 'And now the Springs and Sommers which we see, / Like sonnes of women after fifty bee' (*FA*, lines 203–4). Despite his imperious tone, Donne often justifies and qualifies his figuration. With Drury in place as the 'type', figures of comparison can proceed now cautiously, now boldly:

> And had the world his iust proportion,
> Were it a ring still, yet the stone is gone.
> As a compassionate Turcoyse which doth tell
> By looking pale, the wearer is not well,
> As gold fals sicke being stung with Mercury,
> All the worlds parts of such complexion bee.
>
> (*FA*, lines 341–6)

Commencing the analogy in the subjunctive mode, Donne ends by employing, typically, an enthymeme to make his absolutist claim.

Figuration in the *Progres* opens with a bold gambit: a four-part, richly empirical simile arguing 'there is motion in corruption' links the theme of 'decay' troubling the *Anatomie* with the thirst for ascent dominating the *Progres*:

> But as a ship which hath strooke saile, doth runne,
> By force of that force which before, it wonne,
> Or as sometimes in a beheaded man,
> Though at those two Red seas, which freely ran,
> One from the Trunke, another from the Head,
> His soule be saild, to her eternall bed,
> His eies will twinckle, and his tongue will roll,
> As though he beckned, and cal'd back his Soul,
> He graspes his hands, and he puls vp his feet,
> And seemes to reach, and to step forth to meet
> His soule; when all these motions which we saw,
> Are but as Ice, which crackles at a thaw:
> Or as a Lute, which in moist weather, rings
> Her knell alone, by cracking of her strings:
> So struggles this dead world, now shee is gone;
> For there is motion in corruption.
>
> (*SA*, lines 7–22)

While the first, third, and fourth *comparata* are decorous and concise, the second *comparatum*, the staggering spectacle of the 'beheaded man' and 'those two Red seas', a *hiperbole di simiglianza*, Tesauro would say, imparts extraordinary *enargeia*, pathos, and *grotesquerie*.[104] Yet Donne does not just compare; he also discovers. With the speculative 'As though … / And seemes' clause, he broaches one of the poem's central conceptual, dramatic tensions: the agony of the dying or dead body separated from its 'soule'. Further, the *affectus* of 'those two Red seas' is tempered only if one is willing to read the figure anagogically or typologically, as pointing back to Moses in the closing lines of the *Anatomie* and forward to Christ who guarantees humanity an 'eternall bed'.[105] By thus complicating one *comparatum* – to say nothing of his invocation of shared experience ('all these motions which we saw')[106] – while presenting three others, Donne foregrounds his nimble, restless wit, fixing attention on the how of his thinking as much as on the what.

The how is methodically amplified throughout the poem. A 'Hydropique' (*SA*, line 48) Donne urges his own 'soule' to 'Thinke' about death, to '[f]orget this rotten world' (*SA*, line 49) and to meditate instead on Drury as an ideal *comparandum*, a 'Figure of the Golden times' (*SA*, line 70), who inspires him/us to 'Looke vpward' (*SA*, line 65). To this end, a litany of metaphors and similes works to refigure the already figurative Drury. Still, 'Shee', with her absolute qualities, also defies comparison:

> Thinke these things cheerefully: and if thou bee
> Drowsie or slacke, remember then that shee,
> Shee whose Complexion was so euen made,
> That which of her Ingredients should inuade
> The other three, no Feare, no Art could guesse:
> So far were all remou'd from more or lesse.
>
> (*SA*, lines 121–6)

Similarly, towards the end of the *Progres*, the viability of the very kinds of comparisons propelling both poems is doubted: 'Shee, in whose goodnesse, he that names degree / Doth iniure her; ('Tis losse to be cald best / There where the stuffe is not such as the rest)' (*SA*, lines 498–500). Visiting an inexpressibility topos dear to negative theology, these verses disingenuously but ingeniously suggest the limits of comparison.[107] Having spent some thousand lines comparing the world's 'decay' with Drury's 'goodnesse', Donne now concludes comparison is odious.

Yet again, thinking, comparing figures make his epiphany possible. In the section entitled 'Contemplation of our state in our death-bed' (*SA*, lines 91–156) – the closest the poems get to a narrative of mutability – Donne ponders the nature of comparison. For example, in light of Drury, he doubts the abstract perfection of geometric figures even as he compares her to such figures: 'To whose proportions if we would compare / Cubes, th'are unstable; Circles, Angulare' (*SA*, 141–2). More extensively, in lines 85–219, Donne directs the anaphora of 'Thinke' towards his own 'soule' (*SA*, line 157). Driving the amplification, 'Thinke' becomes an invitation to imagine, figure, and invidiously compare material and spiritual things. So while 'this poor unlittered whelpe / My body' (*SA*, lines 165–6) ostensively recalls the *Anatomie*, with its *contemptus mundi* devaluing all material, corporeal things and the *scientia* that tries to know them, other metaphoric comparisons promote true *sapientia* and belief in spiritual regeneration: 'Thinke that a rusty Peece, discharg'd, is flowen / In peeces, and the bullet is his owne, / And freely flies: This to thy soule allow, / Thinke thy sheel broke, thinke thy Soule hatch'd but now' (*SA*, lines 181–4). Finding first mechanical, then organic *comparata* to figure the body–soul relation, this thought experiment, with all its novelty and potential heterodoxy, has the revelatory force of mystical experience. The condensed speed of the comparisons – matched, if you will, by the speed of the liberated soul, which 'Dispatches in a minute all the way, / Twixt Heauen, and Earth' (*SA*, 188–9) – also dissuades us from dissecting their improbability. Ramie Targoff persuasively shows how Donne's account of 'bodie' and 'soule' yields a 'surprising' conclusion, the 'paradox' that sees the body reluctant to leave its fleshy prison.[108] At the same time, I would add, Donne's *oratio*, playing with 'matters of fact' (*SA*, line 285), clearly disdains the limits of *ratio*.

Simile toys with this very tension. Heightening further the contrast between the sub- and superlunary spheres, but still plumbing his soul's epistemological desires, Donne quickly rehearses then dismisses several cosmological cruxes only to conclude with a marvellously conceited, three-part simile glorifying death:

> And as these stars were but so many beades
> Strunge on one string, speed vndistinguish'd leades
> Her through those spheares, as through the beades, a string,
> Whose quicke succession makes it still one thing:
> As doth the Pith, which, least our Bodies slacke,
> Strings fast the little bones of necke, and backe;
> So by the soule doth death string Heauen and Earth,
> For when our soule enioyes this her third birth,
> (Creation gaue her one, a second, grace,)
> Heauen is as neare, and present to her face,

> As colours are, and obiects, in a roome
> Where darknesse was before, when Tapers come.
> This must, my soule, thy long-short Progresse bee
>
> (*SA*, lines 207–19)

Remarkably, each term in the simile metonymically informs the other terms. The first *comparatum* is a radical meiosis, a novel analogy reducing speeding 'stars' to 'beades' for a necklace or dress (there is also the Spenserian pun on 'still' followed by a pun on 'fast'); the second *comparatum*, by analogy with the first, anatomizes the body, so that 'the little bones of necke, and backe' are like the 'stars', while the spinal cord ('Pith') resembles the 'string'. When we arrive at the *comparanda*, then, not only is 'death' paradoxically equated with the life-sustaining 'Pith' and the artful 'string', but the 'soule' becomes a tailor/anatomist. But Donne does not stop here; remaking the commonplace of death as rebirth, he evokes the proximity of 'Heauen' with an additional analogy in which dying resembles the experience of seeing 'Tapers come' into a dark room. This witty, chiaroscuro vision of life and death, of the soul trying to escape the body and materiality, then concludes with three pointed figures of thought: deixis, apostrophe, and paradox.

With his 'soule' thus illuminated, the main panegyric resumes at line 220, where the hortatory 'Thinke' is soon transferred, via *traductio* and *similitudo*, to the dead Drury:

> Shee, or whose soule, if we may say, t'was Gold,
> Her body was th'Electrum, and did hold
> Many degrees of that; we vnderstood
> Her by her sight, her pure and eloquent blood
> Spoke in her cheekes, and so distinckly wrought,
> That one might almost say, her bodie thought
>
> (*SA*, lines 241–6)

While the two *remedia* 'may' lessen somewhat the conceit's shock, by proposing such a crucial category and theological mistake, Donne propels further conceptual and spiritual overreaching.[109] The following section, 'Her [the soul's] ignorance in this life and knowledge in the next' (*SA*, 251–320), offers an extraordinary series of antitheses. Now an earthly and so metaphoric perspective is contrasted with a heavenly and therefore unfigurable one:

> Thou look'st through spectacles; small things seeme great,
> Below; But vp vnto the watch-towre get,
> And see all things despoyld of fallacies:
> Thou shalt not peepe through lattices of eies,
> Nor heare through Laberinths of eares, nor learne
> By circuit, or collections to discerne.
> In Heauen thou straight know'st all, concerning it,
> And what concerns it not, shall straight forget.
>
> (*SA*, lines 293–300)

'In Heauen' seeing is knowing, not like knowing. There the senses – neatly figured as 'spectacles', 'lattices', and 'Laberinths' – and their Baconian *helps*, are superfluous.

This prized perspective, 'this extasee' (SA, line 321), however, remains more imagined, perforce more proleptic, than realized. Thus Donne commences another prosopopoeia to his 'soule', now urging it to 'Return not ... to earthly thoughts' (SA, lines 321–3). Aided by similes (SA, lines 335–8, 425–33), a conceit whereby 'Shee' becomes 'a state', flirting with allegory (SA, lines 359–75), but, above all, anaphora ('Vp' or 'Vp, vp'), his soule tries ascending again.

In moving from the 'sight' (SA, line 244) of Drury to 'The sight of God', Donne exploits knowledge of geometric figures to figure and 'thinke' the ineffable:

> Then, soule, to thy first pitch worke vp againe;
> Know that all lines which circles doe containe,
> For once that they the center touch, do touch
> Twice the circumference; and be thou such.
> Double on Heauen, thy thoughts on Earth emploid;
> All will not serue; Onely who haue enioyd
> The sight of God, in fulnesse, can thinke it;
> For it is both the obiect, and the wit.
> This is essentiall ioye, where neither hee
> Can suffer Diminution, nor wee;
> Tis such a full, and such a filling good;
> Had th'Angels once look'd on him, they had stood.
>
> (SA, lines 435–46)

Here Donne briefly, subjunctively, realizes his mystical vision – even as he voices conflicting epistemological and religious desires. Initially, the imperious geometric conceit, whose difficulty befits its abstract content, envisions a way of extending the capacity of human 'thoughts' beyond material limits.[110] Yes, the soul's diameter falls abruptly short: 'All' the soul's efforts, all analogy, 'will not serue'. But Donne, leaning on theological commonplaces, can still imagine the perfection of God's thought, which knows itself completely, which 'is both the obiect, and the wit'. He can recall that 'first pitch', a prelapsarian, but also geometric perspective worth of Cusanus. He can even envisage how fallen 'Angels' might not have fallen. Echoing Aquinas and Augustine, Donne explains how these failed to look beyond themselves to see God's face; for, if they had, they would have 'stood'.[111] This contrafactual, where being knows no 'Diminution', where 'hee' and 'wee' rhyme absolutely, indicates a semantic, imagined experience more than an ontological truth. For all the dramatic clarity of 'This is essentiall ioye', the deixis ironically underscores how it cannot be 'enioyd' by the poet, save, perhaps, after the Last Judgement. Put another way, Donne trades *scientia* for *sapientia*, as his totalizing dialectic of *omnis et nihil* moves from the geometric ideal to the kind of situated phenomenological thinking Jean-Luc Marion describes when encountering the 'excess' of divinely 'saturated phenomena'.[112] More cataphatic than apophatic, Donne can name the divine and give acute, verbal expression to his thirst for identity with it, though he only figuratively participates in it.[113] Momentarily immune to mutability, his imagined union with God is immune also to proof, at least while we still have bodies and suffer the Fall's epistemological consequences.[114]

A final sequence of metaphorical configurations (SA, lines 511–28) concludes the *Progres*, as Donne retrospectively equates 'the lawes of poetry' with the 'Lawes of religion'. Fancying himself a 'French convertite' and Drury a 'Saint', he becomes a 'Coine' stamped by God and Drury his 'patterne' and 'Proclamation'. Amplifying this last metaphor, the poet becomes 'The Trumpet', which probably alludes to 1 Corinthians 15:52–5: '[F]or the trumpet shall sound, and the dead shall be raised incorruptible, and we shall be changed ... O death, where is thy sting? O grave, where is thy victory?'[115] To help figure such metaphysical change, Donne constructs another kind of 'patterne'. The repeated ploce and *traductio* of 'all', like his excessive use of anaphora and deixis, lends his poetics a paradoxical, but tangible materialism. Here, as with Spenser's *Cantos*, semantic repetition helps express the ineffable. Like the iteration and conflation of 'we' and 'shee' (and so also the conflation of Donne's 'soule' with Drury's 'soule'), the repetition of 'all' expresses absolute identity and unity – this while similes and other figures of thought play with similarity and difference. Understandably overlooked by most readers hunting for paraphrasable meanings, these iterating figures appeal to the ear as well as the mind.[116]

The poems' most famous lines, for example, tintinnabulate 'all' as Donne details the kind and degree of his scepticism: 'And new Philosophy calls all in doubt' (*FA*, line 205). The spondaic *traductio* of 'calls all' reinforces absolute claims. Had he written 'calls some things in doubt', the line would be prosaic. The subsequent seven lines amplify this 'all', with the help of parison,[117] until Donne strikes the note again, turning it now into an adjective to express the human folly of desiring to be unique and free from contingency:

> 'Tis all in pieces, all cohaerence gone;
> All iust supply, and all Relation:
> Prince, Subiect, Father, Sonne, are things forgot,
> For euery man alone thinkes he hath got
> To be a Phoenix, and that there can bee
> None of that kinde, of which he is, but hee.
> This is the worlds condition now, and now
> Shee that should all part to reunion bow,
> Shee that had all Magnetique force alone,
> To draw, and fasten sundred parts in one
>
> (*FA*, lines 213–22)

Even as the totality and unicity represented by 'man' and 'Shee' are invidiously compared, the ploce of 'all' figures a different kind of 'cohearence'. It provides the material but semantic building blocks with which to construct an absolute, metaphysical antithesis. With this said, 'all' plays more subtle roles, too. It serves as a key end-rhyme and internal rhyme word-sememe. And when, given its ubiquity, '-all' appears in other words without its proper semantic force, oblique, resonant meanings occur; for example: 'Shee that was best, and first originall / Of all faire copies; and the generall / Steward to Fate' (*FA*, 227–9).

More obviously, 'All' has fundamental[l] theological connotations. The *Progres* begins:

> Nothing could make mee sooner to confesse
> That this world had an euerlastingnesse,

> Then to consider, that a yeare is runne,
> Since both this lower worlds, and the Sunnes Sunne,
> The Lustre, and the vigor of this All,
> Did set; t'were Blasphemy, to say, did fall.
>
> (SA, lines 1-6)

With a witty antanaclasis ('Sunnes Sunne'), a jarring enjambment, and the timely figure of thought, epanorthosis or *correctio*,[118] producing fruitful ambiguity, Donne flirts with 'Blasphemy' to embrace the paradox that he is still writing verse in a world that died in the previous *Anniversarie*. Donne's duplicity, if you will, is absolute. Playing with the all-or-'Nothing' topos and hinting at the identity of Drury and Christ, he rhymes 'All' and 'fall', even as he idealizes 'this All'.

The struggle to express 'this All' takes many semantic and syntactic forms. In the face of oblivion, Donne offers this anadiplosis, immediately buttressed by ploce and rhyme:

> Yet a new Deluge, and of Lethe flood,
> Hath drown'd vs all, All have forgot all good,
> Forgetting her, the maine Reserue of all,
> Yet in this Deluge, grosse and generall,
> Thou seest mee striue for life; my life shalbe,
> To bee hereafter prais'd, for praysing thee,
> Immortal Mayd
>
> (SA, lines 27-33)

With Mnemosyne drowned, Donne, with his remembering figures, takes her place. Some three hundred-fifty lines later, he uses the same ploce – augmented by a heterodox hyperbole, a polyptoton, two *comparatios*, and then a dramatic *dissimilitudo* – to again try the absolute:

> As these perogatiues being met in one,
> Made her a soueraigne state, religion
> Made her a Church; and these two made her all.
> Shee who was all this All, and could not fall
> To worse, by company; (for shee was still
> More Antidote, then all the world was ill,)
> Shee, shee doth leaue it, and by Death, suruiue
> All this, in Heauen, whither who doth not striue
> The more, because shee'is there, he doth not know
> That accidentall ioyes in Heauen doe grow.
> But pause, my soule, and study ere thou fall
> On accidentall ioyes, th'essentiall.
>
> (SA, lines 373-84)

Verging on pleonasm, yet insisting throughout on differences, the period ends by asserting an absolute, qualitative distinction, which the remainder of the poem qualifies and amplifies. The twice-repeated (end- and internally) rhyming antithesis of 'all ... fall' prepares the way for the knotty, theological syncrisis that invidiously compares 'accidentall ioyes' and the singular 'essentiall' one. While the former, like a Heraclitan 'riuer' (*SA*, line 395), is riven by 'inconstancee' (*SA*, 400), the latter is firmly grounded in Scripture. Shawcross cites 1 Corinthians 15:28 to gloss 'all this All': 'And when all things shall be subdued unto him, then shall the Son also himself be subject unto him that put all things under him, that God may be all in all.'[119] A key intertext, it obliquely informs all the other poems' figures of speech involving 'all'.

Towards a refigured literary history

Finally, the ways we have seen Spenser's and Donne's figuration converge in this chapter should have implications for any literary history featuring these two poets, particularly if we regard literary history as constitutively figured or 'artificiall'. Any historiography, comparative or not, is also a metaphorology. As Haydn White wrote decades ago: 'Tropic is the shadow from which all realistic discourse tries to flee. This flight, however is futile; for tropics is the process by which all discourse *constitutes* the objects which it pretends to describe realistically and analyze objectively.'[120] History's principal tropes, White argues, are four: metaphor, metonymy, synecdoche, and irony. Periodization, for instance, may work by synecdoche: Spenser stands in for English Renaissance poetry, Donne for metaphysical verse. Or, more promisingly, a metonymic literary history underscores historical causality, contingency, and, yes, mutability. Still, as I have avoided making causal arguments about Spenser's influence on Donne,[121] I would argue that *imitatio* can function indirectly and synchronically. Influence is often more rhizomatic than arboreal. There are always metonymic narratives to tell: within our interpretative, literary-historical frame, Spenser's fragmenting of his moral epic on the anvil of mutability would give way to Donne's generically labile poems, which metaphysically mediate that same mutability. Metonymic literary histories also tend towards the syncritic: for instance, the clichéd tale of the courtly, ethical Spenser ceding his place atop the lyric pantheon to the cosmopolitan, metaphysical Donne. More subtle, perhaps, would be a narrative telling how increasingly untenable allegory ushers in the reign of catachrestic metaphor. Or one might privilege a 'transverse' or Lucretian Spenser over an alchemical, eschatological Donne.[122] Yet by thus complicating linear, causal, or even teleological schemes, metonymical literary history may end in aporia.

Beyond White's schema, literary history can be structured by the figures we encountered above: hyperbole, allegory, icon, *similitudo*, and, yes, syncrisis. In blaming Marino and the 'metaphysical' poets for their hyperbole, Samuel Johnson waxes hyperbolic: 'What they wanted, however, of the sublime, they endeavoured to supply by hyperbole; their amplification had no limits; they left not only reason but fancy behind them; and produced combinations of confused magnificence, that not only could not be credited, but could not be imagined.'[123] As for allegory, beginning with late classical readers of Homer, individual poets (their texts and their lives) have been used as literal pieces in the construction of allegorical schema of various sorts.[124] Or a poet may serve as an *icon* or emblem of a historical style.

As for syncrisis and *similitudo*, these are, for better or worse, the default modes of literary historians. The undulating reception histories of Spenser and Donne confirm the subjective nature of literary taste, but also the syncritic bent of most literary history. Dryden, Johnson, Eliot, Yeats, and many recent readers, whether they admit it or not, treat our poets invidiously. Typological literary histories, which regard one poet as proleptically preparing the ground for another, also function syncritically. Auerbach's 'Figura' essay is a magisterial exercise in syncritic criticism: there Dante towers over other poets because he figures history more brilliantly. But even when comparison does not solicit historical judgements, it perforce finds formal similarities and differences. One poet is like another in some respects, unlike in others. My largely formalist *comparatio* of the *Cantos* and *Anniversaries* puts into relief the dialogic, descriptive, at times ekphrastic aspects of Spenser's verse. Donne, by contrast, neglects narrative and characterization. Yet if, per Joel Fineman's paradigm, Spenser mainly undertakes a mimetic poetics of the 'eye' and Donne a witty poetics of the 'voice', such a distinction is never absolute. Paradoxical wit and wordplay riddle the closing stanzas of the *Cantos*. Donne fancies his poems as public monuments for 'all' to contemplate. And if Spenser's dilated 'sight' demands a very different hermeneutic response from Donne's condensed 'sight', then the bold attempts of both poets to express ineffable relations between physical and metaphysical realms bring them together again. Again, a critical analogy (*similitudo*) insists upon itself: As Mutabilitie is to Nature, so the 'worlde' is to Drury. Conversely, both Nature and Drury serve as recursive ideals, as *comparanda*, fashioned in response to myriad, material contingencies. Both the *Cantos* and the *Anniversaries* figure the impossible, the unfigurable. Or better yet, Spenser and Donne figure the gap between what they know, what they believe, and what they are able to say. With this gap in mind both poets – even as they exhaust figures of thought that think, discover, compare, play, dilate and distil – turn to iterating figures of speech.

Or, as Donne memorably writes in *Devotions upon Emergent Occasions* (1623), this gap is the ontological, Pauline-Augustinian ground on which the thinking poet speaks when he thinks about God:

> My *God*, my *God*, Thou art a *direct* God, may I not say, a *literall* God ... But thou art also (*Lord* I intend it to thy *glory*, and let no *prophane mis-interpreter* abuse it to thy *diminution*) thou art a *figurative*, a *metaphoricall* God too: A *God* in whose words there is such a height of *figures*, such *voyages*, such *peregrinations* to fetch remote and precious *metaphors*, such extensions, such *spreadings*, such *Curtaines of Allegories*, such *third Heavens of Hyperboles*, so *harmonious eloquutions*, so *retired* and so *reserved expressions*, so *commanding perswasions*, so *perswading commandements*, such *sinewes* even in thy *milke*, and such *things* in thy *words*, as all *prophane Authors*, seeme of the *seed* of the *Serpent*, that *creepes*; thou art the *dove*, that flies.[125]

In this, arguably the most self-reflective, performative moment in his oeuvre when it comes to figuration, Donne not only demands one read figuratively but also justifies his own figures of thought and speech as heuristic vehicles to narrow the divide between divine and human *verba*, between flying and creeping 'words'. In this, I think, he implicitly and without invidiousness follows Spenser.

Notes

1. In the 1590s, Shakespearean personae often self-consciously contemplate the means and ends of comparison, e.g., *Richard II* V.v.1–41 ('I have been studying how I may compare'), Sonnet 18 ('Shall I compare thee'), or 129 ('As any she belied with false compare'). As for the commonplace that 'comparison is odious', instances abound in Renaissance literature, e.g., *La Celestina* (9.2), *Don Quijote* (II.23), *The Anatomy of Melancholy* (3.3.1.2).
2. W.J.T. Mitchell, 'Why Comparisons Are Odious', *World Literature Today*, 70.2 (1996), 321–4.
3. Ibid., 322.
4. Ibid.
5. Cited in ibid., 322.
6. John Donne, *The Elegies*, *The Variorum Edition of the Poetry of John Donne*, vol. 2, ed. Gary A. Stringer et al. (Bloomington and Indianapolis: Indiana University Press, 2000), 51–3, 545.
7. Judith H. Anderson, *Reading the Allegorical Intertext: Chaucer, Spenser, Shakespeare, Milton* (New York: Fordham University Press, 2008), 5; see also Judith H. Anderson and Joan Pong Linton (eds), *Go Figure: Energies, Forms, and Institutions in the Early Modern World* (New York: Fordham University Press, 2011). That a figure, like a text or an artwork, might be ascribed conscious agency is subtly advanced by Gordon Teskey in *Allegory and Violence* (Ithaca and London: Cornell University Press, 1996), 52–3.
8. Alternatively, Teskey's promotion of a mode of reading he calls 'entanglement' to break the exclusive reign of close reading in the study of Spenserian allegory should inform any comparison of Spenser's and Donne's thinking figures. See 'Thinking Moments in *The Faerie Queene*', *Spenser Studies*, 22 (2007), 103–25 (111).
9. See C.H. Kneepkens, 'Comparatio', and B. Heininger, 'Gleichnis', in Gert Ueding (ed.), *Historisches Wörterbuch der Rhetorik*, 12 vols (Tübingen: Max Niemeyer Verlag, 1992–2015), 2.293–9, 3.1000–9.
10. Edmund Spenser, *The Faerie Queene*, ed. A.C. Hamilton, textual ed. Hiroshi Yamashita and Toshiyuki Suzuki (Harlow: Longman, 2001). All quotations are from this edition.
11. Anderson, *Reading the Allegorical Intertext*, 1.
12. 'Obsequies upon the Lord Harrington the last that dyed', in *The Anniversaries and the Epicedes and Obsequies*, *The Variorum Edition of the Poetry of John Donne*, vol. 6, ed. Gary A. Stringer et al. (Bloomington and Indianapolis: Indiana University Press, 1995), 178. All quotations from the *Anniversaries* are from this edition.
13. 'Introduction' in Sylvia Adamson, Gavin Alexander, and Katrin Ettenhuber (eds), *Renaissance Figures of Speech* (Cambridge: Cambridge University Press, 2007), 9.
14. *The Mutabilitie Cantos*, ed. S.P. Zitner (London: Thomas Nelson, 1968), 2–4.
15. Even the title, probably given by Gabriel Harvey, hesitates: 'Two Cantos of Mutabilitie: which, both Forme and Matter, appear to be parcell of some following Booke of the Faerie Queene, under the Legend of Constancie'. See Gordon Teskey, 'Night Thoughts on Mutability', in Jane Grogan (ed.), *Celebrating Mutabilitie: Essays on Edmund Spenser's* Mutabilitie Cantos (Manchester: Manchester University Press, 2010), 24–9 (28).
16. As such, it certainly would have been easier to have compared Spenser's *Four Hymnes* (1596) with Donne's *Anniversaries*; see A.C. Partridge, *John Donne: Language and Style* (London: André Deutsch, 1978), 99, 103. However, the greater the dissimilitude, the greater the heuristic rewards may be.
17. See Ayesha Ramachandran, Chapter 7 below.
18. First noted in Hazlitt's 1818 lecture-paragone 'On Chaucer and Spenser'.
19. See G.W. Pigman, 'Versions of Imitation in the Renaissance', *Renaissance Quarterly*, 33.1 (1980), 1–32.
20. See Kathrine Koller, 'Abraham Fraunce and Edmund Spenser', *English Literary History* [*ELH*], 7.2 (1940), 108–20. Koller finds ninety-seven quotations from *Shepheardes Calender* in *Lawyers Logike* (110).
21. Quoted in *Anniversaries*, 240.
22. James Nohrnberg, *The Analogy of* The Faerie Queene (Princeton: Princeton University Press, 1976); Barbara Lewalski, *Donne's 'Anniversaries' and the Poetry of Praise: The Creation of a Symbolic Mode* (Princeton: Princeton University Press, 1973).
23. On the tensions between the visual paradigm that reigned through much of the Renaissance and then its eventual transition to an Enlightenment model of knowing as making ('maker's knowledge'), see Krzysztof Pomian, 'Vision and Cognition', in Caroline A. Jones and Peter Galison (eds), *Picturing Science, Producing Art* (New York and London: Routledge, 1998), 211–31.
24. See George Puttenham's division of the figures into those producing '*Enargeia*' and those yielding '*Energeia*', which roughly corresponds to figures of speech and figures of thought. *The Arte of English*

Poesie (London, 1589), 119. See also Joel Fineman, 'Shakespeare's "Perjur'd Eye"', *Representations*, 7 (1984), 59–86.
25 Philip Sidney, *An Apology for Poetry*, ed. Geoffrey Shepherd (Manchester: Manchester University Press, 1973), 107.
26 See Jane Grogan, *Exemplary Spenser: Visual and Poetic Pedagogy in* The Faerie Queene (Farnham: Ashgate, 2009); Erwin Panofsky, *Studies in Iconology: Humanistic Themes in the Art of the Renaissance* (New York: Harper & Row, 1962), 3–31.
27 See Richard Danson Brown, Chapter 1 above.
28 Gérard Genette, 'La rhétorique restreinte', *Communications*, 16.1 (1970), 158–71. See also Peter Mack, *Elizabethan Rhetoric: Theory and Practice* (Cambridge: Cambridge University Press, 2002); Jenny C. Mann, *Outlaw Rhetoric: Figuring Vernacular Eloquence in Shakespeare's England* (Ithaca and London: Cornell University Press, 2012); J. Knape, 'Figurenlehre', in Ueding (ed.), *Historisches Wörterbuch*, 3.289–342. The philosophical defence made by Sidney's *Apology* is emblematic of this divorce from rhetorical persuasion.
29 Brian Vickers, *In Defense of Rhetoric* (Oxford: Oxford University Press, 1989); *Francis Bacon and Renaissance Prose* (Cambridge: Cambridge University Press, 1968).
30 Adamson et al., 'Introduction', *Renaissance Figures of Speech*, 5.
31 Still, this distinction has been challenged by everyone from Quintilian to Paul Ricœur. Heinrich Lausberg's encyclopaedic account insists on an essential, if admittedly untenable distinction: 'Tropes represent an *immutatio verborum* ... Figures are characterized by the remaining categories of alteration ... (*adiectio, detractio, transmutatio,* [*immutatio*]) and thus behave as a part of the *dispositio* that it oriented towards *elocutio*.' *Handbook of Literary Rhetoric: A Foundation for Literary Study*, trans. M.T. Bliss, A. Jansen, and D.E. Orton (Leiden, Boston, and Cologne: Brill, 1998), §600.
32 Ibid., §603. For allegory, see §§895–901. I'll discuss *similitudo* below.
33 Adamson et al., 'Introduction', *Renaissance Figures of Speech*, 8.
34 Henry Peacham, *The Garden of Eloquence* (London, 1593), 1.
35 Abraham Fraunce, *Arcadian rhetorike: or The praecepts of rhetorike made plaine by examples* (London, 1588), A2v, B8r.
36 Puttenham, *The Arte of English Poesie*, 132–3.
37 Ibid., 3, 115. See Rebecca Wiseman, 'A Poetics of the Natural: Sensation, Decorum, and Bodily Appeal in Puttenham's *Art of English Poesy*', *Renaissance Studies*, 28.1 (2014), 33–49.
38 Peacham, *The Garden of Eloquence*, 156.
39 Ibid., 158.
40 Aristotle, *On Rhetoric*, trans. George A. Kennedy, 2nd ed. (Oxford: Oxford University Press, 2007), III.4. See Heininger, 'Gleichnis', in Ueding (ed.), *Historisches Wörterbuch*, 3.1000–2.
41 Quintilian, *Instititio Oratoria*, trans. H.E. Butler, 4 vols (Cambridge, MA: Harvard University Press, 1985), VIII.3.72; see also VIII.3.81–2; VIII.6.9. For *similitudo* as invention, see Lausberg, *Handbook*, §§422–5; as a figure, see §§843–7. Sidney's *Apology* urges a limited use of *similitudo* to persuade (139). But when it comes to 'similitude' as ornament or simile, his practice is more ambivalent; see e.g., Sonnet 3 of *Astrophil and Stella*: 'Or with strange similies enrich each line'. See also Marsh H. McCall, *Ancient Rhetorical Theories of Simile and Comparison* (Cambridge, MA: Harvard University Press, 1969); Robert J. Fogelin, *Figuratively Speaking*, rev. ed. (Oxford: Oxford University Press, 2011). Often classed with *similitudo* are example (*paradeigma*), parable, and icon.
42 Quintilian, VIII.3.73–4.
43 Peacham, *The Garden of Eloquence*, 158–9.
44 Ibid., 160.
45 Ibid.
46 Samuel Johnson, 'Life of Cowley', in *The Lives of the Poets*, vol. 1, ed. Roger Lonsdale (Oxford: Clarendon Press, 2006), 200.
47 Ibid., 213.
48 Quintilian, X.1.49–51; Raphael Lyne, *Shakespeare, Rhetoric and Cognition* (Cambridge: Cambridge University Press, 2011), 32–3; Christopher Ricks, *Milton's Grand Style* (Oxford: Clarendon Press, 1963), 118–50.
49 Ian Donaldson, 'Syncrisis: the Figure of Contestation', in Adamson et al. (eds), *Renaissance Figures of Speech*, 167–77 (167).
50 See 'Comparatio', in Ueding (ed.), *Historisches Wörterbuch*, 2.295; also Quintilian, II.4.21, VIII.4.9.
51 Peacham, *The Garden of Eloquence*, 162.
52 Ibid., 161.
53 Puttenham, *The Arte of English Poesie*, 163–4.

54 Ibid., 164–5.
55 Ibid., 168.
56 Ibid., 173. See Alexander Gil, *Logonomia anglica* (London, 1621), 112–13.
57 Puttenham, *The Arte of English Poesie*, 170.
58 Gil, *Logonomia anglica*, 123. See Anderson, *Translating Investments* on 'Spenser's complex reflection of and on Renaissance rhetoric at the end of Book III' (113).
59 See Daniel Heller-Roazen, *Echolalias: On the Forgetting of Language* (Cambridge and London: MIT Press, 2005).
60 See Gordon Teskey, 'Mutability, Genealogy, and the Authority of Forms', *Representations*, 41 (1993), 104–22. Spenser may also have been reading Lipsius's *De constantia*, which appeared in Stradling's influential 1595 translation, *Two bookes of constancie*. See Christopher Burlinson, 'Spenser's "Legend of Constancie": Book VII and the Ethical Reader', in Grogan (ed.), *Celebrating Mutabilitie*, 201–19.
61 See Jon A. Quitslund, *Spenser's Supreme Fiction: Platonic Natural Philosophy and The Faerie Queene* (Toronto, Buffalo, and London: University of Toronto Press, 2001), 220–2. Also Katrin Ettenhuber's *Donne's Augustine: Renaissance Cultures of Interpretation* (Oxford: Oxford University Press, 2011) details how 'Donne returned to Augustine's texts throughout his career with almost obsessive frequency' (3).
62 Teskey, *Allegory and Violence*, 181; see also Teskey, 'Allegory', in A.C. Hamilton et al. (eds), *The Spenser Encyclopedia* (Toronto: University of Toronto Press; London: Routledge, 1990), 16–22. Nohrnberg discusses the Elizabethan tendency to equate allegory with the meaning of any literary work (*Analogy*, 92–5).
63 See Mary Thomas Crane, 'Spenser's Giant and the New Science', in Anderson and Linton (eds), *Go Figure*, 19–37, esp. 20.
64 The adjectival 'disfigured' appears twice in the *FQ*: 'Her swollen eyes were much disfigured' (II.i.13); and as a part of a simile: 'She gins her feathers foule disfigured' (II.iii.36).
65 Nohrnberg discusses exemplarity and 'paterne' (*Analogy*, 26–34).
66 For the classical goddess Natura, see *Metamorphoses* XV.145, where Pythagoras dubs her 'novatrix rerum'; also E.R. Curtius, *European Literature in the Latin Middle Ages*, trans. Willard R. Trask (Princeton: Princeton University Press, 1990), 106–27. Zitner regards her as embodying 'law', 'energy and love' (*Mutabilitie Cantos*, 48–9).
67 It is also confirmed by E.K.'s glosses to the *Shepheardes Calender*. In the *glosse* to 'Maye', for instance, in addition to reading Pan as an allegorical figure for Christ, he signposts the figure of speech 'syncope' and the figure of thought 'fictio'. *Spenser's Minor Poems*, ed. Ernest de Sélincourt, 3 vols (Oxford: Clarendon Press, 1910), 1.57–8. See Zitner on 'Rhetoric', in *Mutabilitie Cantos*, 72–5, for an abbreviated account of some of the figures used by Spenser. Zitner cites H.D. Rix, who argues that for Spenser 'rhetorical schemes play a far greater part than the tropes, a fact which accounts for the intense and continuous formal patterning that distinguishes his style from Shakespeare's'.
68 Gil, *Logonomia anglica*, 99.
69 Andrew Fleck, 'Early Modern Marginalia in Spenser's *Faerie Queene* at the Folger', *Notes and Queries*, 55.2 (2008), 165–70 (167).
70 I thus disagree with the acute, invidious comparison sketched by Frank Warnke, in *Versions of Baroque: European Literature in the Seventeenth Century* (New Haven and London: Yale University Press, 1972), 22–30, which would distinguish between the Renaissance and Baroque style by comparing the use of simile in Spenser's *Hymne of Heavenly Beautie* (lines 22–70) and Donne's *Second Anniversarie* (lines 179–218). Simile, at least in the *Cantos*, is less mechanical, mimetic than Warnke grants, and in the *Anniversaries* more tied to material realities.
71 Zitner, *Mutabilitie Cantos*, 125.
72 '"I would abate the sternenesse of my stile": Diction and Poetic Subversion in *Two Cantos of Mutabilitie*', in Grogan (ed.), *Celebrating Mutabilitie*, 275–94 (286).
73 See Paul Ricoeur, *The Rule of Metaphor: The Creation of Meaning in Language* (London and New York: Routledge, 2003), 175–203. Ricoeur also discusses Gilbert Ryle's claim that metaphor is a 'category mistake' (233).
74 Zitner, *Mutabilitie Cantos*, 133.
75 'Tho was I war wher that ther sat a quene / That, as of light the somer-sonne shene / Passeth the sterre, right so over mesure / She fairer was than any creature' (*Parlement*, lines 298–301). In VII.vii.9 Spenser directly indicates his debts to Chaucer's *Parlement* and thus also to Alaine de Lille's *De planctu naturae*. Hamilton (*Fairie Queene*, 702) suggests Wisdom 7:26 as another intertext; there Wisdom is 'the brightness of the everlasting light, the undefiled mirroure of the maiestie of God'.

76 Ruskin's *Stones of Venice*, vol. 2 (London: Smith, Elder and Co., 1867), 271-5, glosses the zodiacal images above the main entrance door of St Mark's partly by invoking Spenser's pageant. Louise Gilbert Freeman doubts our ability to find the truth behind Nature's/Spenser's allegorical 'veile' (VII.vii.5). See 'Vision, Metamorphosis, and the Poetics of Allegory in the Mutabilitie Cantos', *Studies in English Literature 1500-1900*, 45.1 (2005), 65-93.
77 Sherman Hawkins, 'Mutabilitie and the Cycle of the Months', in William Nelson (ed.), *Form and Convention in the Poetry of Edmund Spenser* (New York: Columbia University Press, 1961), 76-102.
78 *Metamorphoses* XV.165; also XV.252-58. For *to pan* ('the All'), see Plato's *Cratylus* 408c. The riddling redundancy of 'all' commences early in the *Cantos*, e.g., VII.vi.5-6.
79 See Puttenham, *The Arte of English Poesie*, on '*Erotema*, or the Questioner', 176-7.
80 See Patrick Cheney, Chapter 4 below.
81 Compare with: 'So turne they still about, and change in restlesse wise' (VII.vii.18). This is the first use of *transverse* to mean 'athwart' according to *OED*.
82 Similarly, in VII.vi.5, the polyptoton of 'establisht ... estate ... statues ... state' underscores how *stasis*, there in the form of God's providence ('did at first prouide'), forms a constant antithesis with '*Change*', one resolved only in the poem's very last stanzas. See also VII.vi.17, 23, 31.
83 In 'Mutability, Genealogy, and the Authority of Forms', Teskey calls this return an *epistrophe* (117). Hamilton cites 1 Cor. 15:36-44 as an intertext (*Fairie Queene*, 711).
84 See Patricia Parker, *Inescapable Romance: Studies in the Poetics of a Mode* (Princeton: Princeton University Press, 1979), 54-64.
85 *The Complete English Poems of John Donne*, ed. C.A. Patrides (London: J.M. Dent & Sons, 1985), 98.
86 *Fairie Queene*, ed. Hamilton, 711. Teskey calls 1 Corinthians 15 'surely one of the most important sources underlying the Mutabilitie Cantos' ('Night Thoughts', 31).
87 The way for this has been prepared in VII.vii.26, 27, 47, 49, 55 (where Mutabilitie concludes her case with the alexandrine: 'Therefore both you and them to me I subiect proue.'
88 See Carol V. Kaske, 'Bible', in Hamilton et al. (eds), *Spenser Encyclopedia*, on the various Latin and English versions Spenser would have used (87-90). I quote from the 1560 Geneva Bible.
89 Form aside, Spenser may also be indebted to the mediated Pythagoreanism of *Metamorphoses* XV.60-478. Grogan opines that neither Nature's argument nor Spenser's poetry 'provides an adequate response to the pressing metaphysical questions raised' (*Celebrating Mutabilitie*, 9).
90 Giorgio Agamben, *End of the Poem: Studies in Poetics*, trans. Daniel Heller-Roazen (Stanford: Stanford University Press, 1999), 109-18 (114).
91 The first of the *Paradoxes and Problems* is the ironic 'A Defence of Womens Inconstancy'.
92 See Ettenhuber, *Donne's Augustine*, 105-35.
93 *John Donne: The Epithalamions, Anniversaries, and Epicedes*, ed. Wesley Milgate (Oxford: Clarendon Press, 1978), xxxiv.
94 *Anniversaries*, 239.
95 Lewalski, *Donne's 'Anniversaries' and the Poetry of Praise*, 50.
96 *Anniversaries*, 240. See Edward W. Tayler, *Donne's Idea of a Woman: Structure and Meaning in 'The Anniversaries'* (New York: Columbia University Press, 1991).
97 On allegory in the *Anniversaries*, see Lewalski, *Donne's 'Anniversaries' and the Poetry of Praise*, 142-7; also *Anniversaries*, 293-317.
98 G.W.F. Hegel, *The Phenomenology of Spirit*, trans. A.V. Miller (Oxford: Oxford University Press, 1979), 459.
99 See Milgate on the 'theological truth' indicated by 'patterne' (*The Epithalamions, Anniversaries, and Epicedes*, xviii-xix). Compare with 'October' in *Shepheardes Calender* where 'In Cuddie is set out the perfecte paterne of a Poete' (*Minor Poems*, 96).
100 See *Anniversaries*, 293-317.
101 Roland Barthes, 'The Old Rhetoric: An Aide-mémoire', in *The Semiotic Challenge*, trans. Richard Howard (New York: Hill and Wang, 1988), 60; see also J.W. van Hook, '"Concupiscence of Witt": The Metaphysical Conceit in Baroque Poetics', *Modern Philology*, 84.1 (1986), 24-38.
102 Puttenham describes '*Metalepsis*, or the Farrefet' as when 'leaping over the heads of a great many words, we take one that is furdest off, to utter our matter by'; e.g., when Medea curses 'the mountaine that the maste bare' instead of the ship that brought Jason (*The Arte of English Poesie*, 152-3). See also Peacham, *The Garden of Eloquence*, 31-2. Quintilian's description of metalepsis is far more conservative (VIII.6.37-9). See Brian Cummings, 'Metalepsis: The Boundaries of Metaphor', in Adamson et al. (eds), *Renaissance Figures*, 217-33.
103 It flourishes in the earliest love poems, e.g., 'Lovers Infinitenesse', through to the last Sermon ('our deliverance *à morte, in morte, per mortem*, from death, in death, and by death'). *The Sermons of John*

Donne, ed. Evelyn M. Simpson and George R. Potter, vol. 10 (Berkeley and Los Angeles: University of California Press, 1962), 231.
104 See Anthony Low, 'The "Turning Wheels": Carew, Jonson, Donne (and the First Law) of Motion', *John Donne Journal: Studies in the Age of Donne*, 1 (1982), 69–80.
105 Donne later figures the Red Sea as Christ's blood redeeming the world. See *Devotions upon Emergent Occasions*, ed. Anthony Raspa (Montreal: McGill-Queen's University Press, 1975), 101.
106 See Edward LeComte, *Grace to a Witty Sinner: A Life of Donne* (New York: Walker and Co., 1965), 133; June Morris, 'A Study of Donne's *Anniversaries*: "How Witty's Ruin?"', *English Miscellany*, 28–9 (1979–80), 157–70.
107 See Curtius, *European Literature in the Latin Middle Ages*, 159–62; also Seneca, *Epistles* LXVI.8–9 for a possible classical source. Dennis Kay, in *Melodious Tears: The English Funeral Elegy from Spenser to Milton* (Oxford: Clarendon Press, 1990), sees an analogous moment expressing the limits of epideixis in *FQ* VI.x.25–8 (111).
108 Ramie Targoff, *John Donne, Body and Soul* (Chicago and London: University of Chicago Press, 2008), 79–105. The subtitle of the *Progres* distils this tension: 'Wherein: By Occasion of The Religious Death of Mistris Elizabeth Drury, the incommodities of the Soule in this life and her exaltation in the next, are Contemplated'.
109 On *remedium*, see Lausberg, *Handbook*, §§558, 579.
110 In '"Essentiall Joye" in Donne's *Anniversaries*', *Texas Studies in Literature and Language* 13 (1971): 227–38, P.G. Stanwood labels these 'the climatic lines' of the poem, 'indeed of both poems' (234). Donne reconfigures the same geometric conceit in *Elegie on the Untimely Death of the Incomparable Prince, Henry* (1613).
111 See *John Donne: The Anniveraries*, ed. Frank Manley (Baltimore: Johns Hopkins Press, 1963), which cites the *Summa Theologica*, 1. q.63, a.6 and Augustine's *Genesi ad Litteram* 4.22–35 (198).
112 Jean-Luc Marion, *In Excess: Studies of Saturated Phenomena*, trans. Robyn Horner and Vincent Berraud (New York: Fordham University Press, 2001).
113 See Denys Turner, *The Darkness of God: Negativity in Christian Mysticism* (Cambridge: Cambridge University Press, 1995), 20.
114 1 Corinthians 4–5 may be an intertext; see *Anniversaries*, 525.
115 See *Anniversaries*, 535.
116 An exception is Kay, *Melodious Tears*, 109–14.
117 See Russ McDonald, 'Compar or Parison: Measure for Measure', in Adamson et al. (eds), *Renaissance Figures*, 39–58.
118 See Kay, *Melodious Tears*, 113.
119 *Anniversaries*, 517.
120 Hayden White, *Tropics of Discourse: Essays in Cultural Discourse* (Baltimore and London: Johns Hopkins University Press, 1978), 2.
121 See John Hollander, 'John Donne', in Hamilton et al. (eds), *The Spenser Encyclopedia*, 221–2.
122 See Ayesha Ramachandran, 'Mutabilitie's Lucretian Metaphysics: Scepticism and Cosmic Process in Spenser's *Cantos*', in Grogan (ed.), *Celebrating Mutabilitie*, 220–45; Kenneth Gross, 'John Donne's Lyric Skepticism: In Strange Way', *Modern Philology*, 101.3 (2004), 371–99.
123 Johnson, 'Life of Cowley', 200.
124 See Robert Lamberton, *Homer the Theologian: Neoplatonist Allegorical Reading and the Growth of the Epic Tradition* (Berkeley: University of California Press, 1989); Harold Bloom, *Shakespeare: The Invention of the Human* (New York: Riverhead Books, 1998).
125 *Devotions*, 100. Compare with *De doctrina Christiana*, 2.7, 3.9. Raspa suggests this passage may ironically rework Puttenham's and Wilson's definitions of the figures (178).

3

Refiguring Donne and Spenser: aspects of Ramist rhetoric

Niranjan Goswami

Any proposal to discuss aspects of Ramist rhetoric, or even rhetoric at large, in the writings of Donne and Spenser must begin with an imbalance. Donne has always attracted rhetorical criticism, and even the notion that Donne used Ramist logic is old and well debated. It was first proposed by Rosemond Tuve in her seminal book on Elizabethan imagery. Her broad claims regarding the use of Ramist logic in much of Elizabethan and metaphysical poetry attracted criticism of literary purists including William Empson, A.J. Smith and George Watson.[1] Tuve's efforts, however, had a positive outcome: modernist critics were persuaded to read seventeenth-century poetry on its own terms, applying its contemporary poetic theory and, in particular, rhetoric.[2] Rhetoric became indispensable to any discussion of seventeenth-century wit.[3] Tuve's analysis of the role of Ramist logic in Donne's poetry has been more or less accepted by modern critics.[4] It is largely agreed that many of Donne's conceits were witty uses of fallacious arguments, applications of hyperbole and catachresis.[5] Spenser, on the other hand, has been largely neglected in rhetorical criticism, and his use of Ramist logic has gone almost entirely unnoticed. The reason for this oversight, I argue, is a fundamental misunderstanding among scholars of Ramus's division between logic and rhetoric and what this division entailed in practice. For Ramus, rhetoric and logic can be separated only theoretically, but in practice they are similar disciplines and work together almost inseparably. Once we understand Ramist rhetoric from this practical standpoint, it becomes easier to see that both Donne and Spenser deploy strategies of Ramist rhetoric in their poetry, particularly in their frequent use of binary oppositions.

The background to Ramist rhetoric

Before we speak of Ramus's reforms in logic and rhetoric, we should note that these reforms were part of a process that began in earnest with the efforts of Rudolphus Agricola, who emphasized the logic of places, or topical logic, in humanist discourse. Many scholars, the most prominent among them being Peter Mack and Lisa Jardine, have traced this early phase of Renaissance logic and examined the changing curricula of logic and rhetoric brought about by humanists' efforts.[6] The vast number of topics, or heads, in medieval logic created confusion and inconvenience. Agricola's list of topics is a remarkable improvement over that of Cicero, Themistius, and Boethius in that, rather than acting as mechanical heads for generating arguments, these commonplaces emphasize the relations among things. Topics are grouped or merged together according to these relations, and the great number of topics, which previously ran into the hundreds, was brought down by Agricola to twenty-three heads. Peter Ramus greatly benefited from Agricola's reform, and in his *Dialectic* retained the heads according to such relations. In Ramus's logic we have topics of definition, opposition, comparison, and causes. Ramus also further reduced the number of heads to only ten: causes, effects, subjects, adjuncts, disagreements, comparison, interpretation of the name, division, definition, and testimony.

Traditional Ciceronian rhetoric had five parts: invention, disposition, elocution, memory, and delivery – a division that was challenged by Ramus, who streamlined subject boundaries by relegating invention and disposition to logic and restricting rhetoric to a discussion of elocution and delivery. Memory was subsumed by his method of disposition, which was a suitable tool of remembering the parts of a discourse by virtue of its organization by dichotomous division. This was only a pedagogical exercise, and Ramus did not propose any epistemological breach between logic and rhetoric because he believed that despite theoretical boundaries between these two disciplines in practice they worked together.

A study of Ramus in the tradition of humanist logic leads to the following conclusions. The impact of Ramism on literature can be observed in the following four ways.

First, the discourse of poetry was conceived in highest logical terms and was equal in status to the discourse in mathematics and science as probable argument.

Second, poetry consequently became more logically motivated; the logical function was emphasized and could be observed in the rigorous argumentative structure of poems.

Thirdly, the different logical functions of all sorts of arguments were well known to practising writers, and disagreeing arguments especially found extensive use in their writings.

Fourthly, the Ramist conception of 'argument' was both pervasive and all-inclusive. Every part of discourse was an 'argument' and could form a link in the chain of 'arguments' that was method. Under such a conception 'images' became much more logically functional.[7]

If the above analysis is acceptable, then in looking for Ramist logic in the work of a poet we try to answer the following questions:

Does the poet use place logic to generate arguments? Does he have an awareness of the logical relations that these places indicate?

Does the poet exhibit a clear preference for binary arguments in so far as these arguments express the relations of comparison, opposition, repugnance, relation, etc.?

Thus, if we want to understand how poets in the sixteenth and seventeenth centuries used Ramist logic in constructing their discourse, we should adopt the holistic approach of Ramus and demonstrate that the poets used *inventio* and *dispositio* to draw and arrange their arguments from various logical topoi and *elocutio* as means of variation, ornament, and expression of their mythopoeic imagination. As Rosemond Tuve has pointed out, in Ramist logic an 'argument' meant any unit of discourse that had a content or signification indicative of its 'relatableness' to other units; images were often such arguments.[8] Ramus had emphasized place logic, or topical logic, instead of syllogism.[9] Ramist logic was all the rage in England's universities during Spenser's and Donne's lifetimes, and both poets partook in this fashionable craze. I will begin, therefore, with a brief sketch of Ramist logic in Donne, which has already been critically assessed and generally accepted, before proceeding to a more extensive examination of Ramist logic in Spenser. In particular, I will discuss the poems of Donne and Spenser from the perspective of invention theory and the necessary *elocutio* accompanying such invention to create poetry that uses arguments in the Ramist sense.

Rhetoric in Donne

Donne was always interested in new discoveries and trends in arts and sciences. His inclination towards using logic to create sharp and sometimes extreme arguments certainly has an affinity with Ramism, which had rhetoricized logic and logicized poetry.[10] This tendency is particularly evident in his elegies and verse letters, but extends also into his devotional poetry and even sermons. A cursory glance at his *Elegy: On His Mistress* (lines 1–7) shows us his range of invention. The speaker attempts to dissuade his mistress from following him on a military expedition, and explains why he does so by enumerating a series of arguments:

> By our first strange and fatal interview,
> By all desires which thereof did ensue,
> By our long starving hopes, by that remorse
> Which my words' masculine persuasive force
> Begot in thee, and by the memory
> Of hurts, which spies and rivals threat'ned me,
> I calmly beg.[11]

Whereas desires, hopes, memory of hurts, remorse are all elements of conventional love poetry, Donne's signature lies in the metaphor of 'words' as the male organ of insemination that gives birth to all these passions in the lady's mind ('begot in thee'). From a Ramist analysis it would be identified as an argument derived from the topic of efficient cause as his words give birth to desires, hopes, and so on.[12] The monstrous birth of 'impetuous rage' (line 14) can be avoided by tempering her passion: 'Temper, O fair love, love's impetuous rage'. The irreverent tone of the poem makes Donne's treatment of temperance, unlike Spenser's, ironical. The absence of the lover would make their later reunion more enjoyable, but this possibility of happiness is immediately punctured by the strange suggestion that, if the lady dies before this reunion, 'From other lands my soul towards thee shall soar' (line 18). The lady is further advised not to disguise herself as a boy, because her gender would quickly be discerned and would attract the sexual attentions of the diseased French, Italian, and Dutch men. Through a clever innuendo and repetition of 'quickly know thee, and know thee' the speaker suggests that she risks becoming a common whore if she follows him to war. Nor, he says, should she behave melodramatically like a common girl, crying out with sudden premonition: 'Oh, oh / Nurse, Oh my love is slain: I saw him go / O'er the white Alps alone; I saw him, I, / Assail'd, fight, taken, stabb'd, bleed, fall and die' (lines 51-4). These lines not only use the figures of apostrophe, *exclamatio*, vision, and polysyndeton, but also convey through a cathartic displacement the poet's own anxiety of danger and death.

The *Elegy: Love's Progress* also offers advice, this time to prospective lovers. Donne argues first in favour of loving one woman, borrowing his argument-image from alchemy (lines 9-16):

> Perfection is in unity: prefer
> One woman first, and then one thing in her.
> I, when I value gold, may think upon
> The ductileness, the application,
> The wholesomeness, the ingenuity,
> From rust, from soil, from fire ever free.
> But if I love it, 'tis because 'tis made
> By our new nature, use, the soul of trade.

It is not difficult to find the Ramist topic of adjunct here being deftly used to point at the qualities of gold: ductility, pliability, wholesomeness, freedom from rust, soil, and fire. Donne's conceits come from well-known concepts in alchemy and cosmology, but, when images from these subjects are compared to a woman's qualities, it is an instance of *abusio*, or catachresis (lines 33-6):[13]

> Although we see celestial bodies move
> Above the earth, the earth we till and love:
> So we her airs contemplate, words and heart,
> And virtues; but we love the centric part.

The comparison of a woman's qualities to celestial objects and of her 'centric part' to the earth unnecessarily reminds the reader of the debates on geocentric versus heliocentric cosmology. The meiosis, or diminution, of cosmic sciences is countered by the hyperbolic statement about a woman's body. It is followed by a parody of a Petrarchan blazon, in which parts of the woman's body are compared to features of a landscape, giving rise to many a witty and suggestive image. The contemporary discourse of voyages and discovery is wittily applied to a perverse end (lines 59-66):

> These and the glorious promontory, her chin,
> O'erpast; and the straight Hellespont between
> The Sestos and Abydos of her breasts,
> Not of two lovers, but two loves, the nests,
> Succeeds a boundless sea; but that thine eye
> Some island moles may scatter'd there descry:
> And sailing towards her India, in that way
> Shall at her fair Atlantic navel stay.

It is not merely the erotic use of geography that we note here; it is the ability of extending the logic of one argument through a series of arguments of comparison, in the manner of an allegory that makes Donne's conceits unique. Once he makes a witty comparison, there is no stopping; through extension a simile or a metaphor turns into allegory.

While the advice we find in Donne's elegies is often irreverent and perverse, Donne's verse letters to his friends often bring out the moralist in him. The Renaissance pet theme of educating a gentleman, so common to Spenser, finds a youthful treatment in Donne's hands. Unlike Spenser, of course, Donne has no grand scheme when he talks about virtues or vices; rather, virtues and vices are scattered in strange metaphors. In a verse letter to Sir Henry Wotton ('Sir, more than kisses'), for instance, Donne speaks of the inability of city, court, and country alike to provide satisfaction to a young man. Spenser would have much appreciated this sentiment (lines 21–6):

> Cities are sepulchers; they who dwell there
> Are carcases, as if no such there were.
> And courts are theatres, where some men play
> Princes; some slaves; all to'one end, and of one clay.
> The country is a desert, where no good
> Gain'd, as habits, not born, is understood.

The city is imagined to be full of dead people, spiritually degenerate. At court there is no truth as everyone dissimulates. The countryside is no pastoral idyll, and does not produce or foster any good habits. There is no lack of ingenious metaphors: 'Men are sponges, which to pour out receive; / Who know false play, rather than lose, deceive' (lines 37–8). Men absorb the falseness of the place like sponges to pour it out in deception, and are unaware of how this deception transforms them until they 'like strangers greet themselves'. A man who started out as a 'Utopian youth' becomes a degenerate 'old Italian' (lines 45–6). In advising his friend on finding the right balance Donne once again resorts to an alchemical metaphor: 'Only in this one thing be no Galenist. To make / Courts' hot ambitions wholesome, do not take / A dram of country's dullness; do not add / Correctives, but as chemics, purge the bad' (lines 59–62).

Donne's use of alchemical and medical metaphors to describe the life of man occurs in his longest and most ambitious poems, the two *Anniversaries*. The statement of Hermes Trismegistus – 'A great miracle, Asclepius, is man' – found an echo in Pico della Mirandola's philosophy of man and is repeated here.[14] Donne's *First Anniversary: An Anatomy of the World* is also an anatomy of man.[15] The oration in praise of the dead Elizabeth Drury becomes a passionate lament about the human condition.[16] Drury is the epitome of human mortality and frailty and elicits this lament: 'She, she is dead; she's dead: when thou know'st this, / Thou know'st how poor a trifling thing man is, / And learn'st thus much by our anatomy, / The heart being perish'd, no part can be free' (lines 183–6). The figure of epizeuxis is most appropriately applied here.[17] The disintegrating world is expressed in a language that is as much poetic as it is scientific:

> When in the planets, and the firmament
> They seek so many new; they see that this
> Is crumbled out again to his atomies.
> 'Tis all in pieces, all coherence gone;
> All just supply, and all relation:

Prince, subject, father, son, are things forgot,
For every man alone thinks he hath got
To be a phoenix, and that there can be
None of that kind, of which he is, but he.

(lines 210–18)

Apart from the Epicurean theory of atoms what is significant here is the phoenix image; usually it is a positive one symbolizing Christ but here by an inverse logic it stands for man's individual pride that tears the fabric of society. The strange phrase 'All just supply, and all relation:' becomes meaningful only in the list of human relationships that follow in a manner of 'copia' using polysyndeton. Without the relations the list is only 'supply' – meaningless 'copia' of words. Ramist rhetoric emphasizes 'relations' which Tuve explained as 'relatable*ness*'. Arguments are thus similar, dissimilar, opposing, repugning, contrary, equal, and so on. Ramist rhetoric recognizes that the sense would evaporate from language without these relations as Donne envisages in this poem that the world would disintegrate without them.

Elements of Ramist rhetoric are present in Donne's devotional writings as well. If one pursues the thread of Donne's arguments in the *Holy Sonnets*, one finds that each sonnet elaborately builds up an argument only to overthrow it by the end. In Holy Sonnet 4 ('At the round') Donne paints the picture of apocalypse like a fire and brimstone sermon detailing the conditions of the dead, but the argument takes a turn from line 9, 'But let them sleep, Lord, and me mourn a space'. It is a Ramist argument of the dissimilar – unlike others, the poet resolves to repent now. Similarly, in Holy Sonnet 6 ('Death be not proud') Donne employs a figure of diminution to present Death as powerless as opposed to received opinion: 'Thou'rt slave to fate, chance, kings, and desperate men, / And dost with poison, war, and sickness dwell.' The polysyndeton in the line has an effect of breathless accumulation of inferior adjuncts or companions of death. The *interrogatio* in 'Why swell'st thou then?' further diminishes death. The final line reduces death to nothingness from an argument of privation: 'And Death shall be no more. Death, thou shalt die.' In Holy Sonnet 19 the argument is based on the Ramist topos of efficient cause where, defying logic, contraries are presented in a father–son relationship: 'Oh, to vex me, contraries meet in one: / Inconstancy unnaturally hath begot / A constant habit'. Inconstancy is personified and is imagined to have given birth to a constant habit. The poet's condition changes frequently depending upon his religious passion of the moment: 'I durst not view heaven yesterday; and today / In prayers and flattering speeches I court God: / Tomorrow I quake with true fear of his rod.' The final line indicates how our pity for the poet's condition is reversed, since in his religious fervour 'Those are my best days, when I shake with fear.'

I conclude my discussion of Donne's use of Ramist rhetoric with his last sermon and last work, *Deaths Duell*. The explication of the text 'And unto God the Lord belong the issues of death' proceeds by comparing man's soul to a building, and, just as the building is secured by its foundations, buttresses, and 'contignations', the soul is secured from damnation. The God of salvation is its foundation; God's determination of the manner of death acts like the buttresses that embrace the structure; and lastly God's act of saving man, through knitting the dual nature of God and man in Christ and through Christ's death, is like the 'contignation' that knits and unites the building. If the similes are somewhat obscure because they are drawn from theological doctrine, the segmented comparison stands out as an example of rhetoric. A similar tripartite logic is present in Donne's explication of the phrase 'exitus mortis', or 'issues of death', which outlines the various kinds of death, before our birth from the womb, at birth into the manifold deaths of the world, and the death after death, the death of corruption, putrefaction, and vermiculation in the grave. This thought of corruption in the grave leads to the topic of Christ's resurrection from the grave after three days, which was possible because of God's decree and its manifestation. Of course, a mere summary of arguments can only make obvious the logical structure but the arguments are rhetorically fleshed out. Donne expounds eloquently on the theme of man's misery:

> That that Monarch, who spred over many nations alive, must in his dust lye in a corner of that sheete of lead, and there, but so long as that lead will last, and that privat and retir'd man, that though himselfe his owne for ever, and never came forth, must in his dust of the grave bee published, and (such are the revolutions of the graves) bee mingled in his dust, with the dust of every high way, and of every dunghill, and swallowed in every puddle and pond: This is the most inglorious and contemptible vilification, the most deadly and peremptory nullification of man, that wee can consider.[18]

I have argued elsewhere that the Protestant practice of logically dividing and subdividing the body of the sermon was a result of the Ramist habit of logical analysis and organization.[19] Till his last, when he delivered this sermon a few days before his death, Donne proved himself to be an ardent practitioner of logical and rhetorical tools of composition.

Spenser's use of rhetoric

As discussed previously, Spenser's use of Ramist rhetoric has received relatively little scholarly attention. However, Spenser's intellectual milieu was rife with Ramist thought. For one, Spenser quite possibly attended the lectures of Gabriel Harvey, the Ramist thinker, in his student days in Cambridge.[20] He was also a part of the Sidney circle, which 'would make his familiarity with the reformed disciplines virtually certain'. Furthermore, the confirmed Ramist author Abraham Fraunce made extensive use of Spenser's *The Shepheardes Calender* to illustrate tenets of logic in his *Shepherd's Logike*, *The Lawiers Logicke*, and *The Arcadian Rhetoricke*, indicating an affinity between Spenser's work and Ramist rhetoric.[21] More generally, as Sam Meyer has argued, even if we cannot know for sure whether Spenser 'came to adopt the Ramist reorganization', Fraunce's use of Spenser's poetry for logical illustration shows 'how closely proponents of the reformed program of liberal arts continue to associate rhetoric and poetry. ... If Spenser can be counted among those who embraced the new approaches, his adoption in whole or in part of the revised system would not have required any basic readjustment of ingrained habit patterns as regards composition through logical and rhetorical modes.'[22] Ramist rhetoric would have been particularly important to Spenser as a Protestant poet. As Tamara Goeglein has pointed out, the vernacular 'godly dialectics' that were prevalent in the late sixteenth century were 'modeled explicitly after the logical innovations of the French protestant martyr, Peter Ramus', and Ramist dialectical thought became a 'virtual manifesto' for the 'emergent protestant mindset', particularly in matters of scriptural interpretation and 'pedagogical strategies'.[23] My focus, therefore, will be on Book I of Spenser's *The Faerie Queene*, the Book of Holiness. However, I shall begin by commenting more generally on the rhetorical underpinnings of *The Faerie Queene* at large.

If the two words in the title of Spenser's epic give any indication, the poem cannot but be an allegorical poem with a political message. Allegory is the best mode to present fairies to sceptical minds, and the fairy queen can represent a mortal political personage only allegorically, through a kind of verbal displacement, a deliberate ambiguity which is also the soul of poetry.[24] It is therefore unsurprising that the significant critical readings of *The Faerie Queene* would be political, historicist, at best generic as some genres also tend to serve political purposes.[25] The fact that it is an epic poem and that the poet himself in his Letter to Raleigh attempts to direct or misdirect our interpretation of the poem as a moral and political allegory further draws our attention towards the message itself rather than how the message is conveyed, which is probably why there are so few successful analyses of rhetoric in the poem compared to the inundation of message- and motive-oriented interpretations.[26] The word 'motive', however, is wittily used by Arthur Burke to discover a matrix of motives in the poem that could lead to a structural study, for example by looking for the motive of courtship in the poem.[27] Following Burke's lead Michael Dixon wrote a rhetorical interpretation of the poem looking for such structural motives while using the words invention and disposition freely as if they were merely glorious synonyms for content and form. The historically much maligned and shunned cause of rhetoric is not helped when writing to promote a rhetorical understanding of the poem one generates such a sentence: 'Rhetorically, the "motive" of a work is the inventio generating its dispositio; the inventio represents in rhetorical structure a locus corresponding schematically and functionally to both the ultimate term in a structure of courtship and, as noted above, the "end" of induction in a dialectical structure.'[28]

Perhaps a better way to undertake a rhetorical study of the poem is to look at the organization of narration in the poem as is done by Gordon Teskey.[29] The many threads of plot in the poem are woven into a complex web of continuity and discontinuity through appearance, disappearance and reappearance of characters, finished and unfinished action (the poem itself problematically standing unfinished and without closure)[30] yielding the rhetorical critic a sufficient ground for his pursuit of the poet's narrative strategy and his persuasive technology. However, our alienation from the holistic understanding of rhetoric in the sixteenth century is so complete that we only focus on aspects of rhetoric and miss the whole picture. That is the principal reason why the attempts of modern theorists such as Derrida, Barthes, and Jakobson to revive ancient rhetoric have failed. Renaissance rhetoric was, using Dixon's terms, an 'inclusive grammar' and not a 'reductive rhetoric' as it comprehended ethos and pathos, *ars* and *techne*, induction and deduction, brevity and copia, *ratio* and *oratio*. Fortunately, to a Renaissance writer these were not binaries but complementary aspects. Ramus through his relentless divisions into binaries paradoxically remained more holistic than those who indulged in the false dichotomies of Cartesian consciousness. In the Ramist system, the art of grammar was divided into many parts and branches only for the sake of memorizing the whole art and its parts. Similarly, the much-misunderstood Ramist segregation of logic from rhetoric was intended to be only a pedagogical method to prevent duplication of labour, although in practice logic and rhetoric functioned simultaneously and inseparably. Historians of a Cartesian frame of mind often failed to understand Ramus's emphasis on nature and its predominance over art.[31]

How does Ramist rhetoric work in Spenser's *The Faerie Queene*? Before proceeding to a longer examination of Book I, let us consider several shorter examples. In short, hardly any titular virtue in Spenser's allegory is perceived without its binary opposite, as in Ramist logic. For instance, in II.v.1 Spenser spells out the contrast between temperance and perturbation:

> Who euer doth to temperaunce apply
>   His stedfast life, and all his actions frame,
>   Trust me, shal find no greater enimy,
>   Then stubborne perturbation, to the same;
>   To which right wel the wise doe giue that name,
>   For it the goodly peace of staied mindes
>   Does ouerthrow, and troublous warre proclame:
>   His owne woes authour, who so bound it findes,
> As did *Pirrhocles*, and it wilfully vnbindes.[32]

The first four lines constitute a logical proposition: whoever applies temperance to his actions finds that he has to fight against perturbation, which overthrows peace of mind and forces one to make war on others, leading to one's own suffering. The semi-formed syllogism in the stanza, which in logical terms is an enthymeme, gives us the *narratio* or the context of the actions of this canto.[33] The proposition is established from the topos of testimony of the narrator through the apostrophe 'Trust me', an address to the reader.[34] From the argument of 'more' it is stated that there is no greater enemy to temperance than perturbation.[35] From the place of 'name'[36] it is argued that the name perturbation is appropriate and from 'effect' this is proved to be so.[37] From the place of cause it is argued that perturbation causes loss of peace of mind and proclaims war. One who is full of perturbation is the author or efficient cause of his own suffering. Although the logical sinews of a simple stanza such as this may not be apparent unless we make a logical analysis, for Spenser's contemporaries it was normal to expect such argumentative structures in poetry. Guyon situates the real war not in outward combat but in the inner struggle between the baser and the nobler parts of man:

> Fly, O *Pyrrhochles*, fly the dreadfull warre,
>   That in thy selfe thy lesser partes doe moue,
>   Outrageous anger, and woe working iarre,
>   Direfull impatience, and hartmurdring loue;

Those, those thy foes, those warriours far remoue,
Which thee to endlesse bale captiued lead.

(*FQ* II.v.16)

The evil quality of passions was a Renaissance commonplace borrowed from the Stoic tradition in which even love was considered to be evil. The first line has an apostrophe to give the discourse a dramatic turn: 'Fly, O Pyrrhochles, fly …'.[38] The lesser parts in Pyrochles are the efficient cause of the war in his mind created by the jarring passions of anger and impatience. The fifth line has the figure of ploce as it repeats the word 'those' three times for the sake of amplification as well as emphasis.[39] A metaphor of the passions as warriors leading the captive Pyrochles ends the quotation.

Pyrochles' brother Cymochles is his binary opposite, but both brothers are *exempla* of intemperance and stand in opposition to the temperate Guyon.[40] Where Pyrochles is all intemperate action, Cymochles, ensconced in Acrasia's Bower of Bliss, is the extreme of inaction:

> There he him found all carelesly displaid,
>   In secrete shadow from the sunny ray,
>   On a sweet bed of lillies softly laid,
>   Amidst a flock of Damzelles fresh and gay,
>   That rownd about him dissolute did play
>   Their wanton follies, and light meriment;
>   Euery of which did loosely disaray
>   Her vpper parts of meet habiliments,
> And shewd them naked, deckt with many ornaments.
>
> And euery of them stroue, with most delights,
>   Him to aggrate, and greatest pleasures shew;
>   Some framd faire lookes, glancing like euening lights,
>   Other sweet wordes, dropping like honny dew;
>   Some bathed kisses, and did soft embrew
>   The sugred licour through his melting lips:
>   One boastes her beautie, and does yield to vew
>   Her dainty limbes aboue her tender hips;
> Another her out boastes, and all for tryall strips.
>
> He, like an Adder, lurking in the weedes,
>   His wandring thought in deepe desire does steepe,
>   And his frayle eye with spoyle of beauty feedes;
>   Sometimes he falsely faines himselfe to sleepe,
>   Whiles through their lids his wanton eies do peepe,
>   To steale a snatch of amorous conceipt,
>   Whereby close fire into his heart does creepe:
>   So, he them deceiues, deceiud in his deceipt,
> Made dronke with drugs of deare voluptuous receipt.

(*FQ* II.v.32–4)

Spenser's transformation of the classical *locus amoenus* into a Renaissance bower of love is striking in its quantum of sensual images of titillation and voyeurism. Whereas the 'flock of Damzelles' are all out to display their physical wealth giving the poet an opportunity of describing their various stages of undressing, Cymochles is described by words that principally reveal the degenerate and degenerated state of his mind: 'carelesly', 'wandring', 'frayle', 'falsely', and 'dronke'. He lies in 'secret shadow', which is opposed to 'sunny ray' – a binary with an opposing moral charge. The sonic effects in these lines create a sense of softness and languor in which Cymochles' senses are drowned. The immorality of the physical exhibition by the damsels is indicated by 'dissolute', 'wanton', 'light', 'loosely', and 'voluptuous'. This is a kind of *hypotyposis* in which the physical description simultaneously evokes in the mind of the reader a perception of the spiritual degeneration of the actors. The epicurean display of pleasures, chiefly of the eye, as Cymochles plays the voyeur by pretending to be asleep and slyly opening his eyes, is intended to be conveyed as a felt experience for the reader. The description of the physical act of 'bathing kisses' and stripping from above the hips or in full are expressed through simile ('glancing like euening lights', 'sweet wordes, dropping like honny dew'), circumlocution ('did soft embrew / The sugred licour through his melting lips') and ploce (in repetition of 'boasts'). Cymochles is compared to an 'adder lurking in the weedes', which is an allusion to Virgil's 'snake in the grass' (*Eclogue III*) and to Satan hiding in Paradise in the form of a serpent. The Biblical allusion establishes the deceitful nature of Cymochles, which is spelt out with polyptoton in stanza 34, line 8: 'So, them deceiues, deceiud in his deceipt …'. The self-negating nature of deception that turns on the deceiver is a strong moral condemnation of the act. The idea of falsehood and deception in this false paradise has been built up gradually with words like 'wandring', 'deepe', 'faines', 'steals', 'creepe'.[41]

A similar binary opposition, in which a virtue is known by its opposite, occurs early in the Legend of Britomartis in Book III, in which Britomart, representing the virtue of chastity, sojourns in the Castle Joyeous of Malecasta, literally 'badly chaste'. It is important Malecasta be judged prejudicially, because her infatuation with the disguised Britomart is impermissible: firstly, the object of her love is royal, and, secondly, it would lead to same-sex love. Thus, Malecasta is represented as full of lust, not love: 'Such loue is hate, and such desire is shame.' The unchaste characters in this Book are foils to the chaste ones, and the poet takes equal care in creating sordid characters as in creating the major ones. Britomart, however, is not without love, and the object of her love is (safely for the poet) a shadow, the image of Arthegall seen in Merlin's magic mirror. The stanza is worth examining as it contains so many Ramist binaries:

> But wicked fortune mine, though minde be good,
>   Can haue no end, nor hope of my desire,
> But feed on shadowes, whiles I die for food,
> And like a shadow wexe, whiles with entire
> Affection, I doe languish and expire.
>   I fonder, then *Cephisus* foolish chyld,
>   Who hauing vewed in a fountaine shere
>   His face, was with the loue thereof beguyld;
> I fonder loue a shade, the body far exyld.

(*FQ* III.ii.44)

Unlike the mythological lovers who had lewd minds yet good fortune, Britomart has a 'wicked fortune' though her 'minde be good'. She 'die[s] for food' while her desire 'feed[s] on shadowes'. A personification of her desire or affection is followed by a simile of her becoming like a shadow. Then in an epic simile she is compared to Narcissus and from the argument of 'more' she is stated to be more foolish than Narcissus. Several arguments of contrary and comparison thus produce binaries, yielding the safe situation of pseudo-Platonic love where bodies are 'far exyld'. The book on chastity paradoxically leads to the theme of love – not Platonic love, but a love that is capable of generation, in order to create a line of English kings. Spenser's definition of such love receives its sanction from the historically valid argument of dynasty. At the beginning of Canto iii love is described from the place of definition:[42]

> Most sacred fyre, that burnest mightily
>   In liuing brests, ykindled first aboue,
>   Emongst th'eternall spheres and lamping sky,
>   And thence pourd into men, which men call Loue ...

It has been argued from the place of adjunct that the fire burns in the breasts of men and that it has been poured there from the spheres and the sky. Love is sacred because of its divine origin. The next argument is from the place of dissimilitude: 'Not that same, which doth base affections moue / In brutish mindes, and filthy lust inflame'. Any suggestion that Britomart, the mythical progenitor and allegorical mirror of the Queen, might be guilty of lust is shrewdly annulled:

> It was not, *Britomart*, thy wandring eye,
>   Glauncing vnwares in charmed looking glas,
>   But the streight course of heuenly destiny,
>   Led with eternall prouidence, that has
>   Guyded thy glaunce, to bring his will to pas ...
>
> (*FQ* III.iii.24)

The efficient cause here is not Britomart but divine will. The argument from the place of cause was the favourite of Ramist logicians and was dealt with in great details in the Ramist manuals.

As a representation of the Queen, Britomart herself is part of a binary, and possesses a fundamentally binary nature. Citing the inadequacy of his poetry to properly deal with this grave subject, Spenser shows the fissures of the patronage system that requires the poet to praise his patron the Queen and seek pardon in advance:

> But O dredd Souerayne
>   Thus far forth pardon, sith that choicest witt
>   Cannot your glorious pourtraict figure playne,
>   That I in colourd showes may shadow itt,
>   And antique praises vnto present persons fitt.
>
> (*FQ* III.i.3)

The attempt to portray the Queen in Gloriana or Belphoebe (the one representing her rule and the other her chastity) or even in Britomart, who is both chaste and a lover, is a daring project to undertake, although as an artistic strategy it was brilliant on Spenser's part to present facets of the Queen through different characters.[43] True to Protestant aesthetics and sensibilities, the Queen's figure is 'glorious' yet 'playne' as opposed to the poet's representations which are 'coulour showes' (rhetorical colours?), suggesting their false and fictitious nature. The poet can only hope that the Queen will not be displeased with these representations: 'Ne let his fairest Cynthia refuse'. When finally Britomart is represented in Canto i we find the same Ramist opposition of qualities in the divided nature of the martial maid:

> For shee was full of amiable grace,
>   And manly terror mixed therewithall,
> That as the one stird vp affections bace,
> So th'other did mens rash desires apall,
> And hold them backe, that would in error fall;
> As hee, that hath espide a vermeill Rose,
> To which sharpe thornes and breres the way forstall,
> Dare not for dread his hardy hand expose,
> But wishing it far off, his ydle wish doth lose.
>
> (*FQ* III.i.46)

The opposition between the qualities of grace and terror (words associated with divinity) is established from the topos of effect. The effect of grace is to arouse 'affections bace', whereas the effect of terror is to check such 'rash desires'. The epithets 'bace' and 'rash' offer a negative judgement of physical desire, and its possibility is annulled at the moment of inception. The dangerous project of talking about the Queen's sexuality can be possible only through the rhetoric of negation and denial.

Spenser's habit of thinking in terms of binary opposition of arguments in the Ramist fashion seems to be well demonstrated throughout *The Faerie Queene*. That contrary arguments abound in Spenser's poem is no accident. Peter Mack has demonstrated how a large part of Elizabethan schooling in rhetoric comprised disputation, writing of themes and theses.[44] Ramus was the new fashion in logic, and Ramist manuals emphasized opposing binary arguments rather than syllogism. With this in mind, we can proceed now to Spenser's most consistent and extensive use of Ramist logic in the Book of Holiness. From the start, Redcrosse Knight's mission is described through the most important of Ramist rhetorical topics, cause:

> Vpon a great aduenture he was bond,
>   That greatest *Gloriana* to him gaue,
>   That greatest glorious Queene of *Faery* lond,
> To winne him worshippe, and her grace to haue,
> Which of all earthy things he most did craue.
>
> (*FQ* I.i.3)

It is conventional to mention the cause at the beginning of an epic poem. The Redcrosse Knight's cause is to obtain Gloriana's grace by succeeding in the adventure on which he is bound. Being bound on the adventure is derived from the topic of adjunct, as McIlmaine explains: 'The adjoynt is that which hathe a subiecte to the which it is adioined: as vertue and vyce are called the adjoyntes of the bodye or soule: and to be shorte all things that do chaunce to the subiecte ...'[45] The effect of anaphora in the repetition of 'That greatest' stresses not only the greatness of Gloriana but also the great enterprise of Redcrosse for being at her commission and the greatness of the poem, the poet's enterprise.

Spenser's plan of presenting the opposition of virtue and vice went hand in hand with the Ramist practice of favouring disjunctive and 'dissentany' arguments, i.e. arguments of opposition, contrary, contradiction, comparison, relation – arguments that always embraced two terms. In the poem such arguments take on human bodies and fight it out; virtues and vices are personified and put into combat. Let us take the example of the encounter between Redcrosse and the Sarazin Sans Foy:

> The Sarazin was stout, and wondrous strong,
>   And heaped blowes like yron hammers great:
>   For after blood and vengeance he did long.
>   The knight was fiers, and full of youthly heat,
>   And doubled strokes, like dreaded thunders threat:
>   For all for praise and honour he did fight.
>   Both stricken stryke, and beaten both doe beat,
>   That from their shields forth flyeth firie light,
> And helmets hewen deepe, shew marks of eithers might.
>
> So th'one for wrong, the other striues for right:
>   As when a Gryfon seized of his pray,
>   A Dragon fiers encountreth in his flight,
>   Through widest ayre making his ydle way,
>   That would his rightfull rauine rend away:
>   With hideous horror both together smight,
>   And souce so sore, that they the heauens affray:
>   The wise Southsayer seeing so sad sight,
> Th'amazed vulgar telles of warres and mortall fight.
>
> So th'one for wrong, the other strives for right ...
>
> (FQ I.v.7-9)

The first line of stanza 8 gives us the argument of opposition between wrong and right, and to indicate the moral emphasis of this opposition the line is repeated at the beginning of stanza 9. However, the graphic description of the fight is built up in stanza 8 by referring to the physical and mental qualities of the combatants from the place of adjunct: stoutness and strength of the Sarazin and youth and ferocity of Redcrosse. As the knight doubles his strokes, so does the narrator use double words to describe the goal of the two – the Sarazin fights for 'blood and vengeance' whereas the knight aims for 'praise and honour'. The parallelism is continued in 'stricken strike' and 'beaten beat;' these phrases are rhetorically, a form of polyptoton[46] and logically, derived from the topos of 'offspring', i.e. variation of the same word in different voices or case-endings.[47] In the next stanza the two fighters are compared to a gryphon and a dragon, both mythical beasts signifying cruelty and power. The use of the words 'wondrous', 'great', and 'dreaded' make it clear that the fight is of epic proportions, as does the evocation of the 'dreaded thunder's threat' associated with Jove and primal power. In the epic simile the soothsayer and the ordinary men listening to his prognostications create a universal epic ambience. Although the two combatants become nearly indistinguishable in the fierceness of the fight, the first line of stanza 9 reinforces their binary opposition: one strives for wrong, the other for right.

The strong allegorical charge of Book I in the fight between Sans Foy and Redcrosse makes it clear that religion is the prior concern of this book.[48] Of particular importance are allusions to the Reformation tenet of election of the faithful. Book I also incorporates several commonplaces of medieval romance: allegorizing the crusade, the perils of temptation and fall of a wandering knight, and the adventures of an abandoned lady, Una. In Canto iii Una encounters a lion that seeing the fair maiden submits meekly. Though it is an allegory of 'auenging wrong' submitting before 'simple truth' yet the stanzas 5–7 are rhetorically constructed out of the elements of folktale of the beauty and the beast to juxtapose the binaries of truth and wrong in a Ramist argument:

> It fortuned out of the thickest wood
>   A ramping Lyon rushed suddeinly,
>   Hunting full greedy after saluage blood;
>   Soone as the royall virgin he did spy,
>   With gaping mouth at her ran greedily,
>   To haue attonce deuourd her tender corse:
>   But to the pray when as he drew more ny,
>   His bloody rage aswaged with remorse,
> And with the sight amazd, forgat his furious forse.
>
> In stead thereof he kist her wearie feet,
>   And lickt her lilly hands with fawning tong,
>   As he her wronged innocence did weet.
>   O how can beautie maister the most strong,
>   And simple truth subdue auenging wrong?
>   Whose yielded pryde and proud submission,
>   Still dreading death, when she had marked long,
>   Her hart gan melt in great compassion,
> And drizling teares did shed for pure affection.
>
> The Lyon Lord of euerie beast in field,
>   Quoth she, his princely puissance doth abate,
>   And mightie proud to humble weake does yield,
>   Forgetfull of the hungry rage, which late
>   Him prickt, in pittie of my sad estate:
>   But he my Lyon, and my noble Lord,
>   How does he find in cruell hart to hate
>   Her that him lou'd, and euer most adord,
> As the God of my life? why hath he me abhord?
>
> (*FQ* I.iii.5–7)

In stanza 5 the lion is described with its adjuncts 'ramping', 'gaping mouth', and 'greedie'. The present participial forms 'ramping' and 'hunting' present the lion in action, the suddenness of which is impressed upon the reader's imagination by the adverbial modifier 'suddeinly' and the verb 'rushed'. The speed of the action is however checked by the particle 'but' because the lion as it comes near Una is overwhelmed by her beauty and 'forgat his furious forse'. The furiousness of the lion is utterly mitigated by the unexpected verb 'forgat' and the assonance of 'rage', 'aswaged', and 'amazd' creates a lullaby that stupefies both the lion and the readers. The narrator wittily posits two pointers describing Una as the 'royall virgin' encountering the lion. Her royalty and chastity are the adjuncts from which the argument of her strength vis-à-vis the lion is derived. The next stanza is completely devoted to describing the fawning action of the lion.[49] The lion kisses Una's feet and 'lilly hands' in a gesture of submission and she is moved by the transformation of the beast; however, her confused feelings of fear and compassion are only momentary as the narrator quickly draws an argument from the comparison between the lion and Redcrosse who, unlike the lion, does not feel pity for the lady. The lion has turned Una's protector whereas Redcrosse has abandoned that role. McIlmaine would call this an argument of the dissimilitude,[50] and Milton would explain that the usual signs are 'not the same', 'not such as', but '[G]enerally there is no sign when the dissimilarity is more fully explicated' as is the case here.[51] The alliterative polyptoton in line 6 ('yielded pryde and proud submission') and is juxtaposed with the alliteration 'dreading death', reinforcing the contrast through sound. Stanza 7 establishes the power and sovereignty of the lion that yields its pride despite its 'princely puissance' and being Lord of all other beasts. On the contrary Redcrosse, who is Una's Lord, and even 'God of [her] life', apparently abhors her. The 'but' in stanza 5 has its parallel in stanza 7, 'But he my Lyon, and my noble Lord'. The rhetorical question or *interrogatio*[52] and *exclamatio*[53] of stanza 5 – 'O how can beautie maister the most strong, / And simple truth subdue auenging wrong?' – has its parallel in stanza 7 in the genuine question asked by Una, 'How does he find in cruell hart to hate / Her that him lou'd, and ever most adord, / As the God of my life? why hath he me abhord?'

Redcrosse has 'abhord' Una, of course, because he has taken up with her binary opposite, Duessa, who is cast in the role of the Whore of Babylon and later rides the seven-headed beast from the Book of Revelation. When Duessa leads Redcrosse to the House of Pride, there is a typically medieval procession of the seven deadly sins, which foreshadows the fall and defeat of Redcrosse, the future St George. Redcrosse is captured by Orgoglio, not because of his pride (as the name 'Orgoglio' and the House of Pride suggest), but because of his presumption that he has already achieved his goal. The nymph resting in the middle of a race is an image of presumption. Drinking from the stream, the knight is infected with her vice and is morally weakened: 'Yet goodly court he made still to his Dame, / Pourd out in loosnesse on the grassy grownd, / Both carelesse of his health, and of his fame'. Redcrosse must suffer because of his apostasy. For Spenser's contemporaries it might have been sufficient indication that no true Christian would remain unassailable for long if he abandons Una, or true Protestant faith, and associates himself with Duessa, or Roman Catholicism. In order to become England's St George, Redcrosse must go through the ordeal of sin and purgation before he can be restored to his former strength. However, the true contest is not only between a Christian and sin but also between true and false faiths. Spenser's habit of generating contesting arguments in binaries could be the result of a Ramist cast of logical thinking: Truth (Una) versus Falsehood (Fidessa/Duessa), false Redcrosse (Archimago) versus true Redcrosse. The topos of false identity gives rise to the disputation of ontological truth – 'I that do seeme not I, *Duessa* ame'. Yet Spenser would not risk leaving any moral or ethical ambiguity here as his ontological argument is enmeshed within a theological statement; therefore even falsehood has a certain and definite lineage – '*Duessa* I, the daughter of Deceipt and Shame' (I.v.26). Analysed logically, even Duessa is important enough to have her lineage described from the topos of efficient cause.[54]

The endless falsehood, the discrepancy between seeming and being, is finally stopped by Arthur's shield, which was made by a greater magician, Merlin: 'No magicke arts hereof had any might, / Nor bloody wordes of bold Enchaunters call, / But all that was not such, as seemd in sight, / Before that shield did fade, and suddeine fall' (I.vii.35). Arthur first comes to the rescue of Una, and then of Redcrosse. When he inquires as to the cause of Una's sorrow, he engages with her in a witty repartee that sounds like a scholastic disputation:

> O but (quoth she) great griefe will not be tould,
>   And can more easily be thought, then said.
> Right so (quoth he) but he, that neuer would,
>   Could neuer: will to might giues greatest aid.
> But griefe (quoth she) does greater grow displaid,
>   If then it find not helpe, and breeds despaire.
> Despaire breedes not (quoth he) where faith is staid.
>   No faith so fast (quoth she) but flesh does paire.
> Flesh may empaire (quoth he) but reason can repaire.
>
> (*FQ* I.vii.41)

The dispute here is not between truth and falsehood of statements but between unstated grief which finds no expression and its articulation and catharsis. This apparently simple resolution of the problem of Una's grief is intricately embedded in the greater issue of Christian optimism in faith and non-Christian, Satanic despair – a question that will be taken up with greater urgency in the episode of the Cave of Despair. As Kathryn Walls has pointed out, taking an anti-Stoical position, Calvin urged that Christians share their sadness.[55]

When Arthur rescues Redcrosse, or Holiness, from Catholic idolatry, the motive of Redcrosse's deviation from truth and consequent fall logically leads to two actions: the union of holiness with truth and the discrediting of falsehood. The union of Una and Redcrosse is a controlled affair, in which Una's lament about the 'misseeming hew' and marred looks (by which the damaged virtue of holiness is metonymically represented) of Redcrosse is curtly arrested by Arthur: 'The things, that grieuous were to doe, or beare, / Them to renew, I wote, breeds no delight' (I.viii.44). The disrobing of Duessa may be a strong argument for ruthless disclosure of deceit and corruption. The two stanzas describing Duessa in her nakedness are a blazon of blame, describing parts of her body in an aesthetics of the grotesque and revealing the sheer ugliness of Redcrosse's apostasy:

> So as she bad, that witch they disaraid,
>   And robd of roiall robes, and purple pall,

> And ornaments that richly were displaid;
> Ne spared they to strip her naked all.
> Then when they had despoyld her tire and call,
> Such as she was, their eies might her behold,
> That her misshaped parts did them appall,
> A loathly, wrinckled hag, ill fauoured, old,
> Whose secret filth good manners biddeth not be told.
>
> Her crafty head was altogether bald,
> And as in hate of honorable eld,
> Was ouergrowne with scurfe and filthy scald;
> Her teeth out of her rotten gummes were feld,
> And her sowre breath abhominably smeld;
> Her dried dugs, lyke bladders lacking wind,
> Hong downe, and filthy matter from them weld;
> Her wrizled skin as rough, as maple rind,
> So scabby was, that would haue loathd all womankind.
>
> Her neather parts, the shame of all her kind,
> My chaster Muse for shame doth blush to write;
> But at her rompe she growing had behind
> A foxes taile, with dong all fowly dight;
> And eke her feete most monstrous were in sight;
> For one of them was like an Eagles claw,
> With griping talaunts armd to greedy fight,
> The other like a beares vneuen paw:
> More vgly shape yet neuer liuing creature saw.
>
> (*FQ* I.viii.46–8)

If Duessa is the image of falsehood, Roman Catholicism or Mary Queen of Scots, the use of *hypotyposis* here appears to be excessive.[56] The rhetoric of excess here is also demanded by the logic of narrative, the literary aspiration to exceed and surpass through hyperbole the aporia of describing a metaphysical quantity such as falsehood. Not only Duessa's nature is false; her anatomy is also steeped in falsehood, being a medley of different animal parts. As Bakhtin pointed out, Menippean satire and the popular genre of writing in its imitation took as its distinct realm the parts of human anatomy below the waist.[57] The agnomination[58] in the phrase 'robd of … robes' and 'displaid' and 'despoyled', along with the alliteration of 'r' and 'p', sets the tone of an extremely stylized description which ends with a *negatio*,[59] a witty trick of saying something while protesting that it cannot or will not be said. The following two stanzas show little respect for 'good manners' in their most sordid and unchivalrous description of Duessa. From an assumed superior ethical point of view, Arthur need not consider Duessa as a human being, because in the fictive world of the poem she is a monster and in allegorical interpretations she is a vice, or falsehood, or something else by an ever-receding metonymic displacement. Falsehood does not have a stable meaning; she is 'I that do seeme not I', a shifting quantity, a false self. She is the female counterpart of Archimago, an empty signifier, evil because of her emptiness. The virtue of an institution such as an empire or dynasty rests in destroying that which destabilizes the institution. Therefore Arthur, who represents national glory and seeks Gloriana to fulfil the nation's destiny, must seek out and destroy empty signifiers such as Duessa who is represented in the form of a woman but is not truly a woman because she is 'truly' nothing.[60]

A certain 'contrarie constitution' (V.Proem.4) lies at the heart of Spenser's poetics, and developing arguments through binary oppositions is a constant dialectical habit in *The Faerie Queene*. Whether it is image-making or discussion through disputation, the allegorical narrative of *The Faerie Queene* is raised on the structures of binaries, a logical embedding that would be relished by Fraunce and Milton, practitioners of Ramist rhetoric. Although Ramist logic is as yet more closely associated with the wit of seventeenth-century poets such as Donne, I hope this chapter has shown that Spenser too has a place in the discussion of Ramist rhetoric in English poetry. Spenser, like Donne, was an active participant in the fashionable application of Ramist rhetoric in poetry, and deployed it throughout in his most ambitious poetic project, using logic to instruct as well as to delight.

Notes

1 Rosemond Tuve, *Elizabethan and Metaphysical Imagery: Renaissance Poetic and Twentieth-Century Critics* (Chicago: University of Chicago Press, 1947; 3rd impression 1957); Rosemond Tuve, 'Imagery and Logic: Ramus and Metaphysical Poetics', *Journal of the History of Ideas*, 3 (1942), 365–400; William Empson, 'Donne and the Rhetorical Tradition', *The Kenyon Review*, 11 (1949), 571–87; A.J. Smith, 'Some Claims for Ramism', *Review of English Studies*, 7 (1956), 349–59; George Watson, 'Ramus, Miss Tuve, and the New Petromachia', *Modern Philology*, 55 (1958), 259–62.

2 A. Alvarez paid a left-handed compliment to Miss Tuve by saying 'In fact, the only first-rate analytical critic the English Renaissance produced is Miss Rosemond Tuve'. See A. Alvarez, *The School of Donne* (London: Chatto and Windus, 1961), 20.

3 Brian Vickers, *Francis Bacon and Renaissance Prose* (Cambridge: Cambridge University Press, 1968); J.B. Leishman, *The Monarch of Wit: An Analytical and Comparative Study of the Poetry of John Donne* (London: Hutchinson, 1962).

4 Walter J. Ong, *Ramus, Method and the Decay of Dialogue* (Cambridge, MA: Harvard University Press, 1958); Thomas O. Sloan, 'The Rhetoric in the Poetry of John Donne', *Studies in English Literature 1500–1900* [*SEL*], 3 (1963), 31–44; Alvin Sullivan, 'Donne's Sophistry and Certain Renaissance Books of Logic and Rhetoric', *SEL*, 22 (1982), 107–20; Claudia Brodsky, 'Donne: The Imaging of the Logical Conceit', *English Literary History* [*ELH*], 49 (1982), 829–48.

5 Respectively, Sullivan, 'Donne's Sophistry'; Brian Vickers, 'Rhetoric', in Thomas N. Corns (ed.), *The Cambridge Companion to English Poetry: Donne to Marvell* (Cambridge: Cambridge University Press, 1993; 7th printing 2003), 101–20; Sloan, 'The Rhetoric'.

6 Peter Mack, *Renaissance Argument: Valla and Agricola in the Traditions of Rhetoric and Dialectic* (Leiden: E.J. Brill, 1993), *Elizabethan Rhetoric: Theory and Practice* (Cambridge: Cambridge University Press, 2002); Anthony Grafton and Lisa Jardine, *From Humanism to the Humanities: Education and the Liberal Arts in Fifteenth-and-Sixteenth-Century Europe* (Cambridge, MA: Harvard University Press, 1986); Lisa Jardine, 'Lorenzo Valla and the Intellectual Origins of Humanist Dialectic', *Journal of the History of Philosophy*, 15 (1977), 143–64; 'The Place of Dialectic Teaching in Sixteenth-Century Cambridge', *Studies in the Renaissance*, 21 (1974), 31–62. See also W.S. Howell, *Logic and Rhetoric in England 1500–1700* (New York: Russell and Russell and Princeton University Press, 1956); Kees Meerhoff, *Rhétorique et poétique au XVI siècle en France. Du Bellay, Ramus et les autres* (Leiden: E.J. Brill, 1986); Katherine Koller, 'Abraham Fraunce and Edmund Spenser', *ELH*, 7 (1940), 108–20; Peter Sharratt, 'Ramus 2000', *Rhetorica*, 18 (2000), 399–455; Steven J. Reid and Emma Annette Wilson (eds), *Ramus, Pedagogy and the Liberal Arts: Ramism in Britain and the Wider World* (Farnham and Burlington: Ashgate, 2011); Mordechai Feingold, Joseph S. Freedman, and Wolfgang Rother (eds), *The Influence of Petrus Ramus: Studies in Sixteenth and Seventeenth Century Philosophy and Sciences* (Basel: Schwabe & Co. 2001).

7 Niranjan Goswami, *Ramist Logic and Its Influence on Renaissance Literary Practice: Some Studies in the Writings of Philip Sidney, Gabriel Harvey, William Temple, Abraham Fraunce and John Milton* (Ph.D. Dissertation, Jadavpur University, 2001), 227.
8 Tuve, *Elizabethan and Metaphysical Imagery*, 344. '"Argument" is a special, technical word in Ramist writings ... It is that which has a fitness to argue something; every several "respect" (relation, reference) is an argument – as man referred to God is an *effect*, referred to sickness, is a subject, referred to a place he dwells in, is an adjunct ... Any two such "arguments" combine in readiness to be juxtaposed to others and form concepts.'
9 Rosemond Tuve, 'Imagery and Logic: Ramus and Metaphysical Poetics', in P.O. Kristeller and P.P. Wiener (eds), *Renaissance Essays* (Rochester: University of Rochester Press, 1968; reissue 1992), 284–5: 'The regular dialectical places in a Ramist Logic are: cause (efficient, material, formal, final), effect, subject, adjuncts, differing or "dissentany" arguments, "gaynsettes" or opposites, relatives, "repugning" and "denying" arguments, depriving arguments, equal arguments, of the more, of the less, the similitude and dissimilitude, conjugates and notation (nominal arguments from etymology, cognates), distribution, the perfect definition (by causes), the imperfect definition by description, and the last "inartificial" arguments from testimony, divine and human.'
10 The closest that earlier criticism could come to explain Donne's use of arguments was Frank Kermode, *Shakespeare, Spenser, Donne: Renaissance Essays* (London: Routledge and Kegan Paul, 1971), 121: 'We cannot think of Donne without thinking of relentless argument. He depends heavily upon dialectical sleight of hand, arriving at the point of wit by subtle syllogistic misdirections, inviting admiration by slight but significant perversities of analogue, which re-route every argument to paradox.'
11 Donald R. Dickson (ed.), *John Donne's Poetry* (New York: W.W. Norton, 2007), 39. Hereafter cited as Dickson, *John Donne's Poetry*. All quotations from Donne's poetry are from this edition.
12 McIlmaine writes: 'The efficient is a cause from the which the thing hathe his being ... The father also, and the mother which engendrethe, and the nurses which bring by, ar causes efficient.' M. Roll. *Makylmenaeum Scotum*, Peter Ramus, *The Logike* (1574) (Menston: The Scolar Press, 1968), 33. Hereafter referred to as *Peter Ramus, The Logike* (1574).
13 'Catachresis (in English *Abuse*) is nowe growne in fashion (as most abuses are,) It is somewhat more desperate then a Metaphore, it is the expressing of one matter by the name of another, which is incompatible with it, & sometimes cleane contrary'. John Hoskyns, 'Directions for Speech and Style', in Louise Brown Osborn, *The Life, Letters and Writings of John Hoskyns 1566-1637* (New Haven: Yale University Press), 125.
14 Giovanni Pico della Mirandola, 'Oration on the Dignity of Man', in Ernest Cassirer, P.O. Kristeller and J.H. Randall Jr (eds), *The Renaissance Philosophy of Man* (Chicago: University of Chicago Press, 1948), 223–54.
15 For a psychoanalytic interpretation of the poem see Ronald Corthell, 'The Obscure Object of Desire: Donne's *Anniversaries* and the Cultural Production of Elizabeth Drury', in Arthur F. Marotti (ed.), *Critical Essays on John Donne* (New York: G.K. Hall & Co., 1994), 123–40.
16 Harold Love argues that Donne uses several rhetorical proofs to establish his argument about the corruption of the world. See Harold Love, 'The Argument of Donne's *First Anniversary*', in John R. Roberts (ed.), *Essential Articles for the Study of John Donne's Poetry* (Hamden: Archon Books, 1975), 355–67.
17 'it happeneth, therefore, it hath purchased seuerall names of figures as a repeticon of the same word, or sound immediately with or without interposicon of any other is called Epizeuxis ... This figure is not to be vsed but in passion'. Hoskyns, *Directions*, 125–6.
18 John Donne, 'Deaths Duell', in Evelyn Simpson, *John Donne: Selected Prose*, ed. Helen Gardner and Timothy Healy (Oxford: Clarendon Press, 1967), 383.
19 Niranjan Goswami, 'Styling Religion: Puritan Rhetoric in the Sermons of Thomas Hooker, Thomas Shepard and John Cotton', in Suparna Bhattacharya (ed.), *Prose Writings of Seventeenth Century England and New England* (Kolkata: Levant Books, 2014).
20 Harold S. Wilson, *Gabriel Harvey's Ciceronianus (1577)* (Lincoln: University of Nebraska, 1945), 10.
21 Sam Meyer, 'The Figures of Rhetoric in Spenser's Colin Clout', *PMLA*, 79.3 (1964), 206–18; note 11, 207 and 209. www.jstor.org/stable/461022, accessed 19 August 2018.
22 Ibid.
23 Tamara A. Goeglein, 'Utterances of the Protestant Soul in "The Faerie Queene": The Allegory of Holiness and the Humanist Discourse of Reason', *Criticism*, 36.1 (1994), 1–19 (2). www.jstor.org/stable/23116622, accessed 19 August 2018.
24 Hoskyns defines an allegory as 'the continuall followinge of a Metaphor' and that when the two terms of the stretched comparison are in one sentence it is an allegory but if the terms stretch at great length it

becomes a poet's tale: 'Let Spencer tell you such a tale of ffaery Queene and Ovid of Diana and then it is a poets tale.' John Hoskyns, 'Directions for Speech and Style', 122–4. C.S. Lewis thought that Spenser's allegory was different from that of the Italian epic: 'In the first place, Spenser, while borrowing the form of the Italian epic, deliberately modified it by turning it into a "continued allegory or dark conceit"'. C.S. Lewis, *The Allegory of Love: A Study in Medieval Tradition* (New York: Oxford University Press, 1936, rpt 1963), 297.
25 See Alastair Fowler, *Kinds of Literature: An Introduction to the Theory of Genres and Modes* (Oxford: Clarendon Press, 1982); Barbara Kiefer Lewalski (ed.), *Renaissance Genres: Essays on Theory, History, and Interpretation* (Cambridge, MA: Harvard University Press, 1986); Rosalie Colie, *The Resources of Kind: Genre Theory in the Renaissance*, ed. Barbara Kiefer Lewalski (Berkeley: University of California Press, 1973); Annabel Patterson, *Pastoral and Ideology: Virgil to Valéry* (Oxford: Clarendon Press, 1988).
26 The letter has been analysed by critics to decide on its date or to comment on the patronage system. See Jean R. Brink, 'Dating Spenser's "Letter to Ralegh"', *The Library* 6th ser., 16 (1994), 219–24; Andrew Zurcher, 'Getting It Back to Front in 1590: Spenser's Dedications, Nashe's Insinuations And Ralegh's Equivocations', *Studies in the Literary Imagination*, 38 (2005), 173–240; Wayne Ericson, 'Spenser's Letter to Raleigh and the Literary Politics of The Faerie Queene's 1590 Publication', *Spenser Studies*, 10 (1992), 139–74. For a brilliant deconstructive interpretation of the letter see Gordon Teskey, 'Edmund Spenser Meets Jacques Derrida: On the Travails of System', *Spenser Review*, 43.3.51 (2014 Winter). www.english.cam.ac.uk/spenseronline/review/volume-43/433/reflections-editors-choice/edmund-spe nser-meets-jacques-derrida-on-the-travail-of-systems, accessed 12 May 2015.
27 Arthur Burke, *A Rhetoric of Motives* (Berkeley: University of California Press, 1969).
28 Michael F.N. Dixon, *The Polliticke Courtier: Spenser's The Faerie Queene as a Rhetoric of Justice* (Quebec: McGill-Queen's University Press, 1996), 12.
29 Gordon L. Teskey, *The Organization of* The Faerie Queene: *A Study in Rhetoric and Aesthetics* (Dissertation, Cornell University, 1981).
30 There is also the possibility of the poem standing deliberately unfinished.
31 According to Ramus logic is natural and common to all: 'Naturalis autem dialectica, id est, ingenium, ratio, mens, imago parentis omnium rerum Dei, lux denique beatae illius, & aeternae lucis aemula, hominis propria est, cu(m) eoq; nascitur. Ideoque simul atq; natus homo est, ad rationis vsum proprio quodam naturae studio, praestantiore alius atque ardentiore, alius tardiore, atque hebetiore rapitur; & quemadmodu(m) stelle luminis, sic hominess rationis omnes sunt participes: sed vt illic aliae sunt aliis clariores radiis, & illustriores: sic inter homines alij sunt ingenio praestantiores aliis, excellen-tioresque natura.' Peter Ramus, *Dialecticae Institutiones* (Paris, 1543), ed. Wilhelm Risse (Stuttgart and Bad Cannstatt: Friedrich Fromann Verlag, 1964), 6. [Logic, however, is got by birth, it is natural, reason, mind, image of origin, of all things of God, further, the light of his blessedness and rival of eternal light; proper to man, born with him. Therefore, they are simultaneous; to be born a man is to learn the proper use of reason from nature; and to be hastily made somebody more excellent, another more eager, one slower, and again someone more dull; and the manner in which the stars participate in light, similarly all men participate in reason. But in those, some have brighter rays than the others; similarly, among men, some are naturally superior to others. (My translation)]
32 Edmund Spenser, *The Faerie Queene*, ed. A.C. Hamilton, textual ed. Hiroshi Yamashita and Toshiyuki Suzuki (Harlow: Longman, 2001, 2007; Routledge, 2013, revised 2nd ed.), 32. All further references from *The Faerie Queene* are from this edition.
33 'Contrarium (Enthymema) Scaliger (III.lxi) Under tractatio. An incomplete syllogism in which one of the two premises is suppressed or is expressed as part of the conclusion.' Lee A. Sonnino, *A Handbook to Sixteenth-Century Rhetoric* (London: Routledge & Kegan Paul, 1968), 62.
34 'The testimonie humaine is eyther generall or singular.' Peter Ramus, *The Logike (1574)*, 66.
35 'That is more, whose quantity exceedethe: whose notes are, not only, but also: I had rather this then that: seeing this muche more that:' Peter Ramus, *The Logike (1574)*, 44.
36 'Of the notation or Etimologie, The Etimologie is the interpretation of a worde:' Peter Ramus, *The Logike (1574)*, 51.
37 'The effecte is that which rysethe of the cause.' Peter Ramus, *The Logike (1574)*, 29.
38 'Aversio (Apostrophe) Quintilian (IX, ii, 38f) Scheme. It consists in the diversion of our address from the judge [to some other] … our adversary … or some invocation to a god, mute object, country, etc.' Sonnino, *A Handbook*, 33–4.
39 'Copulatio (Ploche) Ad Herennium (IV) 38 Scheme. When one or more words are iterated for the purpose of amplifying our subject or drawing forth feelings of commiseration.' Sonnino, *A Handbook*, 64.

40 'Exemplum (Paradigma) *Ad Herennium (IV, 62)* When we cite something done or said in the past, along with the definite naming of the doer or utterer.' Sonnino, *A Handbook*, 90.
41 I do not comment here on Guyon's destruction of the Bower of Bliss which is an elaboration of the contest of Ramist binaries of lust and temperance that ends in doubtful victory because Acrasia has to be kept 'safe and sound'. See Stephen Greenblatt, 'To Fashion a Gentleman: Spenser and the Destruction of the Bower of Bliss', in Andrew Hadfield (ed.), *Edmund Spenser* (London: Longman, 1996), 112–33.
42 'The definition is an Oration which dothe clearly declare what the thing is.' *Peter Ramus, The Logike (1574)*, 62.
43 David Lee Miller's thesis that Spenser's motif of the search for an ideal hermaphrodite body in the union of Arthur and Gloriana is an overarching catachresis seems a little farfetched to me ('Spenser's Poetics', 171).
44 Peter Mack, *Elizabethan Rhetoric: Theory and Practice* (Cambridge: Cambridge University Press, 2002).
45 *Peter Ramus, The Logike (1574)* (Menston: The Scolar Press, 1968), 33.
46 'Poliptoton or Traductio is a repeticōn of words of the same lynage, that differ only in Terminacōn as <332> exceedingly exceeding that exceedingnes, <183b> by this faultievsing of or faults; sometime the same word in seuerall cases, as <266> for feare hide his feare sometime the same verbe in seuerall voices, as <268> forsaken by all friends and forsaking all comfort'. Hoskyns, *Directions*, 130.
47 'Offspringes are arguments which do begin alike, but end diuersly: as iust, iustice, iustly: freedom, free, freely: loue, louer, louely: good, goodness, goodly: man, manlynes, manly: as, Justice is flede out of the Realme, therfore there is no man iust whithin the Realme. Propertius lib. 2.' *Peter Ramus, The Logike (1574)*, 50.
48 A.C. Hamilton, *The Structure of Allegory in* The Fairie Queene (Oxford: Clarendon Press, 1961); Anthea Hume, *Edmund Spenser: Protestant Poet* (Cambridge: Cambridge University Press, 1984); Carol V. Kaske, *Spenser and Biblical Poetics* (Ithaca: Cornell University Press, 1999); John N. King, *Spenser's Poetry and the Reformation Tradition* (Princeton: Princeton University Press, 1990); James Nohrnberg, *The Analogy of* The Faerie Queene (Princeton: Princeton University Press, 1976); Susanne L. Wofford, 'The Fairie Queene, Books 1–3', in Andrew Hadfield (ed.), *The Cambridge Companion to Spenser* (Cambridge: Cambridge University Press, 2001), 106–24; Claire Falcke, '"Heavenly Lineaments" and the Invisible Church in Foxe and Spenser', *SEL*, 53.1 (2013), 1–29. For a discussion of Calvinist theology in *The Fairie Queene* see Andrew Hadfield, 'Spenser and Religion –Yet Again', *SEL*, 51.1 (2011), 21–46.
49 Kathryn Walls interprets the lion as Christ and Una as the Invisible Church in her *God's Only Daughter: Spenser's Una as the Invisible Church* (Manchester: Manchester University Press, 2013). I owe this reference to the anonymous reader of Manchester University Press.
50 'They be unlyke whose qualitie be diuerse: as 2 Peter 6. Lord God of Israell there is no God lyke the. And therefore the ethnicke Antistenes usethe this argumente. There is nothing lyke God, therefore God can no wyse be knowen, by any image or signe made by men.' *Peter Ramus, The Logike (1574)*, 49.
51 John Milton, *A Fuller Course in the Art of Logic Conformed to the Method of Peter Ramus (1672)*, transl. and ed. Walter J. Ong S.J. and Charles J. Ermatinger in *The Complete Prose Works* (New Haven: Yale University Press, 1982), 290. Hereafter referred to as Milton, *A Fuller Course*.
52 'Puttenham (211) Scheme. When we ask many questions and look for none answer, speaking indeed by interrogation which we might as well say by affirmation.' Sonnino, *A Handbook*, 118.
53 'Fraunce (63ff) Scheme. Exclamation is expressed by some note of exclamation, either put downe, or understood: an excellent instrument to stir up diverse affections, sometimes wonder and imagination ... despair ... wishing ... indignation ... derision.' Sonnino, *A Handbook*, 88.
54 'The efficient is a cause from the which the thing hathe his being ... And first the thing that engendrethe or desendethe is called the efficient cause ... The father also, and the mother which engendrethe, and the nurses which bring up, ar causes efficients.' *Peter Ramus, The Logike (1574)*, 18–19.
55 Walls, *God's Only Daughter*. This point is also suggested by the anonymous reader.
56 The figure *hypotyposis* is listed by Sonnino under Evidentia (Enargia): 'Vivid illustration or representation is something more than mere clearness, since the latter merely lets itself be seen whereas the former thrusts itself upon our notice ... The facts are displayed in their living truth to the eyes of the mind' (Quintilian VIII, iii, 61f). See Sonnino, *A Handbook*, 216.
57 In the manner of Lucianic satire and the carnivalesque Spenser highlights Una's 'angels face' (I.iii.4) in contrast with Duessa's 'rompe' (I.viii.48). Bakhtin writes: 'Finally, debasement is the fundamental artistic principle of grotesque realism; all that is sacred and exalted is rethought on the level of the

lower bodily stratum or else combined and mixed with its images.' See his *Rabelais and His World* (Bloomington: Indiana University Press, 1984), 370–1.
58 Agnomination is listed by Sonnino under Adnominatio (Polyptoton) also known as Paronomasia. See Sonnino, *A Handbook*, 24.
59 'Fraunce (13) Trope. A kind of irony, a denial or refusal to speak ... when nevertheless we speak and tell all.' Sonnino, *A Handbook*, 131.
60 Rosemond Tuve explains Arthur as 'a combined figure for the dynasty, the all-inclusive virtue, the spouse-to-be of the personified realm, [and] the royal house through whom divine power flowed in country and people'. Quoted by David Lee Miller in 'Spenser's Poetics: The Poem's Two Bodies', *PMLA*, 101 (1986), 170–85 (171).

4

Artes poeticae: Spenser, Donne, and the metaphysical sublime

Patrick Cheney

That Donne himself, for not being understood, would perish. (Jonson, *Informations to William Drummond* 5:147)[1]

Spenser, in affecting the ancients, writ no language. (Jonson, *Discoveries* 7:1281–2)

The reading of Homer and Virgil is counselled by Quintilian as the best way of informing youth and confirming man. For besides that, the mind is raised with the height and sublimity of such a verse, it takes spirit from the greatness of the matter, and is tincted with the best things. (Jonson, *Discoveries* 7:1283–6)

This chapter examines the literary relation between Donne and Spenser. It does so by considering their principles of poetic art – their *artes poeticae* – and, by extension, their representations of art and its trajectories. Specifically, the chapter will compare how the two poets use poetics to think. The general argument will be that we can profitably see Donne as a counter-Spenserian poet, one who reads Spenser carefully and responds forcefully to him as England's premier national poet.

Conventionally, Spenser and Donne have been understood as radically different kinds of poets. Spenser is a 'laureate poet': he writes in an eloquent or 'golden' style, rich with mythology and colour, flowery and sweet; he frames this style through major canonical genres, such as pastoral and epic, in imitation of Virgil and other classical, medieval, and Continental authors; and he relies on print to address the nation in the context of a Christian eternity. In other words, Spenser has a 'literary career'.[2] In contrast, Donne is an 'amateur poet': he writes in a 'metaphysical' style, filled with colourless, difficult, intellectual diction, syntax, and cadence; he eschews the major Virgilian genres of pastoral and epic that provide national leadership, instead choosing as a major model the private erotics of Ovid; and he relies largely on manuscript to address a coterie audience of friends in the context of London and the court. That is, John Donne eschews a literary career.[3]

Yet, by looking closely at key poems where Donne represents his own poetic art, we may bring the two poets into closer alignment: we may witness Donne's vigorous engagement with the poetics of Spenser. Donne, we will see, is that uncanny author who breaks apart the conventional binaries: he is an amateur with laureate ambitions; an Ovidian poet who attempts Virgilian genres; a manuscript poet who seeks out, and is deeply implicated in, print; a coterie poet who addresses, and reaches, a national audience.[4]

Yet we can go one step further, to examine a neglected way to view the important literary relation between Donne and Spenser, using a key term borrowed from Ben Jonson in the third epigraph to this chapter: both Spenser and Donne tap into a new aesthetics entering England during the late sixteenth century, one that increasingly affects seventeenth-century literature, on its way to becoming 'the preeminent modern aesthetic category': the 'sublime'.[5] As we will see, Spenser and Donne are among the first leading poets in England to use the word – well in advance of Milton and the late seventeenth century, when the sublime is generally thought to have emerged.[6] In a volume featuring 'thinking poets', the sublime affords an unusual perspective on the relation between these two major authors of the English Renaissance – in part, because this aesthetic category connects to such counter-cognitive vectors as language, space, and emotion; and in part because the sublime is a principle of poetic art that represents the unthinkable. When Jonson tells William Drummond of Hawthornden, in the first epigraph to this chapter, that Donne defies comprehension, and quips in the second epigraph, from *Discoveries*, that Spenser writes a language that does not exist (a splendid impossibility), he gestures to a primary poetic register that Donne and Spenser share: the sublime.[7]

As Angus Fletcher long ago recognized, Spenser is Renaissance England's first truly sublime poet, and *The Faerie Queene* its first sublime poem: heightened in style, vast in space, limitless in thought, and filled with the intoxicating emotions of pain and pleasure, Spenser's poem immeasurably crosses the boundaries between terror and rapture, leaving the reader in the exalted condition of the godhead.[8] Donne's achievement is to render the famed Spenserian golden sublime *metaphysical*. The Donnean metaphysical sublime, I shall argue specifically, constitutes one of the most important innovations in the history of English poetics.[9]

Poetics

What does Donne's poetics look like? And how does it compare with Spenser's? Ilona Bell, in her 2012 introduction to *John Donne: Collected Poetry*, usefully summarizes a well-known template against which we might measure Spenser. In particular, she outlines several vectors for thinking about Donne's counter-Spenserian poetics: language (diction, syntax), representation (imagery, figuration, blazon, mythology), and what these serve, a 'vision of the world', including ethics, theology, and Donne's 'vexed representations of women'.[10]

In Bell's model, Donne's language relies on 'innovative diction' and 'intricate syntax' to invent a 'new-made idiom' that 'reinvigorates' poetry itself. Specifically, 'Donne's language yields chasms where the flat verbal surface doubles over and splits apart, leaving us on the edge of an interpretive divide. Yet the physical world keeps intruding.' For Bell, the topic of Donne's language is inseparable from that of his representation, which she classifies as 'metaphysical'. As she notes, Donne veers from the practice of leading *golden* poets like Spenser in avoiding 'elaborate descriptions of symbolic natural landscapes, classical mythos or female beauty'. Indeed, Donne is 'Suspicious of beauteous language', preferring 'shockingly unpoetic images that dazzle the mind and penetrate the skin', especially through his principle of 'striking … encapsulat[ion]', as when he writes in 'The Relic' of a 'bracelet of bright hair about the bone' to animate the poet's corpse (6). Donne's 'images dramatize the movements of thoughts ... drawn from everyday life: building, medicine, food, law'. At the heart of Donne's metaphysical style, we find 'elaborate tropes, ambiguous inverted syntax and abstract language'.[11]

Bell quotes the *Devotions* as containing 'what is perhaps the best account of Donne's own language – attributed to God himself':

> My God, my God, Thou art a direct God, may I not say a literal God, a God that wouldest be understood literally and according to the plain sense of that Thou sayest? But thou art also ... a figurative, a metaphorical God too: a God in whose words there is such a height of figures, such voyages, such peregrinations to fetch remote and precious metaphors, such extensions, such spreadings, such curtains of allegories, such third heavens of hyperboles, so harmonious elocutions, so retired and so reserved expressions, so commanding persuasions, so persuading commandments.[12]

As Bell analyses, 'Donne's prose is as direct, agitated, hyperbolic, witty and spectacularly metaphorical as his poetry', with both media 'reach[ing] a feverish pitch of perplexity and discovery'. Donne's goal, she says, is to use symbolic language to 'persuad[e]' the reader of his identity as a Christian author, for he attributes to the deity the features of his own style. Yet, Bell adds, Donne's commitment to faith jostles with his 'skeptical distrust of received truth'. Finally, Bell writes, Donne, '[u]nlike Sidney, Shakespeare or Spenser, ... rarely represents himself as a poet', with 'the metaphorical God of the *Devotions* ... as close as he gets to a poetics'. Instead of laureate self-presentation in service of Britain, Donne is 'an egoist, given to self-analysis, self-fashioning and self-advertisement'. Rather than clarifying a national project for the poet and his readers, Donne makes it 'difficult to say exactly what Donne himself thought'.[13]

In contrast to Donne's metaphysical style, Spenser's golden style represents natural landscapes symbolically, relies on classical myths, and offers recurrent blazons of female beauty. While the diction of both poets is innovative and intricate, and both write poetry that compels the reader to think, Spenser tends to use poetry to promote thought, and Donne to complicate it.[14] Spenser's vision of the world is as global and personal as Donne's, although Spenser's might more often be understood as nationalist, even internationalist. If Donne tends towards scepticism, Spenser tends towards idealism.[15] Spenser's poetics is 'Protestant' and 'vatic'; Donne's, Protestant, yet all the while bearing the residue of his Catholic faith, at once ardent and fretful.[16]

While the terms of this comparison are well known, with three chapters in the present volume on style, figuration, and rhetoric, three additional topics pertinent to the *artes poeticae* might initially come front and centre here: genre, fame, and literary career. To what extent may we witness Donne thinking about genre in terms applicable to Spenser? Does Donne ever tap into Spenser's overarching principle of immortality linking poetic fame with Christian glory?[17] And how might we see Donne writing a literary career against the grain of 'England's first laureate poet'?[18] In accord with the volume project, we shall focus on how Donne thinks about Spenser sublimely across the literary topics of genre, immortality, and career. The two major sections below unpack this critical model: the first weaves the three topics together as they unfold in Donne's poetic canon; and the second dilates on the sublime as a key feature of this literary web. A final section speculates on the significance of the argument for Donne studies today.

Genre: fictions and patterns

One of the most striking features of Donne's poetic corpus is its vast experimentation with the backbone of a literary career: genre and poetic form. To cite but one fact: *The Oxford Handbook of Edmund Spenser* has a single chapter on 'Spenser's Genres';[19] in contrast, *The Oxford Handbook of John Donne* has no fewer than nineteen chapters nestled under a section titled 'Genres', with eleven of them on poetic genres: love lyric, epigram, elegy, epithalamion, satire, anniversary poem, verse letter, funeral elegy, epicede and obsequy, liturgical poetry, and religious sonnet. Accordingly, editions of Donne's poetry, from 1633 to the most recent, tend to be organized by genre, with the most recent edition, Bell's, dividing the poetic canon into nine generic units. In contrast, editions of Spenser are organized around *works*.[20] It is not that Spenser fails to write in traditional genres; it is, rather, that Donne's practice has long led editors to make genre the framework of Donne studies.

Donne shares with Spenser the composition of several key genres: sonnet, epithalamion, funeral elegy, and hymn. Yet Donne's sonnets tend to be holy or divine; Spenser's, amorous. The most discussed overlap is the epithalamion, although Donne departs radically from Spenser.[21] A neglected overlap is the funeral elegy, with which, we might claim, Donne aims to succeed or perhaps usurp Spenser's role as national elegist: whereas Spenser had written the elegy on Queen Dido in the 'November' eclogue of *The Shepheardes Calender*, as well as *The Ruines of Time* on the Earl of Leicester, *Daphnaida* on Douglas Howard, and both *Astrophel* and *The Dolefull Lay of Clorinda* on Philip Sidney, Donne writes the *First Anniversary*, *A Funeral Elegy*, and the *Second Anniversary* on Elizabeth Drury, as well as funeral elegies on Lady Markham, Elizabeth Bulstrode, Prince Henry, John Harrington, James Hamilton, and, most innovatively, John Donne.[22] For his part, Spenser produces no body of 'songs', or lyrics to speak of, such as makes up *Songs and Sonnets*, or such forms as epigram, love elegy, verse letter, anniversary, and holy sonnet (cf. *Amoretti* 68).

Most intriguing, however, is the little observed fact that Donne does experiment in the two Virgilian genres forming the foundation of Spenser's career as national poet: pastoral and epic. Rarely does Donne get discussed in studies of pastoral, despite his having written 'Eclogue at the Marriage of the Earl of Somerset', a 238-line poem that its title innovatively identifies as wedding two major Spenser genres – genres that Spenser keeps separate. Similarly, critics see *Metempsychosis: The Progress of the Soul* as a mock-epic, and, in particular, as a mockery of Spenser's epic, *The Faerie Queene*.[23]

The key point is that both Donne and Spenser take a leadership role in writing many poetic genres of the English Renaissance, sometimes doing so in the same genre, sometimes in different ones. While Spenser is the first poet to write an epic in modern English, 'the first English satirist was in fact John Donne'.[24] While both poets use genre as a frame for thinking, do they use genre to think about genre? More precisely, can we find Donne thinking about Spenserian genre?

For starters, Donne names the following poetic genres inside the fictions of his verse: sonnets (four times: in 'The Canonization', 'Image of Her Whom I Love', 'Sonnet. The Token' (title), and 'Countess of Salisbury'); elegy (three times: in 'Mr R. W.' (II), and 'Countess of Huntingdon' (I), and *Funeral Elegy*); lyric (once, in 'Epithalamion on St. Valentine's Day'); ode (once, in 'Countess of Huntingdon' (I)); epitaph (three times: in 'A Nocturnal upon St. Lucy's Day', 'Paradox', and 'Eclogue', line 105); hymn (seven times: in 'The Canonization', 'Countess of Bedford' (III), 'Countess of Bedford' (IV), *Second Anniversary*, lines 37 and 43, 'Lady Magdalen Herbert', and 'Mistress Bulstrode'); psalm (six times, all in 'Psalms by Sir Philip Sidney'); obsequy (once in *Metempsychosis*, line 365); anagram (once, in *Elegy X*); and satire (twice: in 'Rowland Woodward' (I) and 'R.W.' (IV)). The total of such generic terms comes to twenty-nine.[25] Moreover, the following genres show up in the titles of Donne poems, although we cannot always be certain the titles are his own: valediction (four times); anniversary (three); elegy (once); epithalamion (twice); satire (once, as '*Poema Satyricon*', part of the title of *Metempsychosis*); funeral elegy (six times); epicede (once); obsequy (once); eclogue (once); hymn (four times); epitaph (twice); litany (once); and lamentation (once). Here, we might recall that both Donne and Spenser are on record for inventing their own literary forms: Spenser, the prothalamion (or espousal poem); Donne, the valediction.[26] Other genres describe groups of poems, as printed in the 1633 and 1635 editions: songs and sonnets, elegies, satires, epigrams, holy sonnets. While critics determine that most of these groups have formal integrity – in a few cases, thought to be gathered as a collection by Donne himself, such as *Satires*, *Elegies*, and *Holy Sonnets* – most intriguing are what I call Donne's genre fictions: his mini-stories about genre stitched into his verse. I count 55 such fictions.

In Donne's genre fictions, we can find important self-inscriptions underwriting thought in his counter-Spenserian poetics. Probably the most famous is from 'The Canonization', when Donne addresses his beloved on the divinity of their erotic love:

> We can die by it, if not live by love,
>   And if unfit for tombs and hearse
> Our legend be, it will be fit for verse;
>   And if no piece of chronicle we prove,
>   We'll build in sonnets pretty rooms;
>   As well a well-wrought urn becomes
> The greatest ashes, as half-acre tombs,
>   And by these hymns all shall approve
>   Us canonized for love.
>
>   (lines 28–36)

Instructively, the concept of 'The Canonization' appears in the last line of Donne's nine-line stanza, an impressive lyricization of the epic stanza from *The Faerie Queene* (nine lines with the first eight in iambic pentameter and the last an alexandrine). What is surprising – and not always examined – is the way Donne presents the canonization coming about under the rubric of genre, of which the poet names four:

'legend', 'chronicle', 'sonnet', and 'hymn'. He tries to communicate to his beloved a compelling idea: they can become 'canonized' as saints in the pantheon of 'love' through inscriptions in a panoply of literary forms. In this poet's hands, canonization is generic. Importantly, Spenser writes in all four genres.

In the first six lines, Donne imagines two generic routes for canonization with his beloved: if they are 'unfit' to be memorialized through 'legend', they will be 'fit' for 'verse'; and, if they do not prove to be a masterpiece for 'chronicle', they will write 'sonnets' together. A 'legend' is originally 'The story of a life of a saint' (*OED*, Def. 1), but it could also be a secular 'history, story, account' (Def. 3). However, Michael Drayton first identifies a Spenserian provenance for the form: 'Master EDMUND SPENSER was the very first among us, who transferred the use of the word, LEGEND, from Prose to Verse', when calling each book of *The Faerie Queene* a 'Legend': e.g., 'The Legend of ... Holinesse'.[27] Writing well before Drayton, Donne anticipates his generic paradigm: whereas Drayton identifies Spenser's achievement of versifying prose history, Donne says he and his beloved will be fit for poetry if no one will put them into a 'legend'. In these terms, Donne writes that if the lovers are not fit for (Spenserian) epic, they will be fit for (Donnean) lyric, as the parallelism with the second of the two comparisons intimates: between 'chronicle' and 'sonnet'.

'Chronicle' can refer to one of the books of the Hebrew Bible, but it is also a Christian history of kings (Def. 1). In Book II, Canto x of *The Faerie Queene*, Spenser had again versified the form when Prince Arthur reads 'A chronicle of Briton kings' (Argument). Thus, Spenser composes a chivalric epic inside a chivalric epic.[28] When Donne writes that, if the lovers do not prove suitable for inclusion in someone's 'chronicle', they will co-author their own sonnets, he produces one of his most memorable formulations, for 'pretty rooms' is a 'subtle pun on "stanza", the Italian word for "room"'.[29] Wittily, Donne tropes literary form as a piece of architecture. Spenser had no monopoly on sonneteering, but he did produce one of the era's most important sequences, *Amoretti*, and he famously calls his future wife, Elizabeth Boyle, 'My soverayne saynt' (sonnet 61).[30]

The last genre Donne mentions is another Spenserian form: 'hymn'. Spenser had taken a leadership role in making the hymn important to a literary career, when he wrote *Fowre Hymnes* (1596) – when he wrote against his own earlier erotic poetry:

Many lewd layes (ah woe is me the more)
In praise of that mad fit, which fooles call love,
I have in th'heat of youth made heretofore,
That in light wits did loose affection move.
But all those follies now I do reprove,
And turned have the tenor of my string,
The heavenly prayses of true love to sing.

(*Hymne of Heavenly Love*, lines 8–14)

Here, Spenser announces a turn from amorous to divine poetry, in an important modification of the movement consolidated by Guillaume Du Bartas: whereas the French poet had eschewed secular love poetry to write Christian poetry, Spenser innovatively slots love poetry into a career pattern that culminates in divine poetry.[31]

In 'The Canonization', Donne does not merely reveal his understanding of four literary genres; he puts four well-known Spenserian genres into a fiction about the role that literary form can play in memorializing a couple's erotic sainthood.

Donne also uses genre-patterning in 'The Canonization' to *think* about genre as the vehicle of companionate desire. Innovatively, he adapts the classical *recusatio*, or refusal to write in the higher genres. Although the device traces to Callimachus, most likely Donne knew about it from Virgil, Horace, Propertius, Tibullus, and, notably, Ovid.[32] In the *Amores*, Ovid frames his erotic relation with Corinna as the subject of his literary career, for the opening elegy to the first and second books presents the poet trying to write Virgilian epic only to be impeded by love elegy, while the third book opens by presenting the poet in dialogue with Dame Elegy and Dame Tragedy, and the collection concludes with a turn (III.15) from elegy to tragedy. As R.V. Young points out, the 'most obvious candidate for Donne's model' in his own sequence of elegies 'is Christopher Marlowe's ... translation of Ovid's *Amores*'.[33] Marlowe is the first European poet to translate the *Amores*, and thus to inscript the Ovidian *recusatio*.[34] Young, however, is mistaken when claiming that in 'Donne's Elegies we encounter no *recusatio*'. In *Elegy VII: Love's War*, Donne writes, 'Here let me war, in these arms let me lie; / Here let me parle, batter, bleed, and die' (lines 29–30) – the Ovidian pun on 'arms' signalling a rejection not merely of war for love but of epic for elegy.[35]

Critics also miss the *recusatio* in 'The Canonization'. Whereas Ovid and other Roman poets base the refusal to write in the higher genres on eros, Donne locates *recusatio* in a socio-literary standard of *decorum*: if the couple is 'unfit for tombs and hearse'; 'if no piece of chronicle we prove'. The couple's unfitness for public 'legend' and national 'chronicle' compels the poet to tell his beloved that they will turn to other lower, erotic forms for their canonization: they will build 'sonnets' and 'hymns' to earthly love and beauty, as Spenser himself did in *Amoretti* and the first two of *Fowre Hymnes*. When Donne imagines the couple being 'approve[d]' by 'all' as saints of desire, he gestures to the fame the couple will acquire by making the career move he outlines: to be 'canonized for love' by 'all' means that they will become famous for their achievement. Finally, 'The Canonization' is important as a metaphysical meditation on *artes poeticae*. In complex, intense, difficult language, Donne enters the Spenserian list to challenge Spenser himself.

In addition to 'The Canonization' and *Elegy VII: Love's War*, eighteen other passages in Donne's poetry exhibit genre patterning, bringing the total to twenty. With so large a number, we might be unsurprised to discover that the form the patterning takes is complex, multi-faceted. In particular, the total renders messy the recent formulation of Daniel Moss, who none the less invaluably introduces a generic pattern shaping Donne's career: Donne 'recalibrate[s] the narrative of his own soul's progress, from the erotic elegies and satirical epic of his Elizabethan youth to the *Holy Sonnets* and sermons of his Jacobean redemption'.[36] Instead of Donne's generic 'progress' constituting a single trajectory from early elegy and satirical epic to later holy sonnets and sermons, I identify six poetic forms alone implicated in the twenty representations of Donne's progress: erotic elegy, satirical epic, satire, marriage poetry, funeral elegy, and divine poetry. The first five forms we might classify as secular, and the sixth as sacred. Fully thirteen represent a secular genre patterning, with seven representing a sacred one. The works in Donne's career featuring these representations spread from early to late, both secular and sacred poems, and include the following: *Songs and Sonnets* (2); *Elegies* (1); *Satires* (1); *Verse Letters* (9); *Metempsychosis* (2); *Anniversaries* (1); *Epicedes and Obsequies* (1); *Divine Poems* (3).

Fully sixteen of the representations trace a progress from one kind of poetry to another, with nine being from one kind of secular poetry to another, and seven from secular to sacred. Altogether, they show Donne entirely familiar with the classical *recusatio* so popularized by Spenser among English authors. Three we might term abbreviated *recusatio*, since they feature the poet's movement simply to epic (*Metempsychosis*, Epistle and lines 1–10), from satire (*Satire V*, lines 1–6), and from funeral epic ('Obsequies upon the Lord Harrington' 255–8), without specifying the full form of the turn. To take but one example, *Satire V* opens: 'Thou shalt not laugh in this leaf, Muse, nor they / Whom any pity warms' (lines 1–2).[37] We have already discussed the turn from epic to elegy in *Love's War* and the double-turn in 'The Canonization'. Two other forms are generalized: from lower to higher forms ('Mr E. G.' lines 1–4); and from public to private ('Valediction of the Book', lines 1–9, the latter to be discussed below). More concretely, 'Mr Rowland Woodward' announces a turn from songs and sonnets and satires to verse letters: 'she [Donne's muse] to few, yet to too many', 'hath shown / How love-song weeds and satiric thorns are grown, / Where seeds of better arts were early sown' (lines 4–6). In 'To Mr R.W.' (IV), Donne recognizes the potency of R.W.'s verse letters to 'quench' his own 'satiric fires', which he has 'writ / In scorn of all' (lines 6–8). In 'To Mr S.B.', Donne's troping is especially enigmatic, using a well-known conceit that we shall see driving *Metempsychosis*, the poem-as-bark, to trace a 'turn' from 'the vast sea of arts' to 'less creeks' (lines 4–7) – evidently from epic to satire: 'and wisely take / Fresh water at the Heliconian spring. / I sing not, Siren-like, to tempt, for I / Am harsh' (lines 7–10). As Moss recognizes, the most important representations are the eight that turn from secular to sacred poetry – as we have seen, a Spenserian turn: *Second Anniversary*, lines 43–4; Holy Sonnet 13; 'Mr R. W.' (I) – interesting because Donne wonders whether his friend hasn't written to him because he's turned from courtly to divine poetry; 'Countess of Bedford' (IV); 'Countess of Huntingdon'; 'Countess of Salisbury' – also interesting because Donne sees his addressee as 'repair[ing]' the 'sonnets' of 'lovers' with 'God's book of creatures'; and finally, 'Hymn to God the Father', which deserves special attention. For in this traditional crown to Donne's poetic canon, the poet asks God 'forgive[ness]' for 'that sin' – writing secular verse: 'by which I won / Others to sin, and made my sin their door', with the architectural metaphor from Donne's toolbox of representing his poetry already mentioned. And when he concludes the stanza, 'For I have more', he does not merely pun on Ann More's name but promises God 'more' words – more divine poetry – in a poem that recalls Spenser's heavenly hymns.[38]

Arguably the most direct representation of genre patterning in the Donne canon opens *La Corona*, and it seems significant that the turn is from secular to sacred verse:

> do not with a vile crown of frail bays
> Reward my muse's white sincerity,
> But what Thy thorny crown gained, that give me,

A crown of glory which doth flower always;
The ends crown our works, but Thou crown'st our ends.

(lines 5-9)

Here, Donne turns away from a classical idea of a laureate career based on the Roman triumph of a Spenser to a Christian idea of thorny-crowning based on Messianic suffering. In doing so, Donne announces a turn from classical poetic fame to Christian glory.[39]

It is in *Metempsychosis*, however, that Donne most formally challenges the Spenserian idea of genre patterning – and everything else Spenserian to boot, including the New Poet's key idea of printing a literary career that leads to public fame in the context of Christian glory. Significantly, the 1633 and 1635 editions of Donne's poetry both print the importance of *Metempsychosis* to the Donne canon. Whereas 1633 gives it pride of place as the opening poem, 1635 retains its structural significance even when moving the poem to a slot later in the book. As Wyman Herendeen notes, in both editions, 'through … links between the *La Corona* sonnets and *The Progresse of the Soule*, Donne initiates the redefinition of his poetic vocation and effects a transfer from profane to sacred poetic. … [H]e makes his profane progress the beginning of a spiritual triumph that carries his readers through the "Holy Sonnets" and into the rest of the volume.'[40]

Critics from Don Cameron Allen to Anne Lake Prescott agree that Donne responds to Spenser in *Metempsychosis*: in language, genre, stanzaic form, method, intertextual reference, and even self-presentation.[41] Donne's self-presentation begins with the most curious feature of this, his second longest, poem: *Metempsychosis* is that striking anomaly, a manuscript poem prepared for print, the title of which reads:

The Progress of the Soul
Infinitati Sacrum
16 August 1601
Metempsychosis
Poêma Satyricon

There may be some wit in the juxtaposition of the second and third lines: a poem sacred to infinity is tied to a specific date. More formally, contradiction emerges in the juxtaposition of the two Latin phrases, for the serious religious connotation of 'Infinitati Sacrum' is belied by the satyr-like poem. For most readers, such contradictions create the window into a poem of absolute mockery.

The precise classification of the mockery becomes clearer in the Epistle, which announces the poem's epic status: Donne juxtaposes his own poem as a picture (Horace's *ut pictura poesis*) with 'Others' who 'at the porches and entries of their buildings set their arms' (lines 1–2) – likely an evocation of the opening line of the *Aeneid*, 'I sing of arms, and the man'.[42] Donne's mockery of the epic tradition continues when he toys with the idea of poetic imitation as his cardinal methodology: 'I have no purpose to come into any man's debt. … If I do borrow anything of antiquity, … you shall still find me to acknowledge it' (lines 15–18) – an acknowledgement that is not forthcoming. Contradictorily, however, Donne immediately targets the didacticism embraced by Spenser in the Letter to Raleigh: 'I will have no such readers as I can teach' (lines 20–1). According to Theresa M. DiPasquale, here Donne 'rejects a Spenserian poetics that would attempt to mould readers into something better than they were before'.[43] When Donne gets to his title topic, 'the Pythagorean doctrine' of metempsychosis, by which 'one soul from man to man' is carried, or translated (lines 21–2), he introduces not merely a philosophical principle that recycles souls but a literary principle that establishes an authorial genealogy. Ennius first used metempsychosis to claim descent from Homer, but Spenser deploys the principle in his retelling of Chaucer's 'Squire's Tale' in Book IV, Cantos ii and iii of *The Faerie Queene*: 'O most sacred happie spirit, / ... through infusion sweete / Of thine owne spirit, which doth in me surviue, / I follow here the footing of thy feete' (IV.ii.34).[44]

The principle of literary *translation* characterizes the opening line of the poem proper: 'I sing the progress of a deathless soul'. As readers have long recognized, Donne imitates not merely the opening line of the *Aeneid* but the key programmatic line in *The Faerie Queene*, itself an imitation of Virgil (via Ariosto): 'I ... / ... sing of Knights and Ladies' (I.Proem.1–5). Yet Donne humorously inflates his claim of inheritance from Spenser and Virgil by doing something they avoid: he *repeats* the epic formula, for it appears twice more in the opening stanza alone: 'I sing. / ... I draw' (lines 4, 6). When Donne concludes the first stanza with a couplet about the fame his poem will have – 'A work t'outwear Seth's pillars, brick and stone, / And (holy writ excepted) made to yield to none' (lines 9–10) – he adds both Horace and Ovid as authors he will mock-triumph over. Yet Donne goes further than that, for he versifies his frame-target as the author of *The Faerie Queene* in the stanza's form, long recognized as a Spenserian stanza with a tenth line. In this regard, we may classify *Metempsychosis* not only as a 'satirical mock-epic' but as a satirical mock-epic of Spenser's epic.[45]

In the sixth stanza of *Metempsychosis*, Donne selects the bark or ship mentioned earlier as the vehicle for his poem's counter-Spenserian progress: he 'sail[s]' a 'course' from 'paradise' to 'home', Eden to England, the 'Tigris and Euphrates' to the 'Thames' (lines 56–9). From classical times, poets use the ship as a metaphor for poetry, especially Ovid, and Renaissance poets like Spenser make the ship a key image of their poetics, especially in *The Faerie Queene* when it becomes the boat of epic: 'Now strike your sailes yee iolly Mariners, / For we be come vnto a quiet rode, / Where we must land some of our passengers, / And light this weary vessell of her lode' (*FQ* I.xii.42).[46] From Donne's description of the soul's voyage, we learn quite a bit about his poetics: in moving from Eden to England, he combines classical and native poetry; and thereby he depends on a system of imitation of both. Moreover, Donne inserts a heroic ethos into his voyage, although the pun on 'light' makes light of the effort: 'for I will through the wave and foam, / And shall in sad lone ways a lively spright / Make my dark, heavy poem light, and light' (lines 53–5). Donne's intense word play – light and dark, heavy and light – boggles the mind (Donne may also be punning on 'lighter', a word for a barge). When he adds, 'through many straits and lands I roam' (line 56), he uses the concept of romance wandering to question the epic teleology of a voyage progressing from Eden to England. According to the *OED*, the word 'roam' admits of no ambiguity: 'To wander, rove, or ramble' (Def. 1). Yet Donne undercuts the idea in the next line: 'I launch at paradise, and I sail towards home' (line 57). Is this an epic? or a romance? Perhaps Donne represents both an epic and a romance – or even the genre that Colin Burrow uses to classify *The Faerie Queene*, 'epic romance' – except this is not what the poet says.[47] Effectively, Donne splits the Spenserian generic bark apart. Hence, we might recall that the idea of 'progress' organizing *Metempsychosis* – of being translated – taps into the concept at the centre of the Western sublime: transport.

Sublime poetics

What do we mean by 'the sublime'? The concept is infinitely complex. As Philip Shaw puts it, 'We are never certain of the sublime'.[48] James I. Porter, in his magisterial 2016 *The Sublime in Antiquity*, concludes that 'terminology is not the best way to determine the presence or absence of the sublime in an author. The more valid criterion is to measure an author's pulse rate.'[49] In this formulation, Porter locates sublimity in heightened and elevated language that moves the reader to strong passion and bewildering thought.

Acknowledging the difficulty of comprehending the sublime, Shaw ventures a definition: 'The highest of the high; that which is without comparison; the awe-inspiring or overpowering; the unbounded and the undetermined'.[50] *The Oxford Classical Dictionary* remembers that the word derives from the Latin *sublimitas*, and refers to 'that quality of genius in great literary works which irresistibly delights, inspires, and overwhelms the reader'.[51] In *On Sublimity* (the originary treatise on the topic, probably written during the first century AD), Longinus offers the following definition:

> Sublimity is a kind of eminence or excellence of discourse. It is the source of the distinction of the very greatest poets and prose writers and the means by which they have given eternal life to their own fame. For grandeur produces ecstasy rather than persuasion in the hearer; and the combination of wonder and astonishment always proves superior to the merely persuasive and pleasant.[52]

For Longinus, the sublime is a counter-rhetorical language, a form of authorship that defies the art of persuasion, because 'in poetry the aim is astonishment' (15.1).[53] A sublime art does not seek either to please or to instruct but to explode: 'Sublimity … tears everything up like a whirlwind' (1.4).[54] The effect of the sublime is thus neither regulated emotion nor clear thought but something that seems genuinely at home in Donne: heightened emotion defying thought. As Shaw puts it, 'Sublimity … refers to the moment when the ability to apprehend, to know, and to express a thought or sensation is defeated. Yet through this very defeat, the mind gets a feeling for that which lies beyond thought and language.'[55] Such language – and idea – recalls that of Bell earlier: 'Donne's language yields chasms where the flat verbal surface doubles over and splits apart'. By using such words as 'vexed … shocking … dazzle … agitated … feverish … perplexity' – suggestive as they are of the impact of his verse – Bell invites us to locate the language of the sublime in the poetic art of John Donne.

The sublime warrants place in a volume about 'Thinking Poets', because it offers a new dynamic to much criticism today, which aims to show how poets like Spenser and Donne use poetry to think profoundly. The sublime is impressive as an aesthetic that boldly enters the circuit of this paradigm, and rends it. According to Longinus, poets produce sublime poetry through five sources, and he uses them to organize what Brian Vickers calls 'one of the most intelligent works of literary criticism ever produced'[56]: (1) 'great thoughts'; (2) 'strong and inspired emotion'; (3) elevated 'figures of thought and figures of speech'; (4) 'Noble diction'; and (5) 'dignified and elevated word-arrangement' (8.1).[57] By focusing on these sources, Longinus opens up space to a chapter on '*artes poeticae*' in Spenser and Donne. Since we have already accounted for word-arrangement, diction, and figuration, let us see how sublime thought and emotion bear on the volume's two 'thinking poets'.

In art, says Longinus, the relation between 'inspired emotion' and 'great thought' is intimate; the sublime uses intense emotion to explode cognition, in keeping with his shocking idea that great literature does something beside persuade, or even delight. As scholars report, at least one-third of *On Sublimity* is missing from the earliest manuscripts, which date to the eleventh century, and the treatise is first printed by Francesco Robortello in 1554. During the sixteenth century, six other editions in Greek and/or Latin were published on the Continent, and even more by the time of Donne's death in 1633 – right on the cusp of the first English edition, in both Latin and Greek, by Gerard Langbaine in 1636.[58] During the past ten years, scholars have indeed been overturning the received wisdom that the sublime becomes important in England only with Milton. As the present volume emerges, the academy across several fields in the humanities, arts, and even sciences continues to supply the evidence.[59]

The attenuated manuscript of *On Sublimity* interferes with our understanding of what Longinus says about sublime emotion. The treatise, however, does bequeath a detailed account of sublime thought. The overarching paradox is that the sublime makes a poet both 'thinking' and 'beyond thought'. In other words, the sublime takes poet and reader to the limits of thinking. In *The Critique of the Power of Judgment* (1789), Immanuel Kant grasps this complexity philosophically:

> We can say no more than that the object serves for the presentation of a sublimity that can be found in the mind, for what is properly sublime cannot be contained in any sensible form, but concerns only ideas of reason, which, though no presentation adequate to them is possible, are provoked and called to mind precisely by this inadequacy, which does allow of sensible presentation. (2.23)[60]

'[T]he mind', Kant adds, 'is incited to abandon sensibility and to occupy itself with ideas that contain a higher purposiveness' (2.23): 'the sublime is therefore not to be found in the things of nature but only in our ideas' (2.25).[61] In a useful formulation, Kant concludes, 'That is sublime which even to be able to think of demonstrates a faculty of the mind that surpasses every measure of the senses' (2.25; boldfaced in original).[62]

Kant does not invent such speculation. Of course, neither Donne nor Spenser could have known Kant, but it would be especially surprising if Donne had not heard of Longinus, perhaps even read him, despite never mentioning *On Sublimity*. As recent research demonstrates, Longinus was in the English water from the 1570s forward, when Langbaine's tutor, John Rainolds, lectured on Longinus at Oxford in

1573/4; when George Chapman in 1614 became the first English poet-playwright to discuss Longinus; and when Franciscus Junius the Younger in 1636/7 wrote down 'the first sustained response to Longinus in English'.[63] In *Discoveries*, when Jonson defines the 'sublimity of ... verse' as taking 'spirit from the greatness of the matter and is tincted with the best things', he demonstrates how the aesthetic model of the sublime infiltrates English authors' *artes poeticae* during Donne's lifetime.

What does Longinus say about sublime poets thinking? In *On Sublimity*, he devotes no fewer than six sections to this 'most important' of the five sources (9.1): 'Greatness of Thought' (9.1–15.12).[64] As Longinus clarifies in the last sentence of these sections, he discusses 'sublimity of thought' (15.12) under three 'road[s]': 'greatness of mind, imitation, and visualization' (or *phantasia*) (13.2).[65] Briefly, let us take each in turn.

First, says Longinus, the sublime helps 'develop our minds in the direction of greatness and makes them always pregnant with noble thoughts' (9.1). Yet the end of sublime thought is not deep cognition (a form of philosophy) but artistic 'greatness' (a form of aesthetics), the mark of 'noble' poetic invention ('pregnant'): '"Sublimity is the echo of a noble mind"' (9.2; Longinus is quoting himself). The mind is the origin of the sublime, which has the power to create great thoughts, which the poet then 'echoes' in his poetry: 'words will be great if thoughts are weighty' (9.3).[66] The word 'echo' is important: simultaneously, it traces the sublime to the mind and records its status as poetic representation. Clearly, Longinus tries to get at a paradox: the sublime is the product of the thinking poet, but through the sublime the poet moves beyond logic into representation, a symbolic expression that exceeds reason. Longinus adds that weighty or sublime thought likely cannot be continuous in a literary work: 'sublimity exists often in single thought' (12.2).[67] As such, a sublime representation stands out, and can be studied, as Longinus studies many representations in Greek literature, including to illustrate a sublimity distinct from emotion: 'Ossa upon Olympus they sought to heap; and on Ossa / Pelion with its shaking forest, to make a path to heaven' (8.2, quoting Homer, *Odyssey* XI.315–17).[68]

Second, Longinus says that greatness of thought comes when one author imitates 'great writers of the past' (13.2). Ingeniously, he lapses into a mythological allegory about 'the Pythia at Delphi' (14.2) to represent the process of sublime literary imitation: 'She is in contact with the tripod near the cleft in the ground which (so they say) exhales a divine vapour, and she is thereupon made pregnant by the supernatural power and forthwith prophesies as one inspired. Similarly, the genius of the ancients acts as a kind of oracular cavern, and effluences flow from it into the minds of their imitators' (14.2).[69] Longinus presents the story of the Pythia and her relationship with the god of poetry, Apollo, as an allegory of the poet's sublimity arising from greatness of thought. The work of a previous writer functions as an 'oracular cavern' of poetic invention, from which 'effluences' flow into the 'mind' of the imitating author, impregnating him with 'supernatural power'. This allegory makes it clear that great or sublime thought is important to Longinus because it overcomes the problem of the human, rendering the author and reader divine: such 'divine gifts' of the sublime poet make it 'almost blasphemous to call them human' (34.4).[70] One wonders: does Donne write the sublime in order to versify the godhead – to render the godhead ineffable?

Finally, Longinus singles out *phantasia*, which 'some people call image-making', but which his modern translators call 'visualization' (15.1): 'the situation in which enthusiasm and emotion make the speaker *see* what he is saying and bring it *visually* before his audience' (15.1–2).[71] For Longinus, visualization is that special representation in a work when 'the poet is accustomed to enter into the greatness of his heroes' (9.10).[72] Longinus cites Euripides' *Iphigenia in Tauris* when Orestes tries to flee the Erinyes, 'O! She'll kill me. Wherefore shall I escape?' (line 291), about which Longinus concludes: 'The poet himself saw the Erinyes, and has as good as made his audience see what he imagined' (15.2).[73] In this sublime principle of authorship, the poet's 'thought' takes him 'beyond the limits of mere persuasiveness' (15.11), for the simple reason that the sublime takes us beyond the limits – beyond the rational, into the unthinkable, the unpresentable.[74] Such an aesthetic principle operates neither on earth nor in heaven but in a special place that Longinus calls 'the interval between earth and heaven' (9.5),[75] where the boundaries between the human and the divine, the mind and the emotions, the rational and the supernatural, play out an ecstatic mystery. This Longinian 'interval', we shall see, transports us to the centre of Donne territory.

In the final stanza of *Metempsychosis*, Donne's address to the reader allows us to classify his metaphysical poetics as sublime:

> Who ere thou beest that read'st this sullen writ,
> Which just so much courts thee, as thou dost it,
> Let me arrest thy thoughts; wonder with me
> Why ploughing, building, ruling and the rest,
> Or most of those arts whence our lives are blest,
> By cursed Cain's race invented be,
> And blest Seth vexed us with astronomy.
> There's nothing simply good nor ill alone;
> Of every quality comparison,
>   The only measure is, and judge, opinion.
>
> (lines 511–20)

Designed as a direct communication to the reader, this final utterance confounds our understanding: 'Let me arrest thy thoughts'. Donne's 'writ' is more than direct or 'sullen'; it is metaphysical and sublime. The word 'sullen' can mean 'solemn, serious' (Def. 2) but also 'deep' (Def. 3a). Donne's writ is serious partly as a false scent, since humour plays a key role in the mockery; yet the writ is a mockery of depth – so mockingly deep it has long sustained speculation, from Allen to Elizabeth Harvey:[76] no one is sure how to gauge John Donne here. In 'arrest[ing]' our 'thoughts' to make us 'wonder', Donne creates a gleefully serious model for the metaphysical sublime. In lines 515–17, the rapid set of contradictions challenges cognition, as Donne categorizes 'arts whence our lives are blest / By cursed Cain's race', and 'blest Seth vexe[s] us with astronomy': 'blest ... cursed ... blest ... vexed'. This set of paradoxes leads to the conclusion that 'nothing' under the sun is 'simply good' or 'ill' – a challenge to the entire Judaeo-Christian system. In Bell's formulation, 'Like everything else, astronomy is neither wholly good nor wholly evil: though it benefits science, it also attempts to elucidate the inner workings of heaven, a violation of God's authority'.[77]

Donne's metaphysics of sublime authorship explodes the value system of the West, including as epitomized in the poetry of Edmund Spenser.

The concluding couplet is especially mind-bending. Perhaps Donne means that the 'only measure' and 'judge' of a 'quality' is through 'comparison' and 'opinion' – which Bell glosses as 'Moral or political judgement; report, rumour; disputable judgement of belief'.[78] Finally, what is measurable is measureless; what is rational, irrational. Donne's thought takes us into a no-man's land of sublimity, from which no traveller returns, and the poem ends abruptly, in linguistic quicksand. The conundrum we finally confront in *Metempsychosis* comes to this (what a strange artefact): presented for print, left unfinished in manuscript, printed as such.

In his poetic canon, Donne uses cognates of the word 'sublime' four times – three times more than Spenser (*Faerie Queene* V.viii.30), and four times more than two other English Renaissance authors often classified as sublime: Marlowe and Shakespeare.[79] All four of Donne's uses of the word nominally depend on the alchemical process of purifying refinement, but each uses the word metaphorically to mean something 'elevated, superior'.[80] In 'Valediction of the Book', Donne uses 'subliming' to represent his own authorship. In another nine-line stanza designed to surpass Spenser, Donne claims an elevated status for his art; his lyric, inspired by his beloved, will 'out-endure' the public poems of Homer, Virgil, Corinna, Pindar, and Lucan:

> Study our manuscripts, those myriads
> Of letters, which have passed 'twixt thee and me,
> Thence write our annals, and in them will be,
> To all whom love's subliming fire invades,
> Rule and example found.
>
> (lines 10–14)

Donne's 'letters' to his mistress set a 'Rule and example' for the 'annals' of poetic history because they are 'invade[d]' by 'love's subliming fire'. That is, the sublime element of desire takes up residence in Donne's poem – desire that is pure, refined, and elevated. While listing classical poets, he once more challenges Spenser in the very stanza form, using a nine-line stanza, with lines 5–7 in trimeters: Donne counters England's sublime national poet. Yet Donne's real point goes further: his sublime love poetry alone will become immortal, since 'posterity shall know it too' (line 4). His 'book' will be as 'long-lived as the elements, / Or as the world's form, this all-graved tome / In cipher writ, or new made idiom' (lines 19–21). Here, Donne out-sublimes Spenser (and the rest).[81]

In his second poem to 'Lucy, Countess of Bedford', Donne opens with sublimity: 'Honour is so sublime perfection, / And so refined, that when God was alone / And creatureless at first, himself had none' (lines 1–3). Again referring to the alchemical process of 'perfection', Donne metaphorizes honour as 'sublime', meaning refined, purified. The thought is itself in the register of the sublime, for it is difficult to grasp, to work out the metaphysical conceit. Donne seems to be talking about chastity – the very topic of Book III of *The Faerie Queene* – and classifying chastity as a valuable, heightened state, modelled on the deity, who, before the creation of Adam (and Eve), had no honour Himself, since such a principle could not exist until after the Creation.

But only in the third stanza do we reach a degree of clarification, for Donne concludes, 'So from low persons doth all honour flow' (line 7). And only in the fourth stanza do we realize that Donne is talking about his own authorship, which self-reflexively versifies a letter to the Countess: 'Care not then, Madame, how low your praisers lie; / In labourers' ballads oft more piety / God finds than in Te Deums' melody' (lines 13–15). Thus the 'Honour' of which he speaks as 'subliming perfection' is the form of Donne's verse letter, which, despite its 'low' generic status as a 'labourer[']s ballad', has greater 'piety' than a church 'melody' praising God.

In one of his divine poems, 'To Mr Tilman after He Had Taken Orders', Donne uses the word 'sublime' twice. Donne wrote the poem as late as 1618, when, on 20 December, Edward Tilman was ordained a deacon. We might pause on the significance of the one double iteration of the word 'sublime' in the Donne canon, for it appears in a divine poem about a man taking holy orders in the Anglican Church, in sharp contrast to the erotic use of the word in 'Valediction of the Book' or the patronage-use in the letter to the Countess of Bedford. Effectively, then, Donne spreads his use of the word over three of the major co-ordinates of his poetic canon: love lyric, celebrating the relationship between poet and mistress; verse letter, celebrating the relationship between poet and patron; and divine poem, celebrating the poet's relationship with a fellow clergyman. Bedroom, great house, church; mistress, patron, colleague: Donne weaves the 'sublime' into a significant triad of his poetic oeuvre.

In 'Mr Tilman', Donne dilates on what it means to take holy orders – how it changes the essential man: he acquires a 'function … so noble as to be / Ambassador to God and destiny' (lines 37–8). This is a version of the Longinian interval between earth and heaven, the holy office by which the human becomes that 'blest hermaphrodite' (line 54), 'A person embodying opposites, here the imperfections of the flesh and the holiness of the divine'.[82] As Donne puts it to Mr Tilman himself, 'How brave are those who with their engines, can / Bring man to heaven, and heaven again to man' (lines 47–8). The word 'engines' means 'Ingenuity; devices';[83] but it also refers to Donne's poetic engine – a version of the poetry he assigns to the Biblical prophets in 'A Litany': 'Those heavenly poets', who 'did see / Thy will, and it express / In rhythmic feet', which he 'pray[s]' will become a licence for his own 'excess / In seeking secrets, or poeticness' (lines 68–72).

The thought of 'Mr Tilman', only 54 lines long, is impressively complex, so we need to limit ourselves to one relevant passage that challenges thought – Donne's own phrase for Mr Tilman's sublime agency is 'surmount expression' (line 25). Donne discusses the 'foolish world' that scorns his holy 'profession' (line 26), because they spend their days 'In dressing, mistressing, and compliment' (line 29):

> whose trust
> Seems richly placed in sublimed dust
> (For, such are clothes and beauties, which though gay,
> Are, at the best, but of sublimèd clay),
> Let then the world thy calling disrespect,
> But go thou on and pity their neglect.
>
> (lines 31–6)

Unlike in both 'Valediction of the Book' and 'Lucy, Countess of Bedford', here Donne uses the sublime to criticize the foolish world – in particular, its faith in the human body alone. The twinned iteration, 'sublimed dust' and 'sublimèd clay', refers to the Book of Genesis, the creation of Adam out of 'dust' and the red earth or clay ('Adam' means *red earth* in Hebrew): 'And the LORD God formed man *of* the dust of the ground, and breathed into his nostrils the breath of life; and man became a living soul' (1:4).[84] By 'sublimed', Donne again means 'refined', 'perfected', yet in both uses he is being ironic, at the same time that he refers to the original Adamic creation as pristine. Those who place their 'trust' *richly* in the dust of the flesh betray man's original divinity, which animates the body with the 'livng soul' – the word 'richly' evoking a materialist, economic inspiration for living.

It may be crucial that the double use of the sublime here shows up with respect to what Ramie Targoff calls 'the defining bond' of Donne's 'life': the 'relationship between the body and soul'.[85] As such, even at their 'best', worldly people are 'sublimèd clay', exanimated bodies – to quote one of Spenser's more interesting words (*FQ* II.xii.7.5), meaning 'deprived of their souls'.[86] Metaphysically, 'sublimed dust' and 'sublimèd clay' are oxymorons, challenging thought, two opposing words 'interanimate[d]' ('The Ecstasy', line 42).

'The Ecstasy' is one of the most renowned lyrics in English, and features a word in its title that Longinus calls sublime, quoted earlier: 'grandeur produces ecstasy'. In the sixteenth century, writes David L. Sedley, 'Christian ecstasy' was 'just one among a cluster of similar concepts' in 'a vein of interest in aesthetic extremes' that includes sublimity, 'wonder', and Neoplatonic '*furor*'.[87] As an aesthetic extreme, ecstasy is a spiritual experience (Platonic, Christian, Neoplatonic) wherein the soul is transported out of the body to experience exhilarating bliss: 'Our souls (which to advance their state / Were gone out) hung 'twixt her and me' (15–17).[88] As Targoff argues, the 'parting between body and soul is ... the great subject of Donne's writing'.[89] As is well known, the Biblical and Platonic concept that launches the ecstatic experience in Donne's poem was most influentially championed by Spenser: 'we two, one another's best ... makes both one, each this and that', a 'dialogue of one' that 'Interanimates two souls' (4, 36, 74, 42).

Repeatedly in his canon, Spenser scripts the irrational idea that two people can jump the gap to become one – in body and soul. Arguably the most famous occurs in the original ending to Book III, 'The Legend of Chastity', when Britomart rescues Amoret from the House of Busirane, and reunites the newlywed with her husband, Scudamour, who embraces her ecstatically – not as a Tilmanesque 'blest hermaphrodite' but as an Ovidian 'faire Hermaphrodite' (III.xii.46): 'she faire Lady ouercommen quight / Of huge affection, did in pleasure melt, / And in sweete rauishment pourd out her spright' (*FQ* III.xii.45; 1590 version).

Most of Spenser's words come from the vocabulary of the sublime: 'ouercommen ... huge ... melt ... rauishment'. But the key concept appears in the second half of the last line: 'pourd out her spright'. A.C. Hamilton's note seems off key: 'Similar language is used in Castiglione, *Courtier* 315, to describe the kiss by which the souls of lovers "poure them selves by turne into the one into the others bodie, and bee so mingled together, that each of them hath two souls"'.[90] In fact, Spenser does not represent this Neoplatonic process, for Amoret and Scudamour engage in something more ravishing than kissing (as other critics rightly assert): 'pourd out her spright' is a euphemism for orgasm, which renders the couple at once speechless and eternal: 'No word they spake, nor earthly thing they felt' (III.xii.45). Like Donne, Spenser depicts the process of ecstasy as a process of sublime transport: the spirit leaves the body to join the soul of another and to experience the divinity of bliss.[91]

Although 'The Ecstasy' is among Donne's greatest metaphysical poems, I should like to classify it as one of his most sublime poems. From Longinus to the Christian Neoplatonists of the Renaissance, the ecstasy is one form of experience that the sublime takes, but in Spenser ecstasy is formally a literary representation, a form of Ovidian authorship. Donne's 'The Ecstasy' is notorious for its complexity, with many criticizing its masculinist rhetorical leveraging of the female of her virginity: if our souls should experience the ecstasy of an out-of-body experience – sublime transport – 'why do we forbear' in matching such spiritual bliss with the sexual unity of 'Our bodies' (line 50)?[92] Yet we may also reclassify 'The Ecstasy' as a new type of English poem: the *metaphysical sublime*. Like Spenser in the conclusion to Book III of *The Faerie Queene*, Donne represents the sublime process of transport, but, unlike Spenser, he intellectualizes the process, subdues it to thought, content with the enigma of the unknowable: 'This ecstasy doth unperplex / (We said) and tell us what we love; / We see by this, it was not sex' (lines 29–31). Whereas for Longinus (as for Kant and Jean-François Lyotard), the sublime perplexes, Donne's ecstasy claims to 'unperplex', clarifying 'what we love'. However, the very next line contradicts the clarification: 'We see, we saw not what did move' (line 32). Donne's metaphysics proceeds with a teasing rationality, yet it ends enigmatically: in 'Love's mysteries' (line 71).

What finally might be sublime about 'The Ecstasy' is Donne's attempt to secure an erotic rhetorical persuasion through a representation of Longinian transport, 'the free abandon of ... movement and the sense of being, as it were, catapulted out' (*On Sublimity* 21.2).[93] When Longinus says, 'if you take away the sublime element, you take the soul away from the body' (11.2: 156), he beckons us to recall that Donne writes an entire lyric on the concept – and perhaps (taking Targoff's cue) inscripts the soul of a whole corpus.[94]

Conclusion

In his poetry, Donne re-scripts the Spenserian process of sublime transport by which two become one, making it one of his primary metaphysical principles, to be ironized, as perhaps in 'The Ecstasy', or rendered wondrous, as in 'A Valediction: Forbidding Mourning'. This last metaphysically sublime lyric recalls the principle of alchemical refinement from 'The Ecstasy' (line 21: 'by love refined'): 'But we by'a love so much refined / That ourselves know not what it is, / Inter-assurèd of the mind, / ... / Our two souls therefore, which are one' (lines 17–21). Throughout his poetic canon, Donne expresses the sublime idea of individuals who 'knew not what we loved' ('The Relic'). A non-cognitive state of rapture finds its way into many corners of the Donne corpus: as in the word 'rapt' in *Elegy XV: His Parting from Her*, or 'poetic rage' in

'Countess of Bedford' [III] – sometimes formally occupying the Longinian interval between earth and heaven, as in the *Second Anniversary*, when the soul of a young girl 'Dispatches in a minute all the way / 'Twixt heaven and earth' (lines 188-9). Of course, 'The Ecstasy' does not have a monopoly on ecstasy; the word recurs at *Second Anniversary*, line 321, 'Prince Henry', line 26, 'Lord Harrington', line 13. In all these representations, Donne outstrips Spenser's golden-style sublimity by metaphysicking the sublime. His metaphysical sublime might be important in today's criticism because it puts poetry to work in thinking profoundly through questions of identity and destiny – erotic, philosophical, theological, national – and perplexes them.[95]

Notes

1 Jonson quotations come from *The Cambridge Edition of the Works of Ben Jonson*, 7 vols, ed. David Bevington, Martin Butler, and Ian Donaldson (Cambridge: Cambridge University Press, 2012), with citations being to volume and line numbers.
2 On Spenser's 'literary career', see Richard Helgerson, *Self-Crowned Laureates: Spenser, Jonson, Milton, and the Literary System* (Berkeley: University of California Press, 1983), 1-20. On Spenser as a 'golden' poet, see C.S. Lewis, *English Literature of the Sixteenth Century* (Oxford: Oxford University Press, 1954), 347-93; for 'golden' as a concept, see 64-5, 323. On Spenser's style as 'flowery' and 'sweet', see David Scott Wilson-Okamura, *Spenser's International Style* (Cambridge: Cambridge University Press, 2013), 79-84.
3 For Donne as an amateur, see Helgerson, *Self-Crowned Laureates*, 30-5; cf. Arthur F. Marotti, *John Donne, Coterie Poet* (Madison: University of Wisconsin Press, 1986). On the ongoing utility of 'metaphysical', see Michael Schoenfeldt, 'Metaphysical Poetry', in Roland Greene (ed.), *Princeton Encyclopedia of Poetry and Poetics*, 4th ed. (Princeton: Princeton University Press, 2012), 871. On Ovid as an amateur, see Helgerson, 26, 35; for Donne's commitment to Ovid, see, e.g., Kevin Pask, *The Emergence of the English Author: Scripting the Life of the Poet in Early Modern England* (Cambridge: Cambridge University Press, 1996), 136. On Donne as a 'careerist', see John Carey, *John Donne: Life, Mind, and Art* (New York: Oxford University Press, 1981), 69-70. I discuss these topics in 'Donne's Literary Career', in Michael Schoenfeldt (ed.), *John Donne in Context* (Cambridge: Cambridge University Press, (2019), 5-17.
4 On Donne's interest in print culture, see Katherine Rundell, 'Donne in Print', in Schoenfeldt (ed.), *John Donne in Context*, 30-8; and Gary A. Stringer, 'The Composition and Dissemination of Donne's Writings', in Jeanne Shami, Dennis Flynn, and M. Thomas Hester (eds), *The Oxford Handbook of John Donne* (Oxford: Oxford University Press, 2011), 12-25.
5 David L. Sedley, *Skepticism and Sublimity in Montaigne and Milton* (Ann Arbor: University of Michigan Press, 2005), 153.
6 Samuel H. Monk popularized this history: *The Sublime* (1935; Ann Arbor: University of Michigan Press, 1960). For revisionist work, see, in addition to Sedley, David Norbrook, *Writing the English Republic: Poetry, Rhetoric, and Politics, 1627-1660* (Cambridge: Cambridge University Press, 1999), 137-41, 212-21; and Patrick Cheney, *Marlowe's Republican Authorship: Lucan, Liberty, and the Sublime* (Basingstoke: Palgrave Macmillan, 2008).
7 On Jonson as Spenser's laureate heir, see Helgerson, *Self-Crowned Laureates*, 101-84; and Ian Donaldson, *Ben Jonson: A Life* (Oxford: Oxford University Press, 2011), 322. On Jonson's commitment in the masques to *grandeur*, *wonder*, *admiration*, and *magnificence*, see Sedley, *Skepticism and Sublimity*, 90-3. For brief discussion of Donne, sublimity, and Longinus, see Gavin Alexander, 'Literary Criticism', who cites Thomas Carew's 1633 elegy, 'the flame / Of thy brave soul ... shot such heat and light / As burnt our earth, and made our darkness bright', to conclude: 'If th[is is] ... not yet evidence of the influence of Longinus' *On the Sublime*, [it is] ... a clear sign that the intellectual climate was ready for it' (98, in Patrick Cheney and Philip Hardie (eds), *1558-1660* (Oxford: Oxford University Press, 2015), volume 2 in *The Oxford History of Classical Reception in English Literature*, 5 vols, ed. Charles Martindale and David Hopkins.
8 I share Fletcher's classification but here adjust his 'Romantic' model in light of *English Authorship and the Early Modern Sublime: Spenser, Marlowe, Shakespeare, Jonson* (Cambridge: Cambridge University Press, 2018). For Fletcher, *The Faerie Queene* is sublime because it is grand in design, enigmatic in

quality, challenging to the mind, ethically free, and finally ambivalent (*Allegory: The Theory of a Symbolic Mode* (Ithaca: Cornell University Press, 1964), 268–9).

9 In connection with Donne, I introduce the link between the sublime and the metaphysical in *Reading Sixteenth-Century Poetry* (Oxford: Wiley-Blackwell, 2011), 159–62, 280–7.

10 *John Donne: Collected Poetry*, ed. Ilona Bell (Harmondsworth: Penguin, 2012), xxix, xxxv. Quotations of Donne's poetry come from this edition.

11 Bell (ed.), *John Donne*, xxviii, xxix, xxvii, xxxviii.

12 Expostulation 19, quoted in Bell (ed.), *John Donne*, xxxiv.

13 Bell (ed.), *John Donne*, xxxiv, xxxii, xxxv, xxxix, xlv.

14 See Gordon Teskey's essays on Spenserian thinking: '"And Therefore as a Stranger Give it Welcome": Courtesy and Thinking', *Spenser Studies*, 18 (2003), 343–59; and 'Thinking Moments in *The Faerie Queene*', *Spenser Studies*, 22 (2007), 103–25. The fact that Spenser promotes thought does not mean he resolves what Fletcher sees as Spenser's 'core of profound ambivalence' (*Allegory*, 273).

15 On Spenserian 'idealism', see Kenneth Borris, *Visionary Spenser and the Poetics of Early Modern Platonism* (Oxford: Oxford University Press, 2017).

16 See Carey, *John Donne*, on 'the two vital factors in his career, his desertion of the Roman Catholic Church and his ambition' (14). On Donne's Protestantism, see Barbara Lewalski, *Protestant Poetics and the Seventeenth-Century Religious Lyric* (Princeton: Princeton University Press, 1976), 253–82; and Achsah Guibbory, 'Donne and Apostasy', in Shami et al. (eds), *Oxford Handbook of John Donne*, 664–77. For Spenser, see, e.g., Linda Gregerson, *The Reformation of the Subject: Spenser, Milton, and the English Protestant Epic* (Cambridge: Cambridge University Press, 1995); and Claire McEachern, 'Spenser and Religion', in Richard A. McCabe (ed.), *Oxford Handbook of Edmund Spenser* (Oxford: Oxford University Press, 2010), 30–47.

17 See Leo Braudy, *The Frenzy of Renown: Fame and Its History* (New York: Oxford University Press, 1986), 161–7: fame occurs along the horizontal axis of time, on earth, with respect to posterity, while glory occurs along the vertical axis of eternity, in heaven, with respect to God. St Augustine transposes classical poetic fame from Virgil and Horace to Christian glory. See also Philip Hardie, *Rumour and Renown: Representations of Fama in Western Literature* (Cambridge: Cambridge University Press, 2012).

18 Helgerson, *Self-Crowned Laureates*, 100.

19 Colin Burrow, 'Spenser's Genres', in McCabe (ed.), *Oxford Handbook of Edmund Spenser*, 403–19.

20 See, e.g., *The Oxford Edition of the Collected Works of Edmund Spenser*, 6 vols, ed. Patrick Cheney, Elizabeth Fowler, Joseph Loewenstein, David Lee Miller, and Andrew Zurcher (Oxford: Oxford University Press, forthcoming).

21 Heather Dubrow, *A Happier Eden: The Politics of Marriage in the Stuart Epithalamion* (Ithaca: Cornell University Press, 1990), 151–200; and Camille Wells Slights, 'The Epithalamion', in Shami et al. (eds), *Oxford Handbook of John Donne*, 298–307.

22 On Spenser as a national funeral elegist, see Patrick Cheney, 'From Dido to Daphne: Early Modern Death in Spenser's Shorter Poems', *Spenser Studies*, 18 (2003), 143–63. On Donne, see Claude J. Summers, 'The Epicede and Obsequy', in Shami et al. (eds), *Oxford Handbook of John Donne*, 286–97.

23 See Anne Lake Prescott, 'Menippean Donne', in Shami et al. (eds), *Oxford Handbook of John Donne*, 160–3.

24 Annabel Patterson, 'Satirical Writing: Donne in Shadows', in Achsah Guibbory (ed.), *The Cambridge Companion to John Donne* (Cambridge: Cambridge University Press, 2006), 118. Patterson's claim has its importance yet appears tendentious, for Donne competes with both Joseph Hall and John Marston for the title of first to write a book-collection of satires (see, e.g., Hallett Smith, *Elizabethan Poetry: A Study in Conventions, Meaning, and Expression* (1952; Cambridge, MA: Harvard University Press, 1966), 245. Of course, Skelton, Wyatt, Surrey, and even Spenser precede this trio as authors of satirical poetry; for a recent summary, see Cheney, *Reading Sixteenth-Century Poetry*, 106–11, 283–4; for criticism, see 307–8, 310.

25 For the same markers, Spenser totals only twenty-one (one for sonnet; three for elegy; sixteen for hymn; and one for obsequy). Spenser does use other generic names, such as 'pastoral' (twice), which Donne does not use.

26 On Spenser's coinage of 'prothalamion', see *The Works of Edmund Spenser: A Variorum Edition*, 11 vols, ed. Edwin Greenlaw et al. (Baltimore: Johns Hopkins University Press, 1932–57), 8.495. On Donne's coinage of 'valediction', see Ramie Targoff, *John Donne: Body and Soul* (Chicago: University of Chicago Press, 2008), 1.

27 Quoted in *The Faerie Queene*, ed. A.C. Hamilton, textual ed. Hiroshi Yamashita and Toshiyuki Suzuki (Harlow: Longman, 2001), 29.

28 On Spenser's debt to Holinshed and Stowe, see *The Faerie Queene*, ed. Hamilton, 247.
29 Bell (ed.), *John Donne*, 350.
30 See also *Amoretti* 61, 22, and *Epithalamion*, lines 208, 423, in Edmund Spenser, *The Yale Edition of the Shorter Poems of Edmund Spenser*, ed. William A. Oram et al. (New Haven: Yale University Press, 1989); all quotations will be from this edition. In 'November', Spenser calls Dido 'the saynt of shepheards' (line 176).
31 On the Augustinian-based Du Bartas career, see Patrick Cheney, *Spenser's Famous Flight: A Renaissance Idea of a Literary Career* (Toronto: University of Toronto Press, 1993), 56–62 (including scholarship, which does not limit the divine poetry movement to Du Bartas but none the less gives him credit for accelerating the movement in England). On Donne's authorship conforming to an Augustinian narrative, see Pask, *The Emergence of the English Author*, 127.
32 On *recusatio*, see Patrick Cheney, 'Literary Careers', in Cheney and Hardie (eds), *1558–1660*, 177–8.
33 Young, 'The Elegy', in Shami et al. (eds), *Oxford Handbook of John Donne*, 136.
34 See Patrick Cheney, *Marlowe's Counterfeit Profession: Ovid, Spenser, Counter-Nationhood* (Toronto: University of Toronto Press, 1997), 9–13.
35 See Marlowe, *Ovid's Elegies* (I.5–8) in *The Collected Poems of Christopher Marlowe*, ed. Patrick Cheney and Brian J. Striar (New York: Oxford University Press, 2006).
36 Moss, *The Ovidian Vogue: Literary Fashion and Imitative Practice in Late Elizabethan England* (Toronto: University of Toronto Press, 2014), 179.
37 Patterson sees lines 1–6 as a turn away from satire ('Satirical Writing', 125). See Summers on the conclusion to the Harrington elegy as Donne's announcement that he is writing his last funeral elegy – even though, as Summers adds, Donne goes on to write one more ('Epicede and Obsequy', in Shami et al. (eds), *Oxford Handbook of John Donne*, 297). I discuss *Metempsychosis* below.
38 I am grateful to Michael Schoenfeldt for help in sorting the generic cast of this verse out.
39 As we shall see, *La Corona* is important not merely for its robust representation of Donne's genre patterning but also for its central position in the printing of Donne's poems in the early editions.
40 Hereendeen, '"I launch at paradise, and saile toward home": *The Progresse of the Soule* as Palinode', *Early Modern Literary Studies*, 7 (2001), 9.1–28, online at paragraph 5.
41 Allen, 'The Double Journey of John Donne', in Arnold Williams (ed.), *A Tribute to George Coffin Taylor* (Chapel Hill: University of North Carolina Press, 1952), 89, 91; Prescott, 'Menippean Donne', 161.
42 Virgil, *Aeneid* I.1 (*Arma virumque cano*), in H. Rushton Fairclough (ed. and trans.), *Virgil*, Loeb Classical Library, 2 vols (Cambridge, MA: Harvard University Press, 1935), vol. 1.
43 DiPasquale, 'Donne, Women, and the Spectre of Misogyny', in Shami et al. (eds), *Oxford Handbook of John Donne*, 679.
44 See Stuart Gillespie, 'Literary Afterlives: Metempsychosis from Ennius to Jorge Luis Borges', in Philip Hardie and Helen Moore (eds), *Classical Literary Careers and Their Reception* (Cambridge: Cambridge University Press, 2010), 209–26.
45 Cf. Prescott, 'Menippean Donne', 160.
46 See David Quint, *Epic and Empire: Politics and Generic Form from Virgil to Milton* (Princeton: Princeton University Press), 248–6; and Jerome S. Dees, 'Ship Imagery', in A.C. Hamilton et al. (eds), *The Spenser Encyclopedia* (Toronto: University of Toronto Press, 1990), 655–6.
47 Burrow, *Epic Romance: Homer to Milton* (Oxford: Clarendon, 1993).
48 Shaw, *The Sublime* (London: Routledge, 2006), 11.
49 Porter, *The Sublime in Antiquity* (Cambridge: Cambridge University Press, 2016), 228. Porter has performed a huge service for the humanities in untethering the sublime from both Longinus and the word itself, concentrating on the concept and its 'markers': Longinus alone 'has some seventy-odd ways to denominate the sublime' (15), which Porter divides into seven categories (180–3), concluding that '[t]hese are only the most common verbal markers, and often virtual equivalents, of sublimity' (182): '*hupsos*-words'; '*meg*-words'; '*dein*-words'; '*huper*-words'; '*ek*-words'; '*ogk*-words'; and 'additional terms' (180–1).
50 Shaw, *The Sublime*, 156.
51 'Sublime', in Simon Hornblower and Antony Spawforth (eds), *The Oxford Classical Dictionary*, 3rd ed. (Oxford: Oxford University Press, 2003), 1450.
52 Longinus, *On Sublimity*, in D.A. Russell and M. Winterbottom (eds), *Classical Literary Criticism* (Oxford: Oxford University Press, 1989), 143.
53 Longinus, *On Sublimity*, 159.
54 Ibid., 144.
55 Shaw, *The Sublime*, 3.

56 *English Renaissance Literary Criticism*, ed. Brian Vickers (Oxford: Oxford University Press, 1999), 25.
57 Longinus, *On Sublimity*, 189.
58 See Bernard Weinberg, 'Translations and Commentaries of Longinus, "On the Sublime", to 1600: A Bibliography', *Modern Philology*, 47 (1950), 145–51.
59 See Roald Hoffmann and Iain Boyd Whyte (eds), *Beyond the Finite: The Sublime in Art and Science* (Oxford: Oxford University Press, 2011): 'This volume represents a first attempt to extend the discussion of the sublime into the realm of the natural scientist' (vii). On the classical sublime, see Porter, *The Sublime in Antiquity*; on the medieval sublime, see C. Stephen Jaeger (ed.), *Magnificence and the Sublime in Medieval Aesthetics: Art, Architecture, Literature, and Music* (Basingstoke: Palgrave Macmillan, 2010). On the early modern sublime, see Eva Madeline Martin, 'The "Prehistory" of the Sublime in Early Modern France: An Interdisciplinary Perspective', in Timothy Costelloe (ed.), *The Sublime: Antiquity to the Present* (Cambridge: Cambridge University Press, 2012), 77–101; and Caroline van Eck et al. (eds), *Translations of the Early Modern Sublime: The Early Modern Reception and Dissemination of Longinus' Perì hýpsous in Rhetoric, the Visual Arts, Architecture, and the Theatre* (Boston: Brill, 2012).
60 Kant, *Critique of the Power of Judgment*, Paul Guyer (trans.) and Paul Guyer and Eric Matthews (eds) (Cambridge: Cambridge University Press, 2000), 129.
61 Ibid., 129, 134.
62 Ibid., 134. Kant's model 'subjectivized' theories of the sublime then current (Paul Guyer, 'The German Sublime After Kant', in Costelloe (ed.), *The Sublime*, 102).
63 Alexander, 'Literary Criticism', 97. For Rainolds, see *Oratio 3. Post festum natalis Christi. Orationes duodecim* (1573/4) (London, 1619), 327–37, first noted by William A. Ringler, Jr, 'An Early Reference to Longinus', *Modern Language Notes*, 53 (1938), 23–4. For Chapman, see the dedicatory epistle to *The Whole Works of Homer* (London, 1614), in Vickers (ed.), *Literary Criticism*, 522–3. For Junius, see *The Painting of the Ancients in Three Books* (London, 1638), an Englishing of his 1637 *De pictura veterum*, called by Alexander 'one of the most important early seventeenth-century critical works' ('Literary Criticism', 97). In *Sidney and Junius on Poetry and Painting: From the Margins to the Center* (Newark: University of Delaware Press, 2007), Judith Dundas discusses Junius's in-depth treatment of Longinus, and examines it with respect to Sidney's poetics (37–8, 100–1, 106–7, 134, 207). I discuss Junius, Chapman, and Rainolds in *English Authorship and the Early Modern Sublime*, Introduction and Chapters 1 and 4. I have not been able to verify that Donne knew Junius, but they shared a friendship with John Selden, and they both knew Lancelot Andrewes (compare Sophie van Romburgh, 'Junius [Du Jon], Franciscus', *Dictionary of National Biography* online, and both R.C. Bald, *John Donne: A Life* (Oxford: Oxford University Press, 1970), 438 (on Selden), and Peter McCullough, 'Donne and Court Chaplaincy', in Shami et al. (eds), *Oxford Handbook of John Donne*, 559–61 (on Andrewes)). Junius and Donne may also have shared a connection with Thomas Howard, Earl of Arundel (compare Romburgh and Bald, 199). Thanks to Mckenzie Eggers for help with this research.
64 Longinus, *On Sublimity*, 158–62.
65 Ibid., 162, 158.
66 Ibid., 150.
67 Ibid., 156.
68 Ibid., 149.
69 Ibid., 158.
70 Ibid., 177.
71 Ibid., 159.
72 Ibid., 152.
73 Ibid., 159.
74 Ibid., 162. See Jean-François Lyotard, 'Presenting the Unpresentable', *Artforum*, 20 (1986), 64–8.
75 Longinus, *On Sublimity*, 150.
76 See Harvey, 'Nomadic Souls: Pythagoras, Spenser, Donne', *Spenser Studies* 22 (2007), 259.
77 Bell (ed.), *John Donne*, 401.
78 Ibid.
79 See Cheney, *English Authorship and the Early Modern Sublime*, esp. chapters 2–4. The Introduction contains a version of the discussion below on 'Valediction of the Book'.
80 A.J. Smith (ed.), *John Donne: The Complete English Poems* (Harmondsworth: Penguin, 1976), 656.
81 See Wilson-Okamura, *Spenser's International Style*: 'In England, there was during the [Renaissance] ... a broadly based effort to make lyric poetry more astonishing and sublime; and by so doing, to appropriate the sweeping forcefulness of epic style', citing James Biester's *Lyric Wonder: Rhetoric and Wit in Renaissance Poetry* (Ithaca: Cornell University Press, 1997) on 'the rough meter, daring metaphors,

and clipped syntax of George Chapman and John Donne' (110). In Donne's list of five classical poets, Homer, Virgil, and Lucan have been singled out for their contribution to a history of the sublime: on Homer, see Longinus himself, who identifies the *Iliad* as the originary sublime work (e.g., 8.2, 9.5–8, 9.10–15; 149, 150–2, 152–4); see Porter, *Sublime in Antiquity*, 360–81, 542–7); on Virgil, see Hardie, *Lucretian Receptions: History, The Sublime, Knowledge* (Cambridge: Cambridge University Press, 2009), 67–135; and on Lucan, see Norbrook, *Writing the English Republic*, 31–2, 137–9, 212–21; and Cheney, *Marlowe's Republican Authorship*.
82 Bell (ed.), *John Donne*, 447.
83 Ibid., 446.
84 Longinus quotes Genesis 1, 'God said … "Let there be light", and there was light; "Let there be earth", and there was earth', in order to present 'the lawgiver of the Jews' as 'no ordinary man – for he understood and expressed God's power in accordance with its worth' (9.9, 152). On the Biblical sublime, see Erich Auerbach, *Literary Language and Its Public in Late Latin Antiquity and in the Middle Ages*, trans. R. Manheim (New York: Pantheon, 1965), 27–81; C. Stephen Jaeger, 'Introduction' and 'Richard of St. Victor and the Medieval Sublime', in Jaeger (ed.), *Magnificence*, 1–16, 157–78; and Dietmar Till, 'The Sublime and the Bible: Longinus, Protestant Dogmatics, and the "Sublime Style"', in Caroline van Eck et al. (eds), *Translations*, 55–64.
85 Targoff, *John Donne*, 1.
86 Hamilton (ed.), *The Faerie Queene*, 271.
87 Sedley, *Skepticism and Sublimity*, 9 and 157 n.17.
88 On ecstasy, *furor*, and sublimity via *phantasia* in the Italian Renaissance, see Eugenio Refini, 'Longinus and Poetic Imagination', in van Eck et al. (eds), *Translations of the Early Modern Sublime*, 41. On Plato and the sublime, see Porter, *Sublime in Antiquity*, 557–617; on ecstasy, 295–6 (see also Index).
89 Targoff, *John Donne*, 2.
90 Hamilton (ed.), *The Faerie Queene*, 405.
91 In passing, René Graziani cites Spenser's representation as an analogue for Donne: 'John Donne's "The Extasie" and Ecstasy', *Review of English Studies*, 19 (1968), 123.
92 See Andrew Hadfield, 'Literary Contexts: Predecessors and Contemporaries', in Guibbory (ed.), *The Cambridge Companion to John Donne*, 60–3. Also on Donne's poetic project, see Hadfield, 'Donne's *Songs and Sonnets* and Artistic Identity', in Patrick Cheney, Hadfield, and Garrett A. Sullivan, Jr (eds), *Early Modern English Poetry: A Critical Companion* (New York: Oxford University Press, 2007), 206–16.
93 Longinus, *On Sublimity*, 166.
94 Targoff argues that Donne's 'deepest fantasy' was to have 'body and soul to be perfectly joined' (*John Donne*, 23, 22), underscoring Donne's 'interest … in ecstatic experience' (31). Overwhelmingly, Donne critics enter the conceptual terrain of the sublime only to bypass it.
95 I am grateful to Yulia Ryzhik and Julian Lethbridge for their help in revising this chapter. Thanks, too, to my Research Assistant, Mckenzie Eggers, for help in checking quotations and citations.

5

Spenser and Donne look to the Continent

Anne Lake Prescott

Edmund Spenser and John Donne often wrote poetry while keeping an inner ear attuned to Continental verses and an informed eye on European history, from the Trojan War to the religious conflicts that were then bloodying lands only a few wet miles from the southern English coast. The differences between their exploitations of Continental texts and their incorporations of current events remain striking. In this condensed set of observations I focus chiefly on their poetry, including that which looks abroad, often with distress, and offer first some reminders of their responses to Continental events or literature and conclude with comments on their responses to one ancient author, Ovid, and to one geographical feature, the hill. As I hope to show, if at the risk of oversimplification, Spenser recalls the Continent and on occasion, often quietly, appropriates its writers; Donne can do the same, but more often flashes and names them, not always with pleasure.

A longer study would include more on the poets' shared interest in Continental politics, for the religious wars and revolts demanded attention: the Spanish threatened Ireland to a degree more terrifying than we usually remember, for example. Living there, Spenser also observed, with interest, alarm, or grief, not only events in that battered country but also those across the English Channel, especially those involving England itself. Elizabeth's unfulfilled plan to marry the much younger Duc d'Alençon, who after his brother's death had become the Duc d'Anjou and in line to inherit the French throne, dismayed him. The Queen fondly called the Prince her 'frog' (although that nickname for the French was not yet established in England), but the Earl of Leicester's circle, to which Spenser was loosely attached, despised and feared such a match. *Mother Hubberds Tale* (its revised version printed in 1591) hints at this now-past anxiety, and it seems likely that the *Shepheardes Calender*'s 'November' eclogue laments not a literal death for its apparently deceased 'Dido' but rather a metaphorical loss, should she in fact marry that 'frog'. The elegy is explicitly based on an eclogue by the French court poet Clément Marot on the death of the 'Treshaulte et tresillustre princesse, Madame Loyse de Savoye' (1527; Marot's father, Jehan, had indeed called his French queen, Anne of Brittany, 'Nostre Dido', presumably meaning the great founder of Carthage, not the seducer of Aeneas). Marot was a witty writer whose translations of more than forty psalms became the basis of the hugely influential 'Marot-Beza' Psalter and whose patronage by François I, likewise a poet, is allegorized in the grateful poet's 1538 eclogue 'soubs les noms de Pan et Robin' on which Spenser modelled 'December'. This royal largesse might have caused envy in England except that Marot's Evangelical leanings made his nervously Catholic king so vexed that for his safety he had been forced to flee France for a time. Marot's troubles would have rendered Spenser all the more aware of the dangers that can accompany royal attention – dangers Donne would have remembered too, although he ultimately secured even more royal patronage than rewarded Spenser. Such political events or situations often appear allegorized in *The Faerie Queene*, from the windy Orgoglio, that earthquake of a giant who befriends the Roman Catholic Whore Duessa and who represents politically the arrogance shown by Philip II when he sent his Armada sailing, to the barely disguised Spanish efforts in Book V to repress the rebellious Netherlands (what Donne's *Elegy XI: The Bracelet* calls 'mangled seventeen-headed *Belgia*') and the allegorical shield that Spenser invents for 'Sir Burbon', the beleaguered Henri de Navarre who threw away his Protestant faith so he could gain the love of the scene's 'Flordelis' – France, with its floral symbol the *fleur de lys*. Donne is less certain about the rights and wrongs, or affects to be so, when he notes in his erotic *Elegy XX: Love's War* (in the same poem calling Ireland 'Sick') that 'In Flanders, who can tell / Whether the Master presse, or men rebell.' In truth, he almost certainly thought the problem was the master's (Spain's) pressure.

Donne is far less given to allegory, as indeed these allusions suggest, and his treatment of developments on the Continent is usually explicit; after all, he had sailed on expeditions that took him to Cadiz and the Azores, for example, and he knew the Continent well and personally. In Robert Collmer's essay on Donne and Spain the number of Continental names, from the Italian Machiavelli to the (Basque) Ignatius Loyola, from the (Portuguese) Jorge de Montemayor to the medical scientist Paracelsus is impressive, and Donne's letters are a rich source for anyone seeking to see how he situated himself intellectually.[1] Indeed, Donne is more likely than Spenser to name names, or at least allow us to decode his lines with little effort. The 'new Philosophy' that calls all in doubt in Donne's *First Anniversary* for Elizabeth Drury (line 205) came from the Continent, after all, and indeed there is evidence that Donne had met Johannes Kepler, one of the innovators whom Donne's prose *Ignatius his Conclave* locates in hell with Loyola and other novelty-makers.[2] In Donne's day Time itself was subject to innovation, or so many thought, thanks to papal instruction. For instance, readers on the Continent might ask if St Lucy's Day is in fact the 'yeares midnight', as Donne calls it in 'A Nocturnal upon *St. Lucies* Day', being the shortest day' and hence offering us the fewest hours of sunshine. Donne so asserts, but he would have known, as did all the educated, and many merchants and sailors as well, that in 1582 the Pope Gregory XIII had introduced the Gregorian calendar. The blinded and martyred St Lucy keeps her day (13 December), but the winter solstice itself has advanced ten days forward, thanks to such interfering – if correct – innovation-peddlers as the astronomer and Jesuit Christopher Clavius. Donne's poem on St Lucy works for England, but not for the Continent, which had largely followed the Pope's proclamation. The 'Nocturnall' is a powerfully moving poem; it also makes a quiet comment on English and Continental treatments of calendrical time, implicitly rejecting the latter.

Each poet had received a decent education, and each had presumably begun his writing career with memories of Virgil, Chaucer, and the rest of what nowadays we would call, if with increased hesitancy, the 'canon'. The two writers, however, deployed that knowledge with other major differences. One can suspect that Spenser wanted his readers to recognize his clear allusions to famous writers or his incorporation of passages familiar to the well educated, but much of what he noticed and recycled in his writings was more a help to his own discourse than something to flaunt to the reader. Donne can seem more explicit, at times indeed flashy, about what he had read and what he was exploiting; the self he presents, although usually not in print but in what many now call 'manuscript publication', is international, suave, sophisticated, witty, slightly naughty, and non-Spenserian. Let the author of *The Faerie Queene* be the Queen's Virgil. Donne, at least early in his career, would be the Inns of Court's English Ovid, although also with moments, and more often in print, as England's satirical Juvenal, Horace, Martial, or Tibullus (see, e.g., this last's *Delia* I.6 and Donne's *Elegy VII* ('Natures lay Ideot'), which Peter DeSa Wiggins argues forcefully is indeed about adultery).[3]

This is hardly to say that Spenser ignored such writers, or Ovid – far from it, as witness the recent revisionary work by Syrithe Pugh – but whatever recent scholarly doubts and modifications concerning his career, his initial presentation of himself as the humble, anonymous 'Immerito', creator of *The Shepheardes Calender*, and the start of his *Faerie Queene* with its English version of Ariosto's opening of *Orlando Furioso* and of the supposed (but cancelled) first two lines of *The Aeneid* would almost certainly suggest to his readers a path already traced, even if not yet very worn, by the Virgilian *rota*'s move from pastoral to epic.[4]

Of course, as a Christian poet who had almost certainly read Guillaume Salluste du Bartas's two *Sepmaines* on the Creation and early Biblical history (1578, 1584), and who in his 'envoy' to Joachim Du Bellay's 'Ruines of Rome' (printed in *Complaints*, 1591) had explicitly noted that the French Huguenot poet's muse Urania had urged poets to write Biblical verse ('l'Uranie', 1574), Spenser knew he could overgo Virgil by writing Christian hymns. He might also have noticed the promise to Du Bartas by 'Uranie' that divine poetry will make kings promote its authors (and indeed that French poet was close to King Henri de Navarre, celebrating his victory at Ivry in verse translated into English). At the very end of Spenser's career as we know it, though, and after some sceptical anti-court lines concluding the last book of *The Faerie Queene* that he saw into print (lines that seem to adapt similarly sceptical ones in Du Bellay's own disillusioned 'Poète courtisanne', 1558), he wheeled back around that *rota* to hope for a Sabbath sight in words recalling, but reversing, the last sonnet of his early translation of Du Bellay's 'Songe' for the 1569 *Theatre for Worldlings*. The illustration in *Theatre* shows what at first look like the Temple's steps to the 'pillours of Eternity' but that are, in that early poem, merely those of an arrogant Rome as it starts to crumble deep into the image. This reversal could of course be a coincidence, but it remains pleasant to consider how Virgil's 'wheel' brought England's first major epic poet back to his earliest and pre-pastoral verse, verse that he owed to the poet who hoped to do for French poetry what one could argue that Virgil had done for Latin.

For both Spenser and Donne, then, the history and literature of the Continent – always mere miles across water but sometimes like another world – were crucial to their imaginations, but in different ways. Spenser, so far as we know, never set a physical foot on the European mainland. Donne travelled there and knew it well, and indeed in 1619 preached a sermon at The Hague when accompanying James Hay, Viscount Doncaster on a European diplomatic tour.[5] It is no surprise that, as John Carey puts it, Donne's reading 'wasn't that of an Englishman but of a European intellectual'.[6] It is typical of his self-situating that in his letters he can refer to such writers as Montaigne, Rabelais, and the Calvinist leader Theodore Beza, and that he not only probably read the *Beehive of the Romish Church*, an anti-Catholic Menippean satire by Philip Marnix (translated in 1636) but also knew Marnix personally. One of his letters, in fact, was accompanied by a 'book of French Satyrs'.[7] As we might put it, he kept up. Like many tradesmen, moreover, if not always to be expected in a poet, Donne can also pun cleverly on Europe's coins, from *Elegy XI: The Bracelet*'s English 'angels' to largely hairless French 'crowns' that are bald, presumably, because they are not only coins but victims of their owners' 'French disease', the illness that we call syphilis. If coins vary, moreover, so do rivers, and Donne's Menippean satire, *Metempsychosis* or *The Progresse of the Soule*, shows off its snarky breadth by working 'Tagus, Po, Sene [Seine], Thames, and Danow [Danube]' into one line (line 16). National stereotypes are vexing, but Donne can make perhaps semi-satirical verse of them, turning those 'others' even more 'other', for example mentioning in his verse letter 'To Sir Henry Wotton' the 'German schisms, and lightnesse / Of France, and faire Italies faithlesnesse' (lines 65–6), and in *Elegy XVI: On His Mistress* calling the French 'changeable Cameleons, / Spittles of diseases, shops of fashions, / Loves fuellers' and artful actors; as for the Dutch, they are 'spungy' and 'hydroptique' (lines 33–42) – in other words they drink too much. Donne clearly wants to project the image of a culturally experienced sophisticate, if one given to playing with national stereotypes, pleasurable clichés that may or may not represent his real beliefs.

Any scroll through scholarly editions of Spenser and Donne reveals many, many other parallels and sources, and I will mention just a few more instances of such reworkings. Donne's *Satire IV*, for example in good part imitates Horace's satire on the pest who walks through Rome with the exasperated speaker (Satire I.ix), and the stubborn pig in Spenser's Bower of Bliss (*FQ* II.xii), who after Sir Guyon's destruction of that witchy garden refuses transformation back to human form, unquestionably descends from the sophist philosopher Gryllus, victim of Circe's transformative powers who snorts in fine Greek and all too persuasive logic his refusal to return from piggish to human form (*Moralia*, 'Beasts are Rational'). To a greater extent than Donne, however, and as notes to editions of his works make clear, Spenser was also drawn to medieval texts. He knew the English Chaucer, of course: although the genealogy of Book I's Wood of Error has many branches, the tree catalogue in the *Parlement of Foules* (lines 176–82) seems to be one of them, and doubtless he also read the widely known *Piers Plowman*.

Less strictly English, though, is the non-canonical but much-read *Acta Pilati*, a dramatic description of Christ's descent to 'harrow' hell and rescue those who deserve heaven; it is hard not to recall this vivid rescue operation when reading about the descent of Prince Arthur to rescue St George in *FQ* I.viii.40. Similarly deserving attention, although not often cited among the medieval texts that Spenser almost certainly knew and exploited, is Stephen Bateman's *Travayled Pylgrime* (1569), a translation of the Burgundian poet Olivier de la Marche's 1483 *Le Chevalier Délibéré*, by way of the Spanish Hernando de Acuña's version.[8] *Chevalier* is a pilgrimage allegory, one with a structure derived ultimately from St Bernard of Clairvaux, in which the knightly protagonist, accompanied by the lady Memory riding like Spenser's Una on her own horse, visits Error (the illustration in Bateman's translation looks much like the palace belonging to Spenser's prideful Lucifera), then Pride, then Despair, and last finds rest in a heavenly palace; true, George's rest is as yet temporary. The structure fits Spenser's Book I, although at least one scholar has found traces of La Marche in Book II.[9]

It is also good to remember, moreover, when thinking of Spenser's possible awareness of medieval texts with a Continental connection, that the implied *visual* format of the printed *Calender* is not just Ovid's unfinished *Fasti* or some Renaissance Italian and French illustrated texts but also the traditional medieval missals, often printed on the Continent for an English readership before the reigns of Edward and Elizabeth; printers abroad were better equipped to reproduce complex woodcuts: such missals were found without difficulty even in Protestant England. 'Februarie' in such illustrated texts is particularly relevant, for it is often said to be the month when Age should educate Youth before the ordinary (although not the astronomical or ecclesiastical) year begins and age has its last chance to discipline the young. Often the image is of a schoolteacher, switch visibly in hand, with a crowd of schoolboys in front of him and, frequently, one boy in the background being disciplined. Yes, Eld trains Youth, and in Spenser's 'Februarie' Youth is not happy with this. As the months rotate, youth will learn how the old man feels – and will perhaps wield the whip himself.

There are of course, many other 'sources' for these two poets' works, although whether 'intertexts' is a trickier question, for they are not always meant, one suspects, to be noticed. Are we meant to hear Torquato Tasso's birds in *Jerusalem Delivered* (XVI.14-15) twittering though those birds in the Bower of Bliss (*FQ* II.xii)? It is hard to say. But it seems less likely that Spenser intended us to recognize and admire his adaptations of sonnets in Philippe Desportes's *Diane*. *Amoretti* 22, a sonnet linking erotic longing to Christian, indeed almost Catholic, imagery, takes its conceit from that French poet's *Diane* I.43, for example, and *Amoretti* 15, on the lady's beauties, reworks that French poet's own adaptation of a sonnet by the Petrarchan Italian poet Panfilo Sasso (1455-1527). To hear such 'borrowings' at least lets us contemplate how Spenser adds praise of her *mind* to the physical loveliness admired by first the Italian and then the French Petrarchist poet, but, although Desportes's fame in England was real, it is not clear that Spenser intended us to notice such modification, one that suits his shift from Petrarchan frustration to pre-marital compliment to his lady's inwardness. Similarly, are we meant to read *Amoretti* and *Epithalamion*, love poetry to a woman the speaker marries, as a show-off triumph over the usual Petrarchan longing for an unobtainable woman? Perhaps. In his *Rime* 190 and 189, sonnets imitated by Wyatt ('Whoso list to hunt', 'My galley'), Petrarch can neither catch the deer he pursues nor bring his ship to harbour; in sonnet 67 Spenser, who unlike Petrarch had no clerical vows of celibacy to keep, welcomes his deer's surrender in a version of that hunt probably taken from a religious adaptation by Marguerite de Navarre of another erotic hunting poem, and in *Amoretti* 63 he had already made his way closer to shore.[10]

The revision of Petrarch's frustrations is vital, significant, but it seems unlikely that Spenser thought most readers would recall that the Neolatinist poets Giovanni Pontano and Jean Salmon Macrin had also written love poems and epithalamia to women whom they had married. These writers were hardly household names in Anglophone lands. Spenser's adaptations and appropriations, then, can snake through much of Europe, but they do not always do so in hopes of being watched. True, these reworkings can seem significant when examined. Spenser knew Du Bellay's sonnet sequence *Olive*, with its title's complex play on, among other matters, the Petrarchan 'laurel', but did he observe that this sonnet sequence, like his *Amoretti*, carries liturgical allusions in its very structure? Perhaps Spenser noticed, or perhaps with Petrarch's 366 lyrics – a year plus a turn to the Virgin Mary – he had no need of French poets (after all, a fellow English poet, Giles Fletcher, had offered his 'Licia' a year of sonnets with some extra lines because the sequence was printed in 1592, a leap year). It can be hard, then, especially at this distance, to know when we are invited to applaud a reworking or when, in an age largely indifferent to what we would call plagiarism, we are meant simply to admire the author's invention. When Donne writes his clever poem ('The Flea') we might – or might not – recall that flea poems were then fashionable in France.[11] If indeed 'Sapho to Philænis' is Donne's, we can wonder if he had read Ronsard's 'lesbian' poem in *Elegies, Mascarades et Bergerie* (1565; withdrawn in 1584, it was restored in 1609); he does refer to Ronsard in his prose pieces.[12] (It is something to ponder that in both France and England the earliest surviving lesbian poems, in all their ambivalence, and some would add sexual ignorance, are by men.)

I offer here one more example of sources' and roots' complexities: Spenser's ageing allegorical oak in the *Calender*'s 'Februarie', once admired, now neglected and under the threat of imminent fall or felling, strongly resembles a tree in the Roman poet Lucan's *Pharsalia (The Civil War)*, I.136–43, symbol of the older Pompey, who is now facing his rival Julius Caesar. Spenser thriftily re-transplanted this oak, so to speak, both for his *Teares of the Muses* and for the lamenting lost city Verlame in *The Ruines of Time*, grieved by her city's ruination and Time's flow. Lucan's long poem had dreadful relevance to modern war-torn Europe, so it is possible that Spenser wants us to recognize the sources of his (and Du Bellay's) trees, rivers, and tears. Sometimes a 'source' serves also as an 'allusion', but often not. In this case Lucan's senescent and threatened Roman oak lived a long time in Spenser's works, from the *Calender* to *Complaints*.

And now two brief examinations, first of the two poets' transformation of Ovid and then of their use of that ancient topos, the hill.

Spenser's vacations were not always Ovidian, for he took another break from epic by adapting the *Culex*, which (whatever modern doubts) he almost certainly thought was by the author of *The Aeneid*, as *Virgils Gnat*. Like Ronsard, whose unfinished *Franciade* Spenser may have recalled when writing *The Faerie Queene*, Spenser can seem nervous about being unable to bring his epic to a conclusion. No wonder he offers more promises in *Amoretti* 80, although one can wonder if the moon that peeps through his window in *Epithalamion* might not recall a vexed Elizabeth, so often called lunar, wondering where her epic has gone. Certainly in the Proem to Book IV of *The Faerie Queene* there had been a clear allusion to Ovid's own generic discomfort (if perhaps a discomfort more assumed for the judgement of Augustus than in fact deeply personal). When Spenser alludes in that Proem to the 'rugged forehead' who is dissatisfied with the poet's concern for love, he would evoke memories of Ovid's claim in *Amores* I.1 that he writes elegiacs, not epic hexameter, because Cupid had flown by and stolen the syllable he needed for the higher genre. In *Amores* III.1 he explains further that even as elegy came, limping slightly on her uneven feet (a witty allusion to the elegiac alternation of pentameter and hexameter), tragedy – not epic, but a higher genre than elegy – had come striding with a darkened brow. That brow ('fronte … torva') surely anticipates Spenser's perhaps nervous allusion to the 'rugged forehead' that condemns the would-be writer of epic for his recent interest in love. Whose forehead, if anybody's, is not fully clear; perhaps the Cecil family, but in any case presumably somebody waiting for a true Virgilian epic and not amorous Ovidian escapism.

For young John Donne, flashes of Ovid can seem more fanciful, show-off, self-positioning the author as a smart young man with wit and education. In his younger years, imitating Ovid was less a departure from epic, a slip into the erotic that might attract the anger of that furrowed brow with hexameter feet, than an imitation of a smart Roman-about-town, albeit one who would indeed one day draw an emperor's frowns (no one knows the exact cause) and would end his career writing his *Tristia* in exile on the Black Sea shore. Ovid's wit and erotic ingenuity could be modified to show off the cleverness of a young man studying law in London's Inns of Court or perhaps attract the attention and patronage of those able to hire and promote him. Donne's Ovidian moments, as were Spenser's, were almost certainly meant to be noticed and admired as clever reworkings, not mere cleverness purse-picked from another's wit, as Sidney put it even while borrowing from others for *Astrophil and Stella*. In a bravura performance of genre-mixing that combines classical allusion, personification, allegory, and medieval fabliau (*FQ* III.ix.30), Spenser has his would-be adulterer Paridell scribble love-messages in spilled wine – to which the lady Hellenore responds in the next stanza with her own alcoholic scribbles. The educated, doubtless including some amused women readers, would probably recognize Ovid's advice to would-be lovers, even without a footnote.[13] The passage, generically and wittily, recalls exactly the swerve into the erotic that the Proem defends in Ovidian terms. Paridell's adulterous behaviour is a threat not just to his host's marriage but to the author's generic claims as he from time to time deploys them. For a moment, the furrowed brow and epic hexameter (even if in truth, of course, Spenser used pentameter for eight of his stanza's lines and swerves into hexameter only for the ninth) can witness the syllable-stealing Cupid at work, and not for the better.

Although we may be meant to admire his tactics more than his morals, Donne's own Ovidian moments seem to adopt lines from the *Amores* to make the writer appear witty, worldly, well-versed, if not respectable (after all, Ovid boasts of seducing married women). Two moments stand out. In what would seem an anti-Petrarchan and by Donne's time an anti-Platonic move, Donne boasts that 'I can love both faire and browne' ('The Indifferent'). Shakespeare claims that he can be content with dark eyes, not the conventional blue, but Donne can be happy with either. It seems safe to assume that many of his amused readers, holding a manuscript, of course, not a printed book, would remember how in *Amores* II.4 Ovid writes that 'I yield to golden-haired, but also can love the darker' (lines 39–40). Donne's 'The Sunne Rising' is less wayward morally, although his arrogance in first telling the sun to stand still and then allowing it to rest over his bedroom and shine on his bed is delicious. Donne almost certainly hoped that his friends would remember *Amores* I.xiii, in which Ovid anticipates the waking lover's imperious orders to the sun – only to admit at the end that the sun 'rose no later than is its habit' (line 48). Donne's tone is Ovidian: both erotic in its bedroom setting and amusing in its self-mocking, show-off arrogance. If Ovid served Spenser as a way to modify his epic, like a painter adding shading or playing with perspective, the Roman poet of love and (probably assumed) cynicism served Donne as a way of escaping not only Virgil but also Petrarch and his followers, a group perhaps including Spenser.

The complex differences between the two poets show also in their mental Continental geography (although Donne's response to Europe was beyond mental), not least when they were imagining significant hills offering religious challenges to those who climb them, or fail to. Perhaps they also remembered Petrarch's Mount Ventoux or, if as yet less often read in Renaissance England, Dante's Purgatory. In *The Faerie Queene* I.x the Redcrosse Knight – after his training in the House of Holinesse and about to learn his identity as the sanctified but earthy St George (a georgic en route to epic transcendence) – manages, with guidance from the hermit Contemplation, to ascend a hill that Spenser compares to Moses' Sinai, Christ's Olivet, and, with appealing but ambiguous pride, the poets' Parnassus. The high hill is a multi-signifying mount from which St George can see the New Jerusalem. His vision inevitably recalls that of St John on the Isle of Patmos (Revelation 21), a Biblical moment illustrated for one of the sonnets that Jan van der Noot added to those he or somebody asked Spenser to translate for the English version of *Theatre for Worldlings* (D5v; the angel points up, but the city is, curiously, hanging below the earthly hill). Spenser would also, I have argued, have had a mental image of the impressive mount with Biblical parallels in Guy Le Fèvre de la Boderie's 1578 Biblical-Orphic-Platonic *La Galliade* (IV, 649–58).[14] That Spenser expected his readers to make a mental association with Le Fèvre's stirring scene, one resonating with cosmology and number symbolism, seems doubtful, for the Biblical hills were far more famous, but a number of details suggest that he had that French hill in mind, perhaps all the more vividly so because Le Fèvre was attached to the Duc d'Anjou, that prince whose courtship of Elizabeth caused such alarm in England's Sidney/Leicester circle and who figures, as I have noted, allegorized and with distaste, in *Mother Hubberds Tale* (1591).[15]

Contemplation's hill, up which St George climbs, makes an interesting contrast to that on which Donne's Truth stands in *Satire III*, and which nobody in the satire manages to scale. (Why a *hill* and not, say, a cave with an oracle, is intriguing to consider.) Donne's speaker in *Satire III*, although not himself, or not yet, climbing the hill, imagines Truth standing atop it so that, we read, to win her and, presumably, to learn what she knows, we must trudge round and round the slope on an upward but curving path. Nor, furthermore, does Donne promise a hermit of Holiness to lead us around and up to where we can gaze in wonder at the great city visible from its peak, providing us only with the suggestion that we trace religious truth by asking our fathers, grandfathers, and so forth. This advice on how to reach the top of the hill assumes, of course, that all those mothers and grandmothers have been faithful, a grim challenge to husbands that Donne would have known was the chief issue in Rabelais's later books with their dubious and doubting would-be husband, Panurge, who seeks truth from a Sybil with a bottle. It comes as no surprise, then, that in *Satire IV*, which also mentions the Continental Beza, Calepino's dictionary, and the famed obscene pictures by Aretino, the speaker mentions Rabelais's Panurge, also citing him as a fine linguist (line 59; cf. *Pantagruel* 1542 ed., ch. 9, the same text with a list of imaginary books that inspired Donne's 'Courtiers library').

Spenser, then, remembered the Bible and such writers as Tasso but also, I think, borrowed details from a successful Renaissance French writer, Guy Le Fèvre. Donne's hill has such parallels too, of course, although I find no memory of *La Galliade*, but his hill rises in verse satire that hardly achieves such heavenly gaze, alluding rather to very modern dilemmas and figures. Religious indecision is figured as a set of modern Continental names (and one English one): should we listen to the antiquity-claiming 'Mirreus' in Rome, sullen young 'Crantz' in Geneva, or our own 'Graius' (then there are 'Phrygius' who abhors all and 'Graccus' who loves everyone); it will not suffice, says the speaker, to ascribe one's faith to Philip (possibly Philip II, if more likely Philip Melanchthon), (Pope) Gregory, Martin (Luther), or our own Henry VIII. Spenser's hill is one we can climb, if as yet only in contemplation, and the passage looks to Scripture and with a quiet memory of other hills in European literature. Donne's steep and resistant hill arises in a land beset by religious discord symbolized by names of European leaders, including the German, Italian, and Swiss fomenters of that discord. St George has a quiet time of it, and his foreign sources, from the obvious Biblical to the less legible Continental, point to transcendence and peace. Donne's satirist lives in a world made noisy by many opposing voices, a few at home, but most European. The difference between the way the two hills relate to the Continent, explicitly and obviously for Donne and, beyond the biblical, with some quiet borrowing for Spenser, is typical: Spenser performs, if quietly, some intertextuality and appropriation; Donne more often names names.

The Continent was not simply an 'over there' for English (and by Donne's full adulthood more properly 'British') poets; it was the source of much of what Spenser and Donne read in school, a land of greatness and such pleasures as wine, but also a nearby landscape with much that can be feared, from invasion and conspiracy to diseases. That Spenser and Donne exploited its various literatures from various ages is hardly surprising, and neither is their acute awareness of what was happening so close to England. If I may end with a mini-editorial: all too often my fellow professors of early modern English literature forget or at least ignore such awareness of the Continent on the part of England's great poets. We too should keep at least a corner of an eye on the other side of what Shakespeare's John of Gaunt, in *Richard II*, called a defensive watery 'moat'. Not an ocean, just a moat around a house. We benefit from keeping that moat in our eye (on the other side lies more than a mote, more even than a beam) and remember to look to its other shore when we think of what Spenser and Donne saw, admired, stole, flaunted, wanted, and feared.

Notes

1. Robert G. Collmer, 'John Donne: His Spanish Connections', *Mediterranean Studies*, 18 (2009), 168–84; Collmer notes the Spanish associations of the portrait, dated 1591, printed with his 1635 edition of his poems.
2. Wilbur Applebaum, 'Donne's Meeting with Kepler: A Previously Unknown Episode', *Philological Quarterly*, 50.1 (1971), 132–4.
3. On Donne's use of Tibullus (and of many other writers) see Peter DeSa Wiggins, *Donne, Castiglione, and the Poetry of Courtliness* (Bloomington: Indiana University Press, 2000), 81ff. Wiggins quotes Donne's inaccurate assertion that 'I am no great voyager in other mens work, no swallower nor devourer of volumes' (37), in the same passage claiming to have thrown away his Dante. On Tibullus I.6 and Donne see also Wiggins, 'The Love Quadrangle: Tibullus 1.6 and Donne's "lay Ideot"', *Papers on Language and Literature*, 16 (1980), 142–50.
4. On Spenser's exploitation of Ovid and Virgil, see Syrithe Pugh's subtle and revisionary, *Spenser and Ovid* (Aldershot: Ashgate, 2005) and her *Spenser and Virgil* (Manchester: Manchester University Press, 2016). Pugh challenges conventional views of Spenser's response to those two poets, although those views remain useful as assumptions against which we can read her modifications. One friend has complained to me about my relative neglect of what Spenser learned and indeed borrowed from Ariosto and Tasso, I suspect in the hope of such thefts being admired. Admirers of Spenser would also do well to compare his treatment of love in *Amoretti* to that in Tasso's verse. Spenser wins his love, if only after a pause, and how he allegorizes his conquest is also worth comparing to the late medieval treatment of love in the *Roman de la Rose*.
5. On Donne's European travels that included preaching in The Hague, see Paul Sellin, *So Doth, So Is Religion: John Donne and Diplomatic Contexts in the Reformed Netherlands, 1619-1620* (Columbia: University of Missouri Press, 1988); John Carey, *John Donne: Life, Mind & Art* (New York: Oxford University Press, 1980), has much that is relevant here.
6. Carey, *John Donne*, 18.
7. R.E. Bennett, 'Donne's Letters from the Continent in 1611-12', *Philological Quarterly*, 19 (1940), 66–73; 67.
8. 'Spenser's Chivalric Restoration: From Bateman's *Travayled Pylgrime* to the Redcrosse Knight', *Studies in English Literature 1500-1900*, 86 (1989), 166–97.
9. Kathrine Koller, 'The Travayled Pylgrime by Stephen Batman and Book Two of *The Faerie Queene*', *Modern Language Quarterly*, 3 (1942), 535–41.
10. On *Amoretti* 67's sources/intertexts, see my 'The Thirsty Deer and the Lord of Life', *Spenser Studies*, 6 (1986), 33–76.
11. David B. Wilson, '"La Puce de Madame Desroches" and John Donne's "The Flea"', *Neuphilologische Mitteilungen*, 72.2 (1971), 297–301. Wilson, who notes Donne's revisions of the fashion but also finds evidence in the poem's puns that he had a French model, says that the French taste for flea poems was known in England. On the fashion see also Cathy Yandell, 'Of Lice and Women: Rhetoric and Gender in "La Puce de Madame des Roches"', *Journal of Medieval and Renaissance Studies*, 20.1 (1990), 123–35.
12. See Clayton D. Lein, 'Donne and Ronsard', *Notes & Queries*, 21.3 (1974), 90–2; Lein notes, with doubts, work on Donne and Ronsard by Hugh Richmond. On the lesbian poems, see my 'Male Lesbian Voices: Ronsard, Tyard and Donne Play Sappho', in Marc Berley (ed.), *Reading the Renaissance: Ideas and Idioms from Shakespeare to Milton* (Pittsburgh: Duquesne University Press, 2003), 109–29.
13. See Ovid's *Amores* I.4; also, *Ars Amatoria* I.571–2.
14. For similar hills, see A.L. Prescott, 'Hills of Contemplation and Signifying Circles: Spenser and Guy Le Fèvre de la Boderie', *Spenser Studies*, 34 (2009), 155–83. La Marche's journey follows the pattern set by Bernard of Clairvaux, and all such texts reply to the Psalmist's query 'Who shal ascende into the mountaine of the Lord?' (Psalm 24).
15. Prescott 2009 offers more such hills, not all with visions, including one in work by John Dee, and one Rinaldo climbs in Tasso's *Jerusalem Delivered* XI.

6
Ovidian Spenser, Ovidian Donne

Linda Gregerson

How can Ovid help us think about the relationship of Spenser and Donne? How did Ovid help Spenser and Donne to think about their own tumultuous era? About the durable conundrums of change and continuity, division and connection? And about the place of poetry in a perishable and perilous world? I would like to consider here the Ovidian heritage in three poems published in the late, declining years of Elizabethan rule. *Prosopopoia: or Mother Hubberds Tale* looks backward to the beast fables of medieval Europe and forward to the rhymed couplets of eighteenth-century satire. Donne's *Metempsychosis* sets out to trace the progress of a soul from the Garden of Eden to the present age but gets only as far as the first generation of Adam's descendants. The *Cantos of Mutabilitie* have come willy-nilly to serve as conclusion to Spenser's unfinished and unfinishable *Faerie Queene*. Each of these poems is deeply concerned with questions of moral and physical decay, the instability of species, the subversion of hierarchy, the transmission of poetic form,[1] and poetic reputation, and each uses Ovid to sharpen these questions. Two figures in the *Metamorphoses*, Astraea in the first book and Pythagoras in the last, mark the troubled foundations of Ovid's cosmos. In their very separate ways and with varying degrees of explicitness, these figures make their presence felt in the poems considered below, undermining the dream of ordered progression and suggesting a root cause for moral decline.

Astraea

In the Book of Genesis, creation begins with an act of division: 'and God divided the light from the darkness' (Genesis 1:4).[2] Ovid's myth of creation begins in a similar fashion: 'God – or kindlier Nature – ... rent asunder land from sky, and sea from land, and separated the ethereal heavens from the dense atmosphere' (*Metamorphoses* [*Meta*] I.21–3).[3] Ovid's narrator presents this as an unambiguous good: division resolves the 'strife' of undifferentiated chaos. 'Parted off ... within their determined bounds' (*Meta* I.69–70), the elements are 'released ... and freed from the blind heap of things' (*Meta* I.25–6). As in the paradox of Christian obedience, this containment is itself a form of liberation, all things 'bound ... fast in harmony' (*Meta* I.26). Later acts of division are less beneficent, however: Jove's division of perpetual spring into four seasons marks the transition from Golden Age (forever temperate) to Silver (at times too hot, at times too cold). Humans, previously fed by the spontaneous bounty of the earth, now subject the 'lesser' animals to labour ('bullocks groaned beneath the heavy yoke' (*Meta* I.124)) and the earth itself to the 'compulsion' of hoe and ploughshare (*Meta* I.101–2). With the Brazen Age, humans turn against one another, resorting to arms, though they have not yet turned against the gods and nature, are 'not yet impious' (*Meta* I.125–7). In the Age of Iron, division becomes for the first time political: the earth, 'which had hitherto been a common possession like the sunlight and the air' (*Meta* I.135), is now defaced with boundary lines and ripped to its very bowels by men in search of riches (*Meta* I.136–40). Wealth – which is to say, divided and unequal ownership – leads to envy and suspicion, which lead to warfare and worse: husband turns against wife, son against father, host against guest. 'Piety lay vanquished, and the maiden Astraea, last of the immortals, abandoned the blood-soaked earth' (*Meta* I.149–50).

Astraea is the goddess of Justice, but in the Ovidian myth of creation and in the poetry indebted to Ovid's myth it is her absence that is Astraea's most salient aspect. In the fifth book of *The Faerie Queene*, the Knight of Justice is described as her protégé, having been taught by Astraea 'to weigh both right and wrong' and to administer 'due recompence' to each (*FQ* V.i.7).[4] But Justice wields a sword obtained by 'slight' (*FQ* V.i.9); his executive function is delegated to an 'yron man', whose very name and methods locate him squarely in the fourth, debased, era of Ovidian evolution; and Justice finds his efforts progressively thwarted by the ill fit between allegorical and historical allegiances in Spenser's poem. '[L]oathing lenger here to space / Mongst wicked men', Astraea has fled 'to heauen' (*FQ* V.i.11) and left Arthegall to navigate a world grown 'daily wourse and wourse' (*FQ* V.Proem.2). Likewise, in *Prosopopoia: or Mother Hubberds Tale*, it is Astraea's departure from the earth that heralds the month of pestilence with which the poem begins: 'It was the month, in which the righteous Maide, / That for disdaine of sinfull worlds upbraide, / Fled back to heaven, whence she was first conceived' (*MHT*, lines 1–3).[5] To justify their cozening course of 'Adventure' (*MHT*, line 224) and to colour their various disguises, even the Fox and the Ape have learned to cite Ovid under the sign of Astraea: in the beginning of the world, the Fox proclaims, Nature

> gave like blessing to each creture ...
> That there might be no difference nor strife,
> Nor ought cald mine or thine: thrice happie then
> Was the condition of mortall men.
> That was the golden age of *Saturne* old,
> But this might better be the world of gold:
> For without golde now nothing wilbe got.
>
> (*MHT*, lines 145–53)

'This yron world', laments the Ape-disguised-as-cashiered-soldier, 'Brings downe the stowtest hearts to lowest state' (*MHT*, lines 254–5).

The poet/narrator of Donne's *Metempsychosis* promises to encompass in his fable all four of the Ovidian ages of man: all that 'the gold Chaldee or silver Persian saw, / Greek brass or Roman iron, is in this one' (*Metem*, lines 7–8).[6] But the world the poem unfolds is emphatically one of iron: 'unkind kinds' (*Metem*, line 288) exist at one another's expense, larger creatures feed upon the smaller, the smaller undermine the larger, 'weakness invites' not pity but 'oppression' (*Metem*, line 250), justice is nowhere to be found. In Book I of Ovid's *Metamorphoses*, it is the arts of division (boundary lines, extractions of surplus value, subjection for the purpose of material gain) that give birth to envy (*Meta* I.127–50). In *Metempsychosis*, it is envy in the person of Cain that bequeaths us the arts of division:

> Let me arrest thy thoughts: wonder with me
> Why ploughing, building, ruling and the rest,
> Or most of those arts whence our lives are blest,
> By cursed Caïn's race invented be ....
>
> (*Metem*, lines 513–16)

The age of Astraea has given way to the age of Cain, and Donne's 'great soul' is condemned to make its progress through the full spectrum of vice that, according to Ovid, drove Astraea from the earth.

Of the goddess's subsequent stellification, the poet/narrator of *The Faerie Queene* informs his readers as follows: Astraea has

> Return'd to heauen, whence she deriu'd her race;
> Where she hath now an euerlasting place,
> Mongst those twelue signes, which nightly we doe see
> The heauens bright-shining baudricke to enchace;
> And is the *Virgin*, sixt in her degree
>
> (*FQ* V.i.11)

It is as Virgo, in the Mutabilitie Cantos, that she who was once the goddess of justice on earth makes her appearance as part of Mutabilitie's forensic evidence on Arlo Hill. Led by August, sixth in the pageant of months, this 'louely Mayd' is adorned with 'eares of corne', but her power to bless the earth with plenty is described as a thing of the past:

> That was the righteous Virgin, which of old
> Liv'd here on earth, and plenty made abound;
> But, after Wrong was lov'd and Iustice solde,
> She left th'vnrighteous world and was to heauen extold.
>
> (*FQ* VII.vii.37)

This cameo abandonment echoes the earlier account of Astraea in the Book of Justice and, more proximately, Diana's abandonment of Arlo Hill, that 'best and fairest' place now left to wolves and thieves. If Arlo Hill is also the site of Nature's Judgement, what are we meant to understand about the nature of justice to be found there? How durable are Nature's dispensations? Can they cross the boundary between then and the degraded now?

Pythagoras

Before concluding his epic of metamorphosis with the ostensible triumph of imperium, Ovid devotes more than four hundred lines – nearly half – of his fifteenth book to a monologue by Pythagoras of Samos (*Meta* XV.75–478). This begins as a diatribe against the eating of flesh: 'What have the oxen done, those faithful, guileless beasts ... born to a life of toil, who are a part of creation ... When you take the flesh of slaughtered cattle in your mouths, ... you are devouring your own fellow-labourers' (*Meta* XV.120–42). The philosopher's objection to the eating of meat is founded on something more essential than creaturely fellow feeling. Or rather, fellow feeling, as expounded by Pythagoras, has a more material ground than his auditors might at first imagine: 'All things change; nothing dies. The spirit wanders, comes now here, now there, and occupies whatever frame it pleases. From beasts it passes into human bodies, and from our bodies into beasts' (*Meta* XV.165–8). In other words, the distinction between us and them is only, ever, specious and unstable. 'We should permit bodies which may possibly have sheltered the souls of our parents or brothers ... to be uninjured and respected, and not load our stomachs as with a Thyestean banquet' (*Meta* XV.456–62). In Western culture, the horror of the Thyestean banquet is meant to induce a primal recoil that requires no explanation. To eat one's own flesh, knowingly or not, violates the most fundamental and instinctive principles of self-preservation. As does, for Pythagoras, meat-eating of any sort: when we eat the flesh of animals, we eat ourselves.[7]

Pythagoras allows for killing in self-defense ('Kill creatures that work you harm') but draws the line at subsequent consumption: 'even in the case of these let killing suffice. Make not their flesh your food' (*Meta* XV.477–8). On the same grounds that he abhors the eating of meat, he abhors the reading of entrails and animal sacrifice generally: such practices, he argues, make 'the gods themselves partners of ... crime' (*Meta* XV.128). Why should we attribute to the gods our own bloodthirstiness?

Pythagoras's long diatribe has a profoundly ambiguous resonance in Ovid's poem. The *Metamorphoses*, after all, presents a world in which the boundaries between humans and animals, humans and plants, humans and the elements are exquisitely unstable; Pythagoras's account of creation would seem to lend both metaphysical warrant and an impassioned ethical tenor to the Ovidian narratives of immanence and transformation.

> [T]here is nothing in all the world that keeps its form. All things are in a state of flux, and everything is brought into being with a changing nature. Time itself flows on in constant motion, just like a river. For neither the river nor the swift hour can stop its course; but, as wave is pushed on by wave, ... so time both flees and follows and is ever new. For that which once existed is no more, and that which was not has come to be. (*Meta* XV.177–85)

Pythagoras is a physicist: 'And even those things which we call elements do not persist' (*Meta* XV.237); earth, water, air, and fire change perpetually into one another. Pythagoras is a natural historian: 'I have myself seen what once was solid land changed into sea; and again I have seen land made from the sea. Sea-shells have been seen lying far from the ocean, and an ancient anchor has been found on a mountaintop' (*Meta* XV.262–5). He is an archaeologist ('If you seek for Helice and Buris, once cities of Acaia, you will find them beneath the waves' (*Meta* XV.293–4)) and a political philosopher ('Sparta was at one time a famous city ... and ... is now a worthless countryside; proud Mycenae has fallen; and what is the Thebes of Oedipus except a name?' (*Meta* XV.426–9)). Ethicist, philosopher of religion, and known in extra-Ovidian accounts to be a mathematician and geometrician as well, long before any of these were construed as separate disciplines, Pythagoras is 'learned indeed', writes Ovid, but in the one central tenet – metempsychosis – 'not believed' (*Meta* XV.74).

The Ovidian narrator does not directly pronounce on the truth value of Pythagoras's claims, though he endows the philosopher with considerable eloquence on the pathos of sacrificial victims and on the subject of mutability in general. And yet. When Pythagoras ceases to speak, the Ovidian epic and the pageant of Roman power proceed as though he had never existed. Numa, who succeeds Romulus as King of Rome, is imbued with the teachings of Pythagoras and incorporates his ethical vision, in essence at least, into the principles of the Roman state, training 'a fierce, warlike people in the arts of peace' (*Meta* XV.483–4). But with the end of Numa's reign, blood sacrifice and the reading of entrails continue unabated.[8] Ovid's ambiguously ironized tribute to imperium has long been read, of course, as a conspicuous alternative to the resounding endorsements of Virgilian epic.[9] Indeed, Virgil's own celebration of imperial power is now understood to be more complexly pitched than was once thought to be the case; critics have focused afresh, for example, on Dido as a symptom of empire's guilty conscience. More generally, the degree to which triumphalism is meant to be qualified or undermined is a question raised by all encomiastic literature. In the *Metamorphoses*, the vision of Pythagoras, expounded at such length and with such vividness in the penultimate movement of Ovid's poem, is among the poet's strongest suggestions of real queasiness before the consummate spectacle of Rome.

Prosopopoia: or Mother Hubberds Tale

The frame for *Mother Hubberds Tale*, like that for Boccaccio's *Decameron*, is a visitation of pestilence. 'It was the month', says Spenser's narrator, 'in which the righteous Maide'

> Into her silver bowre the Sunne received;
> And the hot *Syrian* Dog on him awayting,
> After the chafed Lyons cruell bayting,
> Corrupted had th'ayre with his noysome breath,
> And powr'd on th'earth plague, pestilence, and death.
>
> (*MHT*, lines 4–8)

The month is August, whose notorious 'dog days' make humans especially vulnerable to disease; the maid is Astraea, whose astral sign, that of Virgo, governs this hottest month of the year.[10] The month is not, not exactly, the month in which Astraea abandoned the earth, though the reader may be forgiven for imagining at first that this is the case: 'It was the month, in which the righteous Maide, / That for disdaine of sinfull worlds upbraide, / Fled back to heaven, whence she was first conceived' (*MHT*, lines

1–3). When the sentence continues, as above, Astraea's 'flight' is revealed to be a subordinate action within a subordinate action: it is Astraea's 'reception' of the Sun, not her flight, that distinguishes the month. But even in its feints and dodges syntax does not lie. The first, the crucial thing the poem would have us know about the righteous Maid is that she is no longer here. She has fled the earth 'for disdaine' and become a constellation; her influence has gone from beneficence to bane; that bane is the occasion for the poem.

Having succumbed to the 'wicked maladie' that rages around him, Spenser's narrator endures a period of enforced idleness, during which his friends seek to distract him with 'pleasant tales' (*MHT*, lines 9, 26). Passing over the numerous tales of knights and ladies, faeries and giants, which, as Spenser's readers knew very well, had found ample latitude elsewhere in his oeuvre, the narrator chooses instead to recount a beast fable told him by a 'good old woman', Mother Hubberd (*MHT*, line 34). 'Base is the style', he warns, 'and matter meane' (*MHT*, line 44). The style, alone among the poems gathered in *Complaints* (1591), takes the rhymed couplet as its scaffolding. Thus, while the poem looks back to medieval tales like those of Reynard the Fox, it also looks forward to the favoured prosodic habit of eighteenth-century satire. The couplet is not exclusive to satire, of course, but it is especially apt for satiric deployment, its close-packed 'wrappings up' easily ironized as the symptoms of simplistic thought or specious resolution.

Mutability itself is a parodic device in *Mother Hubberds Tale*, more a matter of Archimagean disguise than of seasonal succession. And *Prosopopoia*, which Puttenham defines as 'Counterfeit Impersonation',[11] links the poet himself to the protagonists he treats with such sceptical wit. In *Mother Hubberds Tale*, prosopopoia is both a figure of speech (a governing trope) and a figure of narrative (an action performed by characters within the poem). As the poet invites his readers to contemplate human corruption in the figures of Fox and Ape, so the Fox and Ape pursue their own agendas by adopting a series of personae. Aggrievement is their justification and their driving force. Thwarted in their hopes of preferment (*MHT*, lines 59–64), an Ape and a Fox resolve to cast their lots together and seek better fortune 'abroad' (*MHT*, line 48). Posing first as a cashiered soldier and his servant, they seek 'adventure' (and handouts) in mock-chivalric wandering. This degraded version of epic romance gives way to mock-pastoral when Ape and Fox proffer their services as shepherd and sheep dog to a guileless husbandman, imagining – as literary pastoral is wont to do – that the shepherd's life will be free of care and serious labour. When their negligence and greed are exposed, they turn to practising these same vices as clerics. After subsequent careers as scheming courtiers and usurping rulers, they come to well-deserved grief, the Fox 'uncase[d]' (*MHT*, line 1380) and the Ape shorn of his long ears and tail. The digressive narrative allows Spenser to target corruption in a vast array of incarnations: grifters and negligent shepherds, deceitful flatterers and abusive rulers, self-seekers of every sort. While most of the villains appear to be general types, the Fox's machinations as chief counsellor to the royal Ape appear to touch more specifically upon a particular figure: William Cecil, Lord Burghley.

> All offices, all leases by him lept,
> And of them all whatso he likte, he kept.
> Justice he solde injustice for to buy,
> And for to purchase for his progeny.
>
> (*MHT*, lines 1145–8)

Modern readers are not the first to sense a topical reference. Contemporaries noted the venom too, as evidenced by efforts to have *Mother Hubberds Tale* withdrawn from publication. 'Spanning many years and ideological viewpoints', writes Bruce Danner, 'topical annotation and commentary concerning Burghley [as a primary target of satire in *Mother Hubberds Tale*] is broad, diverse, and remarkably consistent ... while the government's long-standing censorship of the offending remarks served only to confirm such impressions'.[12]

In many respects, the premise of the beast fable as a genre is flatly opposed to that of Pythagoras's unifying ecology. It is almost too obvious to be noted, and yet it is worth estranging the obvious for a moment. To represent human vice and folly in the guise of beasts is imagined to be inherently satiric because it represents an insulting 'demotion' on the scale of creation. When the Ape claims inherent right to the role of monarch on the basis of his upright stature, when the Fox claims inherent right on the grounds of 'wit and spirite' (*MHT*, line 1043), their boasts take sidelong aim at humanity's entrenched assumptions about its own (our own) physical and mental superiority. Spenser's satire does not, one hastens to add, seriously challenge the anthropocentric premise. If an Ape or a Fox can pass for human, it is because humans have subordinated their inherent capacities to baser motives. Once again, the logic is circular: Ape and Fox are transparently modelled on human types from the beginning, their ambitions, grievances, and indolence drawn from the lexicon of human vice.

Embedded in the logic of satire is another logic: that of Biblical parable. When the Ape and Fox prey upon the lambs of the trusting husbandman, Spenser's readers might well have remembered Christ's warning against false prophets, 'which come to you in sheep's clothing, but inwardly are ravening wolves' (Matthew 7:15). Given the heated vestarian controversies in Elizabethan England, these same readers may well have discerned a pointed topicality when the quondam minders of sheep equip themselves with 'gowne' and 'cassoke' (*MHT*, lines 353–4).[13] But the broader analogy was not limited to specifically Protestant debates: in the Hebrew Bible, the negligent and abusive leaders of Israel are portrayed as false shepherds (e.g., Jeremiah 23:1–2; Ezekiel 34:1–10). In the Christian Bible, Paul invokes Christ's role as good shepherd to serve as model for every bearer of the Word (e.g., Acts 20:28–9). Pastoral, in other words, has long been used to figure forth both the abuse of power and the possibility of benign, albeit hierarchical, interdependence among God's creatures.

This highlights a distinction, in the *Metamorphoses*, between the vision of Pythagoras and that of the larger poem in which he appears. The one implies a radical levelling of living forms, the other posits enduring differentials of dignity and prestige. In other words, not all metamorphoses are equal. Some are clearly punitive, as when Arachne is transformed into a spider or hard-hearted Anaxarete into a stone. Some are meant to be understood as promotions, as when ants become men or Callisto becomes a constellation. Some are forms of rescue, as when Arethusa turns into a fountain or the Trojan ships, torched by order of Turnus, into water nymphs. Some are acts of mercy, as when Myrrha is allowed to hide her shame in the form of a myrrh tree. All are also, of course, commemorations, embodied allusions to the prior state or the prior dilemma of the creature who has been transformed. Ovid's great book of changes encourages compassion towards all the elements of creation, both high and low; hovering just below its surface is a vision of connection and interdependence that we now call ecological. But the poem in its largest spans does not propose a systematic challenge to the differentials of power. Juno may be cruel and her victims may inspire our pity, but Augustus is on the winning side of history.

Spenser, likewise, is no Leveller. When, at the beginning of *Mother Hubberds Tale*, the Fox speaks in the manner of a political philosopher, he invokes the trope of a lost, egalitarian paradise: In 'the golden age of *Saturne* old' Nature 'gave like blessing to each creture ... That there might be no difference nor strife' (*MHT*, lines 151, 146-8, as cited more fully above). Like Ovid's account of creation, and like the Book of Genesis, this political manifesto is imbued with nostalgia for a state of perfection that can only be imagined in contrast to the evidence, which is therefore construed as a later, fallen age. But Spenser's readers have been well inoculated against sentimental alliance with the Fox, who, far from repudiating the unequal division of wealth, seeks only to make it work in his favour: 'Let such vile vassalls borne to base vocation / Drudge in the world', he says to his ally the Ape,

> ... and for their living droyle
> Which have no wit to live withouten toyle.
> But we will walke about the world at pleasure
> Like two free men, and make our ease a treasure.
>
> (*MHT*, lines 156–60)

That this alternative 'vocation' is yet another testament to avarice is of course a centrepiece of the poet's satiric method.

In its narrative frame and in this early, ironized rendering of moral economy, then, *Mother Hubberds Tale* inscribes coincident patterns. The season is one of pestilence; Astraea has abandoned the earth. Distribution is unjust; we have fallen from a Golden Age. While the Fox and the Ape are objects of contempt and their aggrievement without merit, injustice is real. So how ought we to judge? And what are we to do? Spenser's fable also raises the larger question of periodization per se. Spenser scholars who have shifted their attention from the extended time spans of Aristotelian philosophy and Renaissance humanism to focus on the conflicts and aspirations and political intrigues of Elizabethan England have bequeathed to us a fertile field of enquiry. What do we miss when we forget that Donne, too, came to maturity during the reign of Elizabeth, when we construe him instead as 'belonging to' the political temperament and emergent aesthetic conventions of the subsequent century? What do we occlude by emphasizing the contrasts between Elizabethan and metaphysical poetry rather than looking afresh, as the editor of this volume challenges us to do, at their continuities? What is at stake, more broadly, when humans seek explanatory foothold by dividing the past into separate eras? The issue of course is not unique to literary scholarship. What is at stake for coherence and imaginable action when humans explain the suffering and folly around them as symptoms of a belated, fallen era?

Metempsychosis

In his prefatory Epistle to *Metempsychosis*, Donne explicitly anchors the poem in Pythagorean precedent. 'I will bid you remember', he writes, 'that the Pythagorean doctrine doth not only carry one soul from man to man, nor man to beast, but indifferently to plants also: and therefore you must not grudge to find the same soul in an emperor, in a post-horse, and in a mushroom' (*Metem*, Epistle). And, marrying the mock-Pythagorean to mock-Virgilian ('I sing the progress of a deathless soul' (*Metem*, line 1)) and both of these to Holy Writ, the poet promises to comprehend in his verses 'all times before the Law / Yoked us, and when, and since', distilling in his prospect the wonders of gold, silver, brass, and iron ages (*Metem*, lines 3–8). Satires directed at the pretensions and fallibilities of humankind, of course, were not peculiar to late sixteenth-century England. But what might we gain from considering that *Metempsychosis* is a product of the same decade that saw the publication of *Mother Hubberds Tale* and the first six books of *The Faerie Queene*? Might Donne's poem too derive some of its temperament from the late, disillusioned Elizabethan moment? In August of 1601, the date that appears on his dedicatory epistle, Donne was still serving as secretary to Sir Thomas Egerton, privy counsellor and Lord Keeper of the Seal; he had just beheld at close range the disastrous crash-and-burn of the Earl of Essex; he was about to serve as Member of Parliament; he had not yet cut his ties to power and patronage by marrying Ann More. He might well fear he lived in a world where 'opinion' was 'the only measure' (*Metem*, line 520).

The soul that makes its progress through *Metempsychosis* begins its transit in the 'low but fatal room' (*Metem*, line 70) of an apple on the paradisal Tree of Knowledge; the poem grafts the Pythagorean template to the Judaeo-Christian. It also grafts myth to topical satire, identifying 'this great / soul' with that which dwells 'amongst us now ... and moves that hand and tongue and brow / Which, as the Moon the sea, moves us' (*Metem*, lines 61–3). Whomever readers were meant to identify as their 'great' contemporary, the Cynthia/Ocean trope, famously deployed by Sir Walter Raleigh, touches nearly upon the Queen. Its activation here is an acerbic one and, indeed, acerbity is the salient feature of this poem, which mercilessly satirizes the very system on which Donne still pinned his hopes for livelihood and advancement. Little creatures are eaten by larger; the great are slaughtered by the vindictive little. The fish carried off in the beak of the 'sea-pie', or oyster-catcher, is 'Exalted ... but to th'exalter's good, / As are, by great ones, men which lowly stood: / It raised to be the raiser's instrument and food' (*Metem*, lines 278–80).

Anne Lake Prescott has compared the relationship between *Metempsychosis* and Spenser's *Faerie Queene* to that between Ovid's *Metamorphoses* and Virgil's *Aeneid*, describing that relationship as 'quasi-satirical'.[14] Certainly, Donne expected his readers to recognize that *Metempsychosis* has Spenser in mind. Prosodically, it pays explicit homage to the stanza form invented for *The Faerie Queene*, each stanza consisting in Donne's adaptation of ten lines rather than nine, all but the final alexandrine composed in iambic pentameter.[15] Embedded in this stanza, however, and signalled by the rhyme scheme is another, competing prosodic form, to which the elder poet had turned in *Mother Hubberds Tale*. In *Metempsychosis*, the braided logic of the *Faerie Queene* stanza encounters the contrasting logic of the rhymed couplet. This tension – or is it meant as pleasing syncopation? – was already built into the Spenserian stanza, as it was in English and Italian sonnets. Where quatrains meet, whether the pattern is *abbaabba* or *ababbcbc*, fourth and fifth lines form a shadow couplet. And while the Spenserian stanza concludes on another rhymed couplet, it destabilizes closure by pairing lines of different metrical length. Donne alters the balance by making his single quatrain an 'envelope' quatrain – *bccb* – and surrounding it with couplets, so that the pattern is as follows: *aabccbbddd*. Again and again in *Metempsychosis*, one encounters facile expedition of programmed sentiment ('Is any kind subject to rape like fish? / Ill unto man, they neither do, nor wish', 281–2) and epigrammatic cutting off ('He gave it, she t'her husband; both did eat; / So perishèd the eaters and the meat' (88–9)), both effects heightened by the couplet and its rhyme. And yet.

At times, in the very slipstream of satire, Donne's syntax and argument might almost be that of his later devotional poems, tracing the interlacements of theological and figurative logic:

> Yet no low room, nor than the greatest, less,
> If (as devout and sharp men fitly guess)
> That cross, our joy and grief, where nails did tie
> That All which always was all everywhere,
> Which could not sin, and yet all sins did bear,
> Which could not die, yet could not choose but die;
> Stood in the self same room in Calvary,
> Where first grew the forbidden, learned tree,
> For on that tree hung in security
> This Soul, made by the Maker's will, from pulling free.
>
> (*Metem*, lines 71–80)

Here, the politico-ethical deployment of metempsychosis both satirically recapitulates and willy-nilly portends the logic of figural interpretation. In the *Holy Sonnets*, it is clear that no other syntax can capture the intellectual and emotional strenuousness of Christianity's central paradoxes: man/God, life/death, fulfilment of the law/abrogation of the law, Divine omnipotence/creaturely free will. In the stanza above, the ambiguous syntax of the final phrase plays cynically upon that fourth, essential crux. On the one hand, the apple is 'free from being pulled' and eaten, at least for a time, because it has been forbidden to humans. On the other hand it is prevented, by the Maker's will, from 'pulling itself free'. How are we meant to distinguish freedom from coercion?

As the soul continues its progress through the roughly ascending orders of creation – from vegetable to avian and piscine, from piscine to mammalian, from mammalian to human, the moral prospect darkens to include new versions of 'sins against kind' (*Metem*, line 468). The ape, we learn, was the first to distinguish individuated desire from general lust: 'He was the first that more desired to have / One than another' (*Metem*, lines 461–2), which makes him 'the first true lover' (*Metem*, line 460). This does not, however, signal an advance in either delicacy or discrimination: transgressing the species threshold, he attempts to mate with a not-entirely-unwilling Siphatecia, one of the daughters of Adam. Wordplay mimics the carnal debasement: the Ape is 'prevented' by the 'entrance' of Siphatecia's brother (*Metem*, lines 488–9); the soul, which finds a new lodging in human womb, 'comes out … where th'ape would have gone in' (*Metem*, line 491). This 'where' is ambiguously identified, but, once the soul is 'out', we are meant to understand that the womb from which it has emerged is that of Eve, the origin of all our woe. Human at last, the soul is perfected not in virtue but in vice, here as elsewhere deemed the special aptitude of women:

> Keeping some quality
> Of every past shape, she knew treachery,
> Rapine, deceit, and lust, and ills enow
> To be a woman. Themech she is now,
> Sister and wife to Cain, Cain that first did plough.
>
> (*Metem*, lines 506–10)

In its serial incarnations, the Pythagorean soul might seem to stitch a kind of commonality across the species of creation. But in these later stanzas of Donne's poem, boundaries are quickened with prohibition. The wife is also sister; generations are confused. 'Sins against kind / They easily do, that let feed their mind / With outward beauty: beauty they in boys and beasts do find' (*Metem*, lines 468–70). Too much kinship (incest, pederasty) and too little (bestiality) are imagined as contaminating the orderly genealogies of Biblical creation. Among the sequelae, observes the narrator, is the compromising fact that we owe the arts with which 'our lives are blest' to none other than 'cursed Cain' and his race (*Metem*, lines 515–16).

Kenneth Gross has justly observed that the sequence of incarnations in *Metempsychosis* seems 'oddly accidental', lacking 'that sense of an inner erotic or moral continuity from shape to shape that we find in Ovidian metamorphoses'.[16] Janel Mueller, in an elegant source study, suggests an alternative ordering principle. Her argument is far too intricate to summarize in a sentence or two,[17] but its implications for the logic of sequence are as follows: among the heirs to Pythagoras's doctrine of metempsychosis, Donne might well have encountered one Carpocrates and his son Epiphanes (both second century CE). Carpocrates not only believed in the transmigration of souls, he also argued that no life could be consummated until it had manifested the full range of depravities. The soul, said Carpocrates, 'could assert and attain its own selfhood only by actively … completing its quota of … depravity' and thus 'more quickly escap[ing] the body' and the cycles of reincarnation.[18] Epiphanes extended the logic of commonality: God's 'universal righteousness', he argued, 'is given to all equally', like the sunlight and like the plants of the earth and like access to sexual congress;[19] all divisions into mine and yours are a falling off. Orthodoxy was duly horrified by them both. In their views, however, thanks to Mueller's meticulous excavations, we may discern a logic behind the apparent randomness of metamorphic change in Donne's poem: it is not so much a progress as an anthology of vice (see

Carpocrates) and it emblematizes the chaos entailed in radical levelling (see orthodox rejoinders to Epiphanes).

Whatever its specific lines of Pythagorean heritage may have been, Donne's satire shares a broader structural dilemma with *Mother Hubberds Tale*: both poems are torn between vertical and horizontal systems of logic. The food chain logic – big fish eats little fish, masters abuse their subordinates – is emphatically hierarchical. The Pythagorean logic – the ox you eat may be your brother – is emphatically levelling. And, like the title character in another, closely contemporaneous work, Donne finds the second, levelling, logic implicit within the hierarchical: a king may go a progress through the guts of a beggar.

Donne's poet/narrator dedicates *Metempsychosis* to infinity ('Infinitati Sacrum'), which bespeaks both grandiosity (my poem will encompass All That Is) and possible concession (my poem will be unfinished and unfinishable). Promising to follow the passages of the soul from 'her first making' (Epistle) to the present day, he traces it, in narrative terms, only to the immediate offspring of Adam. The present era, however – what the Epistle calls 'this time' – is amply invoked, often within the confines of an epic simile. The mandrake root, for example, forces a place in the earth,

> Just as in our streets when the people stay
> To see the Prince, and have so filled the way
> That weasels scarce could pass, when she comes near
> They throng and cleave up, and a passage clear,
> As if, for that time, their round bodies flattened were.
>
> (*Metem*, lines 136–40)

More significantly, the poet's present makes its tenor felt in every shift to timeless verity: 'Greatness a period [a fixed trajectory] hath, but hath no station [or resting place]' (*Metem*, line 340).

'Period' is a key term in the poem's invocation as well and, significantly for a project dedicated to infinity, suggests the finitude that motivates the quest for inspiration: 'Great Destiny', the poet writes, 'That hast marked out a path and period / For everything',

> O vouch thou safe to look
> And show my story in thy eternal book,
> That (if my prayer be fit) I may understand
> So much myself as to know with what hand,
> How scant or liberal, this my life's race is spanned.
>
> (*Metem*, lines 31–40)

Does the grand project come down to this then? An effort to know the self in the most diminished of terms, that is, to know the span of one's own mortal life? The poet's age at writing, as noted in the following stanza, is 'six lustres' or thirty years (*Metem*, 41), which he reckons as half a lifetime. We find him in the middle of his way, and afflicted with spiritual confusion. Donne's comedic mode is far from that of Dante, but he does contrive to temper his burlesque with more sobering vistas. Even in its broadest formal outlines – fifty-two stanzas – the poem contrives to move in two directions. On the one hand the number suggests the wholeness of the calendrical cycle; on the other it marks a cycle of perpetual incompletion, a vivid comment on, or contrast to, our own brief days.[20]

The Mutabilitie Cantos

Readers have long noted the deepening shadow of dissolution and inconstancy with which the later books of *The Faerie Queene* are haunted. The Proem to the Book of Justice is merely one example:

> So oft as I with state of present time,
>   The image of the antique world compare,
>   When as mans age was in his freshest prime,
>   And the first blossome of faire vertue bare
>   Such oddes I finde twixt those, and these which are,
>   As that, through long continuance of his course,
>   Me seemes the world is runne quite out of square,
>   From the first point of his appointed sourse,
> And being once amisse growes daily wourse snd wourse.
>
> (*FQ* V.Proem.1)

In the posthumous cantos that have come to serve as the final movement of *The Faerie Queene*, Spenser distils the lament that has increasingly informed his poem:

> What man that sees the euer-whirling wheele
>   Of *Change*, the which all mortall things doth sway,
>   But that therby doth find, and plainly feele,
>   How *MVTABILITIE* in them doth play
>   Her cruell sports, to many mens decay?
>
> (*FQ* VII.vi.1)

The lament serves as preface to the story of the Titaness Mutabilitie and her attempt to claim sovereignty over the heavens and earth. Exemplifying precisely those vices Ovid ascribes to the Age of Iron, Spenser's Mutabilitie is motivated by jealousy, ambition, and greed, and the poetic mode in which her adventures are described is accordingly a low one. The physical struggle between the Titaness and Cynthia, in which the former attempts to pluck the latter from her ivory throne, is one of Spenser's least flattering portraits of majesty in action. But the mode is very far from satire when spontaneous insurrection modulates to juridical argument. Intervening in the undignified tug of war, Jove confronts Mutabilitie to defend his title and that of the Jovean pantheon but grants that competing claims shall be submitted to the 'equal' judgement of Nature (*FQ* VII.vi.35). Once that court convenes, the poem sheds its satiric tenor and grants Mutabilitie forty-eight full stanzas in which to make her case: she invokes the ever-changing earth and its morphology, the panoply of earthly creatures, the astral spheres, the units of seasons, months, and hours, and even the elements themselves; all of these, she claims, establish mutability as the foundational principle of creation. Her argument takes its structure, and each of these components, directly from the extended speech of Pythagoras in the *Metamorphoses*.

As does of course the final judgement of Nature. Spenser's readers would have been well acquainted with the oft-invoked correlate to perpetual change, which is, in classical terms, the eternal continuity of essence. '[N]othing perishes in the whole universe', says Ovid's Pythagoras, 'it does but vary and renew its form' (*Meta* XV.254–5). Spenser's Nature puts it this way:

> I well consider all that ye haue sayd,
>   And find that all things stedfastnes doe hate
>   And changed be: yet being rightly wayd
>   They are not changed from their first estate;
>   But by their change their being doe dilate:
>   And turning to themselues at length againe,
>   Doe worke their owne perfection so by fate:
>   Then ouer them Change doth not rule and raigne;
> But they raigne ouer change, and doe their states maintaine.
>
> (*FQ* VII.vii.59)

Before Mutabilitie is allowed to present her evidence and Nature her judgement, however, Spenser interrupts his narrative with another Ovidian tale, one which sounds a by-now familiar theme: the departure of Astraea from an unjust earth. The story is that of Diana and Actaeon, here become Diana and Faunus. The pretext for this interpolation is the introduction of Arlo Hill, which will be the setting for Nature's judgement. Arlo Hill, though once the 'best and fairest' place and especially favoured by Diana, is now 'most ill' (*FQ* VII.vi.37), abandoned by Diana in the wake of Faunus's transgression. As Richard McCabe reminds us, Arlo Hill, corresponding to the peak of Galtymore near Kilcolman, is the most specific invocation of the Irish landscape in all of *The Faerie Queene*.[21] The Galty mountains were thickly wooded and, during the nine years' war that in 1598 would lead to the sacking of Spenser's castle, was thickly populated with guerrilla fighters, or wood kerns, as Arlo Hill is infested with 'Wolues' and 'Thieues' (*FQ* VII.vi.55). To Spenser's mind, the Cynthia/Astraea who governed the Tudor state had faltered in support of her Irish plantation and its most incisive lieutenants; she was guilty, therefore, of an abandonment parallel to Cynthia/Diana's abandonment of Arlo Hill. The cause, in the fable, of Diana's anger? A goddess objects to the gaze that exposes her nakedness. If that nakedness is failed policy and the gaze is the poet's, his trade becomes a dangerous one. 'By cursing the land', Richard McCabe observes, 'Diana effectively curses the narrator' of Spenser's poem.[22]

Cause and effect, when one considers the poem and the world it inhabits, are circular, like the cycles of transmigration. A poet may praise a monarch for virtues she does not (yet) have, in the hopes of imbuing her with just such virtues. Contrarily, the actions of Diana's earthly avatar may undermine the very project designed as her encomium. The Faerie Queene's recall of Arthegall in Book V leaves her Knight of Justice open to attack by the Blatant Beast, who is also inveterate enemy to 'Poets rime' (*FQ* VI.xii.40). As Spenser became increasingly disillusioned with Elizabeth's colonial policy in Ireland, both poet and monarch suffer periodic declines in poetic mode: Faunus is an Actaeon fit for satire; Cynthia struggling with a Titaness to retain her 'seat' is a figure of burlesque, not epic seriousness.

Distinguishing the human

In the Book of Genesis, the story of humans-as-we-know-them begins with expulsion from the Garden, which is to say, with death. Narratively and etymologically, it is terminus that marks our entrance to the mortal world. *Mother Hubberds Tale* begins in a season of pestilence; plagues bring with them the shadow of end times. *Metempsychosis* both does and doesn't wish to 'understand' the death of the self (*Metem.*, 38). The Mutabilitie Cantos struggle to find consolation in a circuit of continuity that dwarfs, or largely fails to notice, the single human lifespan. That lifespan is laughably little compared to the emergence of planets and natural species, and yet it is the default unit by which we tend to measure. Why posit a garden or a golden age? Why mythic and historical periods at all? In a world where transience, in the vegetable world, in the visible heavens, and in the individual human body, is so palpably the dominant principle, is it so essential to impose an ordering principle, even if that principle casts the present era as part of a downward spiral? One cannot achieve perpetual youth, or stop the flowers from withering; one cannot rely on worldly wealth or power, as witness 'Courts inconstant mutabilitie' (*MHT*, line 723). To make the large scheme legible by marking its boundaries is to exert a form of cognitive control where no other control is possible. But is it enough?

Donne's poet/narrator purports to track the circuits of the 'deathless soul' (*Metem.*, line 1), but what he hopes to learn from Destiny's 'eternal book' (*Metem*, line 37) is something rather humbler: the 'span' (*Metem*, line 40) of his own time on earth. The 'interested' poet/narrator posits an 'interested' reader, one whose motive, uncovering and extending the limits of the self, is poised in anxious contrast to the grandiosity of 'all'. In his Epistle, Donne's narrator promises to track the soul, gendered female, from the Garden of Eden to the present time, 'when she is he whose life you shall find in the end of this book' (*Metem*, Epistle). Who is this 'he'?[23] And whose the 'great soul ... amongst us now' (*Metem*, line 61) who governs the moon and tides? If the 'end of the book' provides an answer, it is a profoundly disillusioned one: '*comparison* / The only measure is, and judge, *opinion*' (*Metem*, lines 519–20, italics mine). Which is to say that you, reader, 'whoe'er thou be'st', can only behold in the poem the face you bring to it. 'Opinion', whose name concludes the poem, is unstable ground on which to build a metaphysic.

Spenser makes gentle fun of this in the very form of *Mother Hubberds Tale*, which turns out, after all its moralizing satire, to be a just-so story. How did the ape get its short ears and tail? The premise of such an 'explanation' is the same as that of Genesis and Ovid's four ages: things might be different than they are now. Once, in fact, they were. In the long unfolding of *The Faerie Queene*, it is not change per se that is lamented, but change for the worse. Noble minds were once naturally allied in chivalrous pursuit (*FQ* I.ix.1), 'good was onely for it selfe desyred' (*FQ* V.Proem.3), justice dwelt happily on the earth, and Arlo Hill was once the 'best and fairest' place (*FQ* VII.vi.37). The present is by contrast a sorry piece of work. But in the fragment of a fragment that has served since 1609 as coda to Spenser's great epical-historical-romance, change itself appears to be ground for despair:

> When I bethink me on that speech whyleare,
>   Of *Mutability*, and well it way:
>   Me seemes, that though she all vnworthy were
>   Of the Heav'ns Rule; yet very sooth to say,
>   In all things else she beares the greatest sway.
>   Which makes me loath this state of life so tickle,
>   And loue of things so vaine to cast away;
>   Whose flowring pride, so fading and so fickle,
> Short *Time* shall soon cut down with his consuming sickle.
>
> (*FQ* VII.viii.1)

Why should change breed loathing? Spenser's posthumous editor positions the Mutabilitie Cantos as central sections in a hypothetical Legend of Constancy. Constancy posits faithful allegiance as well as changelessness; if Mutabilitie is its antithesis, mutability implies a breaking of faith, but faith with whom? Even as he raises his bolt of lightning against the impudent upstart who challenges his sovereignty, Jove's hand is stayed by the sight of Mutabilitie's face:

> But, when he looked on her louely face,
>   In which, faire beames of beauty did appeare,
>   That could the greatest wrath soone turne to grace
>   (Such sway doth beauty euen in Heauen beare)
>   He staide his hand ...
>
> (*FQ* VII.vi.31)

Or, as one of Spenser's heirs has put it, death is the mother of beauty.[24] The face of Mutabilitie is ravishing and God, like us, is imagined as helplessly loving the perishing earth. The contract of faith that is broken by that perishing is a contract we have wishfully invented, a contract that says we may keep what we love, a contract that says there can be a meaningful link between transience and eternity, the longings of the self and the realities of creation.

The penultimate stanza ('When I bethinke me') of Spenser's 'Canto, vnperfite' is followed by one in which the poet converts contemplation ('Then gin I thinke') to prayer and turns his face away from 'all that moueth': 'thence-forth all shall rest eternally / With Him that is the God of Sabbaoth hight: / O that great Sabbaoth God, graunt me that Sabaoths sight' (*FQ* VII.viii.2). Scholars have long been puzzled to adjudicate between the first and second stanzas of Spenser's final fragment, but the lack of continuity between them is surely as eloquent as any of their individual parts. If union is the state from which we have fallen and to which we shall return, this makes the only world we know a fleeting interim, and broken. Much as we would like to ally them, the vision that prompts 'loathing' and the vision that prompts hope are at odds and incommensurate. It is the unhealed division between one vision and the other that will lend its tortured energy to John Donne's *Holy Sonnets*.

What does this mean for the project of poetry? With increasing frequency in the second instalment of *The Faerie Queene*, Spenser's poet/narrator complains of weariness and appears grateful for the temporary (and arbitrary) resting place of canto's end: 'Which, for my Muse her selfe now tyred has / Vnto an other Canto I will ouerpas' (*FQ* IV.xi.53). Completion of the narrative proposed in the Letter to Raleigh begins to seem more and more elusive, as the poet confesses in the *Amoretti* 33:

> Great wrong I doe, I can it not deny,
> to that most sacred Empresse my dear dred,
> not finishing her Queene of faëry,
> that mote enlarge her living prayses dead

Indeed, as in their different ways Patricia Parker and Jonathan Goldberg noted several decades ago, deferral comes to seem the very substance of which the poem is made.[25] At times, the poet seems to suggest that what is at stake in practical terms is the differential between visionary 'completion' and the limited scope of a single human lifespan:

> But lodwick, this of grace to me aread:
> doe ye not thinck th'accomplishment of it
> sufficient work for one mans simple head,
> all were it as the rest but rudely writ.
>
> (*Amor* 33)

But what if one takes an intermediate view? Not the brevity of one poet's contribution, however ambitious, and not the limitless reaches of eternity, but the cumulative aggregation of meaning and resonance as narratives, and poetic forms, pass from poet to poet? Do the continuities of literary history promise something more enduring than a single mortal lifetime?

In a compelling essay, Philip Hardie has proposed that the Pythagoras of *Metamorphoses* is key to Ovid's understanding of the epic genre.[26] No texts by the historical Pythagoras survive, but substantial fragments preserved in the writings of Empedocles amply document the philosopher's theory of metempsychosis.[27] Their influence in turn, Hardie argues, is manifest in the prelude to the *Annals* of Ennius (230–169 BCE), the 'father of Roman epic'.[28] When Ennius continues Homer's story from the Fall of Troy to his own era, he begins with the Dream of Homer, in which the elder poet comes to him and explains the nature of the universe, including the transmigration of souls. Two centuries later, in the *Aeneid* of Virgil, Anchises' speech in the underworld is modelled on the Ennian Dream of Homer. 'To trace the Empedoclean in [Ovid's] Speech of Pythagoras is thus', argues Hardie, to follow the outline of a genealogy that makes the *Metamorphoses* central to the history of epic.[29] And epic, we might add, was long construed as the pre-eminent vehicle for collective memory and the pre-eminent articulation of collective purpose.

Pythagoras is not much cited in the animal rights movement nor in the critical field of 'posthumanism'. Campaigners for environmental and social justice do not invoke Astraea or her despairing departure from the earth. But urgent interrogation of the category we call 'the human', sceptical analysis of the supposed boundaries between 'human' and 'other', bold propositions about the ethical entailments of a single, interdependent world system – what we now call ecosystem – are not new. As editors Joseph Campana and Scott Maisano argue in the Introduction to their recent volume, *Renaissance Posthumanism*,[30] the irony of the field devoted to critique of human exceptionalism is the complacency of its own imagined historical exceptionalism. Our predecessors, including those responsible for the emergence of early modern humanism, were much more tenuous about the centrality and stability of 'the human' than they are often given credit for. The plasticity[31] that cognitive science and biomedical research inform us is at once the special aptitude of humans and the quality that links us to the rest of the biosphere has been powerfully rendered and hypothesized by earlier thinkers, including those who found the prospect profoundly disturbing. It is not that nothing changes, far from it. But if understanding matters at all, it cannot be based upon a caricature of the past. Ovid's brilliant book of metamorphosis is a transit point, consolidating centuries of inherited speculation and providing a figurative vocabulary for centuries of speculation to come. The 'post' in posthumanism clearly signals temporal succession; to that extent it is a flat misnomer. But let us, for lack of a better term, regard the prefix as an imperfect placeholder, meant to signal conceptual dissonance and moral interrogation. This stance may be newly urgent, but it is not new.

Notes

1 In Chapter 4 above, Patrick Cheney describes linked circuitry of *Metempsychosis* thus: 'When Donne gets to his title topic, "the Pythagorean doctrine" of metempsychosis, by which "one soul from man to man" is carried, or translated (21–2), he introduces not merely a philosophical principle that recycles souls but a literary principle that establishes an authorial genealogy.'
2 Citations from the Bible: Authorized King James Version with Apocrypha (Oxford: Oxford University Press, 1997).
3 Ovid, *Metamorphoses*, 2 vols, trans. Frank Justus Miller, rev. G.P. Goold, books 9–15, 2nd ed. (Cambridge, MA: Harvard University Press, 1984).
4 Citations drawn from Edmund Spenser, *The Fairie Queene*, 2nd ed., ed. A.C. Hamilton, textual ed. Hiroshi Yamashita and Toshiyuki Suzuki (Harlow: Longman, 2001).
5 Spenser's syntax here, as is so often the case, will go on to complicate our first impressions. For that discussion, see below. Citations from *The Yale Edition of the Shorter Poems of Edmund Spenser*, ed. William Oram et al. (New Haven: Yale University Press, 1989).
6 Citations are drawn from *The Complete Poems of John Donne*, ed. Robin Robbins, rev. ed. (Harlow: Pearson/Longman, 2010).
7 Xenophanes (Fragment 7) reports that Pythagoras once intervened in the beating of a dog when he recognized the voice of a friend in the dog's yelping. *Stanford Encyclopedia of Philosophy* (online).
8 E.g., the sacrifice and reading of entrails that identify Cipus as the designated ruler of Rome (*Meta* XV.573–82); the sacrifices in honour of Aesculapius's decision to come to Rome (*Meta* XV.695) and his arrival there (*Meta* XV.735); the sacrifice and reading of entrails just prior to the assassination of Julius Caesar (*Meta* XV.794–5).
9 In her excellent book on *Spenser and Ovid*, Syrithe Pugh mounts a powerful challenge to the Virgilo-centric readings that have dominated our understanding of Spenser's career. We have wrongly assumed, she argues, that the Ovidian presence in Spenser's poems is limited to a series of troubling disruptions of or lapses from the primary, Virgilian project. When Spenser, like Ovid, presents himself as 'failing to be Virgil', he is, like Ovid, masking a sweeping and systematic critique, meant to challenge the very ideology that sustains and is sustained by epic. Syrithe Pugh, *Spenser and Ovid* (Aldershot: Ashgate, 2005).
10 This is true only north of the equator, of course. Spenser's universals, like Ovid's, were region-based.
11 George Puttenham, *The Arte of English Poesy*, ed. Frank Whigham and Wayne E. Rebhorn (Ithaca: Cornell University Press, 2007), 324.
12 Bruce Danner, *Edmund Spenser's War on Lord Burghley* (Houndmills: Palgrave Macmillan, 2011), 161. Danner notes that 1591, the year *MHT* first appeared in print, was also the year in which Elizabeth made one of her most conspicuous state visits to Theobalds, Burghley's magnificent country house. Underlying their mutual antipathy, Danner argues, is a subtle kinship between the poet of *The Faerie*

Queene and the host at Theobalds: both attempt to further their ambition by means of strategic (rural) withdrawal.
13 While the more usual strategy for targeting contemporary clerical abuses would have been to couch his satire in an ostensibly anti-Catholic fable, Spenser goes out of his way to introduce the Fox and Ape to priestly hypocrisy by means of a Protestant tutor. See *MHT* 445–78 and the discussion of this passage in Kathryn Walls, 'Spenser and the "Medieval" Past: A Question of Definition', *Renaissance Quarterly*, 70.1 (2017), 35–66.
14 Anne Lake Prescott, 'Menippean Donne', in Jeanne Shami, Dennis Flynn, and M. Thomas Hester (eds), *The Oxford Handbook of John Donne* (Oxford: Oxford University Press, 2011), 158–79 (161).
15 In a seventeenth-century manuscript copy of Donne's poem owned by the Folger Shakespeare Library, Lara Crowley has found an intriguing marginal annotation that reads, simply, 'Spenser'. Lara M. Crowley, 'Cecil and the Soul: Donne's *Metempsychosis* in Its Context in Folger Manuscript Va 241', *English Manuscript Studies 1100–1700*, 13 (2007), 47. I thank Professor Crowley for bringing this essay, and the annotation, to my attention.
16 Kenneth Gross, 'John Donne's Lyric Skepticism: In Strange Way', *Modern Philology*, 101.4 (2004 February), 371–99 (372).
17 Janel Mueller, 'Donne's Epic Venture in "Metempsychosis"', *Modern Philology*, 70.2 (1972 November), 109–37.
18 Ibid., 128.
19 See ibid., 124–5.
20 On numerology in *Metem*, see Prescott, 'Menippean Donne', and Yulia Ryzhik, 'Spenser and Donne Go Fishing', *Spenser Studies*, 31.1 (2018), 417–37.
21 Richard McCabe, *Spenser's Monstrous Regiment* (Oxford: Oxford University Press, 2002), 257–8.
22 Ibid., 263.
23 Or 'she'? The 1635 edition of Donne's *Poems* reads 'when she is she'. *The Complete Poems of John Donne*, ed. Robbins, 426n.
24 Wallace Stevens, 'Sunday Morning', *Collected Poems* (New York: Knopf, 1954).
25 Patricia Parker, *Inescapable Romance: Studies in the Poetics of a Mode* (Princeton: Princeton University Press, 1979); Jonathan Goldberg, *Endlesse Worke: Spenser and the Structures of Discourse* (Baltimore: Johns Hopkins University Press, 1981).
26 Philip Hardie, 'The Speech of Pythagoras in Ovid's *Metamorphoses* 15: Empedoclean Epos', *The Classical Quarterly*, 45.1 (1995), 204–14.
27 Ibid., 215.
28 Ibid., 209.
29 Ibid., 212.
30 Joseph Campana and Scott Maisano (eds), *Renaissance Posthumanism* (New York: Fordham University Press, 2016).
31 'Plasticity' is a key term in the essay Joseph Campana contributes to ibid: 'Epilogue: *H* is for Humanism', 283–316.

7

Cosmic matters: Spenser, Donne, and the philosophic poem

Ayesha Ramachandran

At the conclusion of his classic work *The Individual and the Cosmos in Renaissance Philosophy* Ernst Cassirer describes the singular intellectual intuition of the period, which paves the way for modernity and the new science. 'The Ego', he writes, 'must produce the vision of the universe within itself ... Man finds his true Ego by drawing the infinite universe into himself, and conversely, by extending himself to it ... [he] appears to the universe, the world, at once as the enclosing and the enclosed.'[1] Modern subjectivity, Cassirer argues, emerges in the moment when the individual and the world are no longer held in the hierarchical, symbolic relation of microcosm and macrocosm, but rather in a thoroughly enmeshed, dialectical symbiosis.[2] The revolutionary intellectual labour of the Renaissance, he suggests, lies in this reorientation between the human part and cosmic whole, following it through often surprising byways: in the lyric poetry of Petrarch, in the sculpture of Michelangelo, in the heroic frenzies of Giordano Bruno, rather than through more traditional histories of philosophy. Art, Cassirer suggests, is where the groundbreaking philosophic work of the Renaissance happens; to see it, we must take seriously the question of form.[3]

Taken individually, Edmund Spenser and John Donne offer obvious case studies for Cassirer's claim: both are concerned with the relations between the individual and cosmos; both inherit and respond to the energy of Bruno's heterodox oeuvre; and both grapple with the contradictory philosophical currents of the day in their poetry.[4] But this intellectual-historical view also opens a new perspective on the encounter between the two poets, who are so tantalizingly adjacent in literary history, and yet seem so far apart in critical practice. Looking past the confines of genre, we must trace connections between the 'philosophic work' of both poets – and see surprising continuities despite obvious differences in chronology and biography.

Such an invitation is enticing not only because it draws Spenser and Donne into renewed connection but because the links between the intellectual preoccupations of the two writers shows us how and why we must look across the period barrier of 1600. For the cusp of the century discloses a conjunction of intellectual practices and poetic concerns that demand more nuanced and expansive literary histories to account for them.[5] Spenser's death in 1599 has served as something of a symbolic marker, taking on great historiographic significance as a moment of transition from Renaissance to early modern, from Elizabethan to Jacobean, and from a world of magical correspondence to one of disenchantment.[6] That Spenser's and Donne's major works are published on either side of this great divide – which incidentally also separates

Shakespeare's comedies and 'problem plays' from the tragedies, or Jonson's comic drama from his masques and poems – reinforces a narrative of rupture and disconnection as the primal scene for the emergence of a modern literary voice concerned with questions of subjectivity, political and religious self-determination, philosophical scepticism and self-conscious irony. It is no accident, of course, that this historical narrative is replicated in the nineteenth and twentieth centuries: where T.S. Eliot identified a kind of modernist predecessor in the metaphysical poetry of Donne, the Romantics had exalted Spenser, 'the poet of rest and dream, imagination and wonder, metrical music and pictorial delight'.[7] But to what extent does this tale about the emergence of modernity in the seventeenth century – one that draws force not only from literary historians but also from historians of science and contemporary theorists – depend on the effacing of its deep roots in the sixteenth century with its persistent belief in monsters, angels, stellar influence, scholasticism, humanist authorities and magical correspondence?[8] By uncovering some of the shared philosophical and poetic concerns of Spenser and Donne we can begin to answer this question.

Macrocosm and microcosm

The analogy of microcosm and macrocosm, one of the favourite tropes of the early modern period, is a cultural touchstone because it encapsulates perhaps *the* central philosophic problem of the Renaissance: the relationship of the particular to the universal.[9] When Andrew Marvell concludes *Upon Appleton House* in 1651, he gestures to the breakdown of the ancient systems that gave this analogy philosophic force for almost two millennia: "Tis not, what once it was, the world', he muses.[10] For Marvell and his contemporaries, by the mid-seventeenth century, the crumbling of old systems of explanation had left the macrocosmic world itself suddenly vague and undefined, its intelligibility and extent unmoored by the discovery of a New World and new planetary bodies by colonial and commercial exploration and by intellectual trends of sceptical thought, theological questioning, and astronomical speculation. The human and natural worlds seemed decentred and disconnected from a higher order, no more than 'a rude heap' of individual parts. These particulars now lacked the intelligibility that comes from belonging to a symbolic system in which 'each and every object, if viewed correctly, will be seen to reproduce a cosmic totality'.[11]

By locating the writing of Spenser and Donne in this wider intellectual context, we see at once why they are preoccupied with fundamental questions about the place of human beings within a universe whose contours were being radically reshaped. And while it is hardly new to note that their poems engage deeply with the late sixteenth-century revival of cosmology and natural philosophy, their peculiar similitudes on this matter have been long neglected.[12] Though the two poets have been sporadically connected in terms of genre and style – after all, Donne is the first major writer of epithalamia in English after Spenser, and his Petrarchism is certainly indebted to Spenser's various Petrarchan experiments in both lyric and epic form – their philosophic kinship has rarely been explored.[13] And while Donne's philosophic positions are distinct from Milton's, they are curiously similar to Spenser's: their work forms an extended dialogue with shared themes, intellectual practices, and rhetorical strategies.

If Donne famously laments in the *First Anniversary*, "Tis all in peeces, all cohaerence gone; / All just supply, and all Relation' (*FA*, lines 213–14), Spenser had already portrayed a disordered cosmos in the Proem to Book V of the *Faerie Queene*, published the same year as the *Fowre Hymnes* (1596), in language that seems to anticipate Donne:

> For who so list into the heauens looke,
>   And search the courses of the rowling spheares,
>   Shall find that from the point, where they first tooke
>   Their setting forth, in these few thousand yeares
>   They all are wandred much
> ...
>   So now all range, and doe at randon roue
>   Out of their proper places farre away,
>   And all this world with them amisse doe moue,
>   And all his creatures from their course astray,
> Till they arriue at their last ruinous decay.
>
> (*FQ* V.Proem.5–6)[14]

This is Spenser's allegorical version of the impact of the new philosophies, whose effect was already being sharply felt in the last two decades of the sixteenth century. The concentric spheres of the Ptolemaic cosmos with the still Earth at its centre were being dislodged by the heliocentric Copernican hypothesis, intimations of infinite space, and the increasing decentring of humanity within a contingent universe. Spenser may be thinking here of Giordano Bruno, who lectured at Oxford in 1583 (mentioning Copernicus) and published *The Ash-Wednesday Supper*, a dialogue on Copernicanism dedicated to Sir Philip Sidney, in 1584.[15] Spenser's straying Zodiac is a sign of both moral failure and a failure of epistemic understanding: the random roving of the stars and planets is an obvious mirror of earthly disorder, but it also registers a crisis of human knowledge about the universe, for the old paradigms no longer explain new observations. The image is repeated and developed with almost identical import by Donne in the *First Anniversary* as a particular instance of the decaying world:

> They have impal'd within a Zodiake
> The free-borne Sun, and keepe twelve Signes awake
> To watch his steps; the Goat and Crab controule,
> And fright him backe ...
> For his course is not round; nor can the Sunne
> Perfit a circle ...
> He comes no more, but with a couzening line,
> Steales by that point, and so is Serpentine
>
> (*FA*, lines 263–72)[16]

We have not travelled very far from Spenser's lament in *The Faerie Queene* – in Donne's hands, the trope is enhanced and given a more sinister cast, but it remains a moral and epistemological sign.[17] Donne may be referring here to Kepler's recent work on elliptical planetary orbits, a development of the Copernican hypothesis based on Tycho's observations and published in the *Astronomia nova* of 1609; but this new knowledge leads only to a greater epistemic impasse and a sharper sense of cosmic imperfection.[18] As in Spenser, it becomes a marker of fallenness, 'a couzening line' that tricks human understanding and is therefore 'Serpentine' – the visible heavens are no longer a symbolic guide for human action, but may lead them instead into transgression.

Paradoxically, both Spenser and Donne reassert the analogy of microcosm to macrocosm even as they chronicle its breakdown. For the perfection of symbolic symmetries between individual and cosmos are replaced by symmetries of imperfection and dislocation. The world is out of joint because humans no longer seem to understand the bases of cosmic order and therefore cannot find their own rightful place or course of action. Like Spenser, Donne is concerned with fundamental questions that emerge from reorientations in the analogy of microcosm to macrocosm: is there a predetermined cosmic order, a *scala naturae*, established by a demiurgic deity within which humans took their place? Or can individual humans play a part in knowing and (re)making the cosmos thereby determining their own conditions of possibility and action? How are souls and bodies, spirit/form and matter, connected and how can we account for the separation? How can we intimate eternity when we are confined to the mutable, mortal, and material world?

While these questions run through the works of both poets, they coalesce most sharply in the encounter between Spenser's *Fowre Hymnes* and Donne's *Anniversaries* – though on the surface, the poems have little to do with each other and even seem to face in different historical directions. Spenser's persistent Petrarchism, his syncretic Neoplatonism and his mixing of theology and classical philosophy seem to look backward to the language and concerns of the *quattrocento*, while Donne's frequently enjambed, knotty couplets, metaphysical conceits and careful parsing of natural philosophical and theological arguments look ahead to the later seventeenth-century's literary and intellectual preoccupations. Moreover, the *Fowre Hymnes* and the *Anniversaries* are notoriously obscure poems. Their encrustations of abstruse philosophical detail and their forbidding rhetorical surfaces have led generations of readers to intuit their importance as poetic monuments while struggling to make sense of their meaning. Critics have unravelled their philosophical knots through detailed studies of specific influences and contexts, but it is not clear that such careful annotation, immensely valuable though it is, captures the intellectual appeal or broader stakes of the poems. One reason for this interpretative difficulty is the challenge of locating these poems in a wider literary and philosophical landscape made of complex, shifting terrain. Too often, the poetic and philosophic aspects of the poems are treated independently from each other.[19]

And yet, one clue to their connection is their subject which draws together poetry and philosophy: both are fundamentally concerned with the nature of the cosmos. From the literal sense of the cosmos's structure and substance to the relations between its parts and the spiritual lessons to be drawn from an individual point of view, both poems long for a knowledge of cosmic form, which they exhaustively rehearse in various ways – for this, they hope, will reveal the key to an individual moral order. For both poets, an apprehension of divine control over the universe is connected to the promise of salvation and resurrection of the individual self.

But the cosmos matters to Spenser and Donne not only as a philosophic framework, a moral guide, or a visible sign of a divine plan. It is also a foundational aesthetic value. The Greek *kosmos* presents a distinctly aesthetic understanding of the universe (attributed to Pythagoras), since it signifies order, beauty, form, fashion, and ornament. It is also the shared root of *cosmetic* and its derivatives, emphasizing, by its very etymology, an aesthetically beautiful form. Several Renaissance cosmographers and map-makers allude to this etymology, including Jacopo d'Angelo (the first translator of Ptolemy's *Geography* into Latin), Simon Grynaeus, Abraham Ortelius, Hondius and Blaeu, and it was inevitably a rich metaphor awaiting poetic exploitation.[20] For as an extension of the analogy between (worldly) macrocosm and (human) microcosm, the idea of *kosmos* invited an analogy between the well-crafted, beautiful universe and the well-crafted, beautiful poem, one made by the deity and the other by human hands. This aesthetic understanding of the universe and the microcosmic connection to it, via both the human body and the human work of art, begins to explain Spenser's and Donne's obsessive preoccupation with the representation of cosmic order and its breakdown.

Spenser's combination of love poetry and philosophical speculation in the hymns to earthly and divine love and beauty offer a dialectical meditation on the relations between matter and form, human and divine, mutability and eternity as they dramatize a desire to uncover the underlying order of the universe. Drawing together aesthetics and cosmology, they suggest that the individual mind makes sense of the world by seeking its 'Paterne' (*An Hymne in Honour of Beautie* (*HB*), lines 32–6), that poetic symmetries can recreate intellectual coherence amidst competing philosophic paradigms.[21] In the final hymn to *Heavenly Beautie* (*HHB*), Spenser expands on the book of nature topos by insisting that we see the divine only in contemplating the beautiful cosmos:

> The meanes therefore which unto us is lent,
> Him to behold, is on his workes to looke,
> Which he hath made in beauty excellent,
> And in the same, as in a brasen booke ...
> For all thats good, is beautifull and faire.
>
> (*HHB*, lines 127–33)[22]

The universe is like a book here, beautiful and strong ('brasen' here suggests indestructible as brass), and most importantly, *fashioned* with deliberate skill – much like Spenser's own interweaving poems.

Though seemingly different in form, Donne's elegiac meditations on the death of Elizabeth Drury also grapple with the problem of order in the universe and the individual's ability to discern it at a time of philosophic crisis. As 'new Philosophy calls all in doubt' in the *First Anniversary*, poetry, the source of aesthetic coherence, provides the figurative correspondences that assert a new vision of the individual's extension into the cosmos. The extravagant exploration of the hylozoic world-body on the anatomist's table literalizes the problematic analogy of microcosm and macrocosm, while the stars 'as ... so many beads / Strung on one string' echo 'the pith, which ... / Strings fast the little bones of necke, and backe' (*Second Anniversary* (*SA*), lines 207–12) linking the mortal, material human body to the starry skies above. It is not surprising then that what Donne mourns most emphatically in the *First Anniversary* – and what he is at pains to re-establish in the second – is 'proportion', a version of the ideal *kosmos*. 'The worlds proportion disfigured is ... / And, Oh, it can no more be questioned, / That beauties best, proportion, is dead', writes Donne (*FA*, lines 302–6). It is no accident that Donne's 'proportion' here intersects conceptually with Spenser's 'beautie', and itself becomes a metaleptic term that crosses the two anniversary poems. But 'proportion' also expresses the rhetorical figure of analogy – the figure that holds together the cosmos, as well as Donne's poems.[23]

As Elizabeth D. Harvey and Timothy Harrison write eloquently, 'Donne struggles to contain a sense of cultural crisis by drawing a phenomenological experience of cosmic connectedness into language. The poems attempt to heal the very problem they diagnose ... in a way that makes poetic figuration homologous with the cosmic principle it represents.'[24] But the observation of Harvey and Harrison holds true for Spenser as well and touches on a deeper impulse in Renaissance poetry – the desire to use the shaping power of poetry to remake a broken symbolic system that connects the individual to the cosmos. Poetry, with its formal symmetries, harmonious patterns, and figural tissue, repairs the disordered cosmos in the act of representing it as an ordered whole. It does not merely hold the mirror up to nature; it shapes our understanding of the phenomenological world.

Not surprisingly, early modern thinkers across a range of disciplines repeatedly invoked strategies of poetic figuration as they forged new philosophies.[25] The young René Descartes, for instance, would write in 1618–19 that 'It can seem amazing that there are more profound judgments in the writings of poets than of philosophers. The reason is that poets write through enthusiasm and the force of imagination'.[26] Much of his writing in both the *Discourse on Method* and the *Meditations* self-consciously depends on metaphors that make possible new kinds of philosophic connection. Harvey and Harrison thus shift the terms of the debate over Donne's *Anniversaries* and in so doing demand that we reconsider the intellectual labour of such early modern verse. From this perspective, local debates about the decorum of epideictic, panegyric, or elegaic poetry, or the specific details of scientific or theological allusions, seem less important. What is at stake is an identification of the broader cultural symptoms to which Donne responds as a thinker among other thinkers: how is man connected to or disconnected from the universe? What does the new order tell us about our past and future? How is it connected to the old? These are Spenser's questions too, as they are questions at the heart of the period's struggle to reconfigure the ancient analogy of microcosm and macrocosm to suit modern times.

Even though the passage from an earlier time of macrocosmic connection to a modern one of disconnection is often characterized as a philosophic shift, it is also, as Marshall Grossman has astutely observed, a rhetorical reorientation. Grossman notes that in rhetorical practice the analogy of microcosm to macrocosm is 'an iterative set of metonymies of genus for species and species for genus' where 'species is literally what appears' (the particular) and 'genus' refers to the category into which the species may be assimilated (the universal).[27] Shifts in the rhetorical relations between the terms become an index of more abstract, philosophical shifts; by attending to rhetoric and poetic figuration, we may also attend, more precisely, to philosophical questions. This insight, which helps explain the conjunction of poetry and philosophy in poems such as Spenser's *Fowre Hymnes* and Donne's *Anniversaries*, was thoroughly embedded within early modern culture and participates in the broader drive to achieve *kosmos* at the micro-level of language itself. It also suggests the basis for a strong intellectual alignment between Spenser and Donne that pushes beyond familiar models of influence, allusion, and imitation as we account for the seeming kinship between the two poets' aims and practices.[28]

Poetry and philosophy

If *kosmos* can be understood in aesthetic and rhetorical terms, it might point the way towards a hybrid, ample basis for the encounter between Spenser and Donne through the textual genres that made manifest visions of cosmic order on the page. Chief among these are the hymn and the 'philosophical poem', a mixed but legible genre that frequently included religious and theological themes alongside classical natural and moral philosophy, both of which reached back to the Pre-Socratics and were enjoying a revival in the sixteenth century. By drawing on these interlinked literary and philosophical histories, Spenser and Donne share the literary groundwork of philosophical thought, inviting comparison and thereby enacting a historical copula between the ancients and the moderns even as they highlight fissures and perplexities in the early modern philosophical landscape.[29]

If Pythagoras can be credited with the idea of the universe as a *kosmos*, a 'perfect order and arrangement', it is hardly surprising that Renaissance poets traced the origins of philosophic poetry back to Orphic hymns from where Pythagoras was said to have learned the secrets of number and harmony.[30] A key figure in the Neoplatonic tradition, Pythagoras symbolically held together philosophy and poetry at the level of proportion and metrical order, even as he became an emblem for heterodoxy because of his theory of the transmigration of souls – a trope invoked by Spenser in the Garden of Adonis episode of *The Faerie Queene* and by Donne in *Metempsychosis*.[31] This interest in both cosmic harmony and philosophical heterodoxy underlies the renewed interest in philosophical poetry in the sixteenth century, which emerges in conversation with various verse translations of classical philosophic texts (for instance, Pontano's translation of Ptolemy's *Tetrabiblos*) and heroic Christian poems (such as Vida's *Christiad*), but stands apart in its innovative, integrative, and exploratory energy.

Though under-studied today largely because so many of its most influential examples are Neo-Latin poems, philosophical poetry is an intriguing genre for its astonishing heterogeneity of subject matter, its experimentation with generic form, and its often radical and unsettling modes of thought – all of which respond to the crisis of individual and cosmos and would have been attractive to both Spenser and Donne.[32] The term itself connotes a catch-all category that includes astronomical and cosmological works (such as Pontano's *Urania*, Buchanan's *De sphaera*, Guy Le Fèvre de la Boderie's *L'encyclie des secrets de l'eternité*, Scève's *Microcosme*), hermetic poetry

(Bruno's *Degli eroici furori*), hexameral poetry (Du Bartas's, *La semaine*; Tasso's *Sette giorni del mondo creato*), alchemical poetry (Augurelli's *Chrysopoeia*), medical poems (Fracastoro's *Syphilis*), poems on knowledge (Ronsard, Chapman, Davies), on desire and philosophic fulfilment (Donne, Drayton), on mathematics and science (Bruno). All these are united by their attempt to grapple with that central problem of the relationship between the particular and universal. Despite their differences of genre, all these poems demonstrate a 'will to form', that is, a desire to reshape cosmic order through poetic practice, specifically by recrafting the figurative scope of the macrocosm/microcosm analogy. By 1581, the presence of 'philosophic poetry' is an identifiable phenomenon, underscored by the appearance of a 'Discours philosophique et historial de la poésie philosophique', dedicated to Ronsard, by Jean Edouard du Monin, who called himself a 'poete philosophe' and who was, among other things, the translator of Du Bartas's *La semaine* into Latin.[33] An allegorical defence of philosophical poetry in the form of a dream vision, Du Monin's text establishes a literary history for the genre going back to Orpheus and takes as its core subject the discovery of the nature of things – the order underlying the natural world, the microcosm of the individual, the cosmos itself.

Philosophical poetry, therefore, may be characterized by its focus on epistemological problems and its movement away from the ontological questions that underlie traditional Scholastic philosophy. Grossman, for instance, points out that the *Anniversaries* 'treat of a timely tendency to forgo metaphysics – the futility of which they metaphysically explore – in favour of epistemology, that is, to shift the focus from the world to be known to the knowledge of the world'.[34] While this tendency is a staple in prose treatises of the period, perhaps most famously articulated in Montaigne's 'Apology for Raymond Sebond', it has rarely been identified as a key component in Renaissance lyric poetry.[35] But the thematization of epistemic desire was uniquely suited to the forms and concerns of the sixteenth-century lyric. As Neil Kenny observes in his study on French philosophical poets, philosophic poetry, or the *poésie scientifique* of the sixteenth century, confronts the desire for knowledge in its many forms and the almost inevitably unrequited nature of that desire, for what we can know is finally limited.[36]

In both Spenser's and Donne's poems, desire becomes a metaphor for a process of thinking and knowing, and poetry itself emerges as a unique vehicle for modes of active cognition. The readerly trajectory of the *Fowre Hymnes* consequently traces an arc from materiality to abstraction. The lyrics move from the singular experiential instant through the intellective process that makes meaning and extracts its underlying form; the 'careful wretches' of *An Hymne in Honour of Love*, tormented by their unfulfilled sexual desires, culminate in the final hymn's sublime Sapience, 'the soveraine dearling of the *Deity*', who holds the key to cosmic form. Spenser's presentation of contradictory cosmologies in the *Hymnes* (Empedoclean, Lucretian, Platonic, Aristotelian) is thus not so much a mimetic representation of the cosmos as it is a means of thinking through competing philosophical paradigms through a series of thought experiments.[37] Donne is more directly urgent in the exhortation to thought: the anaphoric 'Thinke … thinke … thinke …' (*SA*, lines 107–21) which appears twelve times in the space of fifteen lines creates a rising crescendo in the *Second Anniversary* that is picked up by a second anaphoric refrain of 'Thou know'st... thou ... know'st ... thou ... know' (*SA*, lines 255–60). Once again, mimetic representation is beside the point; the two *Anniversary* poems highlight their commitment to an alternative, philosophical poetics by dramatizing in their titles the cleavage between 'the whole world ... *represented*' and 'the soul ... *contemplated*' (my emphases). Donne's accent on this gap between representation of the visible, phenomenological world and contemplation of the invisible, spiritual realm of the soul foregrounds poetry's singular ability to bridge the intellectual abyss between the visible and invisible, that which can be known and that which can only be speculated.[38]

Locating Spenser's *Fowre Hymnes* and Donne's *Anniversaries* in this tradition of philosophical poetry explains some scholars' description of Donne's poem as 'metaphysical in the strong sense', that is, in terms of the poem's philosophical purpose rather than as a merely stylistic designation.[39] When Samuel Johnson coined the label 'metaphysical poetry' in his *Lives*, echoing Dryden's witticism on Donne ('He affects the metaphysics, not only in his satires, but in his amorous verses, where nature only should reign; and perplexes the minds of the fair sex with nice speculations of philosophy'), he was belatedly and unconsciously codifying the culmination of a poetic tradition that had its origins in antiquity (Empedocles, Ennius, Lucretius) and had been revived by the *quattrocento* humanists.[40] In this lens, Spenser's mythmaking set-pieces and cosmological ruminations, not only in the *Fowre Hymnes* but also in poems such as *Colin Clouts Come Home Againe*, the *Cantos of Mutabilitie*, and parts of *The Faerie Queene*, are influential predecessors to the metaphysical work of seventeenth-century poets such as Donne.

Just as Spenser's interlaced and mirroring hymns recreate *kosmos* within the rhetorical perfection of a rhyme royal stanza, Donne's *Anniversaries* too recall formal structures of reflection and interconnection that call forth the effect of a stable universal order of things. This similarity may in fact point to their generic connection: Donne himself refers to the paired poems as 'Hymnes' in the *Second Anniversary* (*SA*, 37–44), and, as the first English version of the classical hymn, Spenser's *Fowre Hymnes* are an obvious and crucial touchstone. Of course, with its supposed Orphic origin, the hymn was the paramount genre for a philosophic poem.[41]

Although critical commentary on the *Anniversaries* has focused largely on their generic connection to the funeral elegy and the meditation, placing them alongside Spenser's *Hymnes* highlights structural and figural patterns that explain the poems' vatic, incantatory energies and their desire to analyze and act upon the decaying world through the magic of poetic language. As Barbara Lewalski and Rosalie Colie have both pointed out, the *Anniversaries* have a distinctly hymnic quality and include specific elements of the Renaissance hymn, particularly as it explores the separation between humanity and the divine.[42] Donne in fact mobilizes the conceptual proximity between the elegy and hymn – both seek to make the absent present, to investigate desires for transcendence, and to connect the mortal, phenomenological world with intimations of the divine – and, in this sense, the *Anniversaries* are an exemplary successor to the 'daring assay' of the *Fowre Hymnes*.[43] Like Spenser, Donne draws together the natural philosophical and Christian themes of Marullus's *Hymni naturales* and Vida's Latin hymns, the two models of hymnic practice in the period, thereby uniting the classical and Christian inheritance into a sustained meditation on a shifting world order.

Both the *Hymnes* and the *Anniversaries* have a distinct two-part structure – Spenser's 'earthy and natural loves' in the first two hymns to *Love* and *Beautie* are placed in self-conscious counterpoint to the 'heavenly and celestial ones' in the hymns of *Heavenly Love* (*HHL*) and of *Heavenly Beautie* (*HHB*). This binary opposition is also the overt organizing principle for Donne's two anniversary poems, as the *An Anatomie of the World* stands against the subsequent *Of the Progresse of the Soule*. In both sets of poems, the binaries also encode a narrative of ascent, from low to high, earthly to heavenly, material to immaterial. These binaries, however, are eventually revealed to be murky and thoroughly enmeshed in each other – and it is in the *undoing* of these conventional philosophical polarities, which tend to structure reality for powerful ideological reasons (as Carlo Ginzburg has trenchantly noted), that the poems reveal the stakes of their intellectual labour.[44] Donne may even have learned this technique of using the malleability of poetic figuration against the rigidity of philosophical proposition from Spenser.

Understood as part of a literary historical continuum, Spenser's and Donne's poems reveal an early modern philosophical poetics that confronted the crisis of cosmic order and sought to redress it from a position outside the intellectual confines of the philosophical proposition. By recognizing the broadly epistemological thrust of the new philosophies and incorporating its energy into patterns of thinking unique to poetry, both Spenser and Donne produce poems that simultaneously reflect the need for philosophic stability in an era of transition and respond to this challenge in their very form. Such disclosures, however, also raise theoretical and methodological problems for any comparative study for the two poets, for it brings us back to the thorny question of their encounter: did it happen? And if so, how did it happen? Are all these correspondences merely historical accidents and suggestive coincidences that show two poets responding in similar ways to the similar cultural and intellectual dilemmas? What is the threshold of proof for imagining an encounter between Spenser and Donne?

Given the difficulty of establishing beyond a doubt the historical connection between the two poets on the strength of specific allusions or intertexts, we must, I would argue, turn to other possible models for literary encounter that explain shared patterns and proximities. One such possibility emerges from the notion of 'encounter' itself. In a now-famous address, Mary Louise Pratt evoked the notion of 'contact zones' – 'social spaces where cultures meet, clash, and grapple with each other, often in contexts of highly asymmetrical relations of power' – as opposed to the more cohesive, egalitarian, and stable notion of 'community'.[45] Quickly absorbed into theoretical vocabulary across a range of fields, the idea of the 'contact zone' as a shifting locus of encounter, often identified with trading posts and border cities, is now ubiquitous in discussing early modern colonial, imperial or cross-cultural relations. But it also offers rich metaphorical possibilities for theorizing asymmetrical or historically glancing intellectual encounters that are hard to pin down but suggestive in their proximity. Such an intellectual contact zone might be a rhetorical-philosophical space – a topos – where shared conceptual concerns can converge through the force of genre, form and figure, each of which carries the imprint of prior exchanges. Spenser and Donne – rough contemporaries for a time – certainly shared such an intellectual contact zone and it afforded a discrete literary topography for building a robust poetic response to philosophic crisis.

Towards a philosophical poetics

Love and Beauty in Spenser's hymns become metaleptic keywords that mediate a series of interlinked reflections on the nature of creation, the form of the physical universe, the relationship between the visible, phenomenological world and the invisible heavens, the continuum of human desire and divine compassion, the interpenetration of body and soul, and the promise of the afterlife. While these keywords remain seemingly unchanging through incantatory sequences of repetition within and across the hymns, they take on a range of shifting meanings, containing within themselves entire philosophic histories that the speaker reconciles through poetic conjunction. 'Love', for instance, is deployed across the four hymns in a variety of overlapping, complementary, and contradictory ways:

> The flaming light of that celestiall fyre,
> Which kindleth **love** in generous desyre,
> And makes him mount above the native might
> Of heavie earth, up to the heavens hight.
>
> (*HL*, lines 186–9)

> For **Love** is a celestiall harmonie,
> Of likely harts composd of starres concent,
> Which joyne together in sweete sympathie,
> To worke ech others joy and true content
>
> (*HB*, lines 197–200)

> For **lovers** eyes more sharpely sighted bee
> Then other mens, and in deare **loves** delight
>
> (*HB*, lines 232–3)

> **Love**, lift me up upon thy golden wings,
> From this base world unto thy heavens hight,
> Where I may see those admirable things
>
> (*HHL*, lines 1–3)

> He made by **love** out of his owne like mould,
> In whom he might his mightie selfe behould:
> For **love** doth **love** the thing belov'd to see,
> That like it selfe in **lovely** shape may bee.
>
> (*HHL*, lines 116–19)

> Then shalt thou feele thy spirit so possest,
> And ravisht with devouring great desire
> Of his deare selfe, that shall thy feeble brest
> Inflame with **love**, and set thee all on fire
>
> (*HHL*, lines 267–70)

Love, in these examples, is a cosmogonic force, a cosmic principle, a physical need, a metaphysical foundation, a spiritual comfort, and an ethical principle. It is a term that encompasses all aspects of the world, from the emotions and psychology of the individual to the very substance of the universe, from a basic reproductive impulse to a principle of compassion and the basis of a community, from the desire that brings the deity itself into existence (*HHL*, 116–19) to the ultimate sacrifice of the Son to redeem a fallen humanity. There are conceptual and philosophic continuities between these various meanings, but it is Spenser's use of metalepsis, a rhetorical figure, that pulls these divergent topics into cohesion. Poetic language here generates a series of associations that produces the effect of philosophic order and cosmic cohesion – through the hymns, all parts of the cosmos at every level of experience, from physical to metaphysical, are drawn into tight connection.

In the verses from the *Hymne in Honour of Love* cited above, for instance, the 'flaming light of that celestiall fyre' (*HL*, line 188) invites an ascent ('makes him mount above … up') which is simultaneously imaginative, emotional, and material. The 'light' and 'fyre' contrast with 'heavie earth' in an upward motion that concludes the sentence with 'heavens hight', marking the separation of elements, as well as a psychic trajectory from desire to transcendence. The *Hymne in Honour of Beautie* returns to Love, this time not as a 'celestiall fyre' but as a 'celestiall harmony' (*HB*, line 197), as though to explain how the imagined ascent of the previous hymn occurs: in this poem, love joins 'likely harts … in sweete sympathie', a movement that explains the bonds that hold the universe together. These love-ascents mobilize the central Petrarchan-Neoplatonic conceit of the *Fowre Hymnes* – desire and its fulfilment via a 'ladder of love' – but also transform it through repetition and variation into a device that articulates the epistemological desire and spiritual thirst of the speaker, who in each of the hymns' concluding stanzas seeks the assurance of certain knowledge. In the *Hymne of Heavenly Love*, the speaker reprises the language of the first hymn with the strategic desire/fire rhyme (*HHL*, lines 268, 270; cited above), but transforms its erotic charge into a spiritual one: it is 'thy spirit' which will be 'ravisht with devouring great desire' for the Son. The fires of longing here are for religious apotheosis, which, in the subsequent *Hymne of Heavenly Beautie*, will coalesce with a desire for Sapience, knowledge of the foundations of cosmic architecture.

The repetition and counterpointing of themes across the four hymns create a complex set of interactions: the two hymns on love are arrayed against the two hymns on beauty, matching meditations on the material, desiring body with images of intangible, desired form; but the paired earthly and heavenly hymns also function as units in a dialogue, exploring a different, but related, dualism. At the same time, all the hymns share formal features, most notably distinct creation accounts and 'progresses' of the desiring subject towards a paradisal destination, which shifts its particular contours across each hymn, but may ultimately point towards the same goal. Internally, the hymns juxtapose repeated narratives of ascent and descent, fall and redemption, performing in language the very effort of thought as it struggles to comprehend the mysteries of cosmic order.

Though the *Fowre Hymnes* do not betray overt anxieties over philosophic and cosmic incoherence, their carefully closed symmetries and elaborate structures of framing and repetition make a strong case for what the poet *hopes* is true even if he lacks empirical evidence. The language of the two 'heavenly' hymns is therefore strikingly subjunctive in mode for their figures invoke a closed harmony that they hope to call into being through poetic incantation. 'Ah then my hungry soule', urges the speaker at the conclusion of the *Hymne of Heavenly Beautie*:

> Ah cease to gaze on matter of thy grief.
>
> And looke at last up to that soveraine light,
> From whose pure beams al perfect beauty springs,
> That kindleth love in every godly spright,
> Even the love of God, which loathing brings
> Of this vile world, and these gay seeming things;
> With whose sweete pleasures being so possest,
> Thy straying thoughts henceforth for ever rest.
>
> (*HHB*, lines 294–301)

The rapturous view of 'perfect beauty', celebrated as Sapience or Wisdom earlier in the hymn, is fervently promised in these closing lines, but not actually made available. Poetry here is deployed in its ancient form as invocation, as a calling into being through the imagination of a perceived lack that harkens back to the lyric's roots in magical spells. But, as Thomas Greene observes, 'Magical words might be taken to suggest the possibility of a perfect language in which phonic echoes would mirror metaphysical correspondences … [but] the poem must settle for a *scattered* world barren of correspondence, and it must settle for provisional meanings emergent from incomplete analogies'.[46] In this situation, 'Poetry celebrates, heightens, and tests the act of the mind which situates us as subjects, provisionally and contingently, in the post magical disorderly world'.[47] This is Spenser's condition at the end of the *Fowre Hymnes*. It is no accident that these poems have seemed somehow impenetrable, too gleaming and glib perhaps, gesturing towards a philosophical grand style that never condenses into propositional substance. Their purpose is not philosophic system-building but a therapeutic *poiesis*.[48] The *Fowre Hymnes*, like Giordano Bruno's *Degli eroici furori*, experiments with the possibility of a philosophic poetry that does not engage in philosophic debate, but describes, enacts, and brings a philosophic vision into being through the power of the poetic charm. In this, Spenser's goal is nothing less than the re-establishment of the relations between individual and cosmos through the ties of poetic figuration.

If Spenser's *Hymnes* conclude with an assertion of poetic power and the promise of rapture, Donne's *Anniversaries*, by contrast, seem to dramatize the 'loss of the ritual power of language itself' and the 'lost sacramental potency of art'.[49] Towards the end of the *First Anniversary*, he gloomily cautions: 'What Artist now dares boast that he can bring / Heaven hither, or constellate anything … / The art is lost, and correspondence too' (*FA*, lines 391–6). But by the end of the *Second Anniversary*, Donne too claims the vatic voice of poetic invocation, which joins the classical hymnic suppliant to that of Ezekiel: 'Thou art the Proclamation; and I am / The Trumpet, at whose voice the people came.' The passage from the earlier poem's pessimism to the final triumphant assertion of the poet as prophet, however, is not contradictory or accidental – Donne, like Spenser, makes the intellectual movement from one extreme position to the other the very subject of his *Anniversaries*. Using the death of Elizabeth Drury – a singular, tragic instance – as an emblem of the need to recalibrate the relations between particular and universal, Donne returns to the analogy of macrocosm and microcosm with the tools of early modern philosophical poetics.

The *Anniversaries* in fact take on the mixed genre of philosophic poetry more overtly than the *Fowre Hymnes*. From their individual titles (*An Anatomie of the World* and *Of the Progresse of the Soule*) and their paratextual glosses, which recall the apparatus of philosophical or theological treatises, to their direct engagement with 'Philosophie' as a topic and a discipline, the *Anniversaries* are an extended lament for philosophical stability and theological assurance.[50] But they are also a potent response to this desire through poetic figuration. Elizabeth's death precipitates a confrontation with the implications of mortality as an insurmountable limit that radically separates body and soul, matter and spirit, individual and cosmos, human and divine – and, in response, Donne's poems ruminate on the nature of the created world in order to re-establish the severed connections. Elizabeth's death becomes both representative of the philosophic discontinuities that Donne will bemoan and *subject* to them; healing the philosophic ruptures through poetic integration in the *Anniversaries* becomes a potent act of consolation as well as a creative, resurrective overcoming of mortality's limitation.[51] As in the *Fowre Hymnes*, poetry provides the coherence that philosophy cannot offer, replacing the breakdown of systematic propositions with the glue of metaphoric correspondence.[52] But where Spenser seeks harmony, Donne deliberately emphasizes dissonance and stages a sceptical 'crisis' that can be resolved only by the revelations of poetic utterance. In the *Anniversaries*, the poet begins with the tragic crisis of the loss of Elizabeth's body, expanding it into a cosmic crisis that will be, paradoxically, resolved from within his own body – through the poetic voice ('I am / The Trumpet') that triumphantly pronounces the conjoining and coherence promised at the end of times. This intellectual trajectory, which (re)combines space and time, will be the poems' great labour.

The carefully crafted juxtapositions across the two poems illustrate this scope: the *Anniversaries* open with couplet-rhymes that signal the relationship of microcosm and macrocosm at the most minute poetic level:

> When that rich Soule which to her heaven is gone,
> Whom all do celebrate, who know they have one,
> (For who is sure he hath a Soule, unlesse
> It see, and judge, and follow worthinesse,
> And by Deedes praise it? hee who doth not this,
> May lodge an In-mate soule, but 'tis not his.)
>
> (*FA*, lines 1–6)

> Nothing could make me sooner to confesse
> That this world has an everlastingnesse,
> Than to consider, that a yeare is runne,
> Since both this lower world's, and the Sunnes Sunne,
> The Lustre, and the vigor of this All,
> Did set; 'twere blasphemie to say, did fall.
>
> (*SA*, lines 1–6)

It is no accident that the topics and the rhyme schemes of the two poems are strategically inverted. The *First Anniversary, An Anatomie of the World*, opens with a meditation on souls, while the *Second Anniversary, Of the Progresse of the Soule*, opens with a meditation on the world. This simple crossing of subject matter indicates a mirrored inversion of the poems' conceptual trajectories – the first moves outward and downward from soul to world, while the second moves inward and upward from world to soul – so that the poems themselves perform and struggle with the very dualisms that they discuss. Moreover, Donne reverses the opening rhyme scheme of the *First Anniversary* (*aabb*) to begin the second poem (*bbaa*), cementing the relationship between them at the level of both phoneme and discourse: *gone/one* is echoed by *runne/sunne*, while *unless/worthinesse* is echoed by *confesse/everlastingnesse*. Not surprisingly, the rhymes that complete each full period are also conceptual mirrors: the individualized *this/his* in the *First Anniversary* stands in counterpoint to the universal *All/fall* in the second. As the poems move from individual to cosmos, a repeated internal rhyme in the *Second Anniversary* will be '-all', a word-ending that reaches for totality ('essentiall', 'celestiall', 'accidentall', 'casuall').

Even before a careful parsing of the lines with their nested propositions, Donne's poetry reveals a unique ability to encode and confront complex philosophic problems at the level of sound, language, and affect. The *First Anniversary* is answered by the *Second Anniversary* with a perfect symmetry that is made possible only through rhetorical effects – though these rhetorical effects in turn trace a conceptual scheme. The echoing language of the two anniversaries evoke complementary but distinct epistemological perspectives: the introductory lines of the *First Anniversary*, for instance, are concerned with individuation, with the elements that distinguish particular souls (and thus, particular people) from the multitude, while the *Second Anniversary* insists on the multitude, on the persistence of the whole despite the erasure of (some) individual pieces. At the same time, it is the *First Anniversary* which declares 'the world' as its subject, while the subsequent poem takes up the (individual) topic of the soul. These criss-crossing patterns that undermine any clear hierarchy or priority between the two poems accent the interlocking nature of particulars and universals and foil linear thinking. The poems perform, investigate, and ruthlessly deconstruct various philosophic dualisms through verbal and figural recurrence from the micro-level of the inverted couplet-rhymes to the macropoetic structures of ascent and descent.

Consequently, the cognitive actions of the two poems, placed in seeming counterpoint, are revealed to be in conceptual balance. If the *Anatomie* is a list of singular parts, the *Progresse* deliberately and repeatedly invokes cosmic wholes. The anatomist's dissecting gaze in the first poem breaks down the dying world's material ills to the most minute 'atomis', an analytic, deconstructive process that is both extended and countered by the halting *Of the Progresse of the Soule*, which zooms out to take in the big picture as it connects the minutiae of phenomenological experience to speculations about the nature of creation and the afterlife. The downward tug of the decaying world-body in the *First Anniversary* is therefore opposed by the exhortation to cosmic flight in the second: 'Up, up, my drowsie Soule ...' (*SA*, lines 339ff), urges the speaker, 'Returne not, my Soule, from this extasie ... / To earthly thoughts ...' (*SA*, line 321). The moment almost echoes the *Hymne of Heavenly Beautie*, where the poet had also urged his 'hungry soule' to 'look at last up to that soveraine light'.

By identifying his poems as an 'anatomy' and a 'progress', Donne brings two topical philosophical and spiritual exercises into the realm of verse and highlights poetry's cosmological claim, derived from its very etymology (*poiesis*), against the deconstructive thrust of philosophic argument. Both the anatomy and the progress are precise forms of temporal advancement and spatial reconfiguration along prescribed lines: the anatomist dissects according to a well-established order, taking apart a whole into its component parts as he reveals its essential unity; while a 'progress' implies a deliberate movement through a pre-established series of places on a symbolic itinerary.[53] Both practices connect material substance and spiritual goals as Donne exploits his favourite geographical metaphors to capture specific philosophic actions (natural/scientific and moral/spiritual) in poetic form. In doing so, he also captures particular modes of spatial consciousness through the body, in the mind, and on the page.

An Anatomie of the World grafts a medical practice concerned with individual human bodies on to an anthropomorphized world as Donne builds on a submerged but fairly well-established link between anatomy and geography that runs through sixteenth-century cosmographic discourse.[54] From the first anatomical atlas, Vesalius's *De humani corporis fabrica* (1543), to the first world atlas, Mercator's *Atlas: sive cosmographicae meditationes de fabrica mundi...* (1595), there runs a rhetorical thread of correspondence that weaves back together the links between microcosm and macrocosm through the very practices that seemed most responsible for their severance. By taking up the stance of a moral anatomist-geographer in the *First Anniversary*, Donne draws on this distinct set of empirical practices and the cosmographic language with which it was linked. In keeping with this discursive undertow, the 'progress of the soul' in the *Second Anniversary* also takes up a geographic metaphor: that of the pilgrimage to a sacred site that served as a model and an earthly double for the inward progress of the soul towards God. The metaphor of the journey across uncharted territory here matches and answers the anatomic spectacle of the diseased world even as it makes clear the philosophic stakes of traversing the dissected world in order to reach beyond it. This, as Ramie Targoff has powerfully argued, is in fact the great emotional challenge of the *Second Anniversary* – the speaker's attempt to persuade the soul to leave behind the body and travel towards the afterlife – but it is one that also reinforces Donne's materialism, his desire to cement the connection between body and soul and cancel out the easy philosophic binaries that suggest such separation is effortless.

As both Spenser's *Fowre Hymnes* and Donne's *Anniversaries* suggest, such binaries which may regulate the cosmos do not figure rigid systems of thought; instead, they offer ways of responding to the scattering of the world and the word by creating axes of conceptual relation. Where Spenser juxtaposes contradictory cosmologies, Donne juxtaposes various new technologies of perception – emblematized in the titular anatomy and progress – in an attempt to look at the same problem from a variety of perspectives: the anatomical dissection; net-like maps of 'Meridians, and Parallels'; magnification of spectacles; the elevated view from the 'watch-towre'; the cosmic view from heaven. The epistemological shifts precipitated by these new ways of seeing probe once again at the dialectic of the visible and the invisible: even as they make available new knowledge about the world, they can only gesture metaphorically towards the internal gaze that will transport the poet beyond phenomenal experience. At the same time such perceptual technologies become doubles for poetic vision itself, which surpasses them as it generates a panoramic view of the whole. Like Spenser, then, Donne too identifies in poetry alone the possibility for speculative, synthetic vision. 'Verse hath a middle nature', notes Donne cryptically at the end of the *First Anniversary*, and it is quite literally poetry's mediating power through its associative and accumulative dynamics that gives it a philosophic charge.

Despite the *Anniversaries'* seeming emphasis on dissonance, cosmic breakdown, and rejection of the material world, they also insist on tropes of wholeness, circularity, and cosmic connection. Like the *Fowre Hymnes*, these poems exploit the figures of repetition and return already present in their title – the 'anniversary' itself signals circular, periodic return, a reiteration in time that is echoed by the poetry's repeating cadences and proportions. As Lisa Gorton has noted, Donne's poetry returns almost obsessively to the figure of the circle – the language of the circle, sphere, centre, circumference, and concentric permeates his writing.[55] The perfect shape without beginning or end, the circle figures wholeness and harmony, symbolically uniting both time and space. Central to the aesthetics of *kosmos*, it figures the dilemma of the shift from a Ptolemaic to a Copernican universe – the breaking of the circle – a philosophic process that looms over both Spenser and Donne. And it is in the two poets' determined efforts to re-establish the philosophic circle through poetry's incantatory charms that we see an instance of what Cassirer would describe as the 'will to form', a rethinking of fundamental philosophic questions through the intellectual resources unique to poetic practice.

Notes

1. Ernst Cassirer, *The Individual and the Cosmos in Renaissance Philosophy*, trans. Mario Domandi (New York: Harper & Row, 1964), 189–90.
2. A similar point is made by Martin Heidegger in 'The Age of the World-Picture', in *The Question Concerning Technology and Other Essays*, trans. William Lovitt (New York: Harper Torchbooks, 1977), 115–54.
3. On the significance of Cassirer's formulation for the Renaissance as a period concept, see William Kerrigan and Gordon Braden, *The Idea of the Renaissance* (Baltimore: Johns Hopkins University Press, 1989).
4. Cassirer's comment, quoted above, derives from a reading of Bruno's *Degli eroici furori* – and Bruno's possible influence on Spenser and Donne is a matter of critical debate. It seems clear that both writers knew, at the very least, of Bruno's work and his notoriety; but he is also an important poetic predecessor for the kind of philosophic poetry that both would go on to write.
5. In a sense, a number of studies have already connected sixteenth- and seventeenth-century literature: classic considerations of Spenser and Milton or Shakespeare and Jonson (whose work spans the turn of the century). But many more proximate connections have been ignored in recent scholarship – as for instance, Spenser and Donne, or the persistent influence of the Northumberland circle on natural philosophical debates of the early seventeenth century. From an intellectual-historical perspective, Catherine Gimelli Martin's attempt to put Donne's *First Anniversary* in conversation with debates over Bacon's *Advancement of Learning* begins to tease out some of these strands that cross the barrier of 1600 (see 'The Advancement of Learning and the Decay of the World: A New Reading of Donne's First Anniversary', *John Donne Journal*, 19 (2000), 163–203).

6 See Yulia Ryzhik's Introduction, above.
7 See discussion in the essay on 'rhetorical criticism from E.K. to the present' by Judith Henderson in A.C. Hamilton (ed.), *The Spenser Encyclopedia* (Toronto: University of Toronto Press, 1990), 603. See also Anne Fogarty and Jane Grogan's reassessment of this reception history, Chapter 11 below.
8 See for instance the classic accounts in Michel Foucault, *The Order of Things: An Archaeology of the Human Sciences* (New York: Vintage Books, 1973); Timothy J. Reiss, *The Discourse of Modernism* (Ithaca: Cornell University Press, 1982); and Steven Shapin, *The Scientific Revolution* (Chicago: University of Chicago Press, 1996). A useful examination and corrective of these period definitions is Kerrigan and Braden, *The Idea*.
9 I discuss this broader cultural context and its intellectual ramifications at length in Ayesha Ramachandran, *The Worldmakers: Global Imagining in Early Modern Europe* (Chicago: University of Chicago Press, 2015).
10 Andrew Marvell, *Upon Appleton House*, stanza 96. Andrew Marvell, *The Poems of Andrew Marvell*, ed. Nigel Smith (New York: Longman, 2007).
11 Marshall Grossman, *The Story of All Things: Writing the Self in English Renaissance Narrative Poetry* (Durham, NC: Duke University Press, 1998), 154.
12 Sarah Powrie notes that, in general, Donne's engagement with the history of cosmology is relatively unexplored (Sarah Powrie, 'Transposing World Harmony: Donne's Creation Poetics in the Context of a Medieval Tradition', *Studies in Philology*, 107.2 (2010), 212–35). Catherine Gimelli Martin comes closest to touching on the possible relation between Spenser and Donne's cosmological interests, but keeps them separate (the focus of her discussion is Donne and Milton's cosmologies) – see 'Milton's and Donne's Stargazing Lovers, Sex, and the New Astronomy', *Studies in English Literature 1500–1900*, 54.1 (2014), 143–71.
13 For a useful discussion of Donne's Petrarchism see Heather Dubrow, *Echoes of Desire: English Petrarchism and Its Counterdiscourses* (Ithaca: Cornell University Press, 1995).
14 All citations of *The Faerie Queene* are from Edmund Spenser, *The Faerie Queene*, ed. A.C. Hamilton, textual ed. Hiroshi Yamashita, and Toshiyuki Suzuki (Harlow: Longman, 2001).
15 See Hilary Gatti, *Essays on Giordano Bruno* (Princeton: Princeton University Press, 2011). I am not suggesting that this passage endorses or even directly refers to the Copernican hypothesis, but it is important to consider the particular intellectual-philosophic milieu in which Spenser evokes the old trope of the straying zodiac. The irregularity of planetary motions through the zodiac was an important part of Copernican debates.
16 All citations of Donne's *Anniversaries* are from *The Complete Poetry and Selected Prose of John Donne*, ed. Charles M. Coffin and Denis Donoghue (New York: Modern Library, 2001).
17 Both passages may be influenced by Palingenius's *Zodiacus vitae*, a twelve-book philosophical poem on each of the signs of the zodiac; the text was part of the grammar school curriculum in sixteenth-century England and contains significant thematic continuities with both Spenser's and Donne's oeuvre.
18 Donne's knowledge of and response to Kepler is a matter of considerable critical debate – while he denounces Kepler savagely in *Ignatius His Conclave*, possibly for the new theories contained in *De stella nova* (1606) and the later *Astronomia nova*, he may have also visited Kepler in 1616: see the intriguing discussion in Wilbur Applebaum, 'Donne's Meeting with Kepler: A Previously Unknown Episode', *Philological Quarterly*, 50.1 (1971), 132–4. For more recent accounts and interventions in the debate over Donne's relation to the new astronomy see Martin, 'Milton's and Donne's Stargazing Lovers, Sex, and the New Astronomy'; and R. Chris Hassel, 'Donne's "Ignatius His Conclave" and the New Astronomy', *Modern Philology*, 68.4 (1971), 329–37.
19 A classic example is the scholarship on Neoplatonism and early modern poetry, which too often focuses on identifying specific philosophic tropes and ideas in poems rather than considering how poetry may use philosophic patterns and concepts for its own ends. There are, of course, key exceptions: see for instance Terry G. Sherwood, *Fulfilling the Circle: A Study of John Donne's Thought* (Toronto: University of Toronto Press, 1984), who also discusses this interpretive dilemma.
20 The *OED* notes that 'cosmos' derives from the Greek *kosmos*, meaning 'order, ornament, world or universe (so called by Pythagoras or his disciples "from its perfect order and arrangement").' On the persistence of this trope, see Denis E. Cosgrove, *Geography and Vision: Seeing, Imagining and Representing the World* (London: New York: Palgrave Macmillan, 2008), 34–9.
21 For a more extended discussion of this notion see Ramachandran, *The Worldmakers*, especially chapter 1.
22 All citations from the *Fowre Hymnes* follow *The Yale Edition of the Shorter Poems of Edmund Spenser*, ed. William Oram et al. (New Haven: Yale University Press, 1989).
23 On proportion as analogy and its significance for the *Anniversaries*, see Elizabeth D. Harvey and

Timothy M. Harrison, 'Embodied Resonances: Early Modern Science and Tropologies of Connection in Donne's *Anniversaries*', *English Literary History* [*ELH*], 80.4 (2013): 981–1008.
24 Ibid., 982. I suggest that their observation about the importance of poetic figuration as a kind of 'healing' in Donne's *Anniversaries* points to a wider trend in the period that demands greater analysis across a range of authors and texts.
25 There is a growing literature on the use of poetic tropes in scientific writing in the period: see, for instance, Ronald Levao, 'Francis Bacon and the Mobility of Science', *Representations*, 40, 1–32; Matthew L. Jones, *The Good Life in the Scientific Revolution: Descartes, Pascal, Leibniz, and the Cultivation of Virtue* (Chicago: University of Chicago Press, 2006).
26 'Mirum videri possit, quare graves sententiae in scriptis poetarum, magis quam philosophorum. Ratio est quod poetae per entusiasmum et vim imaginationis scripsere …' The citation is from the *Cogitationes privatae*, a private notebook: I cite from René Descartes, *Oeuvres de Descartes*, ed. Charles Adam and Paul Tannery, nouvelle présentation, en co-édition avec le Centre National de la Recherche Scientifique (Paris: J. Vrin., 1973), X.217.
27 Grossman, *The Story*, 154–5.
28 Many contributors to this volume meditate on how to counter the traditional binary view of the two poets without overstating the case. Thus Richard Danson Brown refers to 'overhearing' while Yulia Ryzhik talks of 'engagement'. The struggle to find an appropriate language and theoretical model for discussing such connection remains a wider critical challenge.
29 On the connection between ancients and moderns via the invocation of ancient philosophies, see Harvey and Harrison, 'Embodied Resonances', 983; and David A. Hedrich Hirsch, 'Donne's Atomies and Anatomies: Deconstructed Bodies and the Resurrection of Atomic Theory', *Studies in English Literature 1500–1900*, 31.1 (1991), 69–94.
30 On the significance of Pythagoras for ideas of harmony and discord see S.K. Heninger, *Touches of Sweet Harmony: Pythagorean Cosmology and Renaissance Poetics* (San Marino: Huntington Library, 1974); and Daniel Heller-Roazen, *The Fifth Hammer: Pythagoras and the Disharmony of the World* (New York: Zone Books 2011). See also Linda Gregerson, Chapter 6 above, for the significance of Ovid's Pythagoras for Spenser and Donne.
31 Spenser's possible invocation of the Pythagorean transmigration of souls in the Gardens of Adonis episode was first noted by Edwin Greenlaw ('Spenser and Lucretius', *Studies in Philology*, 17.4 (1920), 439–64), who rejected the connection. More recently, however, scholars have considered Spenser's interest in Pythagoras via Ovid's representation in *Metamorphoses* XV. For the significance of Pythagoras for the Gardens of Adonis episode see Elizabeth Harvey, 'Nomadic Souls: Pythagoras, Spenser, Donne', *Spenser Studies*, 22 (2007), 257–79, and my own extended discussion in Ayesha Ramachandran, 'Edmund Spenser, Lucretian Neoplatonist: Cosmology in the *Fowre Hymnes*', *Spenser Studies*, 24 (2009), 373–411. For a different, eco-critical account see Todd Borlik, *Ecocriticism and Early Modern English Literature: Green Pastures* (New York: Routledge, 2011), especially chapter 1, 'Reincarnating Pythagoras'.
32 'Philosophical poetry' as I use the term is not, strictly speaking, a genre. It is at best a mixed genre, including poems in a range of verse forms.
33 On Du Monin, see Neil Kenny, '"Curiosité" and Philosophical Poetry in the French Renaissance', *Renaissance Studies*, 5.3 (1991), 263–76. See also more generally Kathryn Banks, *Cosmos and Image in the Renaissance: French Love Lyric and Natural-Philosophical Poetry* (London: Legenda, 2008).
34 Grossman, *The Story*, 165, who notes that Barbara Lewalski also makes a similar point: see *Donne's Anniversaries and the Poetry of Praise: The Creation of a Symbolic Mode* (Princeton: Princeton University Press, 1973), 111.
35 Montaigne's importance for both Spenser and Donne is another important topic that has not received much attention. While it is difficult to trace a clear chain of influence, there are striking similarities of theme and language between the writing of the French humanist and the two English poets.
36 See Kenny, '"Curiosité"'.
37 I discuss the competing philosophical paradigms of the *Fowre Hymnes* extensively in 'Edmund Spenser, Lucretian Neoplatonist: Cosmology in the Fowre Hymnes', *Spenser Studies: A Renaissance Poetry Annual*, 24.1 (2009), 373–411.
38 On the distinction between 'represented' and 'contemplated' see Thomas Willard, 'Donne's Anatomy Lesson: Vesalian or Paracelsian?', *John Donne Journal*, 3.1, 35–61.
39 Grossman, *The Story*, 164.
40 Dryden's comment is taken from the 'Discouse on Satire' in *The Satires of Decimus Junius Juvenalis: Translated into English Verse by Mr. Dryden and Several Other Eminent Hands* (London, 1693).
41 On the Renaissance hymn, see Stella P. Revard, *Pindar and the Renaissance Hymn-Ode, 1450–1700*

(Tempe: Medieval & Renaissance Texts & Studies, 2001); Philip Ford, *Ronsard's Hymnes: A Literary and Iconographical Study* (Tempe: Medieval & Renaissance Texts & Studies, 1997); Philip Rollinson, 'The Renaissance of the Literary Hymn', *Renaissance Papers* (1968), 11–20; P.L. Ciceri, 'Michele Marullo e i suoi *Hymni Naturales*', *Giornale storico della letteratura italiana*, 64 (1914), 289–357; and Michel Dassonville, 'Eléments pour une définition de l'hymne Ronsardien', in Madeleine Lazard (ed.), *Autour des 'Hymnes' de Ronsard* (Geneva: Editions Slatkine, 1984), 1–32.

42 See Lewalski, *Donne's Anniversaries*; Rosalie Colie, '"All in Peeces": Problems of Interpretation in Donne's Anniversary Poems', in Peter Amadeus Fiore (ed.), *Just So Much Honor: Essays Commemorating the Four-Hundredth Anniversary of the Birth of John Donne* (University Park: Pennsylvania State University Press, 1972).

43 Roland Greene, 'Elegy, Hymn, Epithalamium, Ode: Some Renaissance Reinterpretations', in Patrick Cheney and Philip Hardie (eds), *The Oxford History of Classical Reception in English Literature: 1558–1660* (Oxford: Oxford University Press, 2015), 323. Greene insists on the proximity between the elegy and hymn, which has a clear bearing on Donne's *Anniversaries* (though Greene does not make that claim).

44 Ford, *Ronsard's Hymnes*; Rollinson, 'The Renaissance of the Literary Hymn'; Ciceri, 'Michele Marullo e i suoi Hymni Naturales'; Dassonville, 'Eléments pour une définition de l'hymne Ronsardien', see especially 31–2. For another perspective on the two poets' use of binaries, see Niranjan Goswami, Chapter 3 above.

45 Mary Louise Pratt, 'Arts of the Contact Zone', *Profession* (1991), 34.

46 Thomas M. Greene, 'Poetry as Invocation', *New Literary History*, 24.3 (1993), 502.

47 Ibid., 513.

48 I am drawing here on the thinking in Martha Nussbaum, *The Therapy of Desire: Theory and Practice in Hellenistic Ethics* (Princeton: Princeton University Press, 1994).

49 Catherine Gimelli Martin, 'Unmeete Contraryes: The Reformed Subject and the Triangulation of Religious Desire in Donne's Anniversaries and Holy Sonnets', in Mary Arshagouni Papazian (ed.), *John Donne and the Protestant Reformation: New Perspectives* (Detroit: Wayne State University Press, 2003), 196.

50 The Donne *Variorum* has an extended discussion of the philosophic basis of the *Anniversaries*, noting that the poems can properly be understood in terms of *genera mixta*.

51 My argument here extends and complements those of Ramie Targoff, *John Donne, Body and Soul* (Chicago: University of Chicago Press, 2008); and Harvey and Harrison, 'Embodied Resonances'. Also of importance is Harold Love, 'The Argument of Donne's "First Anniversary"', *Modern Philology*, 64.2 (1966), 125–31, who argues that 'Elizabeth Drury exists in the poem not only as the soul of the world whose withdrawal from it has caused its corruption but as the heart of the world, a heart that despite its perfections has been finally unable to avoid becoming involved in the universal process of corruption that began with the fall' (127).

52 Harvey and Harrison, 'Embodied Resonances', examine this through what they called the tropology of 'resonance' in the *Anniversaries*.

53 On the dialectic of the particular/universal and part/whole in Renaissance anatomy, see Devon L. Hodges, *Renaissance Fictions of Anatomy* (Amherst: University of Massachusetts Press, 1985).

54 On the link between anatomy and cartography, see Ramachandran, *The Worldmakers*, 30–3.

55 Lisa Gorton, 'John Donne's Use of Space', *Early Modern Literary Studies*, 4.2 (1998), 23–5.

8

'Straunge characters': Spenser's Busirane and Donne's 'A Valediction of my name, in the window'

Elizabeth D. Harvey

In 'A Valediction of my name, in the window', John Donne carves his signature with a diamond into the glass, a vitreous charm against the imminent separation of lovers:

> My name engrav'd herein
> Doth contribute my firmnesse to this glasse,
>   Which, ever since that charme, hath beene
>   As hard as that which grav'd it, was.[1]

The poem's central premise is that writing can both encrypt and summon a body. Displacing his bodily 'rafters', his skeletal structure, into an autograph, the lover hopes that the 'scratch'd' signs will allow his mistress to 'repaire' and 'recompact' his 'scattered body' until his return. Even as Donne plays on the mortal pun embedded in the act of engraving, he counters it with a fantasy of resurrection enabled by the prosthetic name he leaves behind.[2] His signature operates as a metonym, the figure George Puttenham labelled the 'misnamer' because it substitutes the name of the author for the thing itself.[3] Indeed, Puttenham enacts the metonym by giving it a nickname, a 'misnaming', that creates by means of personification a full-bodied 'character' with implicit social attributes. In analogous ways, the metonymic chain in the 'Valediction' joins the hand, the diamond, the autograph, and the departing lover by contiguities of touch, refusing rupture through the anchoring of a substitute materiality. Donne's 'ragged bony name' has, he imagines, the power to subpoena 'Muscle, Sinew, and Veine' to enflesh and reanimate his bony residue. Radically condensing the lover into vestigial 'characters' stages a translation of self into linguistic marks of ownership that seek to exert a continuing magical influence over his mistress after Donne departs.

I engage Donne's inscription of character in 'A Valediction of my name, in the window' via Spenser's Busirane in *The Faerie Queene* because the production of cryptic or magical graphic signifiers in each text uncovers the 'graphic violence' of erotic love.[4] Spenser works through allegory, and his representation of Petrarchan violence dramatizes and expatiates the theatricality of dissolution that is folded into Donne's metaphors. Some of this difference is, of course, generic, since Spenser's characters dilate in epic-romance what is compressed in Donne's lyric. But in each case, bounded subjectivity is sacrificed in the service of an eroticism that continually courts its own undoing. I argue that this erotic dissolution exists in paradoxical tension with each poet's desire to provide an enduring poetic legacy, to inscribe a poetic signature that will represent his distinct and durable psychological and physical character. My aim in this chapter is to explore the early modern idea of character through the writing of these two poets, each of whom established powerfully recognizable signature styles. My analysis centres on how the act of erotic writing in their poetry reveals a metonymical interface between linguistic inscription and human subjectivity. I examine how physiognomical or allegorical depiction instantiates literary characters on the one hand, and, on the other hand, how the discourses of erotic love can both establish authorial identity and undo conceptions of individually bounded subjectivity through a secret graphic system of character.

One well-known early modern precedent for Donne's engraved signature is the verse that Elizabeth I inscribed in a window with a diamond while she was imprisoned at Woodstock. According to John Foxe in *Acts and Monuments*, she learned that a number of suspects had been interrogated and tortured in the expectation that they would testify to Elizabeth's complicity in the plot against Mary. Elizabeth inscribed these words: 'Much suspected by me / Nothing proved can be', signed '*Quod* Elizabeth the prisoner'. They record her innocence as a kind of juridical deposition, a testament by proxy that could proclaim her innocence even if she were executed.[5] Although Donne does not acknowledge this diamond-engraved precedent directly, he might well have known of Elizabeth's inscription from Foxe or Holinshed.[6] As a poetic couplet that could outlast the extreme political hazard in which Elizabeth found herself, the lines provide an analogue for Donne's carved autograph just before his own enforced departure. Donne wittily adapts his own glassy signature as a prophylactic not against legal evidence of political treason, although he borrows that vocabulary in overt and playful ways, but rather against potential new suitors. Donne fantasizes that his beloved might be eventually 'corrupted' through the seduction of her maidservant by a potential lover's 'gold, and page'. Donne's pun on 'page' suggests that the power to seduce her resides not just in bribable servants but also by means of writing, the inscribed 'page'. If the maid is persuaded to place a suitor's seductive letter on his mistress's pillow, Donne imagines that his own etched name might 'step in, and hide his' (lines 50–4). If his beloved's feared 'treason' 'goe / To an overt act', and if she decides to 'write againe' to her new suitor, he fantasizes a kind of textual or linguistic erasure where 'In superscribing, this name flow / Into thy fancy, from the pane'. The charm of the inscription protects his legacy, for as he tells his mistress in the poem, 'in forgetting thou rememberest right, / And unaware to mee shalt write' (lines 54–60). For Donne and Elizabeth, the carved characters serve as a medium of connection with those who gaze at the inscribed name. They are also a synecdoche for the epistles (a material, fragmentary version of metonymy) that were, or might be, exchanged by parties hostile to their interests. Magical in their efficacy, the characters are imagined to exert a continued potency, literally 'superscrib[ing]' the influence of those who would threaten the amorous or political integrity of the signatory.

The proposition that undergirds 'A Valediction of my name, in the window', that a full person could be resurrected from these vestigial 'grav'd' 'characters', implicates the early modern semantic complexity of 'character'. Character has a long tradition beginning with Aristotle's theorization of character in the *Nicomachean Ethics* and *Poetics*. Aristotle's student Theophrastus inaugurated the tradition of codifying personal qualities as characters, and character-writing in English descends from his *Ethical Characters*, moving through Ben Jonson's humour comedies, Joseph Hall's didactic and ethical *Characterismes*, Sir Thomas Overbury's *Characters* flavored with court gossip, and John Earle's *Micro-cosmographie*.[7] John Donne contributed at least one, probably two, character sketches to the 1622 edition of Overbury's posthumous collection, joining in the fashionable practice of witty character-writing and 'conceited news' that was in vogue among his contemporaries.[8] While the Theophrastian tradition overlaps with my concerns, I am, however, tracing a different way of thinking about character here, one that is grounded in lexical history, in a specifically poetic context, and in the literal and etymological sense of a graphic mark.[9] Depictions of alphabetic characters in early modern writing manuals such as Theodor de Bry's humanized and eroticized letters in *Caracters and Diversitie of Letters* fuse the human and written alphabet as a living conjunction of socially and sexually interacting figures.[10]

Sir Thomas Overbury furnishes an illuminating definition of character that lies at the interface between incised mark and the representation of a person. He notes that 'character' comes of the 'Infinitive moode' 'which signifies to engrave, or make a deepe Impression'. Thus, 'a letter (as A.B) is called a Character'.[11] Overbury remarks that what we learn first is likely to leave a 'strong seale in our memories'; he seems to be referring to the practice of forming our first letters, but he then expands his description to liken character to an 'Egyptian Hieroglyphyck', which he calls an 'imprese', as if the condensed 'short Embleme' could in its abbreviated form produce a strong and lingering impression. He elaborates his conceit in an English idiom, claiming that a 'character' is like a picture with colours 'heightened' by 'shadowing, or like 'wits descant on any plaine song'.[12] This notion of character first as an incised mark and then as a radically condensed form that leaves a lasting impression, a kind of improvisory music or descant, suggests how our notion of dramatic or poetic character expands from incised marks and is implicated in the acts of reading and writing. Overbury's description of learning to form letters evokes the precepts of Renaissance pedagogy, which, following Quintilian's advice, involved tracing letters in incised grooves. The regulation of the student's hand was achieved by moving it within the hollowed out letters, as if the depth of the incision could thus more effectively imprint itself on the memory.[13]

Christy Desmet reminds us, as Overbury does, that 'character' was used primarily as a verb in the Renaissance, and only later became a substantive.[14] Timothy Bright epitomizes this active practice in his 1588 treatise, *Charactery: An Art of Short, Swift, and Secret Writing by Character*. His book maps a method for a cryptic language made of marks or characters that would, he tells us, have three advantages: speed, for it would be a kind of shorthand that could be used for transcribing orations or public speeches; secrecy, since there would be no other language like it; and universality, for it would allow nations of 'strange languages' to communicate with ease.[15] Bright likens his coded writing system to Chinese characters, which, he asserts, allowed the

Chinese to 'traffike' together despite the different language spoken in the diverse provinces of China.[16] Bright's treatise provides an instructive insight into ideas of character, for we can see that, long before the word came to designate distinguishing marks of human subjectivity, it was structured as a cryptic relationship between a symbol or graphic mark and a corresponding body or signified.[17]

Donne and Spenser both 'character' language in self-reflexive ways that are alert to its acoustic, etymological, visual, and symbolic aspects. Spenser archaized words and manipulated orthography in order to reveal the complexity of language's referential and temporal dimensions. His depiction of allegorical characters in *The Faerie Queene* insisted simultaneously on a character's external distinguishing attributes and on complex psychological dimensions that might, or might not, correspond to outside appearance. He exemplifies how Puttenham's definition of the 'courtly figure *allegoria*' as 'False Semblant' is ironically characterized by dissimulation.[18] Donne's elaborate metaphysical images and extended metaphors, his restless wit, and his colloquial manipulations of tone and voice manifest in analogous ways his awareness of linguistic duplicity: language promises to show the true nature of the person or object it claims to depict, even as it simultaneously undermines that possibility. At the same time, Donne and Spenser both exhibit a characteristic poetic style, what Puttenham called *mentis character*. Puttenham thought that the 'warp and woof of [a speaker or writer's] conceits' displayed themselves in 'his manner of utterance'. According to him, there was no aspect of physiognomy as revealing of the nature of the inner mind as language and style. As Ben Jonson famously put it, '*Language* most shewes a man ... It springs out of the most retired, and Inmost parts of us, and is the Image of the parent of it, the mind.'[19]

I juxtapose these two scenes of engraving in Spenser's *Faerie Queene* and Donne's 'Valediction' in order to exemplify how graphic marks transform themselves into authorial character or style. I suggest that these moments capture revelations about the mind of each poet. For Spenser, the magical, hieroglyphic quality of Busirane's cardiac inscriptions illuminates a passage from graphic sign to allegorical figure and reveals individual words as incarnating a secret, often contradictory etymological and significatory history. In 'Valediction', the lover hopes to exert an enduring erotic influence over his mistress through the inscription on the window that promises to 'superscribe' his rivals. Like the lover, Donne seeks to establish a lasting signature style, an enduring poetic fame, through a wrenching of language and thought that remakes poetic convention. What Spenser and Donne share is the crafting of a poetic idiom that defamiliarizes traditional language and replaces it with a newly invented signature style.

Donne emphasizes the prefix 'en' in 'engrav'd' by uncoupling it a few lines later in 'grav'd', accentuating through the echo a sense of becoming literally interred, as if language could accomplish the impossible fantasy of inhabiting death or absence with full consciousness. The idea of infiltrating another's skin, soul, or bodily state haunts Donne's poetry: the intergrafted hands and entwined eye-beams of 'The Extasie', the transmigratory soul of *Metempsychosis*, which sequentially occupies a series of different bodies during the poem's narrative, and the disembodied vision of heaven through Elizabeth Drury's soul in the *Second Anniversary*. These poems imagine selves that could take up residence in another body or sensibility. The cognate promise of shrinking a self to a signature, a kind of linguistic replacement body, and reassembling that person to full somatic and psychic integration enacts what Regina Schwartz has elsewhere called a sacramental poetics of presence. In her account, a sign points beyond itself to invoke an 'entire sensory reservoir'.[20] The early lexical history of character encapsulates this idea. Originally, character meant a mark or sign – magical, numerical, alphabetic – but its meaning expanded in the late sixteenth and early seventeenth century to encompass a new sense: the essential, defining features of a thing or person. If the signature is a synecdoche of a letter, Donne's ideas about letter-writing as a mode of reconstituting presence is pertinent. In a 1604 missive to Sir Henry Goodyer, Donne claims letters as the ideal 'conveyance' for 'knowledge or love', because they imprint the writer's essence: 'Where can we find so perfect a character of Phalaris', he asks, 'as in his own letters'?'[21] Donne's use of 'character' here elicits both the sense of a literal mark and the idea that the self could be inscribed into an epistle, folded, sealed, and conveyed across distance, and then reconstituted by the reader. By the late sixteenth century, character designated both the mark and the hidden essence of a subject, and it thus also invoked the intricate relationship between these two semantic poles. Handwriting or signatures emerged gradually during this time as a declaration of idiosyncratic identity, although, as Jonathan Goldberg notes, the mark was distrusted as a guarantor of identity until cultural structures of control could authenticate individuality more reliably.[22]

We can witness the semantic layering of 'character' in Shakespeare's usage.[23] He most commonly designates 'character' as handwriting that is correlated with a specific person. Innogen recognizes Posthumus's 'characters' in his letter to her (III.ii.28), for example, and Gloucester queries Edmund in order to ascertain if the 'character' of the discovered letter is Edgar's (I.ii.60).[24] In *Julius Caesar*, handwriting metaphorizes facial marks of affect for Brutus, 'the secrets of my heart' expressed in the 'charactery of my sad brows' (II.i.305–7), carrying the imprint of grief into the outward sign of the face. In a similar movement from inner secret to surface expression, the consequence of the 'mutual entertainment' in which Juliet and Claudio indulge in *Measure for Measure* is 'writ' with 'character too gross' (I.ii.131–2) on Juliet. The movement from hidden sexual congress to the bodily visibility of her pregnancy transposes hidden passion into a 'gross' writing visible to all. It is this tracking of inner to outer and of affect to language, not just in Puttenham's more general sense of *mentis character*, the mark of the mind, but as a movement from inexpressible, secret erotic passion to its declaration in writing, speech, or bodily signs that is most pertinent to my understanding of Donne and Spenser.

A graphic mark, incised with a pointed tool, maps on to the violence of erotic language, what Cynthia Marshall called the 'shattering of the self'. She challenges the historicist model of the self-contained emergent early modern self in her exploration of an aesthetic of 'self-negation' that 'constituted a counterforce to the nascent ethos of individualism'.[25] Marshall asserts that shadowing the so-called early modern advent of the individual is a darker possibility that the boundaries of this self may not be as firmly self-contained or impermeable as they are supposed to be. We can reconstitute some early modern understandings of the language of the passions and erotic subjectivity through Donne and Spenser's usages, for both explore the making and unmaking of the self in a crucible of erotic violence that joins inscription with a philosophy of the senses and the passions. Margreta de Grazia's brilliant essay on the philosophical and gendered implication of early modern 'imprinting' shows how metaphors of imprinting – from the wax stamped with a signet to moveable type – figured the operations of the mind and sexual reproduction. The two aspects were complexly intertwined, with the metaphorics of generation or cognition materializing and mechanizing textual reproduction.[26] We can witness a cognate process in the incision of graphic characters, which inscribe marks with a penetrative violence that is at once formative of meaning or identity and also threatens to dissolve that integrity.

If Donne is fascinated by mingling souls and incorporations of various kinds, he is also cognizant of the darker aspect of these 'interinanimated' states. In 'A Valediction of my name, in the window', the 'engrav'd' self is torn from itself, the body 'scatter'd', divided into a 'ruinous Anatomie' where, like a Vesalian écorché, muscle and sinew are flayed from bone. The skeletal figure that he conjures becomes a humanized version of his incised signature, just as the letters de Grazia described have human shapes.[27] Donne's imagery activates the etymology of 'engrave', which is cognate with the High German *begrafen*, to dig or to bury. As Donne prepares to leave his mistress, the consequences of severing the erotic union is a death that he imagines in vividly visceral terms. To find erotic union is to be 'Emparadis'd', and to separate from that joining, as he puts it in 'A nocturnall upon S. Lucies day', is to be 're-begot / Of absence, darknesse, death; things which are not'. The negative implications of his inscription are evident in the action itself, as he makes clear in his wordplay on 'engrav'd'. Intaglio engraving, carving into a metal plate with a sharp instrument called a burin, originated in the fifteenth century in Europe. Descending from goldsmithing, the metal plate or matrix was incised with the image by carving out grooves and furrows. When the ink was poured on to the plate, the ridges in between the negative spaces or channels created lines. The recessed areas thus invisibly enabled the design.[28] Just as engraving emerges from violence and negative space, Donne's erotic poetics reveals itself in moments of separation or absence, where passionate attachment is most precarious.

This negative poetics not only is apparent in the leave-taking that occasioned 'A Valediction of my name, in the window' but is also visually signalled in the second stanza where Donne imagines his beloved gazing at his signature in the glass. Although the properties of glass are 'confessing' and 'through-shine', fully capable of revealing the self's image to the self, they can also function as a mirror, 'reflect[ing] thee to thine eye'. But in this case, 'loves magique' undoes that gaze, producing a visual reciprocity that untethers self and image: 'Here you see mee, and I am you.'[29] The central conceit of the poem is this substitution of selves, or bodily inhabitation of the other, in which the lovers' identities are fused and confused, each becoming the other. Donne's wit belies the violence that subtends this crossing of selves, but it emerges in the extravagance of his reiterated imagery of death, mortality, anatomy, scattered bodies, skeletons. To love is also to sacrifice the bounded integrity of the self.

The speaker in Donne's 'Negative Love' offers a poetic theory of negativity. He wittily defines deprivation in less affective terms, eschewing conventional Petrarchan blazonry, which lingers on 'eye, cheek, lip', repudiating Neoplatonic praise of intangible 'virtue, or the mind', and proffering instead a lexicon of negativity: 'To all, which all love, I say no. / If any who deciphers best / What we know not, our selves, can know / Let him teach mee that nothing'. While his playful sexualized puns on 'nothing' and 'cipher' imagine a poetry that will deliver him efficiently to his mistress's 'centrique part', the structures of erasure also signal the unknown within the *Nosce Teipsum* adage: can one know the self?[30] To be a cipher is to be nothing, and yet to undo that cipher (to de-cipher), to become two by uniting with a lover, opens into a powerful intersubjective knowing of 'ourselves'.[31] The cipher, a figure of occult symbology with magical multiplying capabilities, implicates secret codes and hidden languages, an underworld of signification. In 'Valediction to his booke', Donne, to take one example, imagines a book made from the 'Myriades' of letters that he and his beloved have exchanged, which will be in 'cypher writ'. Or, we can witness the seamlessness of the lovers' union in the souls' colloquy in 'The Extasie', their inaudible 'dialogue of one'. The instantaneity of their discursive intercourse is achieved, however, at the expense of the uniqueness that establishes the self. When negative love collapses the self into perfect union, it destroys the possibility of a linguistic articulation that we could hear. The code for this love is literally 'indecipherable', for it becomes the cipher, the nothing, the perfect O. Donne's 'Negative Love' can gesture only to this inaudible language, just as the 'paradoxically impossible' 'dialogue of one' in 'The Extasie' can be described by multiple hypotheticals that hang off the 'if': 'if any so by love refin'd', if 'he soules language understood', if 'by good love were grown all minde', and if 'Within convenient distance stood', he might '[de]part farre purer than he came'. 'Deciphering' these amatory codes coincides with a desire to preserve through discursive exchange the subjective stability that continually solicits the erasure of self.

In Book III of Spenser's *Faerie Queene*, Busirane holds Amoret captive, bound fast to a 'brasen pillour'. The 'vile Enchaunter' sits in front of her as a kind of Petrarchan poet, 'Figuring straunge characters of his art, / With liuing blood he those characters wrate, / Dreadfully dropping from her dying hart' (III.xii.31).[32] Spenser's use of the word 'character' twice in this passage would seem in the first instance to mean alphabetic letters, graphic symbols of writing. It also gestures to the etymological sense of the word, an instrument used to inscribe, engrave, or stamp a distinctive mark, a tool which is cognate with the 'deadly dart' that transfixes Amoret's 'trembling hart'. Busirane's name suggests multiple associations: the dominating male imagination, 'Busy-reign', of Harry Berger's analysis and the Egyptian tyrant of Ovid's *Ars Amatoria*, who sacrificed his guest's blood in order to restore Egypt's fertility.[33] Spenser's knowledge of Egyptian material through Plutarch, and perhaps the Florentine humanists, would have familiarized him with hieroglyphics. Overbury described the practice of children forming their first letters as 'Egyptian Hieroglyphycks', emblems that condense affective memory into an abbreviated form that leaves a powerful impression.[34] It is these 'characters' that Britomart forces Busirane to 're-verse' in a palinodic moment, to read backwards, in order to undo the magical potency of the spell that would bind

Amoret's heart to his. When Amoret is healed through a Stesichoran charm, she feels herself to be perfect 'hole' in Spenser's famously ambiguous homonym, simultaneously complete in herself and psychically lacking. This restorative healing resutures body and psyche, folding its bleeding organ of passion into the interior operations of the self's erotic life, but not before Busirane has made manifest the sado-masochistic violence implicit in erotic joining. Spenser and Donne both use the tortured, flayed body to figure extreme affective states, displaying the cost of intersubjective merging, which, for all the pleasure associated with erotic yearning, also threatens bodily and psychic disintegration.

In a sermon preached at Lincoln's Inn in 1620, Donne mediates on Job 19:26, which describes corruption in the skin: 'we have the book of God, the Law, written in our own hearts; we have the image of God imprinted in our own souls; wee have the character, the seal of God stamped in us, in our baptism; and all this is bound up in this velim, in this parchmin, in this skin of ours'.[35] The passage encapsulates the wish to have the containing boundaries of the skin infiltrated by God's seal, to have his character imprinted on the heart, a desire that simultaneously destroys the outward covering, even as it remakes the flesh ready for its encounter with God. Donne's gloss on Job borrows images from the anatomy theatre – the excised heart, the flayed body – to depict affective inhabitations of the self by another. Both Spenser and Donne draw on writing technologies; for Donne, 'velim' is the amphibious term as appropriate for describing the cutaneous boundary of the human skin as it is for the parchment pages of a book. When Britomart strikes Busirane to the ground, Amoret stays her hand, reminding Britomart that Busirane inflicted the wound in her heart and only he can 'recure' it. The stanzas that describe Britomart's rescue and the magician's restoration of Amoret's physical and affective integrity are punctuated by words prefixed with 're': 'reuerse', 'rehearse', 'recure', 'restore', words that negate a present state through the act of recovery or return. Undoing Busirane's violent magic entails a recantation of his verses: he must erase and expunge the 'cursed leaues' in his 'balefull booke' (III.xii.36). To 'reuerse' his charm is a poetic erasure accomplished on and through the technologies of writing and reading, but as he reverses, the 'cruell steele' that 'thrild her dying hart', drops softly out, manifesting the linkage we have been exploring between the body and writing.

The lover's desire to be known in his or her essence resonates with early modern beliefs about fundamental cosmic correspondences in the doctrine of signatures. Giorgio Agamben provides an instructive account, asserting that the 'core' of the Paracelsian episteme 'is the idea that all things bear a sign that manifests and reveals their invisible qualities.'[36] The doctrine of signatures according to Paracelsus is the 'science by which everything that is hidden can be found', for all things, 'herbs, seeds, stones, and roots' reveal through their *signatum* their interior nature. One of the principal *signators* in the cosmos is the stars, which imprint nature, including human faces, limbs, and hands, with celestial marks. The divinatory arts, physiognomy, chiromancy, necromancy, and astronomy, among others, seek to explicate these hieroglyphic marks. While the paradigm of every signature is Adamic language, that pure correspondence between an essence and a name, and language is thus the 'archetype of the signature', the revelation of correspondence is necessarily rendered opaque in a post-lapsarian world.[37] Jacob Boehme, the German mystic and theologian who was Spenser's younger contemporary, extends and complicates Paracelsian ideas of the signature's relationship to language. As Boehme explains in *De signatura rerum*, all creation is marked with signs, but it is the signature that renders the sign intelligible. Like a lute that lies still and is dumb until it is played, the sign is a silent essence that must be animated by the action of the signature.[38] The term Boehme uses to describe the moment of animation or revelation by the signatory process is 'character'. Character for him designates the interplay between interior essence and its exterior manifestation, a delicate reciprocity between an innate disposition and external influence. As Boehme notes, inward qualities will be marked or signed in outward form, as inner nature is manifested in the configuration or character of the face.[39] Shakespeare articulated a version of this physiognomic principle in sonnet 59, where exterior marks register an inward disposition that is otherwise invisible: 'mind at first in character was done'. In 'A Valediction of my name, in the window', Donne envisages that his incised 'charme' will allow the 'vertuous powers' of the ascendant stars to 'flow' into his carved 'characters'. His choice of word – character – is instructive, for just as the stars that are in 'supremacie' in the heavens at a child's nativity will imprint their sidereal mark on its character, so too, he hopes, will the ascendant stars instil their potency in his vitreous signature.[40]

The modifier Spenser uses to describe Busirane's characters is 'straunge', a word that conjures connotations of foreignness elicited by its Latin root, *extraneus*, external, and that resonates with Bright's ciphers rendering 'strange' languages comprehensible. To take the heart out of the body and to write with its blood is to turn the body inside out, to expose, make foreign, and manipulate its hidden interior. It is this traffic between inside and outside, domestic and strange, figuration and ontology, that the idea of character evokes. The heart was for Spenser and his contemporaries the seat of the passions and the vital centre of the inner self. Bernard Silvester eloquently captured the centrality of the heart in his twelfth-century *Cosmographia*, describing it as 'the animating spark of the body, nurse of its life, the creative principle and harmonizing bond of the senses; the central link in the human structure, the terminus of the veins, root of the nerves, and controller of the arteries, mainstay of our nature'.[41] If, as Eugene Vance and others have argued, Augustine inaugurated the semiological and textual consciousness of the Christian West, he did so partly through his development of the trope of the heart as book and through his influential cultivation of the heart as emblem of the inner self in the *Confessions*.[42] The location of conscience, understanding, and memory, the heart was for Augustine the fleshly embodiment of the self, the site of interior writing and wounding. The *Confessions* nourished the confluence of erotic love and the cultivation of the inner self through writing that found later authoritative expression in Petrarch's models of amorous inscription on the heart. This legacy is apparent in Spenser's first sonnet in the *Amoretti*, where the apostrophe to the sonnet cycle describes being 'Written with teares in harts close bleeding book'. The Busirane episode in *The Faerie Queene* is striking, however, for the ways in which it departs from the traditional book of the heart metaphor. Whereas the trope of interior writing typically accentuates the link between the agency of the writer and the exploration of the self, Amoret, whose heart is extracted from her body and repeatedly wounded, is captive and passive. Even though Busirane is a magician, a figure of the Petrarchan poet, who has extracted her heart and written in her blood, his 'thousand charmes could not her stedfast hart remoue' (III.xii.31).

The house of Busirane anatomizes the physiological and psychological trauma of erotic love by dramatically pathologizing the very literary conventions that feed and sustain desire. As Britomart moves inward through the three rooms of the house, the images that she sees seem to become progressively interior, moving from the Ovidian episodes of erotic narrative to the room decorated with gold reliefs and hung with the trappings of amorous combat to the masque of Cupid. The masque is announced by a series of sensory events invested with an affect that solicits Britomart's participation as embodied spectator: a 'shrilling Trompet', a 'hideous storme of winde', 'dreadfull thunder and lightning', an 'earthquake', 'a direfull stench of smoke and sulphure', followed by 'a most delitious harmony, / In full straunge notes was sweetly heard to sound, / That the rare sweetnesse of the melody / The feeble sences wholy did confound' (III.xii.2–6). The allegorical figures that appear are each described by a series of characteristics and given a name or signature. Doubt, for instance, is clad in a 'discolour'd cote, of straunge disguyse', and he 'lookt askew with his mistrustfull eyes, / And nycely trode, as thornes lay in his way' (III.xii.10). Daunger is 'cloth'd in ragged weed, / Made of Beares skin, that him more dreadfull made, / Yet his owne face was dreadfull, ne did need / Straunge horrour, to deforme his griesly shade' (III.xii.11). Griefe is all 'in sable sorrowfully clad, / Downe hanging his dull head, with heauy chere'. He holds a 'paire of Pincers' in his hand 'With which he pinched people to the hart' (III.xii.16). The correspondence between the name and the defining functions is an allegorical code similar to a system of signatures, where the mark or name makes manifest qualities. Britomart, and the reader as spectator, provide what Jacob Boehme might term character, that is the animation or recognition of the signatory process.

But the allegorical signatures in the masque are more complicated than this because they embody externalizations of the emotions that inhabit the heart. They are externalizations of the secret interiority of the psychic and emotional life of the lover. The masque becomes, then, a passional version of the literal extraction of Amoret's heart, for it anatomizes affective states. Busirane's spells or inscriptions of 'straunge characters' seem to produce the interior of the heart as a dramatic portrayal of various emotional states. Whereas Arthur and Guyon encounter allegorical figures when they enter the parlour of the heart of the Castle of Alma, here the heart is turned inside out, displaying its passional operations as pageant. The hermaphoditic embrace in the 1590 ending of Book III, where Amoret and Scudamour 'like two senceles stocks in long embracement dwelt' (45a) figures the dissolution of boundaries characteristic of erotic union. Most important to this moment is Britomart's role as spectator to this union, for her 'halfe enuying' the bliss of the lovers not only registers her psychic overlap with Amoret but also points to the violent intersubjective dialectic between self and other, between wholeness as merging and hole as lack, the ciphering and deciphering of the erotic self.

Spenser uses the phrase 'straunge characters' in one other place in *The Faerie Queene*. After Britomart has glimpsed Arthegall in the magic mirror and become consumed with lovesickness, she and Glauce journey to Merlin's cave. Britomart first glimpses Merlin 'Deepe busied', 'writing straunge characters in the grownd' (III.iii.14). Merlin anticipates Busirane in multiple ways, and Britomart is, of course, psychically implicated in Amoret's imprisonment and torture; when she accosts Busirane, he draws a 'murdrous knife' from his pocket, which in their wrestling 'strooke into her snowie chest / That litle drops empurpled her faire brest' (III.xii.33). The gash angers Britomart, even though the wound was 'nothing deepe imprest'. This moment echoes the hurt she receives when she first gazes into the magic mirror that Merlin had given to her father, a 'world of glas' designed to protect the boundaries of the kingdom. The vision of Arthegall 'presented to her eye' in the mirror wounds her, although the arrow is shot so 'slyly' by the 'false Archer' that she does not feel it penetrate her flesh or know the cause of her subsequent lovesickness (III.ii.19–26). Like Donne and his inscription in the glass casement, and Spenser's own reference to Petrarchan window-writing, Britomart has been marked by the 'straunge characters' that will make her alien to her former self, vulnerable to Busirane's enchanted verses, and 'imprest' with the signs of erotic desire.[43]

Donne's lyrics 'concord' with Busirane's inscribed 'heart' charms because both figure the heart as an organ of passion that can be removed, dissected, exchanged, or tortured. Donne's Holy Sonnet 'Batter my heart' urges God to 'bend [His] force, to breake, blowe, burn, and make [him] new', a catalogue of ravishing violence transposed from the Petrarchan idom to spiritual context. Fidelia's tutelage of Redcrosse in the House of Holinesse echoes both Busirane's torture of Amoret and the violence of Donne's God: Fidelia's sacred book is 'with blood ywritt', and with her words she kills and 'rayse[s] againe to life the hart, that she did thrill' (I.x.19). 'The Legacie' is a witty legal meditation on love and death that puts the exchangeability of the heart at its centre. Like the confusion of selves and pronouns in 'A Valediction of my name, in the window', 'The Legacie' plays with pronouns: when 'my selfe (that's you, not I)' kills the speaker, he searches for his heart, 'ripp[ing]' himself and 'search[ing] where hearts / did lye' so that he can bestow it in his will. He finds 'something like a heart', which he means to send 'in stead of mine', but finds that he cannot, 'for twas thine'. In 'The Broken Heart', the speaker brings 'a heart into the roome, / But from the roome, I carried none with mee'. Love with 'one first blow' 'shiver[ed]' it like glass, and he experiences the heart that now inhabits his breast as shards of glass that do not 'unite'. Just as 'broken glasses show / A hundred lesser faces', his 'ragges of heart' are no longer capable of fixing on a unitary love. By contradistinction to the fragility of this glass heart, 'A Valediction of my name, in the window' insists that the medium of glass with its scratched signature will endure the vicissitudes of weather and time: 'showers and tempests' can no more 'outwash' the 'point' or 'dash' that are 'accessaries' to the name than time can alter the 'patterne' of self to which the name refers.

The speaker brackets his farewell with two references to this durability: 'firmnesse' in the opening stanza, which is sometimes glossed sexually, and 'firme substantial love' in the final stanza.[44] The pun embedded within the primary semantic referent of 'firm' – stability – is signature, a meaning that appears in English in the late sixteenth century: the presence of a person is 'confirmed' or ratified through a signature or 'firme'.⁴⁵ The dangers Donne enumerates in the final stanza – sleep, lethargy, death – allude not only to the grief associated with leave-taking but also to his fear that his mistress will forget him and that he will be supplanted by another lover. Even as he catalogues this potential erasure through evocations of sleep, forgetting ('lethargie'), and death in the final stanza, however, he insists on the fantasy that his name, and his poem, will 'flow' into 'fancy', 'superscribing' in the moment of forgetting the lover or poet's living presence.

For Donne and Spenser, the amorous inscription of character gestures to the complexity of erotic representation, to the paradoxical way that desire instantiates a poetic self in the instant that it threatens to dissolve into the beloved. As Spenser figures this process in the *Amoretti* 75, verse will 'eternize' the vertues of his beloved. Even though death threatens to erase them both as surely as the waves wash away her name upon the strand, he insists that their love will endure in his verses. Spenser's sonnet is constructed on the edifice of erasure that always threatens it: mortality and time signaled by the expunging action of the waves.⁴⁶ The endeavour of both poets to depict this fragile equilibrium between self and other, between forgetting and remembering, is bound up with their fashioning of what each hopes will be an indelibly recognizable poetic signature.

Notes

1. *The Complete Poems of John Donne*, ed. C.A. Patrides (London: J.M. Dent &Sons, 1985), 70. Subsequent references are to this edition.
2. Donne's signature is preserved in the 'marriage letters', the correspondence between the poet and his father-in-law, George More, in the Folger Shakespeare Library digital archive. The 'ragged bony' autograph evokes the skeletal image that Donne conjures in his poem: http://luna.folger.edu/luna/servlet/detail/FOLGERCM1~6~6~32007~102238:John-Donne-s-marriage-letters-in?h?sort=call_number%2Cmpsortorder1%2Ccd_title%2Cimprint&qvq=q:donne's%2Bmarriage%2Bletters;sort:call_number%2Cmpsortorder1%2Ccd_title%2Cimprint;lc:FOLGERCM1~6~6&mi=1&trs=7.
3. George Puttenham, *The Art of English Poesy: A Critical Edition*, ed. Frank Whigham and Wayne A. Rebhorn (Ithaca: Cornell University Press, 2007), 265. See the introduction for a fuller discussion of Puttenham's evocation of allegory and the romance tradition (59–60). Puttenham participates in a history of character through his personification of rhetorical figures, converting literary tropes into social figures or types that populate his anatomy of linguistic ornament.
4. 'Graphic' derives from the Greek *graphein*, writing or drawing, which is not an inherently violent activity. But, when Busirane writes with Amoret's blood, the brutality of the enchanter's inscription conjures Donne's pun on the word 'engraving', which comes from Old English *begrafen*, to bury. Although distinct in their etymological roots, *graphein* and *bregrafen* are nevertheless bound together through the violence of these representations.
5. *Elizabeth I: Collected Works*, ed. Leah S. Marcus, Janel Mueller, and Mary Beth Rose (Chicago: University of Chicago Press, 2000), 46; John Foxe, *The Unabridged Acts and Monuments Online* or *TAMO* (1576 edition) (HRI Online Publications, Sheffield, 2011). Available from: www.johnfoxe.org, accessed 1 January 2017, Book 12, 2334.
6. *Elizabeth I: Collected Works*, 46n. Ramie Targoff describes this and other instances of engraving glass in *John Donne: Body and Soul* (Chicago, University of Chicago Press, 2008), 67. See also Julia Bekman Chadaga's description of window writing in *Optical Play: Glass, Vision, and Spectacle in Russian Culture* (Evanston: Northwestern University Press, 2014), 37–8.
7. Wendell Clausen charts this genealogy and the place of Casaubon's translation of Theophrastus in it: 'The Beginnings of English Character-Writing in the Early Seventeenth Century', *Philological Quarterly*, 25.1 (1946), 32–45. The tradition of character that develops from physiognomical readings of the body lays the foundation for psychoanalytic studies of character from Freud and Wilhelm Reich: Sigmund Freud, 'Character and Anal Erotism', *The Standard Edition of the Complete Psychological*

'Straunge characters' 169

    Works of Sigmund Freud, trans. J. Strachey (London: Hogarth Press, 1959), Volume IX (1906–8): *Jensen's 'Gradiva' and Other Works*, 167–76; Sigmund Freud, 'Some Character-Types Met with in Psycho-Analytic Work', *The Standard Edition of the Complete Psychological Works of Sigmund Freud*, Volume XIV (1914–16): *On the History of the Psycho-Analytic Movement, Papers on Metapsychology and Other Works*, 309–33. Wilhelm Reich, *Character Analysis*, trans. Theodore P. Wolfe (London, Vision Press, 1950).
 8 See Evelyn M. Simpson, 'John Donne and Sir Thomas Overbury's "Characters"', *The Modern Language Review*, 18.4 (1923), 410–15.
 9 For a discussion of the sense of character as dramatic or fictional person, see Jonathan Crewe, 'Reclaiming Character?', *Shakespeare Studies*, 34 (2006), 35–40.
10 Theodor de Bry, *Caracters and Diversitie of Letters vsed by diuers nations in the vvorld* (Frankfurt, 1628), n.p. Jonathan Goldberg discusses de Bry, Giacomo Franco, and Erasmus in his account of embodied letters in Renaissance writing manuals in *Writing Matter: From the Hands of the English Renaissance* (Stanford: Stanford University Press, 1990), 226–9. Embodied alphabets have an ancient lineage, as Anne Carson notes in her anecdotes about Greek writers' love for the alphabet, including Sophokles dancing in a satyr-play with an actor who 'danced the letters of the alphabet', and an Athenian play, 'The Alphabetic Revue', in which 'twenty-four members of the chorus acted out the letters of the chorus'. *Eros the Bittersweet* (London: Dalkey Archive Press, 1986, 2000), 58.
11 Sir Thomas Overbury, *His Wife with Additions of New Characters* (Dublin, 1626), n.p.
12 Overbury, *His Wife with Additions*, n.p. Impressing and incising are, of course, distinct ways of creating characters, and Overbury here collapses the differences and multiplies the metaphors in his effort to describe the operations of memory.
13 Goldberg, *Writing Matter*, 158–62.
14 Christy Desmet, 'The Persistence of Character', *Shakespeare Studies*, 34 (2006), 46–55 (47).
15 Timothy Bright, *Characterie: An Art of Short, Swift, and Secret Writing by Character* (1588), A3.
16 Ibid., A3v.
17 Giambattista della Porta's treatise on natural magic includes a cognate chapter on secret writing that overlaps with Bright's concern. Della Porta details all the ways of making and sending invisible or coded writing, and although his emphasis is on technique – how to make letters appear upon crystal by strewing it with fine dust, how to hide letters in stones or the bowels of living creatures, how to use arrows or pigeons as messengers, how to inscribe a secret cutaneous message on the back of human messengers – he notes that we contrive these ingenious methods because we need to speak at a very great distance when friends are absent or lovers are separated, and because erotic, military, and political contexts require secrecy, the creation of a special language that excludes other readers. John Baptista Porta, *Natural Magick* (London, 1669), 340–54.
18 Puttenham, *The Art of English Poesy*, 270–80.
19 Ibid., 233. Ben Jonson, *Timber: Or, Discoveries* in *Ben Jonson*, ed. C.H. Herford, Percy Simpson, and Evelyn Simpson, vol. 8 (Oxford University Press, 1947), 625.
20 Regina M. Schwartz, *Sacramental Poetics at the Dawn of Secularism: When God Left the World* (Stanford: Stanford University Press, 2008), 6.
21 Letter XI. To Sir Henry Goodyer, 1604. *John Donne: Selected Letters*, ed. P.M. Oliver (New York: Routledge, 2002), 17.
22 Goldberg, *Writing Matter*, 244.
23 Jonathan Goldberg's chapter on character and writing in 'Shakespearean Characters: The Generation of Silvia', in *Shakespeare's Hand* (Minneapolis: University of Minnesota Press, 2003) argues against character as a naturalized repository of psychology. He insists instead on the psychoanalytic, even Lacanian, implications of the material letter, both epistles that are exchanged and on the alphabetic characters that constitute writing.
24 All references to Shakespeare's plays and poems are to *The Norton Shakespeare*, ed. Stephen Greenblatt et al., 2nd ed. (New York: W.W. Norton, 2008).
25 Cynthia Marshall, *The Shattering of the Self: Violence, Subjectivity, and Early Modern Texts* (Baltimore: Johns Hopkins University Press, 2003) (Kindle Locations 45–6). Kindle Edition.
26 Margreta de Grazia, 'Imprints: Shakespeare, Gutenberg and Descartes', in Terence Hawkes (ed.), *Alternative Shakespeares*, vol 2 (London: Routledge, 1996), 63–94, 82–3.
27 Ibid., 86–7.
28 I am grateful to Yulia Ryzhik for organizing the session on Donne and Spenser at the 2015 RSA conference, for insights from Ayesha Ramachandran and Ramie Targoff, and for John Parker's suggestion to expand the connection between Donne's negative poetics and engraving.
29 Brian Cummings provides an important reading of these lines in the context of the passions and

Donne's letter writing in 'Donne's Passions: Emotion, Agency and Language', in Brian Cummings and Freya Sierhuis (eds), *Passions and Subjectivity in Early Modern Culture* (Farnham: Ashgate, 2013), 51-97.
30 Sean Ford's 'Nothing's Paradox in Donne's "Negative Love" and "A Nocturnal Upon S. Lucy's Day"', *Quidditas*, 22 (2001), 99-113, offers a detailed consideration of Augustinian and Patristic negative theology.
31 For a useful study of subjectivity and early modern intersubjectivity and the passions, see Christopher Tilmouth, 'Passion and Intersubjectivity in Early Modern Literature', in Cummings and Sierhuis (eds), *Passions and Subjectivity in Early Modern Culture*, 13-32.
32 Edmund Spenser, *The Faerie Queene*, ed. A.C. Hamilton, textual ed. Hiroshi Yamashita and Toshiyuki Suzuki (Harlow: Longman, 2001).
33 Thomas F. Roche, *The Kindly Flame: A Study of the Third and Fourth Books of Spenser's Faerie Queene* (Princeton: Princeton University Press, 1964), 81ff. Harry Berger Jr, 'Busirane and the War Between the Sexes: An Interpretation of *The Faerie Queene* III.xi-xii', *English Literary Renaissance*, 1.2 (1971), 99-121.
34 S.K. Heninger, 'Hieroglyphics', in A.C. Hamilton et al. (eds), *The Spenser Encyclopedia* (Toronto: University of Toronto Press, 1990), 370-1. Overbury, *His Wife with Additions*, n.p.
35 John Donne, Sermon 'Preached at Lincolns Inne, 1620', in John Donne Sermons, BYU Harold B. Lee Library Digital Collections, 13-14: http://contentdm.lib.byu.edu/cdm/compoundobject/collection/JohnDonne/id/3153/rec/10.
36 Giorgio Agamben, *The Signature of All Things: On Method* (New York: Zone, 2009), 33.
37 Ibid., 34-6.
38 Jacob Behmen, *De signatura rerum* (London, 1651), II.
39 Ibid., X.77.
40 See Anthony Grafton's *Cardano's Cosmos: The Words and Works of a Renaissance Astrologer* (Cambridge, MA: Harvard University Press, 1999), and John Dee's *Mathematicall Preface to the Elements of Geometrie of Euclid of Megara* (London: 1570), biii-iiij.
41 Quoted in Eric Jager, *The Book of the Heart* (Chicago: University of Chicago Press, 2000), xv.
42 Ibid., 27.
43 Colin in *Colin Clouts Come Home Againe* describes how in the court 'love most aboundeth', for 'all the walls and windows there are writ, / All full of love'. *The Yale Edition of the Shorter Poems of Edmund Spenser*, ed. William A. Oram et al. (New Haven: Yale University Press, 1989), 555.
44 Targoff, *John Donne: Body and Soul*, 70.
45 *OED*: firm, noun. 1. 1.
46 *Amoretti*, *The Yale Edition of the Shorter Poems of Edmund Spenser*, 645.

9

Marriage and sacrifice: the poetics of the Epithalamia

Ramie Targoff

In his 1894 survey of early seventeenth-century English literature, *The Jacobean Poets*, Edmund Gosse reached the conclusion that the only trace of Spenser's influence on Donne was in Donne's epithalamia. 'These marriage songs', Gosse remarked, 'are elegant and glowing, though not without the harshness which Donne could not for any length of time forgo'.[1] The resonances that Gosse and others have found in particular between Donne's 'Epithalamion Made at Lincoln's Inn' and Spenser's *Epithalamion* turn on perceived similarities in the poets' imagery, prosody, and tone. One critic even noted Donne's 'Spenserian sweetness', and his grasp of Spenser's 'more literary style'.[2]

What is altogether missing from the many comparisons between Spenser's poem to his bride and Donne's 'Epithalamion Made at Lincoln's Inn' – and the commentary in the Donne *Variorum* is a virtual list of examples – is any attention to the poets' shared invocations of sexual violence, and, specifically, the idea of the bride as fulfilling the role of sacrificial offering. The presence of sacrifice as a way of describing marital consummation has not played any role in the critical discussion of the poems' relationship to one another, nor has the theme of sexual violence been very present in the reception of Spenser's poem. And yet there is a strong under-current of sexual violence in Spenser's *Epithalamion*, which Donne may well have known, and certainly incorporated into his own reformulation of the genre. I want in particular to introduce as a critical source for Spenser's poem not only the festive epithalamia of Catullus, which literary scholars have typically identified as his source, but also the much darker tales of Ovid. Once identified, the Ovidian text reveals itself as a kind of counter-plot in the metaphorical field of Spenser's poem, and helps in turn to explain Donne's otherwise seemingly inexplicable allusions to the bride as sacrifice. Donne did not borrow simply or even primarily from Spenser's lovely images of the slow declining sun or his elegant stanzaic form. He also brought to the surface the sexual violence latent both within Spenser's poem and within the genre of epithalamia more broadly.

The Greek term *epithalamion* translates literally as 'upon the bridal chamber' (*epi*-upon, *thalamos* bridal chamber). In ancient Greece, the epithalamion was one of several specific poetic genres associated with wedding festivities: there was a song for the wedding procession, a song for the couple's going to bed, a song for the couple's reawakening the next day, and so on. Only the epithalamion survived, and it ultimately absorbed the other genres within its own form (a description of the wedding procession, for example, became a standard feature of the ancient Roman epithalamion).

The earliest mention of an epithalamion comes in an elaborate ekphrasis in Book XVIII of Homer's *Iliad*. On the shield of Achilles that Hephaestus made for the hero at the bidding of his mother, Thetis, the great blacksmith depicted the city as a place of festive weddings:

> They were leading the brides along the city from their maiden chambers
> Under the flaring of torches, and the loud bride song was arising.
> The young men followed the circles of the dance, and among them
> The flutes and lyres kept up their clamour as in the meantime
> the women standing each at the door of her court admired them.[3]

This invocation of the epithalamion or 'bride song' reappears in a second, famous ekphrasis in a poem of uncertain authorship, but long attributed to Hesiod, *The Shield of Heracles*. Depicted on the shield Heracles puts on as he prepares for battle with Cycnus, son of Ares (whom Ares subsequently transformed into a swan), there is a scene of great urban revelry:

> Beside them was a well-towered city of men, and seven golden gates, fitted to the lintels, encompassed it. The men were at pleasure, in revelries and choruses; some were leading a bride to her husband on a well-wheeled wagon, and a great wedding-song rose up. From afar rolled the blaze of burning torches in the hands of slaves, who walked in front, blooming in revelry, and performing choruses followed them. The men sent forth their voices from their soft mouths, accompanied by shrill panpipes, and around them spread the echo; while the women led the lovely chorus to the accompaniment of lyres.[4]

The echo that the poet describes on the shield (one wonders what this echo looked like) is a typical feature of the epithalamion – this is presumably what lies behind Spenser's refrain at the end of each stanza in his poem, 'the woods may answer and your echo ring' – but in the traditional epithalamion the echo is voiced not by trees, but by humans.[5]

The earliest known examples of epithalamia themselves, and not descriptions of them, come from Sappho, who lived several centuries after Homer and Hesiod in the late sixth century BCE. According to ancient commentaries, Sappho composed an entire book of epithalamia, from which we have, as always, only a few fragments. The most famous of these is poem 111, which Anne Carson has translated as follows:

> Up with the roof!
> Hymenaios –
> Lift it, carpenters!
> Hymenaios –
> The bridegroom is coming in
> Equal to Ares,
> Hymenaois –
> Much bigger than a big man![6]

Hymenaois, or Hymen, was not the god of weddings *tout court*, but specifically the god of wedding hymns – there were particular gods for different parts of the ceremony, once again suggesting how drastically reduced our inheritance of the ancient tradition actually is.

One of Sappho's other fragments – or rather a cluster of three fragments – brings us to the moment of evening, and the poet's leaving the bride and groom behind:

> May you fare well
> Bride
> And let the bridegroom fare well
>
> (117)

> Of polished doors
>
> (117A)

> Evening, sing Hymenaios
> O the song of Adonis
>
> (117B)

The effect of the three-word fragment, 'of polished doors', is wonderfully suggestive – we are at the threshold of the bridal chamber, but hear nothing more.

Less celebrated, but important for our purposes, is the haunting fragment 114, spoken in the voice of the bride at either the moment of entering the bedroom or consummating the marriage:

> virginity
>   virginity
>   where are you gone leaving me behind?
>   no longer will I come to you
>   no longer will I come.

There is very little else in the Greek or Roman tradition that carries the sense of regret and loss in the manner of these few lines from Sappho. The epithalamia that have survived from antiquity are on the whole more decisively celebratory. In Greek literature, the iconic text is from Theocritus's *Idyll 18*, on the marriage of Helen and Menelaus, which is introduced with this description of the nuptial celebration:

> Once upon a time, then, at the palace of fair-haired Menelaus in Sparta, girls with hyacinth blooms in their hair prepared to dance before the freshly painted bridal chamber (there were twelve of them, the most distinguished in the city, a fine sample of Spartan womanhood). When after his successful courtship the younger of Atreus' sons locked in his beloved Helen, daughter of Tyndareus, they all sang in unison, keeping time with their intricate steps, and the palace echoed to the sound of the wedding hymn.[7]

The collective song ringing through the palace ends with this farewell to the newly married couple:

> Farewell, bride; farewell, groom, fortunate in your wife's father. May Leto – that good mother Leto – grant to you both fine children, Cypris – the goddess Cypris – mutual love, and Zeus – Zeus the son of Cronus – endless prosperity, and that it may pass again from noble fathers to noble sons.

Sleep, breathing love and desire into each other's breasts, and do not forget to wake at dawn. We too shall come back in the morning, when after roosting the first cock raises his feathered neck and crows.
Hymen o Hymenaeus, may you take pleasure in this marriage.[8]

This third-century BCE Greek text had enormous influence on the Roman tradition, most famously captured in Catullus 61, the epithalamion that in turn served as the primary model for most Renaissance poets. Catullus 61 is an occasional poem in the strict sense: it follows the bride from her awakening 'on this joyful day', through her dressing, and leaving her home, until she reaches her husband's door, literally the *limen aureoles*, the golden or polished threshold, where her husband, 'reclining on a purple couch', is 'all eagerness' for her. Catullus concludes his epithalamion with a traditional prayer for the couple's offspring – the so-called *allocutio sponsalis* – and then the closing of the bridal chamber doors: 'Maidens, shut the doors. We have sported enough. But ye, happy pair, live happily, and in constant wedded joys employ your vigorous youth.'[9] The epithalamion is a poem of anticipation, before and not after love.

As Thomas Greene observed in his 1957 essay, 'Spenser and the Epithalamic Convention', Spenser's *Epithalamion* conforms in the deepest sense to the conventions of the genre as exemplified in Catullus 61.[10] In the broadest terms, those conventions include the social context ('a wedding attended by guests participating in a commonly shared jubilation'); a reference to a specific day, fictive or real; the poet-speaker's involvement in a complex, highly stylized role, as chorus leader or master of ceremonies (it is the poet who invokes Hymen, urges the maidens to sing, and so on); the couple's membership among the nobility or elite. Greene recognizes that Spenser's poem departs from the last two of these features – he both combines the role of poet and bridegroom into one (he is celebrating his own marriage to an Englishwoman named Elizabeth Boyle) and also brings down the social bar of the marriage being celebrated, since he did not count himself among the English nobility. Spenser himself draws attention to the unusualness of his own position, comparing himself, with a rather uncharacteristic lack of modesty (more typical of Milton), to Orpheus in the first stanza of the poem:

> Now lay those sorrowfull complaints aside,
> And having all your heads with girland crownd,
> Helpe me mine owne loves prayses to resound,
> Ne let the same of any be envide:
> So Orpheus did for his owne bride,
> So I unto my selfe alone will sing,
> The woods shall to me answer and my Eccho ring.
>
> (lines 12–18)

Outside of this collapse of poet and groom, Greene reads Spenser's poem as entirely – and this is a compliment – conventional.

What Greene completely overlooked, therefore, is the idiosyncratic representation of the sexual consummation of the marriage. To understand something about this, we need to turn to Spenser's contemporary George Puttenham, whose 1589 *Arte of English Poesie* gives a full, and much less unequivocally ceremonial, account of the epithalamion as a genre. For Puttenham, the epithalamion is centrally – even more or less exclusively – concerned with the sex act itself. As he explains it, the poem is divided into three 'breaches', for three different 'fits or times to be sung'. The first 'breach' was sung in the first part of the night, outside the bridal chamber's door, by a 'good store of ladies or gentlewomen of their kinsefolkes, & others who came to honor the marriage' in a manner 'very loude and shrill'. They did this, Puttenham explains, 'to the intent there might no noise be hard out of the bed chamber by the shreeking & outcry of the young damosell feeling the first forces of her stiffe & rigorous young man, she being as all virgins tender & weake, & vnexpert in those maner of affaires'.[11] In the second 'breach' of the epithalamion, performed around midnight by the musicians alone (the ladies having all retired by this late hour), the song was meant to revive the spouses' 'faint and weried bodies and spirits, and to animate new appetites with cherefull words'. This was done, according to Puttenham, in order to 'auance the purpose of procreation': whereas the first embraces earlier in the evening were filled with passion, these later 'assaults' were more likely to 'bre[e]d barnes'. The final 'breach' of the wedding song occurred the next morning, several hours before the young wife needed to make her appearance before her kinsmen, in order that they might determine, as he puts it, 'whether she were the same woman or a changeling, or dead or aliue, or maimed by any accident nocturnall'. The role of the musicians in the preparations for this examination is not clear: we are told only that they came to greet the spouses with a 'Psalme of new applausions', and to encourage them to 'make a louely truce and abstinence of that warre till next night'.[12]

There is no way to determine with absolute certainty that Spenser knew Puttenham's book. But there were roughly five years between its publication in 1589 and Spenser's composition of the *Epithalamion*, which seems in many ways an anxious response to his contemporary's description of the genre. Spenser's poem begins more or less conventionally, adhering to the standards of the genre as exemplified in Catullus 61, albeit in an early modern English context: the bride awakens and is dressed at the hands of her 'damzels'; the townspeople pipe music to welcome her appearance; the church doors are opened and she is led to the high altar, and she returns home to the wedding feast. This brings us to stanza 16, when Spenser breaks out of the convention with an expression of spousal impatience:

> Ah when will this long weary day have end,
> And lende me leave to come unto my love?
> How slowly do the houres theyr numbers spend?
> How slowly does sad Time his feathers move?
>
> (lines 278–81)

Spenser's wedding to Elizabeth Boyle took place on 11 June, St Barnabas's Day, which in the old calendar was the longest day of the year, but there was nothing in the poem preceding this moment to indicate his frustration with the slow unfolding of the day or his eagerness to get to bed. In stanza 17, much to his apparent relief, this process finally begins, and, resuming his post as master of ceremonies, Spenser instructs

Elizabeth's bridesmaids to bring her into their private chamber, undress her, and place her in bed:

> Now ceasse ye damsels your delights forepast;
> Enough is it, that all the day was youres:
> Now day is doen, and night is nighing fast:
> Now bring the Bryde into the brydall boures.
> Now night is come, now soone her disaray,
> And in her bed her lay;
> Lay her in lillies and in violets,
> And silken courteins over her display,
> And odourd sheetes, and Arras coverlets.
>
> (lines 296–304)

It is at this point that something entirely outside the traditional epithalamion occurs. For when Spenser imagines seeing his bride in bed, what comes to his mind does not remotely resemble Catullus's evocation of the bride lying in her chamber, 'shining with flowery face, like a white daisy or yellow poppy'. Instead, it resembles what Puttenham conjures up in his image of the 'shreeking and outcry' of the bride. 'Behold', Spenser declares,

> how goodly my faire love does ly
> In proud humility,
> Like unto Maia, when as Jove her tooke,
> In Tempe, lying on the flowry gras,
> Twixt sleepe and wake, after she weary was
> With bathing in the Acidalian brooke.
>
> (lines 305–10)

Maia was the eldest of the famous daughters of Atlas known as the Pleiades; thanks to her union with Jove, she is best known as the mother of Hermes. In the Homeric *Hymn to Hermes*, Maia is described as 'a shy goddess, for she avoided the company of the blessed gods, and lived within a deep shady cave'. The encounter with Jove, given his general habits, was almost certainly non-consensual – as Spenser himself describes it, Maia was nearly asleep, and very 'weary' when she was surprised by the chief of the Olympian gods.

Why Spenser would compare his bride awaiting him in bed on their wedding night to a shy and reluctant goddess hiding in a cave when she was taken against her will by Jove is not clear. But lest we imagine the implication of a non-consensual and forcible sexual encounter as somehow accidental, Spenser gives us a much less ambiguous example in the very next stanza. There, as he welcomes Night, which has been so long in coming, he asks that she 'spread thy broad wing over my love and me', so that they can be enshrouded in privacy:

> Now welcome night, thou night so long expected,
> That long daies labour doest at last defray,
> And all my cares, which cruell love collected,
> Hast sumd in one, and cancelled for aye:
> Spread thy broad wing over my love and me,

that no man may us see,
And in thy sable mantle us enwrap,
From feare of perrill and foule horror free.
Let no false treason seeke us to entrap,
Nor any dread disquiet once annoy
the safety of our joy:
But let the night be calme and quietsome,
Without tempestuous storms or sad afray.

(lines 315–27)

He then adds this example of the kind of 'calme and quietsome' night he wishes for: 'Lyke as when Jove with fayre Alcmena lay / When he begot the great Tirynthian groome' (lines 328–9).

In a space of twenty lines, Spenser invokes two episodes of Jove's predatory sexual behaviour, the second more disturbing than the first. For if the story of Maia was only partially sketched in the tradition, the tale of Alcmena was extremely well known, and had no ambiguity about it whatsoever. Alcmena was the wife of Amphitryon, who accidentally killed her father, Electryon, forcing the couple to flee her homeland. She refused, however, to consummate her marriage until her husband had avenged the death of her brothers. Amphitryon does so, but, before he can return to Alcmena, Jove comes to her disguised as her husband, and reports the good news of his victory in order to claim his sexual reward. Jove sleeps with Alcmena that night, a night that he arranges to stretch out to three nights in length – this is why in Statius's telling of the tale in the *Thebaid* he wonderfully describes Alcmena as having 'triple moon about her hair'.[13] The result of this very long night stretched to three was the conception of Heracles. All of this, needless to say, infuriated Jove's wife, Hera, who decided to punish Alcmena by pitting Ilithia, the goddess of childbirth, against her. As a result, Alcmena's labour in giving birth to Heracles rivalled the labours he was forced to perform later in his life. Thus Alcmena explains to Iole in Book IX of Ovid's *Metamorphoses*,

> [W]hen the natal hour of toil-bearing Hercules was near and the tenth sign was being traversed by the sun, my burden was so heavy and what I bore so great that you could know Jove was the father of the unborn child; nor could I longer bear my pangs. Nay even now as I tell it, cold horror holds my limbs and my pains return even as I think of it. For seven nights and days I was in torture; then, spent with anguish, I stretched my arms to heaven and with a mighty wail I called upon Lucina and her fellow guardian deities of birth.[14]

Like so much of Ovid's extraordinary poem, this is a story that involves sexual deception and physical pain. Alcmena did not choose to lie with Jove, and was subsequently punished for it by Hera. As always, there is no ethical system governing the *Metamorphoses*.

Let us return now to Spenser's poem to ask the simple question: why would Spenser choose to compare Elizabeth lying in her bridal chamber to Alcmena? The easiest answer is that he was focused on the length of the night Jove and Alcmena enjoyed – after such a long wedding day, he wanted the darkness to last as long as possible. It was in this context that Chaucer invoked Alcmena in *Troilus and Criseyde*, when the lovers complain about the shortness of the night:

> 'Myn hertes lyf, my trist, al my plesaunce,
> That I was born, allas, what me is wo,
> That day of us moot make disseveraunce!
> For tyme it is to ryse and hennes go,
> Or ellis I am lost for evere mo!
> O nyght, allas! Why nyltow over us hove,
> As longe as whan Almena lay by Jove?'[15]

For Spenser to liken his own blessed and sanctioned wedding night to Troilus and Criseyde's illicit meeting is not much better than the comparison to Jove and Alcmena: in neither case do we find a good model for the chaste and lawful marriage that he wanted to ensure. The fact that the very next stanza in the *Epithalamion* following the invocation of Alcmena begins, 'Let no lamenting cryes, nor dolefull teares / Be heard all night within nor yet without' (334–5) seems a quiet gesture of warding off the unhappy circumstances he has just described.

Another possible explanation for Spenser's invoking of Alcmena is that he regarded her as having actually enjoyed Jove's love for the long three nights – this is how he represents her in Book III of the *Faerie Queene*, where she surfaces as one of the figures in Busirane's tapestry. In that ekphrasis, Alcmena comes at the very end of a long list of women whom Jove has deceived – Europa, Danaë, Leda, Semele – and she is differentiated from the others in terms of her supposed pleasure (although he does describe Leda, in fact, as secretly smiling – 'She slept, yet twixt her eielids closely spyde / How towards her he rusht, and smiled at his pryde', *FQ* III.xi.32).[16] It is Alcmena, however, who is explicitly described as taking more pleasure from Jove than the others: 'But faire *Alcmena* better match did make, / Ioying his loue in likenes more entire; / Three nights in one, they say, that for her sake / He then did put, her pleasures lenger to partake' (III.xi.33). The reason for her increased pleasure rests on the fact of his disguise – she thought she was making love to her husband. The second reference to pleasure in these lines, although ambiguous, almost certainly refers to Jove's prolongation of his own – his pleasure, as it were, in her.

The most likely reason for Spenser's bringing the myths of both Alcmena and Maia into his *Epithalamion* precisely at the moment of his bride's arrival 'into the brydall boures' has nothing to do with pleasure or pain in the sexual encounter, but depends instead on the sons that each of them bore. From these two encounters with Jove came no less than Hermes and Heracles, two of the noblest offspring imaginable. Given the aim of the epithalamion as a genre – to give blessings for the bearing of noble children – Spenser may well have overlooked the conditions of the sexual encounter in favour of its ultimate fruits. Indeed, Spenser ends his poem by anticipating his and Elizabeth's 'fruitfull progeny' (403), and begs Genius (a male spirit linked to fertility) to 'send us the timely fruit of this same night' (404). He also strikingly asks Genius to keep the nuptial bed 'without blemish or staine', as if even the shedding of Elizabeth's virginal blood is more than he can bear to contemplate.

This fantasy of a clean consummation shapes Spenser's description of Chrysogone's giving birth to Belphoebe and Amoret in Book III of *The Faerie Queene*: 'Vnwares she them conceiu'd, vnwares she bore; / She bore withouten paine, that she conceiu'd / Withouten pleasure' (III.vi.27). In that poem, he is willing to sacrifice the mother's pleasure in order to erase the pain, a fate he does not seem to wish upon his own bride. Instead, in the *Epithalamion*, he quietly acknowledges the role that his own art plays in masking the inevitable pain of consummation – that is, he acknowledges the complicity of poetry in sexual violence. The examples of Maia and Alcmena stand out both as exceptions to the otherwise celebratory tone of the poem and as the foundational stories that lie at the heart of the genre's not-so-secret, procreational purpose.

Over the course of his career, Donne wrote three epithalamia: 'Epithalamion Made at Lincoln's Inn', 'An Epithalamion, Or marriage Song on the Lady Elizabeth, and Count Palatine being married on St. Valentine's day', and the 'Epithalamion' for the Earl of Somerset. My focus in this chapter is on the Lincoln's Inn poem, which is the earliest and most enigmatic of the three. Unlike the other two, whose occasions are announced in their titles, it is not clear when or for whom the 'Epithalamion Made at Lincoln's Inn' was written. Most critics agree, however, that Donne wrote it soon after Spenser's *Epithalamion*, which was published in 1595. Donne was a student at Lincoln's Inn at this time, and may well have composed his poem for the marriage of a fellow student or member of the Inn. It has also been suggested that Donne's poem was not written for an actual wedding, but for a mock wedding included in the midsummer revels at the Inn. This hypothesis does not work in relation to Donne's describing within the poem the wedding's occurrence during 'winter days', but, were it the case that the poem was written for revels, midsummer or no, it becomes a kind of commentary on the genre, or even perhaps a parody – an epithalamion that draws attention to what is problematic about the genre itself. I will not delve further into the arguments about the occasion for Donne's writing this poem, but I mention this last possibility only to establish that some of its especially jarring or indecorous features may stem from its being, in effect, a meta-epithalamion.

My focus on Donne's Lincoln's Inn epithalamion stems from its direct engagement with the questions of sexual consent and violence that are implicit in Spenser's poem. Indeed, Spenser's rather anxious representation of the sexual consummation at the end of his wedding day seems, in effect, to hang over Donne's poem from the very beginning. Hence in the first stanza, in which Donne instructs the bride to rise from her bed, he already anticipates her return to bed that night, in terms that seem far from the festive spirit of either Catullus or Spenser:

> The Sun-beames in the East are spread;
> Leave, leave, faire Bride, your solitary bed,
> No more shall you returne to it alone,
> It nurseth sadnesse, and your bodies print,
> Like to a grave, the yielding downe doth dint;
> You and your other you meet there anon.
> Put forth, put forth, that warme balme-breathing thigh,
> Which when next time you in these sheets will smother,
> There it must meet another,

> Which never was, but must be, oft, more nigh;
> Come glad from thence, goe gladder then you came;
> *To day put on perfection, and a woman's name.*[17]

This is a rather sobering introduction to a supposedly celebratory poem: the bride's bed has itself become – due to its 'solitariness' – a grave, and she herself has been reduced to the synecdoche of her thigh, which emits a balmy heat. Donne is interested in balms throughout his poetry – it is a 'balm' that cements the lovers' hands, for example, in 'The Extasie', or keeps the body and soul together in the *Second Anniversarie*, or preserves the youth and beauty of Lady Bedford in one of Donne's verse epistles – but here I think it has a specifically sexual connotation, having to do with what the bride's thighs emit, and therefore anticipating the sexual act described in the next line, when the thigh (or the bride) will be smothered in those sheets.

After several more conventional stanzas in which Donne directs the bride and groom as they proceed in and out of the temple, he comes to the evening hour – in this case, thankfully early in the day, as it is winter – 'O winter dayes bring much delight / Not for themselves, but for they soon bring night' (49–50) – and the preparation of the bride to receive the groom. The transition from day to night begins in the sixth stanza (there are eight in all), as Donne addresses the 'amorous evening starre', and tries to bring the public festivities to a close:

> Release your strings,
> Musicians, and dancers take some truce
> With these your pleasing labours, for great use
> As much wearinesse as perfection brings;
> You, and not only you, but all toyl'd beasts
> Rest duly: at night, all their toyles are dispensed;
> But in their beds commenced
> Are other labours and more dainty feasts;
> Shee goes a maid, who, least she turne the same
> *To night puts on perfection and a Womans name.*
>
> (lines 63–72)

The emphasis here on labour shifting from the entertainment without to the bed within sets the stage for the preparation of the bride, whom Donne treats, unapologetically, as a sacrificial offering. The idea of the bride as sacrifice could in fact be understood to lie behind the poem's refrain, 'put on perfection and a womans name', since in the Hebrew Bible the sacrificial animal is described as needing to be 'perfect'. Thus God instructs Moses in Leviticus 22, '*Ye shall offer* at your own will a male without blemish, of the beeves, of the sheep, or of the goats. *But* whatsoever hath a blemish, *that* shall ye not offer: for it shall not be acceptable for you', and likewise Moses warns in Deuteronomy 17, 'Thou shalt not sacrifice unto the LORD thy God *any* bullock, or sheep, wherein is blemish, *or* any evil-favouredness: for that *is* an abomination unto the LORD thy God.' Although Donne presumably imagines the bride's 'putt[ing] on perfection' through the act of consummating the marriage – the sex act becomes the act of perfecting – the image none the less seems more suitable to the tabernacle than to the bedroom.

That Donne has something like Biblical sacrifice in mind becomes explicit in the next, and penultimate, stanza of his poem, in which he describes the bride as being offered up on to her nuptial bed, which is now no longer a grave but Love's Altar:

> Thy virgins girdle now untie
> And in thy nuptiall bed (loves altar) lye
> A pleasing Sacrifice: now dispossesse
> Thee of these chaines and robes, which were put on
> T'adorne the day, not thee; for thou, alone,
> Like vertue and truth, art best in nakednesse.
>
> (lines 73–8)

This fantastic enjambment, 'In thy nuptial bed (loves altar) lye / A pleasing sacrifice', delivers his central instruction to the bride: this, Donne suggests, is how she should imagine herself. She is Isaac being offered to God, she is the paschal lamb. The image of the paschal lamb is at the heart of Donne's second enjambed commandment in these lines: 'And at the Bridegroomes wish'd approach doth lye, / Like an appointed lambe, when tenderly / The priest comes on his knees t'embowell her' (88–90). 'Embowell' is an archaic term for disembowel, but it also carries with it the sense of the priest, or groom, filling her bowels – the *OED* in fact lists 'offspring' as a now obsolete but then current meaning for 'bowel', so that to embowel was also to impregnate. This is not to take away from the more overt and disturbing sense of the disembowelment as part of the ritual preparation for the 'appointed' lamb to be offered to God. On the contrary, it only deepens the uncomfortable mingling of procreation and sacrifice as the climactic image of the poem.

If all of this were simply an example of Donne's idiosyncratic, metaphysical imagination – what Dr Johnson disparaged as *discordia concors*, when 'heterogeneous ideas are yoked by violence together',[18] or what Edmund Gosse presumably had in mind when he referred to the 'harshness' of Donne's epithalamia – we could dismiss it as particular to this poet alone. But in laying bare, in such chilling, uncompromised terms, the indifference to the will of the bride in the epithalamion's climactic act, Donne brings us back to one of the genre's earliest examples: the sad regret of Sappho's bride, who called out 'Virginity, virginity, where are you gone leaving me behind?' The epithalamion is officially meant to celebrate the day of marriage, but it is anything but a *carpe diem* poem (this is not, for example, 'Corinna's going a-Maying'), and its focus is far more forward-looking. What Donne brings to the surface of the 'Epithalamion Made at Lincoln's Inn' is what Spenser more obliquely acknowledges in his invocation of Maia and Alcmena – namely, the bride's involuntary role as sacrifice as the *telos* of the marriage ritual. The fanfare of the traditional epithalamion with its burning torches, its flutes and lyres and circles of dancers, its marjoram and myrtle and tight-clasping ivy, ultimately culminates with the song that remains outside the bedroom doors, designed both to mask and to expose the noise that occurs within. As perhaps Donne understands best of all, the epithalamion is a complicit genre, a form of art made to co-operate with pain.

Notes

1. John Donne, *The Variorum Edition of the Poetry of John Donne: The Epigrams, Epithalamions, Epitaphs, Inscriptions, and Miscellaneous Poems*, general ed. Gary A. Stringer et al. (Bloomington and Indianapolis: Indiana University Press, 1995), 333.
2. Ibid., 345. The quotation is from Robert S. Hillyer.
3. Homer, *The Iliad*, trans. Richmond Lattimore (Chicago: University of Chicago Press, 1951), XVIII.490-4.
4. Hesiod, *The Shield. Catalogue of Women. Other Fragments*, ed. and trans. Glenn W. Most. Loeb Classical Library 503 (Cambridge, MA: Harvard University Press, 2007), lines 270ff.
5. Edmund Spenser, *The Yale Edition of the Shorter Poems of Edmund Spenser*, ed. William A. Oram et al. (New Haven: Yale University Press, 1989). All references to Spenser's *Epithalamion* are from this edition.
6. Anne Carson, *If Not, Winter: Fragments of Sappho* (New York: Vintage Books, 2002). All references to Sappho are from this edition.
7. Theocritus, Moschus, Bion, *Theocritus. Moschus. Bion*, ed. and trans. Neil Hopkinson, Loeb Classical Library 28 (Cambridge, MA: Harvard University Press, 2015), *Idyll* 18, lines 1-8.
8. Ibid., lines 50-8.
9. Catullus, Tibullus, *Catullus. Tibullus. Pervigilium Veneris*, trans. F.W. Cornish, J. Postgate, J.W. Mackail, rev. G.P. Goold (Cambridge, MA: Harvard University Press, 1913), Poem LXI, lines 8, 165-6, 224-8.
10. Thomas M. Greene, 'Spenser and the Epithalamic Convention', *Comparative Literature*, 9.3 (1957 Summer), 215-28.
11. George Puttenham, *The Arte of English Poesie* (London, 1569), 41. Electronic text available at http://web.archive.org/web/20081012044941/ http://etext.lib.virginia.edu/toc/modeng/public/PutPoes.html. All references to Puttenham are to this edition.
12. Ibid., 42.
13. Statius, *Thebaid, Volume I: Thebaid: Books 1-7*, ed. and transl. D.R. Shackleton Bailey (Cambridge, MA: Harvard University Press, 2004), 6:289.
14. Ovid, *Metamorphoses, Volume II: Books 9-15* trans. Frank Justus Miller, revised G.P. Goold (Cambridge, MA: Harvard University Press, 1916), Book IX, lines 285-94.
15. Geoffrey Chaucer, *The Riverside Chaucer*, gen. ed. Larry D. Benson (Oxford: Oxford University Press, 1987), *Troilus and Criseyde*, III.1422-9.
16. Edmund Spenser, *The Faerie Queene*, ed. A.C. Hamilton, textual ed. Hiroshi Yamashita and Toshiyuki Suzuki (Harlow: Longman, 2001). All references to *The Faerie Queene* are from this edition.
17. John Donne, *The Poems of John Donne*, ed. Herbert J.C. Grierson (Oxford: The Clarendon Press, 1912), lines 1-12. All references to Donne's poetry are from this edition.
18. Samuel Johnson, *The Lives of the English Poets* (London: Charles Tilt, Fleet Street, 1840), 'Life of Cowley', 7.

10

Spenser's and Donne's devotional poetics of scattering

David Marno

'In no poetry more than the religious did the English genius in the seventeenth century declare its strong individuality, its power of reacting to the traditions and fashions which, in the Elizabethan age, had flowed in upon it from the Latin countries in Europe', announced Herbert Grierson in the introduction of his 1921 *Metaphysical Lyrics and Poems*.[1] One of the 'traditions and fashions' to which Grierson alludes is of course Petrarchism: from Donne's choice of the sonnet as a locus of repentance to Herbert's or Quarles's amorous addresses to God, seventeenth-century devotional poets made frequent use of forms and tropes familiar from the *Canzoniere*. In fact, it is tempting to go further and say that towards the end of the sixteenth century a turn to Petrarchism *within* devotional poetry marks the beginning of the kind of religious poetry in England for which Grierson has such high praise. Petrarch's earlier English followers did write religious poetry, of course, but they kept it rather strictly separate from their love lyrics, and one of the first things readers who compare Petrarch's poems with Wyatt's or Sidney's Petrarchist sonnets notice is that nowhere do the latter display the kind of fundamental and programmatic concern with devotion and theology that the poems of the *Canzoniere* do. Devotional poetry in sixteenth-century England consists primarily in verse translations and paraphrases of Biblical materials from the Psalms to the Song of Songs. When in turn a new kind of authorial devotional poetry emerges towards the end of the sixteenth century, its rise coincides with an increasing use of Petrarchan forms and tropes within devotional verse. From Barnabe Barnes's *A Divine Centurie of Spirituall Sonnets* to Donne's *Holy Sonnets*, lyrics in this trend claim a new authority for the devotional poet by departing from the text of the Bible and by merging devotional content with Petrarchan style.

How and why does Petrarchism become once again an available model for devotional poetry? In this chapter, I seek to answer this question by focusing on the appropriation of the Petrarchan trope of scattering in devotional poetry. This might seem a counterintuitive place to start. Scattering is central to the *Canzoniere*, and it might be said that Petrarch's programme in the volume is to produce a poetics of *spargimento*, of dwelling in fragmentation and distraction. In contrast, while it is difficult to define devotional poetry as such, a minimum requirement for a poem to qualify as devotional seems to be to include an attempt to focus one's attention on divine matters. My argument in the following is that it is precisely as a poetry of distraction that Petrarchism provides a bridge from the Biblical translations and paraphrases that dominate sixteenth-century devotional poetry in England to the authorial devotional poetry that emerges at the end of the sixteenth century and flourishes in the seventeenth century.[2] The reason, I suggest, is that the Petrarchan trope of scattering allowed poets to articulate poetry's association with distraction, fiction, and imagination, and to work towards dissociating their own devotional poems from such errors.

I have suggested an interpretation of Donne's poetry in this context of Petrarchan *spargimento* elsewhere, and, although I will briefly reiterate that argument here, my main goal is to see how or indeed whether Spenser's lyrics fit into this story of appropriation.[3] Since Grierson's edition, scholars have proposed numerous genealogies for the period's religious verse.[4] Curiously, Spenser's poetry is rarely considered in this context, presumably because of a perceived difference between his *religious* poetry on the one hand and the *devotional* poetry of Donne and others on the other. I hope to show that Spenser does have a place in the story, and that placing him in it will help us recognize that the boundaries between 'religious' and 'devotional' poetry are less firm than usually assumed. In the next part of the chapter, then, I describe in broad terms what I mean by a Petrarchan poetics of distraction, and show how the formal solutions of Philip Sidney's verse translation of Psalm 1 enact this poetics. In the following part, I read the *Fowre Hymnes* and argue that Spenser's poem appropriates the Petrarchan trope of scattering in order to use it as a foil against which it can articulate its own vision of a devotional attention devoid of imagination. In the final part I turn to one of Donne's *Holy Sonnets* to show how Donne turns lyric distraction into an aspect of meditation and thus a condition of the kind of attention that prayer requires.

Petrarchan distractions

References to scattering are ubiquitous in the *Canzoniere* (Nancy Vickers counts forty-three times the verb *spargere* and its adjectival forms appear in the *Canzoniere*), but a clear example of how Petrarch uses the trope to frame the sequence in terms of distraction appears as soon as the first poem's famous first line:[5]

> Voi ch'ascoltate in rime sparse il suono
> di quei sospiri ond'io nudriva 'l core
> in sul mio primo giovenile errore,
> quand'era in parte altr'uom da quel ch' i' sono.
>
> [You who hear in scattered rhymes the sound of those sighs with which I nourished my heart during my youthful error, when I was in part another man from what I am now.][6]

In a purely formal sense, the *Canzoniere* is 'rime sparse' because it lacks the kind of prose tissue into which Dante inserted his own lyrics in the *Vita Nuova*. The lack of prose in the *Canzoniere* means that the lyric recollections of affective episodes gain a life of their own, taken out of and potentially independent from Petrarch's. But the proem's reference to the rhymes as 'scattered' is of course more than a formal departure from Dante's work; it is also the first indication of the devotional framework that the *Canzoniere*'s readers are invited to keep in mind as they begin reading the poems. Before the proem would reveal that the stuff of the *Canzoniere*'s poems is the speaker's 'giovenile errore', the reference to the form as scattered prefigures the penitential motive by tying the volume's first poem to *Beatus Vir*, the first of the psalms:

> Blessed *is* the man that walketh not in the counsel of the wicked, nor standeth in the way of sinners, nor sitteth in the seat of the scornful. But his delight *is* in the Law of the Lord; and in his law doth he meditate day and night. And he shall be like a tree planted by the rivers of water, that bringeth forth his fruit in his season; his leaf also shall not wither; and whatsoever he doeth shall prosper. The ungodly *are* not so: but *are* like the chaff which the wind driveth away. (Psalms 1:14)[7]

The psalmist's double imagery suggests that the final scattering that sinners will suffer at judgement day is foreshadowed by the unfocused life they live on earth: their fate is to be fruitless, dried out, weightless husks blown abroad by the wind of divine judgement. Petrarch's sonnet retains the same transformation but reverses the order: the poems of the *Canzoniere* are scattered because they are the already judged, fruitless shells of the poet's youthful wanderings. Palinode, enabled by the speaker's partial conversion, replaces prophecy.

The proem's allusion to the psalm suggests that the whole from which the lyrics of the *Canzoniere* are scattered is the divine law. Petrarch's other subtext in the proem, Augustine's *Confessions*, suggests that it is more precisely God himself from whom human life is a distraction. Augustine's revelation that his life is distraction ('distentio est vita mea') comes not only as a conclusion to his attempt to recall the story of his life leading up to the conversion but in the context of attending to God. The *Confessions* begins with an address to God (*Magnus es, domine, et laudabilis valde*), and, when in Book XI Augustine begins to ponder the difficulties of turning to God in language, he takes as his main example the recitation of a psalm.[8] But the meditation that follows makes it clear that not only is attending to God impossible; devoting full attention to anything, including such a humble object as one's own words, is impossible as well. The problem of human *attentio* in Augustine's account is that it does not have temporal extension, that in any given instant it can only mark a temporal singularity.[9] The simultaneously metaphysical and theological result of this problem is that every act of attention is also an act of distraction, and the paradox of human acts of attending is that they are ultimately responsible for distractedness (*distentio*) as the human condition.

Comparisons between Augustine and Petrarch often suggest that Petrarch fundamentally subverted Augustine's thought. In one of the most influential articulations of this view, in Petrarch's hands 'the thematics of idolatry [is] transformed into a poetics of presence'.[10] But this transformation appears less significant if we translate 'idolatry' into distraction, and 'presence' into intention; in other words, if we read Petrarch's *Canzoniere* as a poetic performance of the Augustinian attempt to overcome distraction in acts of attention as well as a performance of the necessary failure of such attempts. On this reading, the poems of the *Canzoniere* will be seen as individual attempts to re-gather the poet's shattered world into the intention of the poetic act itself. The success of such acts is always and necessarily transient ('un breve sogno'), hence the *Canzoniere*'s double achievement: thematically and theologically, it reinforces the Augustinian thesis that life is distraction and offers a chronicle of

Petrarch's serial distractions, the poems themselves; poetically and aesthetically it constitutes a monument for the author by recording the traces of his intention. The paradox of the *innamoramento* is similar to the paradox of Laura: like Laura, who is both a sign of Christ and an idol distracting the poet from Christ, the *innamoramento* is both a poetic fiction of the Fall and an intimation of redemption. But what the poems do is not a Platonic recollection of the *innamoramento*. Instead, every poem is an immense effort of attention, an intention to create a kaleidoscopic totality in which the given, the pieces of a broken mirror are used to rebuild the mirror so that attention can return from a state of distraction by attending to an image of eternity to which Petrarch dedicates the name (*senhal*) 'Laura'. Confirming Augustine's account of attention's dialectic production of distraction, every poem is also a 'failure': even if they individually succeed as acts of intention, they at the same time necessarily perpetuate the distention they were supposed to remedy. The *Canzoniere* itself is thus a chronicle of the speaker's chronic distraction. This is one of the reasons the book begins with a poem that calls the collection 'rime sparse', scattered rhymes: the book as a collection is a work that imitates Augustine's *Confessions* in collecting a scattered self into the artificial unity of the book.

Due at least partly to Protestant concerns about authorial devotional poetry's reliance on imagination and fiction, Petrarch's sixteenth-century English followers rarely delved into the theological and metaphysical intricacies that the *Canzoniere*'s poems thematize. Devotional poets, however, began to appropriate Petrarchan forms and tropes early on, and, whether or not Anne Locke's verse translation of Psalm 51 should be read as the first Petrarchan sonnet sequence in England, it seems clear that Locke was one of the first poets who merged Petrarchan forms with devotional content. While Philip Sidney's use of Petrarchism is less obvious in his psalm translations, a look at the first poem of his sequence will show that Sidney evokes scattering with a full awareness of the trope's devotional and metaphysical implications:

> He blessed is, who neither loosely treads
>   The straying stepps as wicked Counsel leades;
> Ne for bad mates in way of sinning waiteth,
>   Nor yet himself with idle scorners seateth:
> But on God's law his heart's delight doth bind,
>   Which night and day he calls to marking mind.
>
> He shall be lyke a freshly planted tree,
>   To which sweet springs of waters neighbours be,
> Whose braunches faile not timely fruite to nourish,
>   Nor withered leafe shall make yt faile to flourish.
> So all the things whereto that man doth bend,
>   Shall prosper still, with well succeeding end.
>
> Such blessings shall not wycked wretches see:
>   But lyke vyle chaffe with wind shal scattred be.
> For neither shall the men in sin delighted
>   Consist, when they to highest doome are cited,
> Ne yet shall suffred be a place to take,
>   Wher godly men do their assembly make.

> For God doth know, and knowing doth approve
> The trade of them, that just proceedings love;
> But they that sinne, in sinnfull breast do cherish;
> The way they go shal be their way to perish.[11]

This is a formally striking poem: after the first three sestets' complex but confident adaptation of the psalm's parallelisms, the limping fourth stanza breaks the poem's symmetry. When Mary Sidney revised the poem, she must have thought it was unfinished because she erased the last stanza and replaced the jarred, dilated third one with a more concise rendition of the psalmist's last three lines:

> Not so the wicked, but like chaff with the wind
> Scattered, shall neither stay in judgment find
> Nor with the just, be in their meetings placèd:
> For good men's ways by God are known and gracèd.
> But who from justice sinfully do stray,
> The way they go, shall be their ruin's way.[12]

Mary Sidney's version is far more elegant than her brother's, and in so far as it gives a better impression of the psalm's parallel structure it may also be characterized as a more accurate translation. But it overlooks the very poetic innovations that in Philip Sidney's version highlight the speaker's concern with Petrarchism and distraction. In Philip Sidney's rendition, the Petrarchan association between sin, distraction, and poetic form becomes the poem's leitmotif. The first stanza distinguishes between the godly and the sinners both thematically and formally. The godly is characterized by his *skopos*: he 'neither loosely treads' but constantly 'calls to marking mind' God's law. Sinners, in contrast, stray, wander off, become distracted. Influenced by French poetry, Sidney figures this distinction between attentive godliness and distracted sinfulness through the use of feminine rhyme. The stanza begins and ends with masculine lines describing the godly; but, as we move into the stanza's centre, the feminine lines express the speaker's own straying away from the godly *skopos* and dwell in the act of imagining the wicked.

Such distraction remains neatly contained in the first two stanzas: the feminine rhymes and the straying they voice are framed and controlled by the strong, masculine lines with which each stanza begins and ends. But in the third stanza, the containment comes under threat. The wicked are no longer safely contained in the weak middle parts but break out of their imprisonment and contaminate the entire stanza. Notably, this contamination happens precisely in the stanza that paraphrases the psalmist's line about the wicked as 'chaff', which Sidney renders as scattering: 'lyke vyle chaffe with wind shal scattred be.' As if understanding the association between sin and distraction only now, the speaker utters the middle feminine lines with a hesitation and a jarring enjambment: 'For neither shall the men in sin delighted / Consist, when they to highest doome are cited.' The intriguing solution of rendering 'stand' as 'consist' gives voice to the speaker's anxiety about himself becoming distracted – an anxiety that concerns both the spiritual coherence of the subject and the poetic coherence of the sequence.[13]

It makes sense, then, that Sidney adds a last, seemingly fragmented stanza to his translation, a stanza in which the feminine rhymes that until this point have occupied the middle position within each stanza are no longer answered and controlled by masculine lines. The virus of distraction has spread to the end of the poem; the final condemnation of the wicked is uttered in weak lines, with fading attention, a fading away that was foregrounded by the poem's growing anxiety about distraction and its gradual loss of focus. The continuity between Petrarch's and Sidney's poetics is clear: both accept the Augustinian thesis that fallen life *is* distraction. But the differences are just as important: while in the *Canzoniere* the serial distractions of the poem are recorded as monuments of Petrarch's poetic glory, in Sidney's psalm translations it is poetic authorship itself that creates and spreads distraction on to its Biblical materials, so that poetic form becomes a figure of distraction, condemning its own author.

Attention and iconoclasm in *Fowre Hymnes*

In his dedicatory letter to the Countesses of Cumberland and Warwick at the beginning of the *Fowre Hymnes*, Spenser claims he wanted to retract the first two hymns 'in the praise of Love and Beautie', but was 'unable so to doe, by reason that many copies thereof were formerly scattered abroad'.[14] Critics have wondered whether Spenser's statement refers to autobiographical facts, or should rather be read as a modesty topos familiar from other printed collections of love lyrics in the late sixteenth century.[15] To be sure, these two options are not mutually exclusive. In the dedication to the Countess of Pembroke at the beginning of *Delia*, for instance, Samuel Daniel complains that he 'rather desired to keep the private passions of my youth, from the multitude, as things uttered to my selfe, and consecrated to silence: yet seeing that I was betraide by the indiscretion of a greedie Printer, and had some of my secrets bewraide to the world, I am forced to publish that which I never meant.'[16] *Pace* Daniel's complaint, there is a possibility that the 'greedie Printer', Thomas Newton, who indeed had published twenty-eight of Daniel's sonnets at the end of a pirated copy of Philip Sidney's *Astrophil and Stella*, had in fact collaborated with Daniel on the volume. Binding Daniel's poems together with the now dead Sidney's sonnet sequence would have certainly been shrewd advertising for Daniel's subsequent publication of *Delia* in 1592. Indeed, in the letter to the Countess of Pembroke, Daniel goes on to remind Sidney's sister that the 'holy Reliques' of Sidney's *Astrophil and Stella* had to endure the same 'sacrilidge'. If it is true that Daniel had a hand in the printing of his poems at the end of Newton's edition of *Astrophil and Stella*, this is a case in which the modesty topos has a manufactured but nevertheless real foundation in actual facts. Whether Spenser had similar factual grounds for his claim is difficult to tell, but the comparison with Daniel throws into relief the specific language that both Daniel and Spenser use: read by unintended audiences, love lyrics are fragments, the relics of the dead poet in Daniel's statement, and abused copies 'scattered abroad' in Spenser's case. If retraction is a popular Renaissance cliché, in framing their decisions to print the poems as an attempt to undo a previous scattering, Daniel and Spenser rely on a specifically Petrarchan version of it.

Yet in Spenser's case the function of this initial Petrarchism is not immediately clear. Spenser's choice of the hymn suggests that his intention was to compose a formally more coherent work than Petrarch's sonnet sequence. Moreover, the central trope of flight (figuring both imagination and speculation) in the *Fowre Hymnes* means that instead of a Petrarchan record of repetitive mood swings we read an at least relatively teleological lyric programme of sublimation, a programme that has given rise to debates about the poem's Neoplatonism and for the most part sidelined Spenser's allusions to Petrarchism.[17] Indeed, scattering in the *Canzoniere* is primarily a figure of the errors and distractions that the poems recall; in Spenser's letter, the scattering refers to the actual, physical dissemination of the first two hymns' copies. The literalizing is almost comic, and it might indicate that parody was not too far from Spenser's intentions when he wrote the letter. Yet is also serves a serious function: by describing the copies of the poems as scattered rather than the poems themselves, Spenser disclaims responsibility for their potentially erroneous character. As the poems are not inherently scattered, they are also not inherently sinful:

> Having in the greener times of my youth, composed these former two Hymnes in the praise of Love and Beautie, and finding that the same too much pleased those of like age and disposition, which being too vehemently carried with that kind of affection, to rather sucke out poison to their strong passion, then hony to their honest delight, I was moved by one of you two most excellent Ladies, to call in the same.[18]

The blame for any misreading of the poems is placed on the readers. In the next sentence, Spenser uses at least three different phrases to describe how the printed *Fowre Hymnes* are supposed to replace the supposedly original two hymns on earthly love and beauty: 'I resolved at least to *amend*, and by way of *retractation* to *reforme* them, making in stead of those two Hymnes of earthly and naturall love and beautie, two others of heavenly and celestiall.'[19] Readers have understandably been confused by this statement: is Spenser claiming here that he actually rewrote the earthly hymns? Or is he suggesting that the heavenly hymns supplant the earthly ones? If the latter, why did he nevertheless include the first two hymns in the printed volume? It seems to me that Spenser's resistance to calling the poems scattered in some inherent and figurative, Petrarchan sense suggests an answer to these questions. If readers are to blame for the erroneous interpretation of the first two hymns, the addition of the heavenly hymns amends not so much the earthly hymns as their possible readings. Gordon Teskey's provocative suggestion that Spenser's poem is 'better' if read in reverse order, from the last hymn towards the first, is based primarily on aesthetic criteria, but it is tempting to apply it also to the poem's devotional programme.[20] In themselves, the earthly hymns could yield either poison or 'hony' because they are scattered in the Petrarchan sense of distraction and hesitation; but the heavenly hymns impose a retrospective order on them and thus provide instructions to the reader for reading them in the right way.

How, then, do the heavenly hymns suggest a way of reading the entire group of poems? What are the fundamental differences between the earthly and the heavenly hymns? Of course, the two pairs of hymns are different in their subject matters. But the difference we need to look for is a difference in the movements of their thought. At first sight, these movements appear rather similar in each of the four hymns, following a logic of error and amendment *within* the individual poems. In each hymn, the speaker sets out to praise a specific subject: earthly love and beauty in the first two hymns, and heavenly love and beauty in the second pair. But in each hymn, the initial attempt to identify this subject turns out to be erroneous. Let's see some examples. In *An Hymne in Honour of Love* (*HL*), the speaker first praises love as a force that forms and propagates the universe. But, starting with stanza 15, the speaker recognizes that the subject he meant to praise is actually an exception to this universal force because 'man, that breathes a more immortall mynd, / Not for lusts sake, but for eternitie, / Seekes to enlarge his lasting progenie' (*HL*, lines 103–5). The recognition directs the speaker's attention away from the idea of love as a cosmic force to love as the passion that both probes and rewards one's 'truth and loialtie' (*HL*, line 176). *An Hymne in Honour of Beautie* (*HB*) begins with a praise of beauty as the 'wondrous Paterne' (*HB*, line 36) of creation. But the recognition that beauty cannot be identified with such perceptible qualities as colour or proportion redirects the enquiry from the cosmic to the experiential, and in the final analysis the speaker identifies beauty as an invisible inner light that requires love to become visible. In both cases, the turn from an initial error to its correction is also a move from a hypothetical universal to a more specific case.

The heavenly hymns appear to repeat the earthly hymns' movement from error to reform, and they do so once again by moving from the universal to the particular.[21] In *An Hymne of Heavenly Love* (*HHL*), the speaker's initial attempt to praise divine love leads him to a contemplation of creation. But as he retells the story of divine creation, the repeated failure of the creatures to acknowledge and obey their creator forces the speaker to realize that the divine love he set out to praise is most evident not in the act of creation but in the act of redemption. This shift from creation to redemption yields a uniquely devotional and Christological episode in the *Fowre Hymnes*, with the speaker performing an *imaginatio loci*, an ekphrastic and affective exercise that places him in the presence of Christ's passion. Nevertheless the last hymn returns to the earlier method and begins with a praise of creation, from which the speaker ascends in a speculative flight to an image of God. But the vision of God provided in the hymn's central stanzas turns out not to be identical with the divine beauty that the speaker has sought to praise. Instead, he finds heavenly beauty in the vision of Sapience, the 'soveraine dearling of the *Deity*' (*An Hymne of Heavenly Beautie* (*HHB*), line 184).

While this movement from error to amendment is shared by all four hymns, the way in which the initial error is revealed and the amendment is proposed differentiates the earthly hymns from the heavenly hymns. In *HL* and *HB*, the initial attempt to praise love and beauty in universal and cosmogonical terms is abandoned when the speaker turns to his own experience and examines it in terms of what might be called a Platonist phenomenology. The stanzas of *HL* in particular provide mesmerizing visions of how desire generates the imaginative and cognitive processes that in turn give a new object to desire:

> Such is the powre of that sweet passion,
> That it all sordid basenesse doth expell,
> And the refyned mynd doth newly fashion
> Unto a fairer forme, which now doth dwell

In his high thought, that would it selfe excell;
Which he beholding still with constant sight,
Admires the mirrour of so heavenly light.

(*HL*, lines 190–6)

In *HL*'s account, desire is self-purgative, and it achieves its own purgation because it inevitably turns into imagination and cognition. In *HB*, the correction of the initial cosmogonical praise of beauty is likewise replaced by an account of beauty that is grounded in the speaker's examination of experience. Colour or proportion cannot be the source of beauty because 'Why doe not then the blossomes of the field' (*HB*, line 78) also generate love? Moreover, once the speaker examines love as an inner light, he comes to believe that such beauty therefore depends on love's imaginative and cognitive power to actually appear, which in turn leads him back to a restatement of *HL*'s account of true love.

This reliance on experience in recognizing and amending error in the earthly hymns is replaced by typology in the heavenly hymns. *HHL* initially seeks to praise divine love in the image of creation, but it eventually finds it in the image of Christ's passion that redeems creation. In *HHB*, the issue is complicated by the critical disagreement on what or whom Sapience represents in the poem. But whether one emphasizes Neoplatonic or Scriptural precedents for Spenser's figure, the poem suggests a contrast between the speaker's vision of God and Sapience.[22] The God who appears in stanzas 21 to 26 is distinctly Old Testamental: sitting on a throne harder than diamond, he is surrounded by symbols of judgement, and 'underneath his feet are to be found / Thunder, and lightning, and tempestuous fyre, / The instruments of his avenging yre' (*HHB*, lines 180–2). While this vengeful God demands 'feare and awfull reverence' (*HHB*, lines 141), Sapience's incomparable beauty evokes 'extasy' and 'such joy and pleasure inwardly, / That maketh them all worldly cares forget, / And onely thinke on that before them set' (*HHB*, 264–6). In fact, the contrast between the speaker's visions of God and Sapience is not just in their respective affects but in the routes through which they are available to a human observer. While the vision of the righteous God was reached as a result of a flight of speculation that went from the earth to his throne, the vision of Sapience may only be experienced by those whom she selects: 'None thereof worthy be, but those whom shee / Vouchsafeth to her presence to receave' (*HHB*, lines 253–4). Ellrodt's suggestion that Sapience is Christ or the idea that Sapience's election represents a Calvinist view of predestination might be too reductive, but we need not accept either to still see in Sapience a New Testamental, graceful alternative to the speaker's vision of a righteous God.

The amendments that the first two hymns perform as they seek to address their subjects are grounded, then, in experience, whereas the heavenly hymns move beyond their initial errors by relying on typology. This suggests that typology is the kind of reading that would have led readers of even the earthly hymns to find in them 'hony' instead of poison. Indeed, if we consider the account that each hymn offers of the experience of attending to their objects, we will see that these accounts themselves undergo a typological development in the course of the four hymns. In *HL*, once desire undergoes the self-purifying process and creates a 'fairer forme' of the beloved, the mind experiences complete attentiveness to this idealized image:

> Thereon his mynd affixed wholly is,
> Ne thinks on ought, but how it to attaine;
> His care, his joy, his hope is all on this,
> That seemes in it all blisses to containe,
> In sight whereof, all other blisse seemes vaine.
> Thrise happie man, might he the same possesse;
> He faines himselfe, and doth his fortune blesse.
>
> (*HL*, lines 204–10)

In *HB*, despite the speaker's intention to focus on beauty instead of love, the account the poem offers of the experience of attention reiterates closely the previous hymn's description. The lover admires the 'mirrour of his owne thought',

> Which seeing now so inly faire to be,
> As outward it appeareth to the eye,
> And with his spirits proportion to agree,
> He thereon fixeth all his fantasie,
> And fully setteth his felicitie,
> Counting it fairer, then it is indeede,
> And yet indeede her fairenesse doth exceede.
>
> (*HB*, lines 225–31)

Spenser's ominous rhyming of 'felicitie' with 'fantasie' in this stanza already signals the fragility of the experience: the mirror may fracture at any time, leaving the subject alone, stripped of the imaginary object of his attention. The problem with love here is not so much idolatry as the fact that the narcissistic lover runs the risk of solipsism. When in *HHL* Spenser's speaker turns to Christ, the object of his attention changes, but the way in which the mind attends still resembles the lover's devotion to the image of his beloved. Having imagined Christ's passion,

> Then shalt thou feele thy spirit so possest,
> And ravisht with devouring great desire
> Of his deare selfe, that shall thy feeble brest
> Inflame with love, and set thee all on fire
> With burning zeale, through every part entire,
> That in no earthly thing thou shalt delight,
> But in his sweet and amiable sight.
>
> Thenceforth all worlds desire will in thee dye,
> And all earthes glorie on which men do gaze,
> Seeme durt and drosse in thy pure sighted eye,
> Compar'd to that celestiall beauties blaze,
> Whose glorious beames all fleshly sense doth daze
> With admiration of their passing light,
> Blinding the eyes and lumining the spright.
>
> (*HHL*, lines 267–80)

Spenser's and Donne's devotional poetics 193

In the structural progression of the *Fowre Hymnes*, this experience of undistracted attention to Christ is already after the conversion that takes place in the gap between the earthly hymns and the heavenly hymns. Yet it is difficult to forget that, in the earthly hymns, the speaker spoke in strikingly similar terms when he described the lover's attention to the image of his beloved. What the two experiences have in common is not just the ravished nature of attention but the fact that attention is bound up with imagination. Much like the lover who creates a perfect image of his beloved and then pays complete attention to it excluding the rest of the world, here the speaker envisions a devotional process that ultimately gives 'Th'Idee' of Christ's 'pure glorie' (*HHL*, line 284) to the mind's attention. In this sense, even though the object of heavenly attention in *HHL* is different from the object of earthly attention in the first two hymns, the way in which the object is given to attention remains comparable.

This is why it is so important that, when we reach the final description of devotional attention in the last hymn, the imaginative process that is shared by the first three hymns disappears, and with it the danger of idolatry and solipsism also fades away. This is also why those who are selected by Sapience to see her face experience an attentiveness that for the first time in the *Fowre Hymnes* includes contentment:

> So full their eyes are of that glorious sight,
> And senses fraught with such satietie,
> That in nought else on earth they can delight,
> But in th'aspect of that felicitie,
> Which they have written in their inward ey;
> On which they feed, and in their fastened mynd
> All happie joy and full contentment fynd.
>
> (*HHB*, lines 281–7)

The experience is full because there is no danger that it might turn out to be a work of imagination:

> But who so may, thrise happie man him hold,
> Of all on earth, whom God so much doth grace,
> And lets his owne Beloved to behold:
> For in the view of her celestiall face,
> All joy, all blisse, all happinesse have place,
> Ne ought on earth can want unto the wight,
> Who of her selfe can win a wishfull sight.
>
> (*HHB*, 239–45)

The experience of attending to Sapience in the *Fowre Hymnes* provides a paradigm from which all previous experiences of attention prove to be distractions. We are now in a position that allows us to see the reason: attending by grace escapes the threat of a scattering of the image of attention's object, leaving the subject in solitude. Perhaps the greatest paradox of Spenser's *Fowre Hymnes*, then, is that it imagines an experience of devotional attention whose value and superiority over erotic attention and even over devotion to Christ is that it does not rely on imagination.[23] It is impossible to tell whether Spenser was aware of the inherent contradictions of the poem's vision, but, in articulating an experience of attention to God that does not rely on imagination, he has foreshadowed some of the main concerns of seventeenth-century devotional poetry that are first fully articulated in Donne's *Holy Sonnets*.

Donne's distracted devotion

While the *Songs and Sonets* often portray experiences of erotic attention, Donne's devotional poetry never offers an image of heavenly attention comparable to Spenser's in the *Fowre Hymnes*. Indeed, it is far more tempting to describe Donne's *Holy Sonnets* as poems that tend to dwell in the kind of scattering and distraction one knows from Petrarch.[24] One of the most conspicuously distracted poems in the group is the eighth sonnet in the Westmoreland sequence, a poem that focuses on the moment when all that is scattered should be recollected one last time:

> At the round Earths imagind corners blow
>   Your trumpets Angels, and Arise Arise
>   From Death you numberles infinities
> Of Soules and to your scattered bodyes go,
> All whome the Flood did and fyre shall overthrow
>   All whome Warr, dearth, age, agues, tyrannyes,
>   Dispayre, Law, Chance, hath slayne, and you whose eyes
> Shall behold God, and never tast deaths wo.[25]

This is a mimetic-performative enactment of the tumult at the Last Judgement; the ecstatic, apocalyptic tone, the way the paratactic urgency of the first call is further intensified and reaches its climax in the last two lines' long asyndeton all fit in with the notion of the Ignatian *compositio loci* that Louis Martz identified as a major source of Donne's *Holy Sonnets*.[26] The initial address to the angels shifts to a general address to all participants of the general resurrection, and the work of attention dissolves into the act of imagining the actors of the Last Judgement. Yet after the two-quatrain long, resounding invocation for the dead to rise, for the Last Judgement to begin, the speaker suddenly changes his mind: 'But let them sleepe, Lord, and me mourne a space'. What brings about this *volta*, one of the most clear and emphatic turns in all of the *Holy Sonnets*? After the *volta*, the speaker's former enthusiasm is supplanted by an altogether different, penitential voice that mixes argument and repentance:

>   For if above all these my Sins abound
> Tis late to aske abundance of thy grace
>   When we are there: Here on this lowly ground
> Teach me how to repent, for that's as good
> As if thou hadst Seald my pardon with thy blood.

While in the poem's first eight lines the speaker was concerned with imagining the resurrection as a universal event, in these six lines he seems to have shifted his attention entirely away from the universal to the particular, which in this case is his own singular case. Indeed the seemingly scandalous closing couplet makes this focus on the self particularly clear. What the strange counterfactual ('As if thou hadst Seald my pardon with thy blood') signals is not any scepticism concerning the validity of Christ's redeeming sacrifice. But knowing that Christ *has* sealed every elect's pardon with his blood is different from believing that I, the speaker, am also included in the works of redemption. In other words, and this is what Protestant authors in the period name 'application', a cognitive assurance about a universal truth such as the truth of Christ's redeeming sacrifice does not guarantee that the self can believe the sacrifice's validity for his own case.

What this tension between the universal and the particular means for the poem is that the *volta*'s poetic work coincides with the devotional work of application, that is, with the movement from the general to the particular, from the universal to the self. If we now go back to the moments just before the *volta*, we find traces of what could have motivated it. The clause immediately preceding the *volta* is 'and you whose eyes / Shall behold God, and never tast deaths wo'. In his enthusiastic attempt to imagine the moment of the resurrection by listing all of those who would participate in it, the speaker almost by accident moved from the dead to those who would be *alive* at the time of the Last Judgement. But this gives birth to a new thought: what up until this point was imagined as an event safely placed in the distant future and happening to others suddenly becomes a real possibility that could happen right here, right now – to this very speaker, to me. This is what awakens the speaker to the severity of his situation, and this is what prompts him to abandon the exercise of imagining the Last Judgement in favour of repenting in preparation for it.

But this is not all; the last six lines of the poem further argue that repentance is urgent because 'if above all these my Sins abound / Tis late to ask abundance of thy grace / When we are there'. What does the deictic 'these' refer to? The previous lines did not really include sins, the enumeration focused instead on common causes of death. We could perhaps name 'Dispayre' as sin from a Christian perspective, but that would still not be satisfying as a reference for the deictic 'these'. Is it possible that 'these' refers to the tumult of the dead that the parataxis enumerated? That would seem to be a category mistake. But perhaps we *should* look at it as a category mistake, as a strange instance of mis-speaking, a technique Donne often uses as a moment of grammatical impropriety that suddenly refocuses the scattered attention of the poem. Here the deixis unveils not previous sins, not even the tumult of the dead, but rather the 'these'-ness of the octave, the parataxis, the asyndeton itself. If so, then 'these' refers to the words themselves, the scattered words of the poem, the wordiness of the poem; it is the moment when the speaker realizes that he has more sins than words in his poem.

Within one poem, then, we have two cases of 'mis-speaking'. First, carried away by the paratactic structure, the speaker includes the living, and thus himself, among the dead that he calls on to rise; this discrepancy between form and content, the inattentive collapsing of the living with the dead, 'wakes up' the speaker from the dream of the poem's imagination of the Last Judgement. The second instance of 'mis-speaking', however, is intentional: the 'above all these' is the awakened speaker's recognition of his previous dream, and of the fact that he needs to repent. Repentance, and thereby the devotional conversion that is expressed by the poem's *volta*, is thus prepared by the poem's own mistakes. We might recall, then, that 'metanoia', conversion and repentance, are also rhetorical categories; indeed this is how Puttenham defines the trope, which he also calls 'The Penitent', in the *Arte of English Poesie*:

> *Metanoia*: Otherwhiles we speake and be sorry for it, as if we had not wel spoken, so that we seeme to call in our word againe, and to put in another fitter for the purpose: for which respects the Greekes called this manner of speech the figure of repentance: then for that vpon repentance commonly followes amendment, the Latins called it the figure of correction, in that the speaker seemeth to reforme that which was said amisse.[27]

Indeed, the sudden withdrawal from the apocalyptic tone in the poem occurs right after another Pauline line. Those whom the poem names by their 'eyes', those who 'Shall behold God, and never tast deaths wo', are the subjects of Paul's 'secret thing' in 1 Corinthians 15, just a few verses before Paul announces the death of Death: 'Behold, I shew you a secret thing; We shall not all sleep, but we shall all be changed, In a moment, in the twinkling of an eye at the last trumpet; for the trumpet shall blow, and the dead shall be raised up incorruptible, and we shall be changed' (1 Cor. 15:51-2). One of Paul's most apocalyptic passages, this announcement promises that the end of the world, the Last Judgement, and the resurrection will arrive so soon that some of those who are alive at the time of the announcement will witness it alive. In one sense, then, Donne's poem was actually right: the resurrection will affect everyone, dead and alive, in the same way. But in another sense, the poem's mistake becomes all the more visible when compared with the Pauline passage. For if the poem was supposed to call forth the resurrection, it should not have *imagined* the many, the scattered, the dead, but instead it should have *attended* to the 'twinkling of an eye' itself; it is this 'twinkling of an eye' that contains the 'last trumpet' and the 'secret thing'. The 'twinkling of an eye' is a moment of imperceptibly small extension; yet it is long enough for the body to shed its flesh and change into its new, incorruptible form.

This is what escaped, and indeed necessarily escaped, the attention of the poem from the very beginning; instead, the poem must have distended in time so that it can enlist the multiplicity that the apocalyptic last moment would entail. In this consisted the poem's own sin; and this is why 'above all these' does, in fact, refer back to previous sins – the sins of the poem itself. By now, it should be also clear not only that the 'mourning' here refers to the sins for which the self, recalled from distraction, is repenting but also that these sins are coextensive with the dead of the octave: mourning thus means mourning sins, mourning the dead, but also mourning and creating the space that separates the time of the living from the time of the dead. Augustine says of death that it is nothing but flesh falling off the bones; what 'above all these' does to the poem is to tear off the flesh of words from the skeleton of the octave's syntax to create the 'twinkling of an eye', the moment of death that concentrates attention and forces it into the 'mourning space', the *locus penitentiae* of the poem.

At the core of Donne's poem, then, there is a moving discrepancy between form and content, between sound and sense. The sonnet begins by performing the given, by giving form to the given. But this form turns out to be slightly inadequate and it does not subject the given to attention in its givenness but rather distracts from it. The poem then dwells in this distractedness much like Augustine's *Confessions* dwells in sin before conversion. In this, it is different from Petrarch's poetics. But it is also different from Sidney's figuring of poetic form as distraction: in Donne, distraction is the substance out of which a new, intransitive attention can emerge. In other words, the poetic programme that we saw in Spenser's *Fowre Hymnes* becomes a poetic performance in Donne's sonnet, the root of an experimental poetics that affords the reader the occasional experience of attention emerging through the cracks and crevices of language, out of the very distraction that words create.

Conclusion

While the two most influential literary-historical accounts of the reasons devotional poetry came to flourish in seventeenth-century England remain Louis Martz's *The Poetry of Meditation* (1962) and Barbara Lewalski's *Protestant Poetics and the Seventeenth-Century Religious Lyrics* (1979), in recent years the question of what led to the flourishing of seventeenth-century devotional poetry in England has received new emphasis. For instance, Kimberly Coles's *Religion, Reform, and Women's Writing in Early Modern England* (2008) challenges Lewalski's category of 'Protestant poetry' by arguing that the transition from Scriptural translations and paraphrases to authorial devotional poetry in the sixteenth and seventeenth centuries was performed primarily by female poets including Anne Locke and Aemilia Lanyer. One of the most attractive aspects of Coles's argument is that unlike Martz or Lewalski, who account for the rise of English devotional poetry by reducing it to its various sources (Catholic meditations, Protestant sermons, etc.), Coles takes particular care to articulate how difficult it was for poets in Protestant England to conceive a collaboration between devotion and poetry, given the latter's association with fiction and imagination. In this chapter, I have argued that Spenser and Donne relied on the Petrarchan trope of scattering as one way of negotiating this difficulty. For them, scattering was attractive as a figure of distraction inherent to poetic and imaginative acts of attention, a figure that allowed them to work toward its opposite, a devotional act of attention without imagination.

Notes

1 Herbert Grierson, *Metaphysical Lyrics and Poems of the Seventeenth Century* (Oxford: Clarendon, 1921), 49.
2 I use the phrase 'Biblical poetry' in a restricted sense to refer to verse translations and paraphrases of concrete Scriptural texts, in contrast to the broader and somewhat vague sense in which for instance Herbert's voice in *The Temple* is sometimes called Biblical because it resembles the Psalmist's.
3 In those portions of the chapter that concern themselves with Donne I rely on the argument that I make about the *Holy Sonnets* and their role in early modern devotional poetry in *Death Be Not Proud: The Art of Holy Attention* (Chicago: Chicago University Press, 2016), chapter 5.
4 The two most influential early works are Louis L. Martz's *The Poetry of Meditation: A Study in English Religious Literature of the Seventeenth Century* (New Haven: Yale University Press, 1954) and Barbara Kiefer Lewalski's *Protestant Poetics and the Seventeenth-Century Religious Lyric* (Princeton: Princeton University Press, 1979); a powerful recent account is Kimberly Coles, *Religion, Reform, and Women's Writing in Early Modern England* (New York: Cambridge University Press, 2008).
5 Nancy Vickers, 'Diana Described: Scattered Women and Scattered Rhyme', *Critical Inquiry*, 8 (1981), 273. While a full account of distraction's role in Petrarch's poetry is beyond the scope of this chapter, interested readers should consult James Chiampi's important essay on the subject: 'Petrarch's Augustinian Excess', *Italica*, 72 (1995), 1–20.

6 *Petrarch's Lyric Poems*, ed. and trans. Robert M. Durling (Cambridge, MA: Harvard University Press, 1976), 36–7.
7 KJV quoted from the Oxford World's Classics Bible, ed. Robert Carroll and Stephen Prickett (Oxford: Oxford University Press, 1998).
8 Augustine, *Confessions*, 2 vols, ed. and trans. William Watts (Cambridge, MA: Harvard University Press, 1997), 1.3. Augustine's praise is composed of several passages from the Psalms, including 95:4, 144:3, and 47:2 in the Vulgate, and in the second half of the sentence he quotes 146:5.
9 'Et quis negat praesens tempus carere spatio, quia in puncto praeterit? Sed tamen perdurat attentio, per quam pergat abesse quod aderit' [And who can deny that the present moment has no space, because it passeth away in a moment? But yet our attentive marking of it continues so that that which shall be present proceedeth to become absent] (XI.28).
10 John Freccero, 'The Fig-Tree and the Laurel: Petrarch's Poetics', *Diacritics*, 5.1 (1975), 40.
11 *The Poems of Philip Sidney*, ed. William A. Ringler, Jr (Oxford: Clarendon Press, 1962), 270–1.
12 Hannibal Hamlin et al., eds, *The Sidney Psalter* (Oxford: Oxford University Press, 2009), 11.
13 On 'consist', see Roland Greene, 'Sidney's Psalms, the Sixteenth-Century Psalter and the Nature of the Lyric', *Studies in English Literature 1500–1900*, 30.1 (1990), 28.
14 *The Yale Edition of the Shorter Poems of Edmund Spenser*, ed. William Oram et al. (New Haven: Yale University Press, 1989), p. 690.
15 See for instance the editor's introduction to the *Fowre Hymnes* in the *Shorter Poems*, 683–684, and more recently David Lee Miller's essay 'Fowre Hymnes and Prothalamion (1596)', in Richard A. McCabe (ed.), *The Oxford Handbook of Edmund Spenser* (Oxford: Oxford University Press, 2010), 295. Miller suggests that the Petrarchan precedent of Spenser's poem is not so much the *Canzoniere* as the *Trionfi*.
16 Samuel Daniel, *Delia* (London, 1592), 1.
17 Though Spenser's Petrarchan allusions in the poem are widely acknowledged, they are usually marginalized as minor initial gestures that cease to be important as the poem passes beyond its first addresses to Love. In contrast, debates about the poem's Neoplatonism, which started in the early twentieth century with John Smith Harrison's *Platonism in English Poetry in the Sixteenth and Seventeenth Century* (New York: Macmillan, 1903) and J.B. Fletcher's 'A Study in Renaissance Mysticism: Spenser's *Fowre Hymnes*', *PMLA*, 26 (1911), continue into the twenty-first century, as shown by the recent special edition of *Spenser Studies* (Kenneth Borris, Jon Quitslund and Carol Kaske (eds), *Spenser and Platonism* (New York: AMS Press, 2009)), a substantial part of which is dedicated to the *Fowre Hymnes*.
18 *Shorter Poems*, 690.
19 Ibid. (emphases mine).
20 Gordon Teskey, 'A Retrograde Reading of Spenser's *Fowre Hymnes*', in Borris et al. (eds), *Spenser and Platonism*, 481–98.
21 In calling errors the hymns' initial, cosmological and cosmogonic quests to imagine and define the proper objects of their praises I do not mean to dismiss the possibility that the errors themselves are significant, either in the parallels they provide for Spenser's psychology and phenomenology, as Harry Berger argues, or in themselves as Spenser's genuine attempts to articulate his cosmogony, as Ayesha Ramachandran suggests. See Harry Berger, Jr, 'The Spenserian Dynamics', *Studies in English Literature*, 8 (1968), 1–18, and Ayesha Ramachandran, 'Edmund Spenser, Lucretian Neoplatonist: Cosmology in the *Fowre Hymnes*', in Borris et al. (eds), *Spenser and Platonism* (New York: AMS Press, 2009), 373–412. But it does seem to me that, from the perspective of the poem's devotional programme, the cosmological beginnings fulfil a specific function as errors and distractions.
22 See for instance the chapter on Sapience in Robert Ellrodt, *Neoplatonism in the Poetry of Spenser* (Geneva: Libraire E. Droz, 1960), 183–95.
23 Compare this with Ayesha Ramachandran's elegant reading of the concluding stanzas of Spenser's poem: 'The rapturous view of "perfect beauty", celebrated as Sapience or Wisdom earlier in the hymn, is fervently promised in these closing lines – but not actually made available. Poetry here is deployed in its ancient form as invocation, as a calling into being through the imagination of a perceived lack that harkens back to the lyric's roots in magical spells' (Chapter 7, p. 149 above). While Ramachandran reads the absence of a final vision as a replacement of a philosophical ambition with a therapeutic and poetic one, my suggestion is to see it as the completion of a devotional programme.
24 Donne's complex relationship to Petrarchism in the *Songs and Sonets* has been treated extensively in the scholarship; the Petrarchist elements in the *Holy Sonnets* have also received some, though not as much, attention. For a classic study of Donne's Petrarchism, see Donald L. Guss, *John Donne, Petrarchist: Italianate Conceits and Love Theory in the Songs and Sonets* (Detroit: Wayne State University Press,

1966). For an exquisite recent account of Petrarchism in the *Holy Sonnets*, see Gary Kuchar, *The Poetry of Religious Sorrow in Early Modern England* (Cambridge: Cambridge University Press, 2008), 151–83.
25 *The Variorum Edition of the Poetry of John Donne, Volume 7, Part 1: The Holy Sonnets*, ed. Gary Stringer et al. (Bloomington: Indiana University Press, 2005), 14.
26 Louis Martz's *The Poetry of Meditation* (New Haven: Yale University Press, 1962), 27.
27 George Puttenham, *The Arte of English Poesie*, ed. Frank Whigham and Wayne A. Rebhorn (Ithaca: Cornell University Press, 2007), 184.

11

Eliot, Yeats, Joyce, and the modernist reinvention of Spenser and Donne

Anne Fogarty and Jane Grogan

The modernist encounter with Renaissance poetry was a highly productive one, particularly in the realm of poetics, involving revitalized approaches to literary history and tradition. The attempt to look past the Romantics, to rescue English Renaissance writing from sentimentalizing Victorian and Edwardian readings united Eliot, Yeats, Pound, and Joyce, helping them forge a new modernist poetics in a 'direct line' (as Eliot put it) with early modern poetic practices.[1] All of them wrote critical essays or lectures on 'the Renaissance' or on specific Renaissance writers that substituted interrogation for reverence, finding in Renaissance literature useful articulations of the modern.[2] All of them mined Renaissance poets for models, techniques, images, metrical forms, and rhetorical possibilities, and the construction of the individual 'voice' of each of our writers owes something to their engagements with Renaissance poets. Partly interrogative, partly self-serving, the modernist redescription and reuse of Renaissance poetry – even recasting of the canon of Renaissance poetry – gave impetus to poetic innovation in both theory and practice, if in strikingly different ways.

Our focus in this chapter is primarily on the critical writings on Spenser and Donne by Eliot, Yeats, and Joyce, of whom Eliot was the most prolific, Joyce the least. But theory and practice are never entirely separable, and we also draw on their creative work to demonstrate significant uses as well as shifts in their engagement with Renaissance authors. Certain commonalities emerge: encountering Spenser and Donne in the context of the university curriculum proves important in different ways for all three. Allusion, predictably, serves as a key mechanism, but not the only one; each of the modernists has a deep and abiding interest not only in Renaissance writers, but also in the current critical work on them. By and large, all three accept a perceived literary-historical divide separating Spenser from Donne, or make different kinds of use of each poet. Then there is the issue of the intertextual triangulations between Renaissance and modernists poets: if the most Spenserian section of Eliot's *Waste Land* was shaped by readings of and by Joyce and Pound, what intertextual modernist work does Spenser do? If Eliot responds unfavourably (indeed with prejudice) to Yeats's writings on Spenser, how does Yeats respond to Eliot's writings on Donne, and how far does each other's critical work shape their creative responses to Renaissance poets? These are the kinds of questions that the present chapter seeks ultimately to enable, but only after studying carefully the rich and varied uses of Spenser and Donne by these leading modernist authors. Beginning, therefore, with a survey of the broader implications for poetics and literary history of modernist reinventions of Renaissance poetry, we move to three discrete but linked sections examining the influence of Spenser and Donne on Eliot, Yeats, and Joyce respectively. Finally, we seek to begin a new critical conversation about the place of Spenser and Donne in modernist intra- and intertextuality, a task too large for the present chapter.

Modernism's early modern interests involved literary history as much as practice, the remoulding of 'Tradition' as well as of individual talents – but this was a case of 'both/and', not 'either/or'. Famously, Eliot declared that writers must have 'a perception, not only of the pastness of the past, but of its presence', such that the writer must write 'not merely with his own generation in his bones, but with a feeling that the whole of the literature of Europe from Homer and within it the whole of the literature of his own country has a simultaneous existence and composes a simultaneous order'.[3] Which is not to say that literary history should lack historicity. For Yeats and Eliot, for example, the English Renaissance stood as the last unified or harmonious period of literary expression before a sea-change in poetic values, for the worse. This involved a shift from a period of mythic unity and 'unification of sensibility' to 'disintegration' and 'dissociation of sensibility' (Eliot), a 'last struggle' (Yeats), giving way before a harsher modern order.[4] For both Eliot and Yeats, these changes were social as well as poetic. But Eliot wrote of the striations within the intellectual currents of the Renaissance more substantively than Yeats: 'our ideas, vague as they are, about the Elizabethan mind are derived mainly from the work of the humanising poets – Wyatt, Surrey, Spenser, with the derivations from French and Italian literature, Fulke Greville and the Senecals – or from the work of the dramatists'. From poets, in other words, rather than 'professional men', Eliot derives the most familiar characteristics of Renaissance poetry. From this point of view, Roger Ascham seems to Eliot more modern than John Donne, a man defined by 'theological politics' to the extent that other powerful literary influences (Montaigne, Seneca, Machiavelli) appear to bypass him altogether.[5] And yet, Eliot makes a valiant (and successful) case for the modernity of Donne, against the now-impossible optimism of the 'humanizing' writers of the Tudor age, among whom Eliot counts Spenser. If some of this argument is a projection of his own poetic values, it is one he makes good through his lifelong habit of thinking with and alongside Donne. For all this Donnean alignment, however, in Eliot's own poetic practice, Spenser ultimately proves a richer and more complex source of allusion and poetic innovation than Donne, we will suggest. Indeed, the fitful and unstable presence of Spenser and Donne in the work of Yeats, Pound, and Joyce may be due in part to the increasing marginalization of the former and the relatively recent re-evaluation of the latter by Herbert J.C. Grierson and Eliot. Pound and Joyce, moreover, were less wedded to the ideal of an English Renaissance, probably because of their stronger instincts for the European tradition of Homer and Dante and their interest in breaking down divisions between the medieval and early modern periods. But they still found it useful for their own self-fashioning, if only to overgo it. For Pound, the integrity of the Renaissance itself provided a viable model of literary achievement: as Jewel Spears Brooker writes, 'Pound thought of the modernist movement as Renaissance II'.[6] But however useful it was to cast their own more or less antagonistic individual relationships to an English literary tradition represented by Spenser and Donne, Shakespeare and Marlowe, it was the specific formal qualities of English Renaissance poetry that provoked Eliot, Yeats, and Joyce into experiments in their own literary art, experiments that put them at the vanguard of modernist literary innovation, diverse though their efforts were.

Allusion, often conspicuous, is central to modernist literary practice – just as it was in Renaissance literary practice.[7] An article of faith for Eliot and Joyce, allusiveness in the modernist tradition differs from early modern intertextual practices in its subordination of the original context to the new poetic artefact, and in its willingness to countenance and explore the jarring or uncooperative effects arising from these new terms. But much more than allusion is involved. As Eliot noted in a 1923 essay on John Donne, engagement with Renaissance writers is no mere search for literary ancestors, but illuminates the modern condition: 'Our appreciation of Donne must be an appreciation of *what we lack, as well as of what we have in common with him*. What is true of his mind is true, in different terms, of his language and versification. A *style, a rhythm*, to be significant, must embody a significant mind, must be produced by the necessity of a new form for a new content.'[8] For Yeats, reading 'the great old masters' of English literature (he names Spenser, but not Donne, among them) was vital to the production of modern Irish literature, a feeling Joyce shared as part of his even more pluralist aesthetic. Despite the broader modernist habit of attending more strongly to the Renaissance poem than its context, for the Irish writers, Spenser would prove a trickier forebear and model than Donne. Spenser's history in Ireland and his uncompromising writings on the subjugation of the native Irish made Yeats and Joyce especially sensitive to the embedded politics of the English literary 'tradition', though each of them none the less found ways to make Spenser serve their purpose. And yet, the 'English Renaissance' adduced by all three writers presented a bifurcated poetic tradition, with Spenser and Donne pitched in different camps: Spenser standing for the lush, self-regarding heights of Elizabethan convention, Donne for a more cerebral, hard-won and personal verse involving a truer 'feeling' or 'sensibility' cherished by the likes of Eliot. Despite its provenance in just those Victorian critics whose values they challenged, and in the university curricula they studied, it was a distinction that modernist writers tended not to disentangle, at least not explicitly.[9] What Eliot, Yeats, and Joyce learned from Spenser and Donne they learned and kept separately, for the most part. Yeats and Joyce, moreover, put Spenser and Donne to different uses and drew on them in disparate and often wilful ways. Yeats wrestled with the duality of Spenser whom he viewed both as a congenial role model and as terrible proof of the corruptibility of the imagination. He ultimately worked to free himself of the influence of Spenser, and gravitated towards Donne at a midpoint in his career when he programmatically set about to simplify his style, rid it of Romantic idiom and make it conspicuously more colloquial and modern. Joyce, for his part, annexed aspects of Spenser in order to add pointed ironies to his symbolic renderings of the abject nature of Irish colonial identity in *A Portrait of the Artist as a Young Man*, but also in order to dismantle the authoritativeness of *The Faerie Queene* and to co-opt it for the subversive and layered wordplay and shifting mythic configurations of *Finnegans Wake*. Donne, by contrast, he posited as a less inimical figure, but he also insisted on redisposing him by casting him as essentially medieval, thereby allying him with a worldview that he saw as a necessary counter-weight to the modern and an inherent aspect of the recalcitrance and Otherness of Irish culture.[10]

Eliot, Spenser, Donne

For Eliot, at least, the separation of Spenser and Donne originated in the educational curriculum he followed, both as a student and later as a teacher. And if Spenser seemed the establishment poet cherished by the Victorians, Donne was the unsettling skeleton in the closet of English Renaissance poetry. At Harvard, as Dayton Haskin has shown, Eliot's instructors presented Donne as 'discontinuous' with Spenser, with courses including 'Death of Spenser to the Closing of the Theatres'.[11] Haskin argues that Barrett Wendell's theory of the 'fall' from Spenser and high Elizabethan literature at the hands of Donne was integral to the teaching of Renaissance literature at Harvard during Eliot's years there – and that it was a theory Eliot sought to counter with his own postulations about the 'dissociation of sensibility' in later seventeenth-century poetry.[12] We know from an August 1920 list of his books at his mother's house that Eliot owned an impressive range of work by Renaissance writers. He took a keen interest in critical work on these writers, who had benefited not just from the attentions and interest of nineteenth-century editors such as A.B. Grosart but also from critics such as Pater and Symonds, and more recently, Dowden and Grierson. Matthews suggests that the very crowdedness and venerability of this area suggested opportunity to the young Eliot: 'For Eliot, then, the critical "field" of his topic remained in his view outmoded at best, and void of critical understanding. It was a field, in other words, that could rapidly be occupied by a new writer who was fascinated by the early modern period, and by an American citizen anxious to assimilate himself to Old World "tradition"'.[13] Eliot would produce critical writings on the English Renaissance throughout his life, in turn influencing his creative output.

Throughout his career, Eliot found in early modern writers – poets and dramatists – powerful lines, images and voices that could be harnessed to express the experience of the modern. Spenser and Donne are only two of a company of early modern writers upon whom Eliot drew in his poetry and criticism. Dramatists (notably Middleton, Shakespeare, and Massinger) and religious writers (including preachers such as Lancelot Andrewes and poets such as George Herbert) feature again and again, shaping Eliot's poetry, drama, and prose.[14] It was early in his career that Eliot engaged most strongly with English Renaissance writing – the 'apprentice years', as the editors of his prose works term it, in which he was establishing himself as a poet, critic, and man of letters in English intellectual society. In particular, from 1918 to 1924 we find Eliot's literary energies, both as poet and as critic, invested in early modern writers. This period takes in the 'extension lectures' on Elizabethan Literature he gave at the University of London in 1919 (which included lectures on *The Faerie Queene* and Donne), the first of his editorial appointments, and the sharp increase in his literary reviewing activities, often of new editions or essays on metaphysical or early modern writers.[15] These reviews resulted in his first published collection of prose works, *The Sacred Wood* (1920), of which a quarter of the essays were devoted to the English Renaissance, with individual essays on Jonson, Marlowe, Massinger, and *Hamlet*. It also included the seminal essay 'Tradition and the Individual Talent', in which Eliot made a powerful and sophisticated argument for the necessity for writers to engage with the literary tradition preceding them. The Introduction set out a key role for the critic, declaring that 'It is part of the business of the critic to preserve tradition – where a good tradition exists'.[16] The 'tradition', in other words, was to be a collaboration between writers and critics. Eliot would soon make good his own stipulation. In 1921 his seminal review-essay of Grierson's anthology of *Metaphysical Poetry: Donne to Waller* appeared in the *TLS*, later to be reprinted as the highly influential essay 'The Metaphysical Poets'. Wittingly or not (and Eliot later denied this), it ensured the canonicity of Donne and Marvell for the rest of the century and empowered the New Critics. The years 1921 and 1922 were also the difficult years of composition, editing and eventual publication of *The Waste Land* (1922), famously peppered with quotations from and allusions to Spenser, Shakespeare, Kyd, Webster, Marvell, and Middleton (to mention only those explicitly identified in Eliot's published notes to the poem). This period of intense engagement with early modern poets culminates in 1926, when Eliot presented the Clark Lectures at Cambridge: eight lectures titled 'On the Metaphysical Poetry of the Seventeenth Century with Special Reference to Donne, Crashaw and Cowley'. For a long time afterwards, Eliot would contemplate incorporating this material into a book, potentially entitled *The Disintegration of the Intellect*, with three sections on 'The School of Donne', 'Elizabethan Drama', and 'The Sons of Ben', though ultimately it never came about.[17] His conversion and baptism into the Church of England in 1928 saw a major shift in Eliot's thought and poetry, as well as a turn to drama in the mid-1930s, and he looked more frequently to early modern drama than to the poets in his later writings.

Eliot's critical engagement with Donne is well known, not just his interest in Donne's ideas of love, sex, and death but especially his 'metaphysical' poetic techniques and values. His encounter with Spenser is less obvious and has been much less studied, yet in some of his critical writings Eliot praised Spenser as a 'master of versification', an 'innovator' and 'elaborator' 'with a sensitiveness to words almost equal to that of Chaucer'.[18] These virtues of innovation and elaboration resemble those for which Eliot values Donne, particularly in the Clark Lectures and Grierson review. And yet, Eliot elsewhere returns to the divided Renaissance of the curriculum to present Spenser as a skilful, mellifluous versifier, eclipsed by Donne the modern innovator. In the essay on Marlowe published in *The Sacred Wood*, for example, Eliot turns to Spenser, crediting 'this great master of melody' as the force behind the '"lyric"' effects of Marlowe's *Tamburlaine* plays.[19] 'This is not Spenser's movement', he writes, 'but the influence of Spenser must be present. There had been no great blank verse before Marlowe; but there was the powerful presence of this great master of melody immediately precedent; and the combination produced results which could not be repeated.'[20] Marlowe's synthesis and multiple reformulations of a single Spenserian line are, of course, close to Eliot's own poetic practices; here, Spenser is merely what is practised on, it seems. But Eliot's theory of the necessity of engaging with the literary tradition re-amplifies the significance of Spenser in Marlowe's hands. Roughly contemporary though Marlowe's use of Spenser might be, his drawing strength from Spenser stylistically, even as he subjugates the Spenserian line to his own innovations and repetitions, gives his poetic practice a significance within literary history, allowing it to make its mark on the tradition. In so doing, the Spenserian line re-emerges from within Marlowe's verse, and asserts itself with a prior historic authority, wrenching open a crucial critical distance, the space of reinvention and renewal.

As scholars have often pointed out, allusion, even to the point of polyvocality, is central to Eliot's poetic practice, particularly in *The Waste Land*. Although Donne certainly informs his poetic technique, the few uses of Spenser in his poems take the form of clear and elaborated allusion rather than emulation. His allusions to Spenser thus advertise a crucial disjunction between the values of the English Renaissance and those of the modern moment. Eliot's ascription of difficulty, 'variety and complexity' to metaphysical as well as modern poetry means that this disjunction is less strongly felt in his uses of Donne.[21] The modern experience of self-alienation can be more closely felt through alienation from the poetic achievements of a Spenser than a Donne, at least in *The Waste Land*. Allusiveness demands intensive readerly work, as Eliot reanimates perhaps not just a particular quotation but also its tone and contexts, even where such allusions are barely visible.[22] This holds true more strongly of his allusions to early modern plays than to poems, but tone and context are crucial to Eliot's most famous use of Spenser: 'Sweet Thames run softly, til I end my song.'

Signalled by Eliot himself in his own notes to *The Waste Land* (1922), the refrain of 'Sweet Thames run softly til I end my song' in the third section ('The Fire Sermon'), which served as a refrain in Spenser's *Prothalamion*, certainly draws on the 'calm' (also *Prothalamion*'s first word), measured tone of Spenser's bridal song for the two daughters of the Earl of Somerset.[23] The nature and extent of Eliot's irony in quoting Spenser in this way have been much debated. That the rubbish-strewn river of Eliot's poem contrasts with the full-flowing river of 'merry London' in Spenser's poem is unquestionable; less clear is how much conviction or animus enlivens that contrast. Scholars have been quick to see it exemplifying the corruption of the modern condition, but in a 1958 letter Eliot asserted that the conspicuous difference between Spenser's river and his 'is not to glorify the past in contrast to the present or to give any suggestion of futility'.[24] Nor is it clear in what direction the ironic effect runs – to satirize Spenser (as Richard Danson Brown suggests), or to chasten modernity.[25] Michael Whitworth complicates the situation by pointing out that Eliot may well have had in mind some of the intervening uses of Spenser's line, citing two poems (including a pastoral by Pope in imitation of Virgil), and two prose works that use the 'Sweet Thames' line.[26] More recently, Ricks and McCue enrich the allusion by juxtaposing the debris of Eliot's Thames with Spenser's swans so white 'That euen the gentle streame, the which them bare, / Seem'd foule to them'.[27] They also tentatively suggest a Spenserian echo in 'leman', which appears in the description of the storm that leads Redcrosse and Una to seek shelter in the wandering wood (*FQ* I.i.6), and further distant echoes of *Prothalamion* in 'To Carthage then I came'.[28] Certainly, the speedy shifts in this opening section through allusions to Shakespeare, twice more to Spenser, then Marvell soon after situate us firmly in the English Renaissance, but Whitworth's remembrance of Pope's poem is especially interesting, because the 'Sweet Thames' lines appear in the revised opening of 'The Fire Sermon', replacing (on Pound's advice) an extended pastiche of Pope's *The Rape of the Lock*.

With these critiques in mind, the composition of 'The Fire Sermon' bears revisiting. While much of Part III was written while Eliot was at Margate, on sick leave and recuperating for a few weeks before travelling to a Lausanne clinic, it was revisited and revised in light of Ezra Pound's editorial suggestions.[29] 'The Fire Sermon' had originally begun with 89 lines parodying Pope's *The Rape of the Lock* and had its protagonist, Fresca, immersed 'in a soapy sea / of Symonds-Walter Pater-Vernon Lee'. Pound advocated deleting this completely in January 1922, along with a host of other changes to the poem.[30] So it was while he was still in Pound's company in Paris in early 1922 that Eliot wrote the Spenserian opening of 'The Fire Sermon'. But something of the original remained in the focus on water to link with the Thames-maidens at the end of Part III, and of the well-known Renaissance interests of Fresca's fashionable triumvirate of writers. There are further Spenserian echoes in 'The Fire Sermon' not noted by Ricks and McCue, many clustered around the image of Elizabeth flirting with Leicester upon Eliot's river Thames. The 'nymphs' and 'sweats' of the river recall the poet's command that the walls be doused in wine and 'sweat', the 'nymphs' evoking those Spenser commands to his own nuptial purposes in *Epithalamion*. More deeply buried, the 'departed nymphs' may also allude to the Mutabilitie Cantos, specifically the departure of the goddess Diana and her nymphs from Ireland upon being betrayed by Molanna and surreptitiously viewed bathing in a 'sweet stream' (VII.vi.54) by lustful wood-god Faunus, who had tempted Diana's nymph with 'Queene-apples' (VII.vi.43) and flattery. If she appeared as Cynthia (the moon) peeping in the window on Spenser's wedding night in *Epithalamion*, in the *Cantos of Mutabilitie* Queen Elizabeth became the spied-upon Diana; the nymphs who celebrated Spenser's wedding now depart the pristine pastoral scene with her, ushering in a darker, cursed world. The openness of Eliot's allusions enable this triangulation of sources – rivers, nymphs, Elizabeth, marriage – through the *Epithalamion* as well as *The Faerie Queene* in this section, and serves to make the ironic contrast between what looks like a Renaissance idyll and an apocalyptic modernity much more dynamic, more dialectical, and even more mythic.

Contrast this web of myth, history, and autobiography with the rather functional allusion to Donne in the 'Exploring hands' of the typist's would-be lover later in 'The Fire Sermon' (l. 240).[31] Similarly, the arms braceleted with hair in 'The Love Song of J. Alfred Prufrock' recall a favourite Donne poem of Eliot, 'The Relic' (in 'The Burnt Dancer' Eliot compressed the opening two lines of 'The Relic' in the image 'O broken guest').[32] But such allusions to Donne are relatively rare, and hardly to be found in *The Waste Land*: most significantly, the 'Exequy', one of the short poems with which Eliot wanted to intercalate his long poem, had used the opening of 'The Relic' for its own opening – but Eliot complied when Pound strongly counselled against including it.[33]

Eliot's Spenserian allusions elsewhere are not nearly as conspicuous, though they can be as hard-working. The editors labour through an intermediary Shakespearean reference to locate a rather slight Spenserian antecedent (only a simile in *The Faerie Queene*) in the use of the word 'dreaming' in the Shakespearean epigraph to 'Gerontion'.[34] The rhyming of 'gems' and 'Thames' in 'Airs of Palestine no. 2' again reminds them of Spenser's so doing in *Prothalamion*, while the phrase 'Time's ruins' in 'Burbank with a Baedeker: Bleistein with a Cigar' recalls for them the title of Spenser's *The Ruines of Time* (in *Complaints*). Some early critics found echoes of *Epithalamion* in 'East Coker', but Ricks and McCue demur, instead trusting in Eliot's own account of the passage's debts to the work of Sir Thomas Elyot.[35] As he had outlined in 'Tradition and the Individual Talent', Eliot worked through both Spenser and Donne, poets of his education and youth, unspooling their techniques as innovators and avatars of the modern before re-stitching them into the rich strangeness and recursive polyvocality of his own verse. But the dynamism of his poetics, and even of his allusions to these poets, has perhaps been lost in the sheer force and extent of his own poetic achievement. Recently, for example, as part of the cultural festivities associated with London's hosting of the 2012 Olympics and Paralympics, Eliot's Spenser made an unusual appearance: in a piece of graffiti. 'Sweet Thames run softly til I end my song' was inscribed on a riverside wall on the south bank of the Thames. A Thames festival commission in collaboration with the Forward Arts Foundation, the work was created by the artist Moose, a leading practitioner of 'reverse graffitti', a process in which stencils and a high-powered water-hose are used to create graffiti not by writing over the urban surface but instead by inscribing it temporarily within the layers of accumulated urban grime, eventually to be re-absorbed into the patina of dirt and pollution. But in all the supporting materials and advertising, Spenser's line was silently presented as the poetry of T.S. Eliot, and Eliot's estate thanked for granting permission for its use.[36] Despite Eliot's bleak framing of Spenser's melliflu-ous line in *The Waste Land*, the festival organizers favoured Eliot over Spenser in borrowing these lines, the City clerk rather than the colonial servant, making clean again the paratextual fabric of the dirty, storied Thames.[37] By asserting an originary authenticity and pureness made visible and tenable again precisely by its projection into a degraded modernity, 'reverse graffitti' – like Eliot's own Spenserian allusion – does not just make an Eliot of Spenser, but a new Spenser of Eliot.

Yeats, Spenser, Donne

The work of Edmund Spenser played a talismanic role for Yeats throughout his career and was especially important for the embryonic poet who enthusiastically and reverentially imitated and adapted his English predecessor. Yeats found his own voice through his emulation and appropriation of Spenser; by contrast, Donne became a pronounced influence from 1912 onwards in his middle and late poems and propelled his quest for a more concrete, modernist style. In making Spenser over, Yeats as an apprentice writer began gradually to formulate his own aesthetic and to pinpoint themes that would remain hallmarks of his work. He saw Spenser at once as a touchstone of artistic values and as a testing ground for his changing views of the social role of the writer and of the political, spiritual, and intellectual importance of poetry. Thinking with and about Spenser was a regular reflex of his ruminations. Yet, even though Spenser was fundamental to Yeats's vision and practice as a poet and an unfailing part of a personal canon on which he perennially drew, Yeats constantly revised his view of him and recalibrated his legacy at different junctures in his life. It may, moreover, be mooted that Yeats would later use Donne to mitigate the influence of Spenser and the political divisions that he embodied. If modernism elsewhere was, in Ezra Pound's phrase, intent on making things new, Irish modernism was alert always to the problems posed by the unappeased aspects of a troubled and divided colonial past and insistent on the necessity of rethinking, not of jettisoning, tradition.[38]

Spenser was key to Yeats's incessant reinterrogations of the literary forebears that he designated as shaping forces for his own work. In particular, Yeats was drawn to the complex symbolic systems constructed by Spenser both in his shorter poems and in *The Faerie Queene* and to the heterodox mystical and philosophical beliefs that they evince. Yeats's views of Spenser evolved as he matured and aged. If for the young Yeats Spenser's texts served as exemplars for the workings of the imagination and provided compelling instances of how literary worlds could be envisaged in poetry, for the older poet Spenser was essential for counteracting what he saw as the vulgarity and effeteness of contemporary language and style. Increasingly, Yeats questioned his youthful lionization of Spenser and interrogated his earlier assumptions about the poet. He particularly worried about the political dimensions of Spenser's oeuvre, its embeddedness in early modern English colonialism and its reification of racial and ethnic prejudices. He made Spenser a sparring partner in his ongoing endeavour to articulate Irish nationalist cultural values and to engage in searching conversations with the canon of English literature to which he acknowledged himself to be completely beholden. He also reflected on Spenser in the context of the Irish-Ireland philosophy of political commentators such as D.P. Moran who decried external influences, especially those stemming from Britain, as corrupting and foreign and advocated a return to the Irish language. Contrary to such arguments, Yeats called upon Spenser and other key English poets to defend the radical potential of Irish nationalist writers who aimed, as he himself did, to effect a political awakening of the country through composing works in English.

An examination of the disparate allusions to Spenser in Yeats's essays and correspondence provides an insight into the manner in which his views of him modulated and were strategically redisposed depending on the political occasion or the polemical claims that he wished to press home. Such a survey also evidences how he uses the Renaissance poet as scaffolding for arguments on the aesthetic and its links with the numinous and the visionary. In part, it is the very pliability and contradictoriness of his vision of Spenser that made him useful to Yeats. He saw the sixteenth-century writer as a figure in transition between an ancient, cohesive world order rooted in folk culture and a modernity attached to a courtly politics that is divided and compromised. But he also viewed him as a herald of the modern, forming part of a continuum interlinking Renaissance poetry, Romanticism, and modernism and guaranteeing a pathway to art forms that are shaped by organically sustaining primitive values and act as vehicles for otherworldly wisdom and communication.

In an early allusion to Spenser in a letter to the editor of *The Bookman* in November 1892, Yeats profiles him as a poet who managed to elude if not quite transcend the worst effects of his allegiance to Elizabethan imperialism.[39] However, in a missive from November 1902, to Thomas MacDonagh (the poet, academic and playwright, who would later be one of the executed leaders of the 1916 Easter Rising), Yeats's intellectual regard for Spenser is far less wary. He advises the younger man that reading the 'great old masters of English', amongst them Spenser, Ben Jonson and Thomas Browne, was the most effective apprenticeship for an aspiring poet.[40]

Two review pieces from the 1890s on folklore evince further vital grounds for his espousal of Spenser: his tapping into a world of inherited folk understanding. This facet of Spenser is further elaborated on in the prefatory essay to the volume of selected passages from Spenser that he was commissioned to compile for the Golden Poet Series that appeared in 1906. In 'The Message of the Folk-lorist', an essay published in the *Speaker* in 1893, he contended that folklore supersedes literature and is in fact its bedrock. He pronounced that great writers were 'folk-lorists with musical tongues' and that the peoples of countries such as Ireland, Yugoslavia and Sweden had immediate access to such knowledge and 'had need neither of Dante nor Spenser to tell them of the living trees that cry or bleed if you break off a bough'.[41] Spenser's works here are deemed to enshrine ancient esoteric wisdom, and indeed a Spenserian motif from *The Faerie Queene*, Book I, is nicely deployed to reinforce this point. In a similar vein, his 1894 review of William Larminie's *West Irish Folk Tales* in the *Bookman* praises the author's ability to draw on a reservoir of inherited stories and myths in the manner of Homer and Spenser.[42]

It is however in his 1906 preface to his edition of Spenser, which he subsequently revised for inclusion in *The Cutting of the Agate*, a collection of essays first published in the US in 1912 and republished in the UK in 1919, that he most thoroughly enunciated and picked over his views of Spenser.[43] The fresh account of the Renaissance poet that he unfolded differed from his earlier pronouncements in that it unblinkingly reviewed the role played by the poet in the late sixteenth-century colonization of Ireland. It is these sections of the essay that have most frequently been cited. Yeats castigated Spenser for being a political functionary and for giving 'his heart to the State'.[44] He contended that when Spenser wrote about Ireland he did so as an official and that he neither 'pictured the true countenance of Irish scenery' nor understood the people amongst whom he lived.[45] Despite these chilling conclusions, Yeats's essay is ultimately a highly precarious balancing act in which he endeavours to weigh up numerous countervailing views of Spenser which pull against one other and cannot readily be made to cohere. On the one hand, Spenser is Puritanical, a moralist, and incapable of emotion; on the other hand, he is the poet of 'the delighted senses', a supremely pictorial artist, and a mouthpiece for the pagan values of 'indolent, demonstrative Merry England' and the civilities of an Anglo-French feudal order.[46] Even though Yeats takes issue with these contradictions, they are also the very facets of Spenser that attracted him. Moreover, he posited Spenser as a transitional figure who existed on the cusp of two worldviews, torn between the 'religion of the wilderness' and the bureaucratized order brought in by the Reformation and the Elizabethan settlement.[47] Indeed, as David Gardiner has observed, the tensions laid bare in Spenser have a kinship with those faced by Yeats himself, who felt divided between the demands of being a public figure and political activist and a poet and visionary.[48] The scission between imagination and politics is a burden for the writer, whether as supporter of the violent suppressions of early modern colonialist policies or of the Irish nationalist impetus for independence and liberation. The sacred qualities of the Merry England that Yeats values in Spenser's poetry also appear to have much in common with the profane ancient lore of Celtic Ireland which he was at pains to retrieve and to use as a force for regeneration and renewal.

The sections from Spenser's work featured in Yeats's anthology bore out his preoccupation with the esoteric and Neoplatonist dimensions of his writing as well as his fascination with the magical, otherworldly spaces that he constructed. Indeed, Elizabeth Bergmann Loizeaux has contended that Yeats learnt the importance of region and the intense visualization of place from Spenser.[49] In his preface he declared his aversion to allegory, but this is belied by the excerpts that he chose, which include many of the pivotal symbolic scenes of *The Faerie Queene*, such as the Cave of Despair, the Garden of Adonis, the House of Busirane and the islands of Phaedria and Acrasia. Yeats's selections from Spenser serve as a personal poetic primer and florilegium and excise those aspects of the poet's writings that he found problematic. In his *Autobiographies* Yeats recorded that as a young man he 'wrote poetry in imitation of Shelley and Spenser', in a quest to produce the exalted dramatic pieces favoured by his father.[50] *The Island of Statues* is an example of one such early work composed under the influence of Spenser, which appeared in the *Dublin University Review* in 1886. The poet ultimately withheld it from his Collected Poems because he felt it to be clumsy and inchoate. It counterpointed two worlds, an effete Arcadia inhabited by quarrelling shepherds and a fateful island in a lake, ruled over by an Enchantress. Those who travel to this realm in quest of a flower that promises joy are turned to stone if they alight on the wrong plant. Alminter, a hunter, who goes in search of this flower in order to prove his love for Naschina, is duly calcified. Naschina, disguised as a shepherd, travels herself to the island and manages to outwit the enchantress and undo the spell placed on Alminter and others. At the end, she becomes the sole ruler of this island world, exchanging the lassitude of Arcadia for a sphere in which heroic self-realization is possible. R.F. Foster has noted that lurking beneath the archaisms of this poem was a 'hard philosophical question about the utility of "dreaming"', thereby suggesting how Spenserian motifs and themes were to be evolved and developed by the poet.[51] *The Wanderings of Oisin* is a much more successfully devised quest narrative that takes its bearings from Spenser; it centres on the fated love between Oisin and Niamh and depicts the differing island worlds to which they retreat.[52] It ultimately counterweighs the rival claims of the fairy sphere and of historical reality, and of paganism and Christianity. At the end of the poem, the lure of fairy land is shown to be a corollary of the mortal world to which Oisin succumbs. Indeed, the facility to project images of the ineffable or of idealized female beauty and to parse them on several disparate but intertwined symbolic levels is a central aspect of Yeats's work and an imperative that he learnt in part from Spenser. Thus, readers are enjoined to decipher the Neoplatonic image of the Rose in 'The Secret Rose' and to interrogate the meaning of the alluring artificiality of the gilded world in which the poet takes refuge in 'Sailing to Byzantium'.[53] Additionally, the dialogue poem in which differing figures reflect on metaphysical issues or questions about art, politics, and patronage in the manner of *The Shepheardes Calender* and the epithalamic poem are further Spenserian modes whose lineaments can be discerned in Yeats's works such as 'Solomon to Sheba', 'Ego Dominus Tuus', and 'Shepherd and Goatherd'.[54]

Spenserian effects seem frequently to intrude in Yeats's searing late poems that attempt a reckoning with the personal and political involvements of the past and self-reflexively to ponder the esoteric wisdom of art. This is the case with 'A Bronze Head', a meditation from 1939 on a bust of Maud Gonne, the woman whom he had celebrated, idealized, and unavailingly loved throughout his life, displayed in the Municipal Gallery in Dublin.[55] Writing in rhyme royal, the poet responds to the bust as to a terrible *memento mori*, thus turning the poem into a proleptic elegy. The beloved in this new emanation appears to be eerily unnatural and spectral: 'Human, superhuman, a bird's round eye / Everything else withered and mummy-dead.'[56] The final stanza returns to the mystery of Gonne as a supernatural being and conjures with the implacable essence of her nature as it is laid bare in this art work and by implication in Yeats's own poem:

> Or else I thought her supernatural;
> As though a sterner eye looked through her eye
> On this foul world in its decline and fall;
> On gangling stocks grown great, great stocks run dry,
> Ancestral pearls all pitched into a sty,
> Heroic reverie mocked by clown and knave,
> And wondered what was left for massacre to save.[57]

As Helen Vendler has observed, Yeats ends the poem with a Spenserian alexandrine, thus fracturing its metrical pattern.[58] In so doing, he intimates the devastating truths uncovered in his final ruminations and also cross-associates Gonne with a Renaissance poem written in homage to a female ruler conceived of as a divinity, who is similarly distant and unyielding in her impartiality and regal untouchability. Gonne is envisaged here as a destructive deity or cosmic principle. But even as Yeats acknowledges her immortal power he also admits to its remorseless and inhuman nature. Spenserian metrics allow him to crystallize this stark recognition while giving it subtle poetic shape.

Other references to Spenser in Yeats's late work evince the degree to which he still cleaved to him as an intellectual resource and literary wellspring. In 'The Municipal Gallery Revisited', a group elegy, the poet contemplates paintings and sculptures of his dead friends, and assesses what has become of their erstwhile dreams and ambitions:

> My medieval knees lack health until they bend,
> But in that woman, in that household where
> Honour had lived so long, all lacking found.
> Childless, I thought, 'My children may find here
> Deep-rooted things', but never foresaw its end,
> And now that end has come I have not wept;
> No fox can foul the lair the badger swept –
>
> (An image out of Spenser and the common tongue).[59]

The enjambment between the fifth and sixth stanzas renders the allusion to *The Ruines of Time* self-conscious and overdetermined. The couplet in Spenser's poem,

'He now is gone, the whiles the Foxe is crept / Into the hole, the which the Badger swept', is condensed and inverted. Yeats mourns the passing of Lady Gregory and the demolition of her house in Coole Park in a manner akin to Verlame's vehement lament for the death of the Earl of Leicester. Yet, in Yeats's elegy, death creates an abiding absence; far from being defiled, Coole retains its aura despite being effaced. In gleaning motifs from Spenser, Yeats reworks them thoroughly, adds a distantiating and arch commentary and cross-connects them with the 'common tongue', the demotic idiom from which modernist poetry derives its dynamic and unruly energy. Notably, Spenser is cast as a modernist precursor; his images are ransacked and pressed into service by the twentieth-century poet, their original pungency is turned to effect in a highly self-conscious act of literary borrowing and reinvention. In a similar manner, Spenser is cited in the revised version of *A Vision*, in a passage in which the writer struggles with the issue of the computation of the equinoctial precession and the number of years it takes the soul to move through the twenty-eight phases of the wheel of time.[60] He acknowledges that Spenser has reckoned the precession of the equinox differently in the 'Proem' to *The Faerie Queene*, Book V, but notes that his instructors (that is, the visionary voices and personae that guide him and provide him piecemeal with esoteric wisdom) have arrived at a different measurement of the Platonic Year. Spenser, in this context, is included as part of the visionary company that informs *A Vision*, but as in 'The Municipal Gallery Revisited' he is referenced only to be revised and rethought. [61]

In 'A General Introduction to My Work', published in 1937, Yeats declared that he owed his 'soul to Shakespeare, to Spenser and to Blake, perhaps to William Morris and to the English language in which I think, speak and write'. Spenser, it is evident, remained until the end of his life an irremovable member of his personal pantheon of literary progenitors. John Donne is never accorded such status, but he is a crucial figure for Yeats's reinvention of his style. Indeed, Donne more than Spenser facilitated Yeats's transition to modernism, and Grierson's gift of the two volumes of his edition of *The Poems of John Donne* to the poet in 1912 played a vital role in Yeats's reworking of his poetic. Yeats expressed his enthusiasm in a letter of thanks to Grierson in November 1912 and indicated the extent of his intellectual connectedness with the seventeenth-century poet: 'Your notes tell me exactly what I want to know. Poems that I could not understand or could but understand are now clear and I notice that the more precise and learned the thought the greater the beauty, the passion; the intricacy and subtleties of his imagination are the length and depths of the furrow made by his passion'.[62] Yeats aimed always to balance contraries in his poetry and the example of Donne strengthened his resolve to maximize such counterpointing of thought and feeling. It is evident that he is especially invigorated by the latter's facility for interfusing learning and passion, the religious and the profane. As Wayne K. Chapman has noted, Yeats's intermingling of the spiritual and the sexual in his 1912 volume *The Green Helmet and Other Poems* and in *Responsibilities*, published in 1914, becomes 'recognizably Metaphysical and unmistakably Donnean in manner'.[63] The yoking of opposites, the sudden affluxes of intense emotion, and the precise rendering of paradoxical affective states in 'The Cold Heaven', for example, are reminiscent of Donne's meditations.[64] Indeed, what Patrick Cheney dubs Donne's 'metaphysical sublime', states of being and emotion that explode cognition, appears particularly to attract Yeats.[65] By contrast, the dualities between nature and art, the physical and the spiritual, the material and the transcendent in his early allegorical and symbolist work influenced by Spenser issue often in the failure of his Romantic questers, such as Oisin or Red Hanrahan, or are evinced as ineffable forms of longing that can never be fulfilled. Antinominalism remains a constant facet of Yeats's writing, but under the influence of Donne's poetics, sexual, mythic, and experiential oppositions are marshalled to allow the poet to engage directly with reality, to meditate on it philosophically, and to gain fleeting access to arcane and otherworldly knowledge. The bringing together of the poetic and philosophic and the juxtaposing of arcane details of esoteric wisdom with a pungent earthiness in the manner of metaphysical poetry become a particular hallmark of his most accomplished modernist sequences such as 'Meditations in Time of Civil War' in *The Tower* (1928) and 'Words for Music Perhaps', the poems written from the perspective of the Crazy Jane persona, in *The Winding Stair and Other Poems* (1933). 'Chosen' and 'Parting' in the latter volume were distilled from a longer adaptation of Donne. These lyrics at once imitate, retool, and are in dialogue with Donne's *Elegy XII* and 'Break of Day', a rare aubade conceived from the viewpoint of the female lover. The fantasy of male power and the misogynist berating of the beloved in Donne's elegies are commuted in Yeats's 'The Parting' into a more evenly balanced meditation by the woman on the mystery of a physical love that also betokens mystical union:

> I struggled with the horror of daybreak,
> I chose it for my lot! If questioned on
> My utmost pleasure with a man
> By some new-married bride, I take
> That stillness for a theme
> Where his heart my heart did seem
> And both adrift on the miraculous stream
> Where – wrote a learned astrologer –
> The Zodiac is changed into a sphere.[66]

Consonance between the sexes, however, remains as much out of reach in Yeats's poems about sexual love as in those of Donne; the unity envisaged here is wistfully rendered and invoked not triumphantly but in an ironic vein, as the playful allusion to the 'learned astrologer' intimates. Above all, Yeats's espousal of metaphysical poetry and his intense study of Donne convinced him of the imperative of finding befitting syntax and stanzaic moulds for his work. This necessitated the adoption and alteration of traditional metres and forms to suit his ends. A skilled and continuous repurposing of the inherited forms from the Renaissance period, such as *ottava rima*, the elegy and the sonnet, especially the hybrid sonnet practised by Donne, fuels his output. As he evinced in his summation of his poetic and his quest to evolve a passionate syntax that would closely mirror the rhythms of everyday speech, 'ancient salt is best packing'. [67] Hence, 'Chosen' not only cleaves to the thematic preoccupations and repertoire of conceits specific to Donne but also borrows the complex stanzaic form and rhyme scheme of 'A Nocturnal upon St Lucy's Day'. Yet, as Helen Vendler has perceptively observed, even in this regard Yeats reserves the right to put his stamp on the poetic form that he assiduously reproduces. He elongates Donne's lines, adding one foot to each of the lines in the central tercet of the poem, thereby mirroring sexual climax and also subtly signalling the licence exercised by the modernist poet who adeptly reworks those very features of metaphysical poetry that he most keenly admires.[68] Purposefully, appropriation and retooling are conjoint activities.

Joyce, Spenser, Donne

Joyce's reflections on Spenser and Donne are more scattered, fragmented, and less amply articulated in his occasional and critical writings than those of Yeats, but are no less compelling. Spenser and Donne rarely feature in his essays or letters, but his engagement with the work of these Renaissance writers is implicated in the protean intertextuality of his fiction. His links to them are of a different order to those of Yeats and Eliot as he subsumes their influence into texts which revolutionize and break with all the inherited practices and structures of the novel. Their poetry forms part of a web of intertexts from which he generates his art and against which he offsets its radical experimentation. Joyce's compositional practices for all of his works involved intensive periods of reading and note-gathering. In the Paris/Pola notebook from 1904, he recorded multiple passages from Ben Jonson and in the so-called 'Subject Notebook' from 1918, compiled as he was writing *Ulysses*, he created lists of English authors in which John Donne features.[69] The 'Oxen of the Sun' episode of *Ulysses* plays with the canon of English literature by drawing on phrases from leading anthologies of English literature. It juxtaposes the birth of Mina Purefoy's baby with what appears to be a gestational history of the development of English literature that ends in the varying demotic forms of spoken English in the twentieth century. Even though Joyce criticism long held that the pastiches of the styles of English authors were arranged in chronological order in 'Oxen', Sarah Davison has persuasively shown that in fact the episode interleaves their writings, thereby tampering with and upending any putative order.[70] 'Scylla and Charybdis', the episode in *Ulysses* in which Stephen Dedalus unfolds his much heralded theory of Shakespeare, also encourages a crossing of contexts as it moves between a depiction of the Renaissance dramatist and the early twentieth-century Irish Literary Revival. Hence it may be mooted that Joyce's approach to the early modern is playful and iconoclastic. Even as he appropriates and imitates it, he also intervenes in it and mischievously disrupts its authority. The games he plays with temporality allow him to ransack literary history and to pilfer and realign texts at will. In particular, Joyce shifts the boundaries of the early modern and the medieval.

Spenser and Joyce are rarely coupled. The pervasive influence of Shakespeare on Joyce has been extensively explored but the importance of Spenser has seldom been considered.[71] The glossaries on his works, such as Don Gifford's annotations to *Ulysses*, Roland McHugh's to *Finnegans Wake* and Adaline Glasheen's census of the *Wake*, contain sparse entries for Spenser. Indeed, Patrick Parrinder has argued in his summation of Joyce's relationship to English literature that Spenser was irrelevant to Joyce (if not anathema to him) because of his Protestant orthodoxy.[72] However, such an evaluation not only misconstrues Spenser but is also over-categorical in its refusal to countenance the multiple connectivities that may be discerned between the Renaissance poet and the modernist author. The documented allusions to Spenser in Joyce's writings make clear that he had a compendious knowledge both of *The Faerie Queene* and of the shorter poems and that he took pains to weave references to these texts into his writing in order to achieve an artistic and political reckoning with Spenser as a literary predecessor, an agent of English colonialism and a London author. It will be argued here that Spenser, albeit often an implicit presence in Joyce's work, serves multiply as a source, literary model, poetic Other, agonistic rival, and ramifying intertext. Joycean intertextuality is dynamic, complex, and multi-faceted and always goes beyond mere citationality. Intertexts in Joyce are plagiarized, mocked, deconstructed, reassembled, overwritten, buried, disinterred, echoed, and re-echoed. Spenser may be conceived of as a ghostly, vestigial presence in all of Joyce's work, but his influence is particularly of moment in *Finnegans Wake*.

In a series of conversations with Jacques Mercanton that took place in Paris in 1931, Joyce elucidated the compositional processes of the *Wake* and provided clues on how to interpret the text. Mercanton was one of the many friends whom Joyce was priming to act as exegete and promoter of his final revolutionary but perplexing text.[73] In his account of these exchanges, Mercanton several times noted Joyce's passion for Spenser and his recourse to him as a source. During a meeting in Lausanne he recounted that Joyce asked him to get him 'the books he needed, *Le Rime* of Petrarch, Spenser's *Epithalamium*' so he could add to 'Anna Livia Plurabelle', the section of *Finnegans Wake* that enlarges on Anna Livia, as a representation of the river Liffey, wife of HCE, and maternal archetype, as well as the closing pages of Book IV which depict her final meditations before she enters the sea.[74] On another occasion, Mercanton observed: 'He extolled the marvellous music of Spenser's "Prothalamium" repeating softly the refrain, of which he never tired, "Sweet Thames, run softly till I end my song"'.[75] Joyce draws upon Spenser not just to add density to the central skein of river imagery in the *Wake* but also as a suggestive model for the reworking of archetypal images that are capacious enough to encapsulate precise, local inferences while also carrying geopolitical and universal weight. Joyce's predilection for this line in the *Prothalamion*, moreover, is scarcely innocent as it silently references Eliot's *The Waste Land* while also circumventing it in favour of Spenser. Spenser eclipses Eliot and allows Joyce to bypass his influence.

In the 'Scylla and Charybdis' episode of *Ulysses*, John Eglinton pronounces that 'our young Irish bards ... have yet to create a figure which the world will set beside Saxon Shakespeare's Hamlet' and A. E. (George Russell) later challengingly quotes George Sigerson's supposed declaration that 'our Irish epic has yet to be written'.[76] Although George Moore in *Ulysses* is tipped by A., E. as the author most likely to topple the supremacy of the imperializing English canon of literature, Joyce tacitly but demonstrably took up the gauntlet himself in producing in *Ulysses* a text that not only reworks the epics and capstone works of Western literature but also remakes, modernizes, and hibernicizes them. If *Ulysses* in part refashions and redeploys *Hamlet*, it may be argued that Spenser's *The Faerie Queene, Colin Clouts Come Home Againe* and *Prothalamion* are prominent amongst the plethora of intertexts informing *Finnegans*

Wake. In one collocation in the *Wake*, Persse O'Reilly / HCE, the central male principle of the text, are cross-associated with Walter Raleigh / Spenser, 'sponsor to a squad of piercers, ally to a host of rawlies', casting them accordingly as piercers or invaders.[77] However, Joyce does not just conceive of Spenser as an inimical colonizing force and literary rival, he also views him as a coeval and double. In particular, he identifies with Spenser as a London author and a mythographer of the city especially when viewed through the lens of the exile.

In the 'Cyclops' episode of *Ulysses*, which uses a pastiche of styles from Irish-language epics to describe the truculent, racist Citizen who peddles a virulent form of Irish nationalist grievance, a lengthy catalogue lists the totemic effigies dangling from his belt. Amongst the many heroes that are invoked is the cryptic but vaguely familiar P.W. Shakespeare. At first this seems merely to be a comic misrecognition of Shakespeare's name. However, a more subtle melding of identities is actually at work here as Joyce in this restyling conflates two precise figures, P.W. (Patrick Weston) Joyce and William Shakespeare. (In the process of course he succeeds in fusing his own name with that of Shakespeare as well, thus rendering himself a descendant or modern avatar of the Bard.) P.W. Joyce was an Irish polymath, held in regard in particular for his activities as linguist, ethnographer, historian, and cultural commentator. Amongst his best-known works are an influential and pioneering account of Irish-English, *English as We Speak it in Ireland*, and an essay on Spenser's Irish rivers.[78] While the Gaelic tribe of the Joyces originated in Galway, a second branch, to which Joyce through his Cork-born father was related, settled in Munster. P.W. Joyce grew up in the historic area of Glenosheen in North Cork, celebrated for its folklore and music, that borders on Spenser's estate at Kilcolman. The contiguity in part explains P.W. Joyce's interest in the writer and his quest to understand the degree to which local lore informs his poetry. Family genealogy and the implicit topographies and locations of *The Faerie Queene* with its largely unvoiced Irish backdrop and contexts thus interlink Spenser and Joyce.

In a redolent narrative in chapter 5 of *A Portrait of the Artist as a Young Man* set precisely in this Spenserian terrain, Davin, a nationalist university friend of Stephen Dedalus, relates an uncanny incident: walking home after a hurling match, he encounters a woman who offers him milk and also invites him to stay the night with her.[79] The erotic and darkly suggestive story discomfits Stephen as it redisposes a familiar Irish narrative about the treacherous woman who invites the stranger into the house, a plot often deployed to allegorize the conquest of Ireland by the English and the perfidy of sexual alliances with the invader. Suggestively, this disturbing fable about modern Irish identity emanates from the self-same setting of the Ballyhoura mountains and 'Arlo Hill', or Galtymore, which Spenser depicts as at once paradisal and conflict-ridden in the *Cantos of Mutabilitie* and in *Colin Clouts Come Home Againe*. The mythic figures of Cynthia, Mutabilitie, Faunus, and Colin Clout now cede to the forward country woman and the directionless student with his nationalist longings and suppressed sexuality. Like Spenser, Joyce projects an archetypal story centring on the encounter with an enticing female Other on to the North Cork landscape, thus partially wresting the terrain from Spenser but also tapping into his mythologizing imaginary.

The marriage of the rivers, *The Faerie Queene*, Book IV, Canto xi, is a further potent Spenserian intertext that Joyce feeds off, annexes, and refashions. Spenser's disposition of the marriage of the Thames and Medway with its hierarchical and politically skewed listing of the river guests has spawned much commentary and led to many conflicting readings. Richard McCabe has seen it as a fusion of poetry and ideology, the projection of what he dubs 'a mindscape onto a landscape', while Andrew Hadfield and Willy Maley have argued that it is a mythography of imperialism that ultimately undermines itself by involuntarily registering aspects of the troubled recent history of sixteenth-century Ireland.[80] Richard Helgerson has pointed to other fissures in the narrative as he holds that the endeavour to produce a universal political narrative runs counter to the demands of the mode of chorography that Spenser is ostensibly drawing upon.[81] P.W. Joyce, interestingly, worked to supplement and complete Spenser by supplying his readers with the fertile local legends that subtend Spenser's accounts of Irish rivers, thereby casting the poet as a practitioner of what is known in Irish as *dinnseanchas* or place-lore.[82] Harry S. Berger instructively contended that Spenser is aware of the flawed and inexact nature of the perfect circle as a portrayal of the eternal recurrence of the same.[83] He observed that 'the river's tendency to return to the source is not in its pure or abstract form an ideal for human imitation; the actual river bears with it more than it knows and this interchange between geography and history, between the eternally recurrent flow-through of water and the continually changing organisation of society is Spenser's theme'.[84] In this light, Spenser's marriage of the rivers problematizes the primitivism and ancient archetypes that it invokes, and works to wriggle free of them. It is this oscillation between the modern and the primitive that is of moment for a conjoint analysis of the mythic rendering of rivers in Joyce and Spenser. Further, as Elizabeth Bellamy has contended, Spenser's 'spectral geographies' that pull against imperial fantasies of domination provide suggestive tropes for the modernist writer.[85]

Joyce is attracted to the malleability of textual, literary rivers, but he embraces them precisely because they can include the regressive and the primitive as well as the modern. History and language in *Finnegans Wake* are made up of layerings, accretions, and sedimentations. In constructing the text, Joyce was particularly influenced by Giambattista Vico's theory of history as moving through three successive cycles: the divine, the heroic, and the human. The ages cede to one other, repeat, and overlap in the *Wake*; they mutate and cycle round, wheeling back to the initial phases of civilization at moments of *ricorso* or return. Anna Livia, in one of her many aspects, concretizes the *corsi* and *ricorsi* (courses and returns) of history, the coincidences of different temporalities, mythic phases, and political conflicts. Vico insisted on the need to return to primitive ur-phases of civilization and to understand those 'first nations who thought in poetic characters, spoke in fables and wrote in hieroglyphs'.[86] Further, he dubbed poetic geography the other eye of poetic history. For him, a spatialized and toponymic imaginary was the best means of going back to the roots of language and culture.[87]

It is just such a narrative that Joyce creates in the Anna Livia episode, *FW*, I.8.[88] In this dialogue between two Dublin washerwomen on opposing banks of the Liffey, Joyce insinuates hundreds of names of rivers into the onward propulsion of his linguistic invention. The names are scattered, dispersed, often masked and randomly threaded through the flow of words. He thus continues the 'endlesse worke' of which the narrator complains in the Proem to *The Faerie Queene*, Book IV. If Spenser's marriage of the Thames and Medway is in part a colonial fantasy of concord, Joyce's text is chaotic and demotic. He wrenches the river narrative away from the ideological instrumentality with which it was freighted in Spenser by giving it to two Dublin working women who see HCE and ALP as further members of the degraded urban poor. However, it retains its association with timelessness and the regressive, as these women are also primitive archetypes: they transform into a stone and a tree at the end of the episode. Their gossiping about Anna Livia serves, moreover, to occlude her rather than make her more knowable or discernible. Her story may be a universal one that encompasses an open-ended catalogue of the rivers of the world but it remains darkly ominous, murky and obscure, diluted and sedimented in the speculative exchanges about her. The washerwomen's conversation begins with a description of the dirty water that results from washing the linen of ALP and HCE; this pollution leads in turn to their suggestive commentary on the guilty sin that taints the link between this couple. The quicksilver, hydrodynamic nature of their discourse captures the fluidity of ALP and mirrors the elemental non-language that Joyce invents and charges with meaning. In *Finnegans Wake* I.8, Anna Livia is depicted as a mother bestowing gifts on her offspring and a Pandora unleashing death on the world, thus conjoining creative and destructive urges. The ending of the first book of the *Wake* sees the passing of the Viconian divine age (Shem and Shaun, the warring brothers, calcify) and the fading out of Anna Livia. The narrative follows her out to sea and into the subterranean depths and unfathomable dreamspace that is the locus of the text as a whole. Joyce may upturn the overall order associated with the Spenserian marriage of the rivers, but both writers use the confluence of the rivers of the world to grapple with intractable problems in their symbolic plots and to concretize quintessential aspects of their poetics. The micronarratives in Spenser's account of the marriage of the Thames and Medway undermine the harmony this union is designed to suggest, while the pluralibities of the Anna Livia episode confront us with the fundamental chthonic disorder of history and the social. But the elemental, fluvial energies driving Joyce's materially realized language above all capture the quixotic and ever-transmuting nature of the central female principle of the *Wake*.

As stated before, Joyce's predilection for the *Prothalamion* hinged specifically on its refrain, 'Sweete Themmes run softlie, till I end my song'. He thus fastened attention not only on the counterpoint between the river and art in the poem but also on the contrast it posits between harmony and the recurrence of loss, political rivalry and the ongoing need for patronage. In a similar fashion, the ending of *Finnegans Wake* follows eddies and counter-eddies of meaning as it tracks the estuarial Liffey into the Irish Sea. Anna Livia's monologue that rounds out the text is at once a *Liebestod* in the manner of Wagner's *Tristan and Isolde*, a relinquishment and a violently erotic union in which she, as mother and daughter, surrenders to the spousal and paternal ocean. This lyrical conclusion with its many dark, embittered notes is simultaneously ecstatic and transcendent, poignant and painful. Death, loss, and erasure are rendered in a final fluvial cascade of words. The oppositions and tensions in Spenser's marriage of the Thames and Medway have been rewritten, pointedly hibernicized, and infinitely extended in the 'constant of fluxion' (*FW* 297.28) of *Finnegans Wake*.

The work of Donne is rarely referenced by Joyce but it is clear that he is a vital component in his lifelong sparring with and rethinking of English literature. The so-called Subject Notebook reveals that Donne is listed by Joyce in a compilation of English authors whose writing he planned to rearrange and redispose in the 'Oxen of the Sun' episode of *Ulysses*. In the event, Donne is not explicitly drawn upon in this section of *Ulysses* that splices together the altering styles of English prose through the centuries in a wilful pastiche that mimics the birth throes of Mina Purefoy but also casts doubt on any account of the evolution of language as progressive. Exchanges with an Irish friend, Arthur Power, in the 1920s, however, point to an intimacy with the writing of Donne and also a strategic and even idiosyncratic positioning of the poet that allowed him to refute the work of other British writers whom he abjured on ideological grounds.[89] Joyce thus used Donne to dismiss Tennyson, who in his view played only with 'one stop'. By contrast, he lauded the achievements of Donne because of the intricacy of his love poetry and the fact that reading 'a poem of his is an adventure in which you do not know where you will end'.[90] In his further ruminations, he came to the conclusion that Donne was quintessentially a medievalist who had a fundamental kinship with Chaucer. Ultimately, for Joyce, what he dubbed the 'excitement' of Donne's writing stemmed from his 'paganism, unorthodoxy and love of life', qualities that he equates with the author's medievalism.[91] An even more telling token of Joyce's regard for Donne is borne out by Harriet Shaw Weaver's Christmas gift to Joyce in 1922, the year in which *Ulysses* was first published, of what Jane Lidderdale and Mary Nicolson describe as 'a pocket-sized volume of Donne' bound in the colours of the Greek flag to mimic the binding of Joyce's epic text.[92] Weaver was Joyce's patron, mentor, and publisher and also a close creative associate to whom he communicated his artistic aspirations in a detailed, lively correspondence that spanned several decades. They regularly exchanged gifts of books but only ones that fitted in with particular reading agendas that connected with Joyce's work. Even though the volume has not survived in Joyce's libraries now housed in the University of Buffalo and in the Harry Ransom Centre, there can be no more tangible proof of Joyce's high regard for Donne than this now lost volume that symbolically fused their work and literally coalesced it. Indeed, it may be mooted that Donne was of moment for Joyce as a predecessor whose unconventionality and originality fed into and reinforced his own predilection for experimentation. Donne, it would appear, appealed to him because of that rebelliousness and unorthodoxy, on the one hand, and ability to create self-sufficient symbolic universes, on the other, that he saw as the hallmarks of the contrarian medieval writer.[93] Joyce absorbed Donne's tropes and rhetorical strategies into the deep structures of his texts, particularly in his treatment of the human body, of sexuality, and of the interplay between microcosms and macrocosms and his abiding concern with the symbolism of the ordinary. The misprisions and play on metempsychosis in *Ulysses*, a term transliterated as '[m]et him pike hoses' by Molly Bloom, suggests a shared interest in exchange and movement in the physical realm and a desire to pinpoint the essence of the human.[94] Ramie Targoff has persuasively argued that valediction is a literary figure that is peculiar to Donne and one which he invented.⁹⁵ The trope of valediction is likewise prominent in Joyce's works and seems likely to have been prompted at least in part by his passionately attentive reading of Donne's texts: it provides the basis for the enigmatic ending of 'The Dead' in which Gabriel's consciousness breaks loose from existence and undertakes a journey westwards towards Connemara, a national heartland, across a symbolically snow-covered Irish landscape, in Molly Bloom's night-time musings on her life and her wistful but acerbic recreation of her girlhood in Gibraltar and her youthful trysts on the hill of Howth with Leopold Bloom, and in Anna Livia's threnody acknowledging while also forgiving the multiple sins of HCE as she rushes to her death by flowing into Dublin bay. Donne may be a silent and cryptic presence in Joyce's texts but his intermittent allusions to the poet in his occasional writings uncover an association between the metaphysical poet and the modernist author that is deeply felt, considered, and suggestive.

Bernard O'Donoghue has argued that modern writers have treated medievalism as a 'semantically empty term' and used it to embody values from which they want to dissociate themselves.⁹⁶ Given the predilection for allusion, intertextuality, layered meanings, disruptive chronologies, and porous historical sources, a similar claim could be made about the deployment of Renaissance texts by modernist authors. However, this chapter has shown that the engagement with Spenser and Donne by Eliot, Yeats, and Joyce, for all its playfulness, is also deep-seated and rigorous. It is spurred by intellectual curiosity and a penchant for erudition as well as the desire to appropriate and recast the work of predecessors. Allusions to these early modern poets are never merely embellishments or empty flourishes, but permit ramifying, multi-directional meanings and carefully constructed ironies to accrue. Spenser and Donne are animating forces in the works of Eliot, Yeats, and Joyce and give rise to a textual dynamics that is necessary and enlivening and always warrants careful scrutiny as it reveals the complicated ways in which modernism commandeers, interacts with, and playfully redisposes Renaissance poetry. Such scrutiny will, we hope, continue to complicate our sense of the allusive, often elusive, and highly intertextual ways in which these early modern writers figure for their modernist readers.

Notes

1 All quotations from Eliot are from *The Poems of T.S. Eliot*, ed. Christopher Ricks and Jim McCue, 2 vols (London: Faber & Faber, 2015).
2 As detailed below, Yeats made frequent allusion to Renaissance writers in his essays and letters. He also edited a selection of Spenser's poetry *Poems of Spenser*, selected with an Introduction by W.B. Yeats (Edinburgh: T.C. and E.C. Jack, 1906). This volume was reprinted in London by the Caxton Publishing Company in 1906 in the Golden Poets Series. The copious notes that Joyce took for a series of twelve lectures on *Hamlet* which he gave in the Università Popolare in Trieste 1912–13 are held in the Joyce collection at Cornell University. For a transcription, see W.H. Quillian, 'Shakespeare in Trieste: Joyce's 1912 "Hamlet" Lectures', *James Joyce Quarterly*, 12 (1974–75), 7–63.
3 'Tradition and the Individual Talent' (1919), reprinted in *The Sacred Wood* (London: Methuen, 1920), 42–53.
4 From T.S. Eliot's seminal review of *Metaphysical Lyrics and Poems of the Seventeenth Century: Donne to Butler* selected and edited, with an essay, by Herbert J.C. Grierson (Oxford: Clarendon Press, 1921) in the *Times Literary Supplement* (20 October 1921), 669. 'Thoughts and qualities sometimes come to their perfect expression when they are about to pass away, and Merry England was dying in plays, and

in poems, and in strange adventurous men' (xxiii). Yeats contrasts this to 'the triumph of the Puritan and the merchant' ('Edmund Spenser', *The Poems of Spenser*, xx–xxi, xxiii). 'Edmund Spenser' was first published as the introduction to *The Poems of Spenser* and reprinted in *The Cutting of an Agate* (New York: Macmillan, 1912); the British Macmillan edition appeared in 1919.
5 From Eliot's Clark Lectures, on Donne, in *The Varieties of Metaphysical Poetry, by T.S. Eliot*, ed. Ronald Schuchard (London: Faber & Faber, 1993).
6 Spears Brooker in the *Cambridge Companion to 'The Waste Land'*, ed. Gabrielle McIntire (Cambridge: Cambridge University Press, 2015), 112.
7 On its uses within a culture of commonplaces, see Harry Berger's seminal essay 'The Discarding of Malbecco: Conspicuous Allusion and Cultural Exhaustion in *The Faerie Queene* III.ix–x', *Studies in Philology*, 66 (1969), 135–54.
8 From 'John Donne', *The Nation and the Athenaeum*, 33:10 (9 June 1923), 331–2; emphasis added.
9 For a different assessment of the unwarranted 'ontological chasm' that obtains between Spenser and Donne, see Richard Danson Brown, Chapter 1 above.
10 For Joyce's pronouncements on the inherently medieval nature of the Irish, fundamentally setting them at odds with the English who are all 'Renaissance men', see Arthur Power, *Conversations with James Joyce* (1974; Dublin: Lilliput Press, 1999), 107.
11 Haskin, *John Donne in the Nineteenth Century* (Oxford: Oxford University Press, 2007), 224–33.
12 'Wendell made his treatment of Donne an integral, in fact climactic, part of a thesis that he developed out of Edmund Gosse, according to which, after the death of Shakespeare, Donne was principally responsible for the "fall" from the glories of the Elizabethan age "into the affectations of a mannerism which grew lifeless the moment the master who vitalized it fell asleep".' Haskin, *John Donne*, 232–3. See also chapter 8, 'A subject not merely academic', for the working-out of the Spenser/Donne division through the nineteenth century.
13 See Steven Matthews, *T.S. Eliot and Early Modern Literature* (Oxford: Oxford University Press, 2013), 27.
14 See ibid. Matthews argues for the 'allusive, but also the often subliminal presence of Early Modern writers within the development of Eliot's own poetry' (6).
15 Matthews, *T.S. Eliot*, 26. On the Extension lectures on Elizabethan Literature see ibid., chapter 1.
16 *The Sacred Wood*, 1920, xiii–xiv.
17 This, at least, was the understanding of Mario Praz, who corresponded closely with Eliot about the subject (and transcript) of his Clark lectures. See *The Varieties of Metaphysical Poetry*, ed. Schuchard, 19–23.
18 In Eliot's essay 'Sir John Davies' (1926), in *The Complete Prose of T.S. Eliot: The Critical Edition*, ed. Anthony Cuda and Ronald Schuchard (Project Muse/Baltimore: Johns Hopkins University Press, 2014), 2:860–7 (860); from 'The Spoken Word', in *Festival of Britain 1951: London Season of the Arts, Official Souvenir Programme* (London: Lund Humphries, printed for the Arts Council of Great Britain, May–June 1951), cited in *The Poems*, ed. Ricks and McCue, 651.
19 *The Sacred Wood*, 81–2: 'Marlowe [in *Tamburlaine*] gets into blank verse the melody of Spenser, and he gets a new driving power by reinforcing the sentence period against the line period' (82–3).
20 Ibid., 81–2.
21 'Our civilization comprehends great variety and complexity, and this variety and complexity, playing upon a refined sensibility, must produce various and complex results. The poet must become more and more comprehensive, more allusive, more indirect, in order to force, to dislocate if necessary, language into his meaning', he famously writes. In 'The Metaphysical Poets', in *The Complete Prose of T.S. Eliot*, ed. Cuda and Schuchard, 1.381.
22 Matthews finds early modern literature 'subliminally' present even in Eliot's prose. *T.S. Eliot*, 5.
23 His slightly puckish notes were first published in December 1922 and invariably printed alongside the poem in editions ever since. In fact, although they were originally produced to fill out the publication, Willy Maley finds something Spenserian about Eliot's notes, comparing them to the quasi-editorial notes of E.K. attached to *The Shepheardes Calender* (1579). See Willy Maley, 'Spenser's Languages: Writing in the Ruins of English', in Andrew Hadfield (ed.), *Cambridge Companion to Spenser* (Cambridge: Cambridge University Press, 2001), 162–79, where he describes the notes of E.K., Eliot, and Alasdair Gray in *Lanark*, as being 'highly selective, ironic, punning, playful and parodic, sending up classical scholarship – and academic politesse generally – rather than merely imitating it' (173).
24 Letter to Dr Abraham Minola, 5 November 1958: 'I should say that there is a difference between the two aspects of the river, but that it is not to glorify the past in contrast to the present or to give any suggestion of futility. As for the nymphs, this word is used merely to indicate the young ladies whom the young gentlemen took out in punts on the river.' Cited in *The Poems*, ed. Ricks and McCue, 650.

25 'MacNeice in Wonderland', in J.B. Lethbridge (ed.), *Edmund Spenser: New and Renewed Directions* (Madison and Teaneck: Fairleigh-Dickinson University Press, 2006), 352–3.
26 Whitworth argues that, if Eliot knew the Spenserian source of the allusion when he published the notes to it in December 1922, 'the texts of Spenser's descendants may have weighed equally on his mind' when he was composing it months earlier ('"Sweet Thames"', 42).
27 *The Poems*, ed. Ricks and McCue, 1.650–1 (651).
28 More obviously, 'leman' also recalls Lac Léman, or Lake Geneva, beside which Eliot wrote some of this section 652. 'To Carthage here I came' reflecting Spenser's 'At length they all to mery London came' (ibid., 680).
29 For an account of Pound's changes, see *The Annotated 'Waste Land'*, ed. Lawrence Rainey (New Haven and London: Yale University Press, 2005), 22–4.
30 See *The Poems*, ed. Ricks and McCue, 1.672.
31 Donne, *Elegy: To His Mistress Going to Bed*.
32 *The Poems*, ed. Ricks and McCue, 1.1137. Ricks and McCue note the frequency of Eliot's return to 'The Relic': 'in *Reflections on Contemporary Poetry* I (1917), *The Metaphysical Poets* (1921) and *The Varieties of Metaphysical Poetry* 125 (Clark Lecture IV)', 1.1137.
33 See *The Poems*, ed. Ricks and McCue, 1.1190 where, following Lawrence Rainey, they date it to November 1921.
34 The epigraph, 'Thou hast nor youth nor age / But as it were an after dinner sleep / Dreaming of both', is loosely adapted from *Measure for Measure*. Ricks and McCue take a cue from the 'dry brain' of the closing line of the poem, using John M. Major's argument that the phrase in *As You Like It*, to suggest a deeper link to Spenser's 'As one then in a *dreame*, whose *dryer braine* / Is tost with troubled sights and fancies weake' (*FQ* I.i.42, emphasis added). See *The Poems*, ed. Ricks and McCue, 1.469–71, citing John M. Major, 'Eliot's "Gerontion" and *As You Like It*', *Modern Language Notes*, 74.1 (1959), 28–31.
35 See *The Poems*, ed. Ricks and McCue, 926, 933. The argument was made by G.W. Stonier, 'Mr Eliot's New Poem', *New Statesman*, 20 (14 September 1940), 267–8; it is reprinted in *T.S. Eliot: The Contemporary Reviews*, ed. Jewel Spears Brooker (Cambridge: Cambridge University Press, 2004), 433–4.
36 This included a YouTube video of its manufacture, embedded in this official website for the piece: http://totallythames.org/events/info/sweet-thames-run-softly.
37 See Michael Whitworth, '"Sweet Thames" and *The Waste Land*'s Allusions', *Essays in Criticism* (1998), 35–58, for an account of uses of Spenser's line before Eliot. Completely silent on the line's provenance, Shakespeare's Globe theatre recently adopted 'Sweet Thames, Run Softly' as the title for its 'free annual festive celebration of the past, present and future of Southwark', held 10 December 2015. www.shakespearesglobe.com/education/events/performances/concertforwinter.
38 Michael North, however, has shown that the Poundian slogan is frequently cited out of context and misrepresented. It was never intended as a modernist rallying cry and stems from the poet's interest in Confucian philosophy. See Michael North, *Novelty: A History of the New* (Chicago: University of Chicago Press, 2013), 162–70.
39 W.B. Yeats, *The Collected Letters: Volume I: 1865–1895*, ed. John Kelly and Eric Domville (Oxford; Clarendon Press, 1986), 326.
40 W.B. Yeats, *The Collected Letters: Volume III: 1901–04*, ed. John Kelly and Ronald Schuchard (Oxford: Clarendon Press, 1994), 247.
41 W.B. Yeats, *The Collected Works of W.B. Yeats, Volume IX: Early Articles and Reviews: Uncollected Articles and Reviews, 1886–1900*, ed. John P. Frayne and Madeleine Marchaterre (New York: Scribner, 2015), 210.
42 Ibid., 240.
43 'Edmund Spenser', *The Cutting of an Agate*, 182–223. All references to the essay will be to the 1919 Macmillan edition.
44 Ibid., 207.
45 Ibid., 189.
46 Ibid., 203 and 194.
47 Ibid., 214.
48 David Gardiner, *'Befitting Emblems of Adversity': A Modern Irish View of Edmund Spenser from W.B. Yeats to the Present* (Omaha: Creighton University Press, 2001), 48–85.
49 Elizabeth Bergmann Loizeaux, 'Yeats's Early Landscapes', in Richard J. Finneran (ed.), *Yeats: An Annual of Critical and Textual Studies* (Ithaca: Cornell University Press, 1984), 144–64.
50 *The Collected Works of W.B. Yeats Volume III: Autobiographies*, ed. Douglas Archibald and William O'Donnell (New York: Touchstone, 1999), 81. On Yeats's frequent conflation of Shelley and Spenser,

see George Bornstein, 'The Making of Yeats's Spenser', in Richard J. Finneran, ed., *Yeats: An Annual of Critical and Textual Studies* (Ithaca: Cornell University Press, 1984), 21–9, and *Yeats and Shelley* (Chicago: Chicago University Press, 1970). For an astute analysis of Yeats's willingness to accentuate and embrace Spenser's links with Ireland and his endeavour to explicate the gap between Spenser as lyric and public poet, see Jane Grogan, 'After Mutabilitie: Yeats and Heaney Reading Spenser', in Grogan (ed.), *Celebrating Mutabilitie: Essays on Edmund Spenser's Cantos* (Manchester: Manchester University Press, 2010), 295–314.
51 R.F. Foster, *W.B. Yeats: A Life. Volume I: The Apprentice Mage, 1865–1914* (Oxford: Oxford University Press), 38.
52 *The Variorum Edition of the Poems of W.B. Yeats*, ed. Peter Allt and Russell K. Alspach (New York: Macmillan, 1966), 1–63. All further references will be to this edition.
53 Ibid., 169–70 and 407–8.
54 Ibid., 332–3, 367–71, and 338–43.
55 Ibid., 618–19.
56 Ibid., 618.
57 Ibid., 619.
58 Helen Vendler, *Our Secret Discipline: Yeats and Lyric Form* (Oxford: Oxford University Press, 2013), 353. An affinity may be mooted between Yeats's echoing but fracturing of Spenserian metrics and Donne's propensity to repeat Spenserian figures with a difference. See Christopher D. Johnson, Chapter 2 above.
59 *VP*, 601–4.
60 W.B. Yeats, *A Vision: The Revised 1937 Edition*, ed. Margaret Mills Harper and Catherine E. Paul (New York: Scribner, 2015), 148–9. See 391 for commentary by Harper and Paul on this passage and its allusion to Spenser.
61 For a penetrating analysis of Yeats's adaptive complex and the different phases of his engagement with Spenser throughout his career, see Wayne K. Chapman, *Yeats and English Renaissance Literature* (London: Macmillan, 1991), 68–101 and 185–218.
62 *The Letters of W.B. Yeats*, ed. Allan Wade (London: Rupert Hart-Davis, 1954), 571.
63 Wayne K. Chapman, *Yeats*, 162. See 142–84 for Chapman's astute account of the influence of Donne on Yeats.
64 *VP*, 316.
65 See Patrick Cheney, Chapter 4 above.
66 *VP*, 534–5.
67 'A General Introduction to My Work' (unpublished); reprinted in W.B. Yeats, *Essays and Introductions* (London: Macmillan, 1961), 522.
68 Helen Vendler, *Our Secret Discipline: Yeats and Lyric Form* (Oxford: Oxford University Press, 2013), 410.
69 See Luca Crispi, 'Commentary on James Joyce's National Library of Ireland Early Commonplace Book: 1903–1912. (MS 36,639/02/a)', *Genetic Joyce Studies*, 9 (Spring 2009), and Wim van Mierlo, 'The Subject Notebook: A Nexus in the Composition History of *Ulysses* – A Preliminary Analysis', *Genetic Joyce Studies*, 7 (Spring 2007), accessed 9 June 2016.
70 Sarah Davison, 'Joyce's Incorporation of Literary Sources in "Oxen of the Sun"', *Genetic Joyce Studies*, 9 (Spring 2009), accessed 9 June 2016.
71 See Vincent Cheng, *Shakespeare and Joyce: A Study of 'Finnegans Wake'* (Philadelphia: Pennsylvania University Press, 1983); Laura Pelaschiar (ed.), *Joyce/Shakespeare* (Syracuse: Syracuse University Press, 2015); and William Schutte, *Joyce and Shakespeare: A Study in the Meaning of 'Ulysses'* (New Haven: Yale University Press, 1957).
72 Patrick Parrinder, 'The English Literary Tradition', in John McCourt (ed.), *James Joyce in Context* (Cambridge: Cambridge University Press, 2009), 205–15.
73 Jacques Mercanton, 'The Hours of James Joyce', in Willard Potts (ed.), *Portraits of the Artist in Exile: Recollections of James Joyce by Europeans* (Dublin: Wolfhound Press, 1979), 205–52.
74 Ibid., 218. Mercanton confuses the *Epithalamium* and the *Prothalamium*.
75 Ibid., 220.
76 *U*, 9.43–5 and 9.309. All references will be to *Ulysses*, ed. Hans Walter Gabler with Wolfhard Steppe and Claus Melchior (London: Bodley Head, 1986).
77 For an illuminating discussion of this nexus of images linking Spenser, Walter Raleigh, and HCE, see Brad Tuggle, '*The Faerie Queene* at *Finnegans Wake*', *Explicator*, 74 (2016), 129–32.
78 P.W. Joyce, 'Spenser's Irish Rivers', *Proceedings of the Royal Irish Academy*, 10 (1866–69), 1–13, and *English as We Speak it in Ireland* (Dublin: Longmans Green and Co., 1910).

79 James Joyce, *A Portrait of the Artist as a Young Man*, ed. John Paul Riquelme (New York: Norton, 2007), 159–60.
80 Richard McCabe, *Spenser's Monstrous Regiment: Elizabethan Ireland and the Poetics of Difference* (Oxford: Oxford University Press, 2002), 199; Andrew Hadfield, *Edmund Spenser's Irish Experience: Wilde Fruit and Salvage Soyl* (Oxford: Clarendon Press, 1997), 141–5; and Willy Maley, *Salvaging Spenser: Colonialism, Culture and Identity* (London: Macmillan, 1997), 78–98.
81 Richard Helgerson, 'The Land Speaks: Cartography, Chorography and Subversion in Renaissance England', *Representations*, 16 (1986), 51–85.
82 P.W. Joyce, 'Spenser's Irish Rivers', 3–13.
83 Harry S. Berger, 'Two Spenserian Retrospects: The Antique Temple of Venus and the Primitive Marriage of Rivers', *Texas Studies in Literature and Language*, 10 (1968), 5–25.
84 Ibid., 23.
85 Elizabeth Jane Bellamy, *Dire Straits: The Perils of Writing the Early Modern English Coastline from Leland to Milton* (Toronto: University of Toronto Press, 2013), 87.
86 Giambattista Vico, *New Science*, trans. David Marsh with an introduction by Anthony Grafton (London: Penguin, 2001), §429.
87 Ibid., §§741–69.
88 *Finnegans Wake*, ed. Robbert-Jan Henkes, Erik Bindervoet and Finn Fordham (Oxford: Oxford University Press, 2012). All references will be to this edition.
89 Arthur Power, *Conversations with James Joyce* (1974; Dublin: Lilliput Press, 1999), 117–18.
90 Ibid., 117.
91 Ibid., 117 and 118.
92 Jane Lidderdale and Mary Nicolson, *Dear Miss Weaver: Harriet Shaw Weaver, 1876–1961* (London: Faber and Faber, 1970), 213. They do not give further details and the volume does not seem to have survived, but it is probable that it was Grierson's edition of Donne's poetry.
93 On Joyce's peculiar views of the medieval, see Umberto Eco, *The Aesthetics of Chaosmos: The Middle Ages of James Joyce* (Cambridge, MA: Harvard University Press, 1989).
94 *U*, 8.112.
95 Ramie Targoff, *John Donne, Body and Soul* (Chicago: University of Chicago Press, 2008).
96 Bernard O'Donoghue, 'Dante's Versatilities: Seamus Heaney's Modernism', in Nick Havely (ed.), *Dante's Modern Afterlife: Reception and Response from Blake to Heaney* (London: Macmillan, 1998), 242–57 (243).

Index

Note: All titles of poems by John Donne have been modernised, and may appear differently in the text, depending on the edition used in the chapter. Donne's *Elegies* and *Holy Sonnets* are identified by title and first line, respectively, to avoid confusion due to different numbering systems. Longer titles by both Donne and Spenser may appear abbreviated in the text. 'n.' after a page reference indicates the number of a note on that page.

Acuña, Hernando de 112
aesthetics 7, 15, 19, 21, 34, 37–8, 74, 78, 87, 95, 97–8, 101, 125, 141, 143, 153, 161, 186, 189, 202, 207–8
Agamben, Giorgio 46, 164
Agricola, Rudolphus 62–3
alexandrine 15–19, 89
    see also Spenserian stanza
allegory 25, 32–5, 40–1, 47, 52, 65–6, 69–70, 76, 80, 97, 108–9, 117n.4, 139, 144, 157–8, 160, 166, 210, 213
Allen, D.C. 93, 98
allusion 2–3, 5, 7–8, 14–15, 24, 28n.22, 28n.26, 31n.70, 72, 76, 109–10, 113–14, 125, 142–3, 146, 171, 185, 189, 200–2, 204–8, 211, 213, 215, 220
    see also intertextuality
Alpers, Paul 19, 28n.32
anatomy 3, 27n.18, 51, 79, 141, 152, 156n.53, 162, 164, 166, 168n.3
    see also Donne, John, *Anniversaries*
Anderson, Judith H. 11n.28, 14, 27n.9, 33
Andrewes, Lancelot 106n.63, 203
Apocalypse 67, 194, 196
    see also Last Judgement
Aquinas, Saint Thomas 52
Aretino, Pietro 116
Ariosto, Ludovico 94, 110, 117n.4
Aristotle 32, 37, 40, 125, 144, 159
Ascham, Roger 201

attention 8, 183–97 *passim*
    see also distraction
Auerbach, Erich 56, 107n.84
Augurelli, Giovanni Aurelio 144
Augustine, Saint 8, 34, 39, 46, 52, 56, 59n.61, 104n.17, 105n.31, 165, 170n.30, 185–6, 188, 196, 198n.8

Bacon, Sir Francis 36, 39, 51, 153n.5, 155n.25
Bakhtin, Mikhail 79, 83n.57
Barnes, Barnabe 183
Barthes, Roland 69
Bate, Walter Jackson 5
Bateman, Stephen 112
Bedford, Countess of *see* Russell, Lucy, Countess of Bedford
Bell, Ilona 86–7, 88, 95, 98, 99
Bellamy, Elizabeth 217
Bender, John B. 15
Berger, Harry S., Jr. 163, 198n.21, 217, 221n.7
Berry, Craig A. 30n.57
Beza, Theodore 108, 111, 116
The Bible 37, 38, 39, 72, 90, 100–1, 107n.84, 110, 115, 116, 124, 128, 180, 181, 183, 188
    Acts 124
    Corinthians 45, 46, 55, 60n.86, 61n.114, 196
    Deuteronomy 180
    Ezekiel 124
    Genesis 101, 107n.84, 118, 125, 132

The Bible (cont.)
  Jeremiah 124
  Job 164
  Leviticus 180
  Luke 37
  Matthew 42, 124
  Psalms 89, 108, 117n.14, 183–8, 197n.2, 198n.8
  Revelation 77, 115
  Romans 46
  Song of Songs 183
Blake, William 212
Bloom, Harold 11n.40, 14, 27n.9
Boccaccio, Giovanni 122
Boehme, Jacob 165, 166
Boethius 62
Borris, Kenneth 27n.10, 104n.15, 198n.17
Boyle, Elizabeth 90, 174, 175–8
Braden, Gordon 153n.3
Brahe, Tycho 139
Bright, Timothy 159–60, 165, 169n.17
Brink, Jean 21, 29n.51, 82n.26
Brown, Richard Danson 5, 6, 28n.29, 41, 155n.28, 205, 221n.9
  author of chapter 1
Browne, Sir Thomas 209
Browning, Robert 2, 9n.11
Bruno, Giordano 39, 137, 139, 144, 149, 153n.4, 154n.15
Buchanan, George 143
Burghley, Lord *see* Cecil, William, Lord Burghley
Burke, Arthur 69
Burke, Edmund 32
Burrow, Colin 95
Bush, Douglas 27n.5

Callimachus 91
Campana, Joseph 11n.36, 134, 136n.31
Carew, Thomas 2, 13, 15, 26, 35, 103n.7
Carey, John 13, 27n.5, 103n.3, 104n.16, 111, 117n.5
Carpocrates 128–9
Carson, Anne 169n.10, 172
Cassirer, Ernst 137, 153
Castiglione, Baldassare 101, 117n.3
catachresis 35, 55, 62, 65, 81n.13, 83n.43
Catullus 171, 174, 175, 176
'Cavalier' 4

Cecil, Robert, Earl of Salisbury 20, 114
Cecil, William, Lord Burghley 20–1, 31n.76, 114, 123–4, 135n.12
Chapman, George 97, 106n.63, 106n.81, 144
Chapman, Wayne K. 212, 223n.61, 223n.63
character 8, 40, 69, 74, 123, 157–68, 217
  see also graphic writing
Chaucer, Geoffrey 21–2, 24, 29n.49, 30n.55, 30n.57, 35, 39, 41–2, 59n.75, 94, 109, 111, 178, 204, 219
Cheney, Patrick 6, 7, 106n.79, 135n.1, 212–13
  author of chapter 4
Christianity 39, 41, 44, 77–8, 85, 87, 93, 101, 110, 112, 118, 127, 143, 145–6, 195, 210
  see also The Bible; devotional poetry
  Catholicism 23–4, 77–9, 87, 109, 111, 136n.13, 197
  Protestantism 23, 31n.70, 68–9, 74, 76, 87, 104n.16, 109, 112, 124, 186, 195, 197, 214
Cicero 29n.40, 37, 62, 63
classical literature 2–3, 7, 21, 55, 59n.66, 71, 85–7, 91, 93–5, 99, 114, 131, 140–9 *passim*
  see also Catullus; Homer; Horace; Juvenal; Lucretius; Ovid; Sappho; Virgil
Coleridge, Samuel Taylor 2, 9n.11
Coles, Kimberly 197
Colie, Rosalie 145
Collmer, Robert 109, 117n.1
Comes, Natalis 39
comparatio 7, 33–8, 41–2, 45, 48, 54, 56
conceit 26, 32–4, 50–2, 62, 65, 92, 99, 140, 148, 159–60, 213
Copernicus, Nicolaus 3, 27n.9, 139, 153, 154n.15
Corthell, Ronald 81n.15
cosmology 3, 7, 44, 50, 65, 115, 138–9, 141, 143–5, 152, 154n.12, 198n.21
  see also Copernicus, Nicolaus; *kosmos*; macrocosm-microcosm; Ptolemy
Cowley, Abraham 25, 204
Crashaw, Richard 204
Crowley, Lara 136n.15
Cummings, Brian 60n.102, 169n.29

d'Alençon, Duc *see* Francis, Duc d'Alençon, Duc d'Anjou

d'Angelo, Jacopo 141
Daniel, Samuel 41, 188
Danner, Bruce 29n.46, 124, 135n.12
Dante Alighieri 24, 42, 46–7, 56, 115, 117n.3, 129, 184, 201, 209
Davies, Sir John 144, 221n.18
Davison, Sarah 214
debate 7, 18–19, 28n.35, 65, 124, 142, 149, 153n.5, 154n.15
  see also dialogue
de Bry, Theodor 159, 169n.10
de Grazia, Margreta 10n.22, 162
De Quincey, Thomas 2, 9n.11
Derrida, Jacques 69, 82n.26
Descartes, René 70, 142, 155n.26
Desmet, Christy 159
Desportes, Philippe 112
Devereux, Robert, Second Earl of Essex 1, 126
devotional poetry 3, 5, 6, 8, 64, 67, 127, 183–4, 186, 189–90, 193–7
dialogue 7, 18, 34, 91, 139, 148, 210
  see also debate
DiPasquale, Theresa 11n.34, 20, 25, 94
distraction 183–9, 193–4, 196–7
  see also attention
Dixon, Michael 69
Dolven, Jeff 11n.36, 22, 30n.58
Donaldson, Ian 38
Donne, John
  Anniversaries 1, 6, 7, 32–5, 39, 46–8, 56, 66, 92, 140, 142–6, 149–53
    First Anniversary, An Anatomy of the World 3, 34, 47–9, 50, 66–7, 109, 139–42, 149–53
    A Funeral Elegy 88–9
    Second Anniversary, Of the Progress of the Soul 48–55, 88–9, 92, 103, 141–5, 149–52, 161, 180
  Biathanatos 46
  La Corona 92–3
  The Courtier's Library 116
  Devotions upon Emergent Occasions 56, 87
  'Eclogue and Epithalamion at the Marriage of the Earl of Somerset' 89, 179
  Elegies 46, 64, 66, 89, 91–2, 113, 213
    The Anagram 89
    The Bracelet 109, 111
    The Comparison 32
    The Dream ('Image of her whom I love…')
    His Parting from Her 102
    Love's Progress 65–6
    Love's War 91–2, 109
    Nature's Lay Idiot 110
    On His Mistress 64–5, 111
    Sappho to Philaenis 113
  'Elegy on Mrs Bulstrode' 88–9
  'Elegy upon the Untimely Death of the Incomparable Prince Henry' 88, 103
  Epicedes and Obsequies 88–9, 92
    'Obsequies upon the Lord Harrington' 92, 103
  'Epithalamion Made at Lincoln's Inn' 5, 6, 8, 171, 179–81
  'An Epithalamion, or Marriage Song on the Lady Elizabeth and Count Palatine being Married on St Valentine's Day' 89, 179
  Holy Sonnets 6, 8, 46, 67, 89, 91, 93, 127, 133, 183–4, 194
    'At the round earth's…' 67, 194–7
    'Batter my heart…' 167
    'Death be not proud…' 67
    'If poisonous minerals…' 19
    'Oh, to vex me…' 67
    'What if this present…' 92
  'A Hymn to God the Father' 31n.74, 92
  'A Litany' 89, 100
  Metempsychosis: The Progress of the Soul 6, 13–19, 23, 26, 88–9, 92–5, 98–9, 111, 118–20, 126–30, 132, 143, 160
  Paradoxes and Problems 46
  Satires 6, 13, 46, 89, 92
    Satire III 20, 29n.42, 115–16
    Satire IV 6, 20, 23–5, 111, 116
    Satire V 46, 92
  sermons 3, 64, 67–8, 91, 111, 164,
  Songs and Sonnets 46, 88–9, 92, 194
    'The Anniversary' 17
    'Break of Day' 213
    'The Broken Heart' 167
    'The Canonization' 89–92
    'The Ecstasy' 101–3, 160, 163, 180
    'The Flea' 17, 113
    'The Indifferent' 19, 114
    'The Legacy' 167
    'Negative Love' 163

Donne, John (*cont.*)
  Songs and Sonnets (*cont.*)
    'A Nocturnal upon St Lucy's Day' 89, 109, 162, 213
    'The Paradox' 89
    'The Relic' 17, 86, 102, 206
    'Sonnet. The Token' 89
    'The Sun Rising' 115
    'A Valediction: forbidding mourning' 26, 37, 45, 102
    'A Valediction: of my name, in the window' 157–8, 160–2, 165, 167
    'A Valediction: of the book' 92, 99–101, 163
    'Woman's Constancy' 46
  'To Mr Tilman after he had taken orders' 100–1
  'To the Lady Magdalen Herbert, of St Mary Magdalen' 89
  'Upon the Translation of the Psalms by Sir Philip Sidney, and the Countess of Pembroke his Sister' 89
  Verse Letters 64, 66, 88, 92, 100, 111
    'To Mr E. G.' 92
    'To Mr R. W.' ('Kindly I envy…') 89, 92
    'To Mr R. W.' ('Muse not…') 89
    'To Mr R. W.' ('Zealously my muse…') 92
    'To Mr Rowland Woodward' 89, 92
    'To Mr S. B.' 92
    'To Sir Henry Wotton' ('Sir, more than kisses…') 66, 111
    'To the Countess of Bedford' ('Honour is so sublime') 99–100
    'To the Countess of Bedford' ('T'have written then…') 89, 92
    'To the Countess of Bedford' ('You have refined me…') 89, 102–3
    'To the Countess of Huntingdon' ('That unripe side of earth…') 89, 92
    'To the Countess of Salisbury' 89, 92
Dowden, Edward 203
Drayton, Michael 90, 144
Drummond, William, of Hawthornden 29n.49, 85, 86
Drury, Elizabeth 47–54 *passim*, 56, 108n.61, 66, 88, 109, 141, 150, 156n.51, 161
Dryden, John 2, 21, 26, 31n.80, 56, 145, 155
Du Bartas, Guillaume 90, 105n.31, 110, 144

Du Bellay, Joachim 16, 110, 113
Dubrow, Heather 11n.31, 154n.13
Dudley, Robert, First Earl of Leicester 88, 108, 115, 206, 212
Du Monin, Jean Edouard 144

Earle, John 159
ecology 7, 124–5
  see also species
Edward VI, King of England 112
Egerton, Sir Thomas 126
Eliot, T.S. 2, 8, 15, 56, 138, 200–7, 214–15, 220
Elizabeth I, Queen of England 3, 18, 21, 108, 112–13, 115, 125, 131, 135n.12, 158, 206, 208–9
elocutio 37, 58n.31, 63–4
Elyot, Sir Thomas 207
emblem 15, 43, 55, 143, 150, 159, 163, 165
Empedocles 134, 145
Empson, William 17, 19, 62
enargeia and *energeia* 35, 37, 49, 57
Ennius 94, 134, 145
epic (poetry) 2, 6, 16, 28n.26, 55, 69, 74, 82n.24, 85, 88–95, 106n.81, 110, 113–15, 122–3, 134, 138, 215
Epicurus 67
epithalamion 7, 88–9, 113, 138, 171–6, 181
  see also Donne, John, 'Epithalamion Made at Lincoln's Inn'; Spenser, Edmund, *Epithalamion*
eroticism 7, 8, 65, 85, 89–91, 100, 102–3, 109, 112–15 *passim*, 148, 157–62, 164–8, 169n.17, 193–4, 216, 218
eschatology 39–40, 44, 55
  see also Apocalypse; Last Judgement
Essex, Earl of *see* Devereux, Robert, Second Earl of Essex
Ettenhuber, Katrin 59n.61
Euripides 98

Fairfax, Edward 26
figures *and* figuration 5, 6, 7, 8, 23, 32–56, 65–6, 71, 86–7, 96, 116, 118, 123–4, 127, 131, 135, 141–53, 157, 160, 163–8, 188–9, 191, 196–7
Fineman, Joel 56
Fletcher, Angus 86, 103n.8, 104n.14
Fletcher, Giles 113

Florio, John 39
Fogarty, Anne 2, 8, 154n.7
  co-author of chapter 11
form (poetics) 13–18, 20, 22–3, 25, 46, 88,
    90–1, 93–4, 99–100, 118, 127, 147,
    152, 171, 187–8, 197, 213–14
  see also metre (poetry); rhyme; Spenserian
    stanza; style
Foucault, Michel 3, 37, 154n.8
Foxe, John 158
Fracastoro, Girolamo 144
Francis, Duc d'Alençon, Duc d'Anjou 108,
    115
Fraunce, Abraham 35–6, 68, 80, 83n.53,
    84n.59
Freer, Coburn 25

Galen 3, 66
Galileo Galilei 3, 39
Gardiner, David 209
gender 42, 64, 117, 132, 162
Genette, Gérard 36
genre 6, 7, 13–14, 16, 20, 69, 79, 85–95, 103,
    114, 124, 137–8, 143–5, 147, 150,
    171–5, 178–9, 181
Gifford, Don 214
Gil, Alexander 39–41
Ginzburg, Carlo 146
Glasheen, Adaline 214
Goeglein, Tamara 69
Goldberg, Jonathan 134, 161, 169n.10
Gonne, Maud 211
Goodman, Nelson 32
Gorton, Lisa 153
Gosse, Sir Edmund 9n.7, 171, 181, 221n.12
Goswami, Niranjan 6, 7, 156n.44
  author of chapter 3
graphic writing 8, 157–63, 168n.4
Greene, Robert 24
Greene, Roland 156n.43, 198n.13
Greene, Thomas 149, 174
Gregerson, Linda 6, 7, 11n.36, 155n.30
  author of chapter 6
Gregory XIII, Pope 109, 116
Greville, Fulke 201
Grierson, Sir Herbert J.C. 2, 31n.72, 183–4,
    201, 203–4, 212, 224n.92
Grogan, Jane 2, 8, 60n.89, 154n.7, 223n.50
  co-author of chapter 11

Grosart, A.B. 203
Gross, Kenneth 10n.16, 128
Grossman, Marshall 142, 144
Grynaeus, Simon 141
Guilpin, Everard 20, 24, 29n.43

Hadfield, Andrew 27n.7, 30n.61, 107n.92,
    217
Hall, Joseph 48, 104n.24, 159
Hamilton, A.C. 29n.42, 45, 60n.83, 101
Hardie, Philip 134
Harriot, Thomas 39
Harrison, Timothy 142, 155n.23, 155n.29,
    156n.52
Harvey, Elizabeth D. 7–8, 10n.16, 16, 27n.11,
    98, 142, 154n.23, 155n.29, 156n.52
  author of chapter 8
Harvey, Gabriel 57n.15, 68
Haskin, Dayton 9n.11, 13, 203
Hegel, G.W.F. 47
Heidegger, Martin 153n.2
Henri IV, King of France 109–10
Henry VIII, King of England 116
Herbert, George 25–6, 183, 197n.2, 203
Herendeen, Wyman 93
Hesiod 172
Hieatt, A. Kent 28n.22
Holinshed, Raphael 105n.28, 158
Homer 1, 35, 38, 41, 55, 85, 94, 97, 99,
    107n.81, 134, 172, 176, 201, 209
Horace 91, 93–4, 104n.17, 110–11
Hoskyns, John 81n.13, 83n.46
Howard, Douglas 88
Howard, Henry, Earl of Surrey 104n.24, 201
humanism 7, 39, 43, 62–3, 125, 135, 138, 145,
    155n.35, 163, 201
hymn 88–92 passim, 110, 143, 173, 176
  see also epithalamion; Spenser, Edmund,
    The Fowre Hymnes

idolatry 78, 185, 192–3
  see also Christianity
Ignatius Loyola, Saint 109
influence, literary 1, 5, 8, 11n.33, 14, 55, 134,
    143, 174, 187, 201–2, 204, 207, 210,
    213–15, 217
intertextuality 14, 16, 20–1, 24–5, 45, 55, 93,
    112, 116, 146, 200–2, 214–15
  see also allusion

invention 33, 36–8, 47, 63–4, 69, 97, 113
Ireland 1, 21, 33–4, 108–9, 131, 202, 206, 208–10, 216–17, 223n.50

Jakobson, Roman 69
James I, King of England 3
Jardine, Lisa 62
Johnson, Christopher D. 6–7, 223n.58
  author of chapter 2
Johnson, Samuel 37–8, 55–6, 145, 181
Jonson, Ben 3–4, 27n.5, 29n.49, 35, 47, 85–6, 97, 103n.7, 138, 153n.5, 159–60, 203, 209, 214
Joyce, James 8, 200–2, 214–20, 221n.10, 224n.93
Joyce, P.W. 216–17
Junius, Franciscus, the Younger 97, 106n.63
Juvenal 21, 110

Kant, Immanuel 32, 96, 102
Kaske, Carol 60n.88, 198n.17
Kenny, Neil 144
Kepler, Johannes 3, 109, 139, 154n.18
Kermode, Frank 81n.10
Kernan, Alvin 21
Kerrigan, William 153n.3
Kilcolman Castle 131, 216
Kneidel, Gregory 24
Knevet, Ralph 26
kosmos 7, 43, 141–3, 140, 145, 153, 154n.20
  see also cosmology
Kyd, Thomas 204

La Marche, Olivier de 112, 117n.14
Langbaine, Gerard 96
Langland, John 111
Lanyer, Aemilia 197
Larminie, William 209
Last Judgement 40, 46, 52, 194–6
  see also Apocalypse
Lausberg, Heinrich 58n.31, 58n.41, 61n.109
Lee, Vernon 206
Le Fèvre de la Boderie, Guy 115–16, 143
Legouis, Pierre 19, 28n.30
Leicester, Earl of *see* Dudley, Robert, First Earl of Leicester
Lethbridge, J.B. 107n.95

Lewalski, Barbara K. 35, 104n.16, 145, 155n.34, 197
Lewis, C.S. 82n.24
literary career 1, 3, 5, 6, 7, 30n.58, 32, 46, 85, 87–8, 90–3, 103n.2–3, 104n.16, 109–10, 135n.9, 202
literary history 1, 3–5, 8, 13–14, 25–6, 35, 55–6, 134, 137–8, 146, 197, 200–2, 205, 214
  see also periodization
Locke, Anne 186, 197
logic 7, 62–5, 67–8, 70, 74, 80, 97, 124, 127–9, 189
  see also Ramus, Peter
  topic or place logic 62–5, 68, 74
Loizeaux, Elizabeth Bergmann 210
Longinus 95–8, 101–2, 103n.7, 105n.49, 106n.63, 107n.84
Lownes, Matthew 1
Lucan 99, 107n.81, 113
Lucretius 55, 144–5, 155n.31
Luther, Martin 116
Lyotard, Jean-François 102
lyric (poetry) 14, 88–90, 100, 106n.81, 137–8, 144, 223n.50

McCabe, Richard A. 131, 217
McCue, Jim 205, 206, 207, 222n.34
MacDonagh, Thomas 208
Machiavelli, Niccolò 109, 201
McHugh, Roland 215
McIlmaine, Roland 74, 77, 81n.12
Mack, Peter 62, 74
Macrin, Jean Salmon 113
macrocosm-microcosm 3, 41, 48, 137–44, 150–2, 219
Maisano, Scott 134
Maley, Willy 217, 221n.23
manuscript (publication) 2, 5, 25, 26, 30n.59, 31n.70, 85, 93, 96, 99, 110, 115, 136n.15
  see also print (publication)
Marino, Giambattista 55
Marion, Jean-Luc 52
Marlowe, Christopher 91, 99, 105n.35, 202, 203, 204–5, 221n.19
Marnix, Philip 111
Marno, David 5, 6, 8
  author of chapter 10

Index

marriage 7, 8, 15, 91, 108, 112–14, 126, 168n.2, 206
  see also epithalamion
Marshall, Cynthia 161
Marston, John 20, 22, 24, 104n.24
Martial 110
Martin, Catherine Gimelli 10n.15, 11n.32, 153n.2, 153n.5, 154n.12
Martz, Louis 194, 197
Marullus 145
Marvell, Andrew 43, 138, 204, 205
Mary, Queen of Scots 79
Mary I, Queen of England 158
Massinger, Philip 203
Mayne, Jasper 35
medievalism 4, 11n.28, 219, 220
medieval literature 62, 76, 77, 85, 106n.59, 111–12, 114, 117n.4, 118, 123
Melanchthon, Philip 116
Mercanton, Jacques 215
Mercator, Gerardus 152
metamorphosis 2, 28n.22, 39, 46, 124–5, 135
  see also Ovid
'metaphysical' 1, 2, 4, 25, 37, 55–6, 62, 86–7, 98, 102, 125, 138, 140, 145, 160, 181, 183, 203–5, 212–14, 220
metonymy 34, 40, 48, 51, 55, 78–9, 142, 157–8
metre (poetry) 14, 16, 22, 26, 29n.42, 30n.58, 89, 99, 114, 127, 213
Michelangelo Buonarroti 137
Middleton, Thomas 203, 304
Milgate, Wesley 28n.34–5, 29n.42, 31n.70
Miller, David Lee 83n.43, 198n.15
Milton, John 1–2, 4, 27n.9, 38, 77, 80, 86, 96, 138, 153n.5, 154n.12, 174
Mitchell, W.J.T. 32
modernism 2, 8, 13, 62, 138, 200–2, 207–8, 212–15 *passim*, 217, 220, 222n.38
Montaigne, Michel de 39, 111, 144, 155n.35, 201
Montemayor, Jorge de 109
Moran, D.P. 208
More, Ann 92, 126
Morris, William 212
Moss, Daniel D. 12n.45, 91–2
Mueller, Janel 128
myth *and* mythology 7, 15, 34, 73, 75, 85, 86, 87, 97, 118–19, 126, 178, 206, 209

natural philosophy 3, 40, 138, 140, 143, 145, 153n.5
  see also cosmology; macrocosm-microcosm
Navarre, Henri de *see* Henri IV, King of France
Navarre, Marguerite de 112
Neoplatonism 2, 9n.15, 44, 101–2, 140, 143, 148, 154n.19, 163, 189, 191, 198n.17, 210
Netherlands 109, 117n.5
Newton, Thomas 188
Nohrnberg, James 35, 59n.62, 59n.65

O'Donoghue, Bernard 220
Ortelius, Abraham 141
Overbury, Sir Thomas 159, 163, 169n.12
Ovid 6, 7, 39, 40, 43–6, 85, 91, 94, 101–2, 103n.3, 108, 110, 112–15, 117n.4, 118–22, 125–6, 128, 130–2, 134–5, 155n.31, 163, 166, 171, 177

Panofsky, Erwin 35
Paracelsus 3, 109, 164–5
Parker, Patricia 134
Parrinder, Patrick 214
Partridge, A.C. 57n.16
pastoral 85, 88, 104n.25, 110, 123–4, 205, 206
Pater, Walter 203, 206
patronage 1, 33–4, 47, 73, 82n.26, 100, 108–9, 114, 126, 210, 218, 219
Patterson, Annabel 104n.24, 105n.37
Paul, Saint 33–4, 39, 42, 56, 124, 196
Peacham, Henry 36–8, 45
pedagogy 1, 13, 69, 70, 159
Pembroke, Countess of
  see Sidney, Mary, Countess of Pembroke
periodization 1–4, 8, 10n.22, 55, 125, 132, 137–8, 201, 203
Petrarch, Francesco 8, 35, 46, 47, 65, 112–15, 137–8, 140, 148, 154n.13, 157, 163, 165–7, 183–9, 194, 196–7, 198n.17, 199n.24, 215
Philip II, King of Spain 109, 116
philosophic poem 6, 137–8, 143–7, 149–50, 153, 154n.17, 154n.19, 155n.32
physiognomy 158, 160, 164–5, 168n.7
  see also character

Pico della Mirandola, Giovanni 66
Pindar 99
Plato *and* Platonism 9–10n.15, 60n.78, 73, 101, 107n.88, 114–15, 144, 186, 190
ploce 32, 35, 38, 43–5, 53–4, 71–2
Plutarch 35, 163
poetics *see* form (poetics); style
Ponsonby, William 21
Pontano, Giovanni 113, 143
Pope, Alexander 9n.11, 205–6
Porter, James I. 95, 105n.49, 106n.59
Pound, Ezra 200–1, 205–6, 208, 222n.29, 222n.38
Power, Arthur 219, 221n.10
Powrie, Sarah 154n.12
Pratt, Mary Louise 146
Prescott, Anne Lake 6, 7, 16, 93, 126, 136n.14
author of chapter 5
Pre-Socratics 143
print (publication) 5, 85, 93, 99, 103n.4, 110
see also manuscript (publication)
Propertius 91
Ptolemy 3, 139, 141, 143, 153
Pugh, Syrithe 110, 117n.4, 135n.9
Puttenham, George 22, 36, 38, 57n.24, 61n.125, 83n.52, 123, 157, 160–1, 168n.3, 175–6, 196
Pythagoras 7, 29n.40, 59n.66, 118, 120–2, 124, 128, 130–1, 134, 135n.7, 141, 143, 154n.20, 155n.30–1

Quarles, Francis 183
Quintilian 37, 58n.31, 58n.41, 60, 82n.38, 83n.56, 85, 159
Quitslund, Jon 59n.61, 198n.17

Rabelais, François 111, 116
Raleigh, Sir Walter 126, 216
Ramachandran, Ayesha 5, 6, 7, 169n.28, 198n.21, 198n.23
author of chapter 7
Ramist rhetoric 6, 7, 67–77 *passim*, 80
Ramus, Peter 62–4, 69–70, 74
see also rhetoric
Reformation 28n.34, 76, 209
see also Christianity
Renwick, W.L. 22

rhetoric 5, 6, 7, 30n.61, 35–6, 39, 41–2, 58n.28, 59n.58, 62–4, 67–70, 74–80 *passim*, 95, 102, 138, 140, 142–3, 148, 151–2, 154n.7, 168n.3, 196, 200, 219
see also figures; logic; Ramist rhetoric; Ramus, Peter
rhyme 16–20, 22–3, 25, 28n.24, 30n.57, 30n.59, 30n.62, 45–6, 52–4, 127, 145, 148, 150–1, 187–8, 211, 213
Ricks, Christopher 205–7, 222n.32–4
Ricoeur, Paul 58n.31, 59n.73
ritual 8, 149, 181
rivers 55, 111, 113, 121, 185, 205–7, 215–18, 221n.24
Robbins, Robin 20, 31n.81, 136n.23
Robortello, Francesco 96
Roche, Thomas P. 170n.31
Romanticism (poetry) 2, 9n.10, 138, 200, 202, 208, 213
Ronsard, Pierre de 113, 117n.12, 144
Russell, Lucy, Countess of Bedford 100, 180
Ryzhik, Yulia 16, 27n.5, 27n.12, 35, 107n.95, 136n.20, 155n.28, 169n.28
author of Introduction and editor

sacrifice 8, 121–2, 135n.8, 148, 162, 171, 179–81, 195
Sappho 172–3, 181
Sasso, Panfilo 112
satire 3, 5, 6, 11n.33, 15, 21–5, 31n.76, 41, 47, 79, 83n.57, 88–9, 91–2, 94, 104n.24, 105n.37, 110–11, 123–7, 129–32, 136n.13, 145, 205
see also Donne, John, *Metempsychosis*; *Satires*; Spenser, Edmund, *Prosopopoia*: or *Mother Hubberds Tale*
Scaliger, Julius Caesar 38, 82n.33
Scève, Maurice 143
scholasticism 34, 78, 138, 144
Schwartz, Regina M. 161
science 5, 7, 10n.15, 63–5, 96, 98, 135, 137–8, 144
see also anatomy; cosmology
Sedley, David L. 101
Seneca 61n.107, 201
sexual violence 7, 161–2, 167, 179
Shakespeare, William 3, 4, 9n.3, 36, 38, 57n.1, 59n.67, 87, 99, 114, 116, 138, 153n.5, 161, 165, 202–6, 214–16, 221n.12

Index

Shaw, Philip 95
Shawcross, John T. 55
Shelley, Percy Bysshe 210, 222n.50
Sidney, Mary, Countess of Pembroke 187–8
Sidney, Sir Philip 35, 58n.28, 58, 87–9, 106n.63, 114–15, 139 183–4, 186–8, 197
signature 8, 64, 157–8, 160–2, 164–8
Silvester, Bernard 165
simile 32–3, 37–8, 41–3, 48–53, 66, 68, 72–3, 75, 129, 206
similitudo 7, 33–40, 43, 51, 54–6, 58n.41
  see also syncrisis; *traductio*
sin 18–19, 77, 92, 186–7, 195–6
Smith, A.J. 62
sonnet 88–93, 104n.25, 112–13, 115, 127, 183, 185–6, 188–9, 213
  see also Donne, John, *Holy Sonnets*; Petrarch, Francesco; Spenser, Edmund, *Amoretti*
Spears Brooker, Jewel 201
species 18, 118, 128, 132, 142
  see also ecology
Spenser, Edmund
  Amoretti 88, 90–1, 112–13, 117n.4, 133–4, 165, 168
  Astrophel and *The Dolefull Lay of Clorinda* 88
  Colin Clouts Come Home Againe 145, 170n.43, 215–16
  Complaints 15, 20–1, 23, 25, 39, 110, 113, 123, 207
    Prosopopoia: or Mother Hubberds Tale 6, 20–6, 108, 115, 118–19, 122–6, 127, 129, 132
    Ruines of Rome 16, 110
    The Ruines of Time 31n.76, 88, 113, 207, 211
    The Teares of the Muses 113
    Virgils Gnat 113
    Visions of the Worlds Vanitie 15–16, 27n.11, 31n.76
  Daphnaida 88
  Epithalamion 7, 16, 112–13, 171, 174–9, 206–7
  The Faerie Queene 1, 14–15, 19, 22, 26, 34–5, 39, 41, 46, 69–70, 74, 86, 90, 94–5, 145, 160, 202–3, 206–10 *passim*

Book I 6, 41, 69, 74–80, 94, 109, 111, 115, 132, 167
Book II 16–17, 39, 70–2, 90, 110
Book III 41, 72–4, 99, 102, 143, 157–8, 160, 163–7, 178–9
Book IV 94, 114, 133–4, 217–19
Book V 80, 99, 109, 119–20, 130–2, 139, 212
Book VI 131
Letter to Raleigh 15, 27n.17, 40, 69, 93, 134
Two Cantos of Mutabilitie 1, 6, 7, 33–5, 39–47, 53, 56, 118, 120, 130–3, 145, 206, 216
The Faerie Queene (selected characters)
  Acrasia 71, 210
  Amoret 101–2, 163–8, 179
  Archimago 78–9, 123
  Arthegall 72, 119, 131, 166–7
  Arthur 78–80, 90, 111, 166
  Astraea 118–20, 122–3, 125, 131, 134
  Belphoebe 73, 179
  Britomart 33, 72–4, 101, 163–4, 166–7
  Busirane 40, 101, 157, 160, 163–8, 178, 210
  Cymochles 71–2
  Cynthia 34, 130–1, 206, 216
  Despair 19–20, 78, 210
  Diana 120, 131, 206
  Duessa 40, 77–80, 109
  Errour 111–12
  Faunus 131, 206, 216
  Gloriana 73–5, 80
  Guyon 16, 70–1, 111, 166
  Hellenore 114
  Malecasta 72
  Merlin 72, 78, 167
  Mutabilitie 34, 39–45, 47, 130–1, 133, 216
  Nature 40–5, 56, 130
  Paridell 114
  Pyrochles 70–1
  Redcrosse Knight 19–20, 74–8, 115, 205
  Scudamour 101–2, 166
  Una 76–8, 112, 205
The Fowre Hymnes 6, 7, 8, 90–1, 139–41, 143–50, 152–3, 184, 188–94, 197
Prothalamion 1, 14–15, 89, 205–6, 215, 218

Spenser, Edmund (*cont.*)
  The Shepheardes Calender 35, 59n.67, 68, 88, 108, 110 210, 221n.23
    'December' 108
    'Februarie' 112–13
    'November' 88, 105n.30, 108
    'October' 60n.99
  Theatre for Worldlings 110, 115
Spenserian stanza 14–19, 26, 28n.29, 94, 127
  see also rhyme
Stringer, Gary A. 25, 31n.74
style 6, 16, 21–3, 25, 26, 28n.26, 36, 55, 59n.67, 85–7, 103, 106n.81, 123, 138, 149, 158, 160, 171, 183, 202, 207–8, 212, 214, 216, 219
  see also form (poetics)
subjectivity 8, 137–8, 157–8, 160, 162–4, 166, 170n.31
sublime (concept) 7, 32, 55, 86–8, 95–103, 104n.9, 105n.49, 106n.59, 213
  see also Longinus
Surrey, Earl of *see* Howard, Henry, Earl of Surrey
Symonds, John Addington 203, 206
syncrisis 7, 33–8, 42, 44–8, 54–5
  see also simile; *similitudo*

Targoff, Ramie 7, 50, 101–2, 104n.26, 107n.94, 152, 156n.51, 168n.6, 169n.28, 219
  author of chapter 9
Tasso, Torquato 35, 112, 116, 117n.4, 144
Tesauro, Emanuele 49
Teskey, Gordon 33, 57n.7–8, 60n.83, 69, 82n.26, 104n.14, 189
Theocritus 173
Theophrastus 159, 168n.7
Tibullus 91, 110, 117n.3

topos 21, 50, 54, 67, 70, 74–5, 78, 113, 141, 146, 188
  see also logic, topic logic
traductio 35, 38–9, 43–4, 51, 53
Trismegistus, Hermes 66
Tuve, Rosemond 62–3, 67, 81n.8, 84n.60
typology 49, 56, 191

Van der Noot, Jan 115
Vendler, Helen 211, 213, 223n.58
Vesalius, Andreas 3, 152, 162
Vickers, Brian 96
Vickers, Nancy 184
Vico, Giambattista 217–18
Victorian literature 2, 9n.10, 200, 202, 203
Vida, Marco Girolamo 143, 145
Virgil 1, 35, 38, 72, 85, 88, 91, 94, 99, 104n.17, 105n.42, 107n.81, 109–10, 114–15, 117n.4, 122, 126, 134, 135n.9, 205

Wagner, Richard 218
Walls, Kathryn 78, 83n.49, 136n.13
Walton, Izaak 3
Warnke, Frank 59n.70
wars 1, 3, 4, 108–9, 131
Watson, George 62
Weaver, Harriet Shaw 219
Webster, John 204
Wendell, Barrett 203, 221n.12
White, Haydn 55
Whitworth, Michael 205, 222n.26, 222n.37
Wiggins, Peter DeSa 110, 117n.3
Wilson-Okamura, David S. 28n.29, 30n.61, 103n.2, 106n.81
Wyatt, Sir Thomas 104n.24, 112, 183, 201

Yeats, W. B. 8, 56, 200–2, 207–14, 220
Young, R.V. 91

EU authorised representative for GPSR:
Easy Access System Europe, Mustamäe tee 50,
10621 Tallinn, Estonia
gpsr.requests@easproject.com

www.ingramcontent.com/pod-product-compliance
Lightning Source LLC
Chambersburg PA
CBHW030120240426
43673CB00041B/1349